MIDDLE KNOWLEDGE

HUMAN FREEDOM IN DIVINE SOVEREIGNTY

MIDDLE KNOWLEDGE

HUMAN FREEDOM IN DIVINE SOVEREIGNTY

JOHN D. LAING

Printed in the United States of America

18 19 20 21 22 / 5 4 3 2 1

DEDICATED TO
MY WIFE, STEFANA,
AND OUR CHILDREN,
SYDNEY, SOPHIA, AND ALASDAIR,
AND TO MY PARENTS,
ED AND LIZ LAING

CONTENTS

INTRODUCTION

THE DOCTRINE OF PROVIDENCE

One of the most widely held doctrines of Christianity is that of meticulous divine providence. The doctrine of providence refers to God's governance and preservation of the world—his ongoing activity in the creation—and it is "meticulous," because it refers to the smallest details of all events. Thus, we speak of God being "in control" of all things, and as Helm rightly notes, this is no mere academic exercise: "Far from studying what is static or abstract, we are to be concerned with God's action in our world, and with how, according to Scripture, that activity is carried out."[1] Providence is as much a concern of *practical/applied* theology as it is of *systematic* and *philosophical* theology, and therefore, this book should be of interest to all Christians.

Scripture supports belief in meticulous providence, noting that (for example) it is God who makes the clouds rise and the rain fall (Ps. 135:6–7), and ensures the successes of individuals and nations (Job 12:23; Ps. 75:6–7). God is providential over salvation. The apostle Paul assures the Ephesians that their salvation was part of God's plan, noting that God "works all things after the counsel of His will" (Eph. 1:11). Similarly, God's providence applies to the specific destinies of individuals. The Lord declares to both Jeremiah and Isaiah that they were appointed prophets before their conceptions (Jer. 1:5; Isa. 49:1–6). Providence also refers to God's sustainment of the natural order. For example, God causes the grass to grow (Ps. 104:14; cmpr. Jesus's statement that he "clothes the grass of the field," Matt. 6:30). Somewhat related, the Psalmist declares that God gives the lions their food (Ps. 104:28), but this passage also highlights a key difficulty with meticulous divine providence, namely the problem of evil and suffering. Since lions are carnivores, when God provides their food, he hands over a poor zebra or wildebeest. Any robust view of meticulous providence must deal with this issue.

---

1. Paul Helm, *The Providence of God* (Downers Grove: IVP, 1994), 17. Thus, he concludes, the doctrine of providence is uniquely relevant. He writes, "As the word, 'providence' indicates, 'the providence of God' is a rather formal way of referring to the fact that God *provides*. And what could be more practical, relevant or down-to-earth than that?" Ibid., 18.

MODELS OF PROVIDENCE

Several models of providence have been articulated in the history of the church. It is best to group them according to how they explain the relationship between God's control, creaturely (i.e., human) freedom, and evil and suffering. Five basic approaches are discussed in theological circles: Process Theology (or Finite Godism), Open Theism, Arminianism/Middle Knowledge, Calvinism, and Theological Fatalism. Two have been largely dismissed as heretical/unorthodox (Process Theology and Theological Fatalism), one is typically thought to be heterodox (Open Theism), and two have been widely held among orthodox Christians (Arminianism/ Middle Knowledge and Calvinism). I will argue that middle knowledge best deals with the issues at hand. It is my hope to offer a less philosophically rigorous and more biblically and theologically oriented explanation. But first, a word or two about each of the alternatives is in order.

Process Theology

Process Theology is a uniquely American movement. It grew largely out of the philosophical work of Alfred North Whitehead and was popularized by Charles Hartshorne, John Cobb, David Griffin, Shubert Ogden, and others. Much of the discussion surrounding Process Philosophy and Theology is rather technical and can be dense, so we will focus on the basic ideas and their impact upon the Process view of providence.[2]

Perhaps the most characteristic feature of Process Theology is its emphasis on change as fundamental to reality, or in traditional philosophical categories, the primacy of *becoming* over *being*. It is often presented as an alternative to traditional Christian theology. For example, in his provocatively entitled work, *Omnipotence and Other Theological Mistakes*, Hartshorne sets forth what he calls six common errors about God that have pervaded classical theism in the West: God as absolutely perfect and therefore unchangeable; Omnipotence conceived as power to act; Omniscience as knowledge of all things; God's unsympathetic goodness (or impassibility); Immortality as a career after death; and Revelation as infallible. The primacy of change in Process thought extends to God himself, who is conceived as the Process of Reality Itself. It should come as no surprise, then, that Process Theology is *panentheistic* and sees all of reality in God. He is the sum total of all things (to be distinguished from *pantheism*, which says that all things are God/gods), and when things change in the world, God is also changed.

---

2. An excellent introductory text on Process Theology is authored by Mesle. While the book is arguably simplistic in its treatment of some themes, it lays out the basic ideas current in process thought in a way that is accessible to both the layman and the college or seminary student. C. Robert Mesle, *Process Theology: A Basic Introduction* (St. Louis: Chalice, 1993).

While the primacy of *becoming* over *being* is surely a hallmark of Process Theology, most process thinkers have argued that it is not at its heart. Rather, relationality and love are key, as Loomer points out: "To speak technically for a moment, what is distinctive about this mode of thought is not the substitution of 'process' for 'being,' although it does do that. Such a substitution says simply that becoming rather than being is ultimate. . . . It is rather that the distinctive aroma of this outlook occurs when you combine the ultimacy of process with the primacy of relationships. It is really relationships that process is all about."[3]

This emphasis on love is thought to distinguish the God of Process Theology who is eminently loving and relational (requiring change) from the God of so-called classical theism, who is impassible and immutable. Hartshorne argues that if humans add something of value to the life of God, then he can change for the better, and this should not be seen as a defect, but rather a necessary corollary to his relational nature.[4] God's loving nature is also taken to imply that providence has little to do with his *control* of events or history. Instead, it should be conceived in terms of *persuasion*. Two arguments are typically given for this claim. First, true love allows for the freedom of others, as exemplified in human relationships. Cobb and Griffin note, "Process theology's understanding of divine love is in harmony with the insight, which we can gain both from psychologists and from our own experience, that if we truly love others we do not seek to control them."[5] Just as loving human relationships are characterized by respect for the individuality of the other, so also is divine love for creatures. God does not cause events to occur or force persons to act in certain ways; rather, he lovingly suggests or persuades persons to do what he wishes for their good. Second, if God did control everything, then he would be the cause of evil. Process Theology prides itself on the strength of its theodicy. In the Process view, God is in no way responsible for evil because his providence is not causative. In fact, he quite literally *cannot cause or prevent evil* and is simply part of a process that includes evil!

---

3. Bernard M. Looper, "Process Theology: Origins, Strengths, Weaknesses," *Process Studies* 16, no. 4 (Winter 1987): 245.

4. Hartshorne writes, "Do or do not finite things contribute something to the greatness of God? . . .Consider that, according to the tradition, God could have refrained from creating our world. Then whatever, if anything, this world contributes to the divine life would have been lacking. Moreover, if God could have created some other world instead of this one, God must actually lack what the other world would have contributed. If you reply that the world contributes nothing to the greatness of God, then I ask, what are we all doing, and why talk about 'serving God,' who, you say, gains nothing whatever from our existence?" Charles Hartshorne, *Omnipotence and Other Theological Mistakes* (Albany: SUNY Press, 1984), 7–8.

5. John B. Cobb, Jr. and David Ray Griffin, *Process Theology: An Introductory Exposition* (Philadelphia: Westminster, 1976), 53.

Ironically, this strength for its theodicy also serves as a weakness for its eschatology. Providence through persuasion cannot guarantee that God's will can prevail or that he will emerge victorious. Cobb and Griffin admit as much when they note that the Process God cannot prevent specific evil acts.

> Process theism . . . cannot provide the assurance that God's will is always done. It does affirm that, no matter how great the evil in the world, God acts persuasively upon the wreckage to bring from it whatever good possible. It asserts that this persuasive power with its infinite persistence is in fact the greatest of all powers. But it does not find in that assertion assurance that any particular evil, including the evil of the imminent self-destruction of the human race, can be ruled out. God persuades against it, but there is no guarantee that we will give heed.[6]

It is not a far leap from the claim that God is unable to prevent specific evil acts to the claim that he cannot prevent ultimate destruction due to the overwhelming forces of evil.

Nevertheless, most Process thinkers are optimistic about God's ability to persuade humans to goodness and the prospects of humanity's positive response. For example, Suchocki points to God's ongoing loving draw upon man as a source of hope: "It bespeaks the providence of God for increasing opportunities for intensities of harmony within the world. The redemptive reality of God's communal nature is the ground of hope that the world, in all its ambiguities of freedom and finitude, can nonetheless actualize itself in congruity with God's aims. The communal structure of redemption is a constant given in the world, an unfailing resource for our good."[7] Still, she cannot say with any degree of certainty that evil will be overcome; its defeat is seen only as a hopeful possibility. Similarly, but not acknowledged, Process thinkers must also admit the possibility that the *ambiguities of freedom and finitude* (in her words) could eventuate in the defeat of Good and in the total destruction of life.

Process thinkers have criticized traditional theism, arguing that it is primarily based on philosophy (rather than the Bible). This claim cannot be sustained, though it serves as a valuable reminder against allowing speculative philosophy to dictate theological belief. It is true that most Christian theologians were trained in classical philosophy and sometimes drew upon it in their conceptions of God, but that proves nothing. After all, there is much that Socrates and Plato got right![8] And just because

6. Ibid., 118.
7. Marjorie Hewitt Suchocki, *The End of Evil* (Albany: SUNY Press, 1988), 124.
8. Justin famously suggested that Socrates and Plato may have been Christians before Christ insofar as they worshiped the true Reason (*logos*) who took on flesh in the person of Jesus Christ. See Justin, *First Apology*.

theologians referred to philosophy or philosophical categories in their writings, they were not necessarily driven by philosophy. In point of fact, the primary emphasis in the theological work of Augustine, Athanasius, Irenaeus, and even Origen, was Scriptural exegesis, and the theological writings of the Cappadocians—Basil of Caesarea, Gregory of Nazianzus, and Gregory of Nyssa—were extensions of their sermons and commentaries on Scripture.[9] Moreover, there was also a tradition within the early church, following Tertullian of Carthage, which argued against the incorporation of philosophy in Christian theological work.[10] Even in the medieval work of Anselm and Aquinas, fidelity to Scripture is the hallmark of theology; Aquinas did not shy away from offering correctives to Aristotle when necessary. It is also worth noting that Process Theology/Philosophy is heavily indebted to Greek philosophy itself. While Process thinkers criticize traditional theism for its similarities in emphases to the philosophy of Parmenides, who highlighted *being* over *becoming* as primary, they ignore the fact that their own thought is at least equally similar to the philosophy of Heraclitus, who argued that *becoming* is fundamental to reality.[11] As Cooper has aptly put it, "If classical theism represents 'the God of the philosophers,' then panentheism counters with 'the *other* God of the philosophers.'"[12] Merely pointing out similarities to ancient Greek philosophy is not a critique.

---

9. Not to mention that they were not "Western," but were from the East.

10. Tertullian's famous words, "What has Athens to do with Jerusalem?," nicely summarizes the basis of this tradition. These words have engendered much consternation, discussion, and debate among scholars. While they have traditionally been seen as a general disdain for philosophy, this does not seem to garner a full appreciation for Tertullian's own understanding of pagan philosophy. Tertullian was most concerned with the adoption of pagan categories uncritically, and warned against an unspiritual worldview. Still, he also argued that the *logos* of which the pagans spoke was/is Christ: "And we, in like manner, hold that the Word, and Reason, and Power, by which we have said God made all, have spirit as their proper and essential *substratum*, in which the Word has inbeing to give forth utterances, and reason abides to dispose and arrange, and power is over all to execute." Tertullian, *Apology* 21.

11. Heraclitus' saying, "You can never step in the same river twice" is emblematic of his commitment to the thesis that reality is constantly in flux. Heraclitus' metaphysic is typically seen as an opposition to Parmenides' belief that all is One and therefore, change is illusory. These two are seen as epitomizing the extremes and introducing the intractable problem of the One and the Many. Is reality unified or is it a multiplicity? If One, then change does not occur and all things are united. This leads to pantheism. If Many, then there is no stability and nothing is real because all is fleeting. In most cases, the Heraclitean view of reality results in either atheism or it devolves into pantheism again (as here, though panentheism—the idea that all is in God—is the position of Process Theologians). Colin Gunton has argued that only a triune God provides a metaphysical basis for holding the two in proper tension. Process Theology's dipolar theism was incapable of doing so, but a singular being who is three distinct persons allows for both One and Many to be true without either superseding the other. See Colin Gunton, *The One, the Three and the Many* (Cambridge: Cambridge University Press, 1993).

12. John W. Cooper, *Panentheism: The Other God of the Philosophers: From Plato to the Present* (Grand Rapids: Baker, 2006), 19.

Open Theism

Open Theism is the name given to a relatively recent development in theology which begins with the concept of divine self-limitation, but extends it to include God's inability to know the future with certainty. Open Theists contend that God's decision to create free creatures limits his foreknowledge because free actions cannot be certain until the free agent acts. That is, statements about how persons will freely act cannot be true prior to the act itself, and therefore, cannot be known (even by God). In saying this, Open Theists are not claiming God has no knowledge of future events, or that God *could not* have comprehensive foreknowledge, for he could have determined the future by causing it to play out in a particular manner, but that would compromise freedom and does not appear to be what he actually did.

Proponents of the Open view offer four basic arguments to prove that God does not have foreknowledge: 1) the traditional model of God (with foreknowledge) is based on Greek philosophy and should therefore be discarded; 2) the Bible suggests that God does not know the future; 3) a relational view of God requires that he be *open* to human actions and reactions, and this precludes his knowing them ahead of time; and 4) divine foreknowledge and human freedom are incompatible, and since human freedom is a given, God cannot know the future.

Open Theists have joined a growing number of theologians and philosophers who have begun to question the traditional attributes of God. Attributes such as immutability, impassibility, omnipotence, omniscience, and eternality have either been called into question or radically reinterpreted. The most common complaint is that they are strongly influenced by Greek thought and hardly reflective of the biblical revelation. For example, John Sanders argues that the early church was made up of people who were constantly in dialogue with Greek contemporaries and who utilized pagan categories to explain and/or defend the Christian view of God. This appropriation led to confusion and a perversion of theology. He writes, "Greek thought has played an extensive role in the development of the traditional doctrine of God. But the classical view of God worked out in the Western tradition is at odds at several key points with a reading of the biblical text."[13]

William Hasker agrees, claiming that many attributes originate in Plotinus and Neo-Platonism rather than the Bible.[14] He argues that they grew out of the Greek philosophical ideal of permanence, which sees

---

13. John Sanders, "Historical Considerations," in *The Openness of God*, eds. Clark Pinnock, et al. (Downers Grove, IL: InterVarsity, 1994), 59.

14. He writes, "The philosophy of neo-Platonism, as seen in Plotinus and later on in Pseudo-Dionysius, was a powerful molding force in ancient and medieval theology. Today, however, neo-Platonism really does not exist as a living philosophy, though it continues to have considerable indirect influence through the theological tradition." William Hasker, "A Philosophical Perspective," in Pinnock, et al., *The Openness of God*, 127.

change as defective. Permanence is virtually synonymous with perfection because if a being were perfect, then a change would diminish him in some way. Therefore, if God is perfect—and it is presupposed that he is—then he must be unchanging in every way: in thought, personality, and being (i.e., immutable, impassible, and eternal understood as timeless). Hasker writes:

> In the philosophical lineage stretching from Parmenides to Plato to Plotinus, there is a strong metaphysical and valuational preference for permanence over change. True Being, in this tradition, must of necessity be changeless; whatever changes, on the other hand, enjoys a substandard sort of being if any at all—at best it may be, in Plato's lovely phrase, a 'moving image of eternity.' And this bias against change has been powerfully influential in classical theology, leading to the insistence on an excessively strong doctrine of divine immutability—which, in turn, provides key support for divine timelessness, since timelessness is the most effective way (and perhaps the only way) to rule out, once and for all, the possibility of any change in God.[15]

Hasker argues that we need not be constrained by such an attitude toward permanence and change.

The problem, then, is that the Greek metaphysic came to be accepted *a priori* (at the beginning), and functioned as a sort of lens through which the biblical text was interpreted. This approach has been handed down through the tradition of the church and serves as a dogma of sorts. Sanders explains, "The classical view is so taken for granted that it functions as a preunderstanding that rules out certain interpretations of Scripture that do not 'fit' with the conception of what is 'appropriate' for God to be like, as derived from Greek metaphysics."[16] According to Sanders, there is a tension within evangelicalism between a *prima facie* reading of the biblical text, and what he terms a *theologically controlled* reading of the text. The Greek ideas of perfection and truth have so pervaded the theology of the West that they often dictate how the text is understood and interpreted, and this has led to an incorrect view of God's nature.[17] Thus, proponents of the Open view claim that a fresh examination of the biblical materials will reveal that God is much more personal and has a more dynamic

---

15. Ibid., 129.
16. Sanders, "Historical Considerations," 59.
17. Sanders writes, "In the history of the church, guidelines were developed, often unwittingly, for interpreting biblical metaphors. The guidelines, once established, functioned like axioms in geometry, taking on incontestable certitude. They were formulated under the belief that the Greek philosophical way of speaking of God (impassible, immutable, timeless, etc.) was superior to the anthropomorphic way (father, changeable, suffering, etc.). The church has followed this path for so long that we now take this way of thinking for granted." John E. Sanders, "God as Personal," in *The Grace of God and the Will of Man*, ed. Clark H. Pinnock (Minneapolis: Bethany House, 1989), 169.

relationship with the creation and this requires change in his knowledge and responses. Since his knowledge can change, he does not have comprehensive knowledge of the future.

One of the favorite passages they cite is found in the book of Exodus, where Moses intercedes on behalf of the people of Israel following the incident with the golden calf. God informs Moses that he intends to destroy the Israelites and make a great nation of his descendents instead. When Moses intercedes for the people, God decides not to go through with the destruction (literally, "changes his mind"; Exod. 32:7–14).

Open Theists argue that this story demonstrates that God is genuinely responsive to the creation and as a result, experiences change in his knowledge, attitudes, and dispositions toward creatures. As Richard Rice puts it, "The repentance mentioned in this case clearly applies to a change that took place in God, not in his people."[18] He is quick to point out that this is not to say God's nature or purpose changed. On the contrary, God's changing of his mind *preserved* his plan for the ages: "his ultimate objectives required him to change his immediate intentions."[19] Sanders agrees, noting that this passage indicates that God is faithful to his project of redemption—to his covenant with Abraham—even though he allows humans to influence the specifics of how his plan will be met.[20] Nevertheless, the key point for Openness advocates is that a real change took place in God; he changed his mind about what he was going to do. As Rice puts it, God's intentions "are not absolute and invariant; he does not unilaterally and irrevocably decide what to do."[21] God takes human response into account as he deliberates.

This reading of the passage raises at least two problems for the idea that God knows everything about the future. First, it seems incoherent to claim that God knows the future and yet changes his mind about how he will act. Commenting on a similar passage that describes God's revocation of his anointing of Saul as king over Israel (even though it seemed to be a perpetual call; 1 Sam. 13:13–14), Sanders writes, "God nevertheless experiences a genuine change in emotion from joy to grieving over Saul. It is questionable whether it is coherent to affirm both that God has always known of this event and that God now has changing emotions about that event."[22]

---

18.   Richard Rice, "Biblical Support for a New Perspective," in Pinnock, et al., *The Openness of God*, 28.
19.   Ibid.
20.   Sanders writes, "But God has different options available, and the one that he will choose is not a foregone conclusion. Sometimes God allows human input in regard to the option that is realized. As God permitted Abraham's intercession for Sodom (Gen. 18:16–33), so now God allows Moses incredible access to him. With or without human input, God remains faithful to his project of redemption." John Sanders, *The God Who Risks: A Theology of Providence* (Downers Grove., IL: InterVarsity, 1998), 66.
21.   Rice, "Biblical Support for a New Perspective," 29.
22.   Sanders, *The God Who Risks*, 72.

Sanders' point is this: Suppose at one moment, God knows that he is going to anoint Saul king over Israel and that Saul will subsequently act in such a way that God will then revoke that blessing. After that, God anoints Saul as king over Israel, and Saul acts in just that way. God is then described as changing his mind regarding his anointing of Saul and removes his spirit from Saul. Since God knew that he was going to revoke it from the beginning, it is not really a *changing* of his mind when he does so. Thus, Sanders concludes, either at that first moment, God did not *know* what was going to happen in the future, or the Bible is in error when it describes God as changing his mind regarding Saul's kingship.[23] Boyd agrees, arguing that a responsible reading of the biblical text requires a rejection of comprehensive divine foreknowledge because God did genuinely repent. He writes:

> We must wonder how the Lord could truly experience regret for making Saul king if he was absolutely certain that Saul would act the way he did. Could God genuinely confess, "I regret that I made Saul king" if he could in the same breath also proclaim, "I was certain of what Saul would do when I made him king"? I do not see how. Could I genuinely regret, say, purchasing a car because it turned out to run poorly if in fact the car was running exactly as I knew it would when I purchased it? Common sense tells us that we can only regret a decision we made if the decision resulted in an outcome other than what we expected or hoped for when the decision was made.[24]

---

23. Sanders considers and rejects the suggestion that the biblical writer was utilizing anthropomorphic language and that therefore, descriptions of God as repenting or changing his mind should not be taken as literal descriptions of the divine cognitive processes. He asks how one is to distinguish between those passages which are literal descriptions of God and those which are not. According to Sanders, the proponents of this view do not offer clear criteria. In reference to divine-repentance passages, he writes, "On what basis do these thinkers claim that these biblical texts do not portray God as he truly is but only God as he appears to us? How can they confidently select one biblical text as an 'exact' description of God and consign others to the dustbin of anthropomorphism?" Ibid., 68. Sanders is not convinced by Ware's discussion of passages which claim that because God is *not human*, he does not repent. See Bruce Ware, "An Evangelical Reformulation of the Doctrine of the Immutability of God," *Journal of the Evangelical Theological Society* 29, no. 4 (1986): 431–46. Sanders points out that Hosea 11:8–9 is problematic for Ware's thesis because it claims that God repents because he is not human: "Following Ware we have a real problem on our hands because the Bible teaches both (1) that God cannot change his mind because he is not human and (2) that God is literally does change his mind because he is not human." Sanders, *The God Who Risks*, 68–69. Sanders does admit, though, that the images of divine repentance found in the Bible are metaphorical in nature. This does not mean that they are not an accurate reflection of God: "The metaphor of divine repentance signifies God's ability to remain faithful to his project while altering his plans to accommodate the changing circumstances brought about by the creatures." Ibid., 72.
24. Gregory A. Boyd, *God of the Possible: A Biblical Introduction to the Open View of God* (Grand Rapids: Baker, 2000), 56.

Second, there appears to be a moral problem with God's anger being provoked by creaturely actions if he knew what those actions would be beforehand. Sanders approvingly quotes Terence Fretheim, who argues that God's anger should be immediate at the point of his knowledge of sin rather than at the point of its occurrence.[25] There seems to be an underlying assumption here that it is somehow dishonest for God to be angry in response to actions that he already knew would occur. A truly responsive anger would be triggered not by the action, but rather by the knowledge of the action. Here, too, Sanders' conclusion is that either God did not know of the creature's sinful actions before they were committed, or the Bible is in error when it describes God's anger being fueled in response to those sinful actions.

Open Theists often claim that God's personal relation to the creation demonstrates that the traditional doctrine is insufficient. For instance, Pinnock presents two models of God for consideration: 1) monarch and 2) loving parent. It is the second model that Pinnock believes to be the correct, biblical one. It offers a picture of a God who is in dynamic relation with free creatures he loves. God creates a world with significantly free personal agents in it, and humanity contributes to the divine life because God allows true freedom in an open future.[26]

Sanders claims that the metaphors used in the Bible to describe God are the best sources for discovering who God *really is*. The anthropomorphic metaphors describe God's relatedness to the creation, most importantly, to humans. He contends that when these metaphors "are allowed to speak within a personalistic conception of God, then a quite different image [of God] emerges" from that in the church's tradition.[27] God is seen as personally involved and related to his creation in such a way that he finds pain in unfaithfulness (of humanity) and joy in love. This depicts him as the defenseless superior power. He is creator and sustainer, but because he chose to create free creatures, he has allowed himself to be *defenseless*, or *vulnerable*. The personal relationship God has with humanity is dynamic, which requires him to be responsive and precludes him from timelessly decreeing his actions before creation. As Sanders puts it, "Yahweh's wrath can change to kindness, his power to defenselessness, and judgment to forgiveness because he is the *living personal God*."[28]

Rice develops these concepts in his claim that divine love is limitless, precarious, and vulnerable. It is limitless because the lover has an unlimited concern for the beloved, it is precarious because it is not controlling but passive (e.g., as the father patiently waiting for the prodigal son,

25. Sanders, *The God Who Risks*, 72. See Terence Fretheim, *The Suffering of God: An Old Testament Perspective* (Philadelphia: Fortress, 1984), 40–44.

26. Clark Pinnock, "God Limits His Knowledge," in *Predestination and Free Will: Four Views of Divine Sovereignty and Human Freedom,* eds. David Basinger and Randall Basinger (Downers Grove, IL: InterVarsity, 1986), 144.

27. Sanders, "God as Personal," 175.

28. Ibid., 176.

Luke 15), and it is vulnerable because the lover grants the beloved power over himself.[29] By loving humans, God makes it possible for them to cause him grief, joy, suffering, or delight. Love is not coercive, and therefore, the outcome is not set. Sanders writes, "God elects to establish a world in which the outcome of his love is not a foregone conclusion. God desires a relationship of genuine love with us and this, according to the rules of the game God established, cannot be forced or controlled and so cannot be guaranteed."[30] The point is that a genuine, personal, loving relationship between God and his creatures can only exist if God does not possess foreknowledge and is not controlling because a loving relationship must be open for both parties. If one party knows how things will turn out or controls the other, then he is not really vulnerable and not really loving.

A final reason some have rejected divine foreknowledge is they see it as incompatible with creaturely freedom due to the asymmetry of past, present and future or to the nature of freedom. While the past and present can be said to exist *now*, the future cannot; instead, it is *open* to development, and this means it does not yet exist to be known. Rice explains:

> Future free decisions do not exist in any sense before they are made. So the real difference between the traditional view of God and the alternate proposed here is not that one attributes perfect knowledge to God, while the other doesn't. Both affirm that God knows everything there is to know. They differ, however, in their concepts of what there is to know. . . . [I]f future free decisions do not yet exist, they are not there to be known until they are made. And the fact that God does not know them ahead of time represents no deficiency in His knowledge.[31]

Similarly, it is argued that statements about free actions cannot be true prior to the person acting because it is *in acting* that a statement about the action is made either true or false.[32] Statements about future free actions cannot be true and therefore, cannot be known, even by an omniscient God.

---

29. Sanders agrees, writing, "God is willing to wait if need be and to give it another try. Waiting implies a degree of passivity and dependency, whereas trying again implies that the efforts of love have failed to achieve the desired end as yet." Sanders, *The God Who Risks*, 177.

30. Ibid., 178.

31. Richard Rice, *God's Foreknowledge and Man's Free Will* (Minneapolis: Bethany House, 1985), 53–54. Originally published under the title, *The Openness of God* (Minneapolis: Bethany House, 1980).

32. Thus, Swinburne concludes that the doctrine of omniscience can only be salvaged if conditional future contingents do not have a truth-value until they come to pass. Statements which describe how creatures will freely choose to act in the future are neither true nor false until the individual is faced with the situation, and makes a decision about how to act. Swinburne asserts, "There seems to be one way in which the theist might avoid this conclusion [that omniscience is incompatible with freedom]. He could coherently assert that there was a perfectly free and omniscient person, if it were the case that all (or certain particular) propositions about the future were neither true nor false. . . . But if propositions about the future actions of

In addition to these considerations, Pinnock argues that the doctrine of divine eternity—that God knows free decisions timelessly—does not alleviate the problem.[33] In fact, most who have jettisoned comprehensive divine foreknowledge have done so only after carefully weighing and rejecting the proposed solutions to reconciling it with human freedom. For example, Swinburne argues that the incompatibility of foreknowledge and freedom can only be overcome if backward causation is possible. Since backward causation is impossible, no one, not even God, can know how an individual will freely choose from among competing alternatives in the future.[34] Hasker agrees, noting that the Open Theist rejection of divine foreknowledge is based in their belief that the past cannot be changed: "what lies at the root of them [controversies over compatibility of divine foreknowledge and human freedom] is a disagreement over a fundamental intuition or metaphysical datum—the intuition often expressed by saying, 'You can't change the past.'"[35] Thus, Open Theists conclude, because arguments for compatibilism fail, incompatibilism follows.

Several answers to Open Theism's objections are available. In response to the claim that the traditional model of God has been greatly influenced by Greek philosophical and metaphysical categories, two comments must be made. First, as already noted this is not really a critique of traditional theology. As Wolterstorff has noted, there are many areas in which the Greeks simply *got it right!*[36] The platonic view of reality may be, in essence,

agents are neither true nor false until the agents do the actions, then to be omniscient a person will not have to know them." Richard Swinburne, *The Coherence of Theism*, rev. ed. (1977; Oxford: Clarendon, 1993), 179. Swinburne makes the further claim that a powerful argument can be constructed along the same lines for the incompatibility of divine foreknowledge and divine freedom. An argument of this sort stands as evidence against an answer to the divine foreknowledge/human freedom problem that simply denies that humans are free, because it is a central tenet of Christianity that, at least, God himself is free!

33.   He writes, "If God knows eternally that A will be the selection and not B, then it is still an illusion that any genuine alternative will exist at the time of the decision. It would appear to me that actions which are infallibly foreknown or timelessly known cannot be free in the required biblical sense." Pinnock, "God Limits His Knowledge," 157.

34.   Swinburne, *The Coherence of Theism*, 174–75.

35.   William Hasker, "Foreknowledge and Necessity," *Faith and Philosophy* 2, no. 2 (April 1985): 121. Hasker surveys several of the proposed answers to the dilemma of foreknowledge and free will, from divine timelessness, to Ockhamism, to the thesis that the past is not really necessary at all. In the end, though, he concludes that those who argue for compatibility ultimately abandon "implicitly if not explicitly," libertarian freedom. Ibid., 154. Bruce Reichenback has challenged this article, claiming that Hasker's argument for incompatibilism equivocates on the use of *bring it about that God has not always believed* such and such. See Bruce Reichenbach, "Hasker on Omniscience," *Faith and Philosophy* 4, no. 1 (1987): 86–92. For Hasker's reply, see William Hasker, "The Hardness of the Past: A Reply to Reichenbach," *Faith and Philosophy* 4, no. 3 (July 1987): 337–42.

36.   Nicholas Wolterstorff, "Address to the Evangelical Philosophical Society" (Address presented at the annual meeting of the Evangelical Philosophical Society, Boston, November 18, 1999). For example, many of our rules of logic come from Aristotle, many of our theories regarding music and harmony come from Pythagoras, and much of our thought regarding law and

fundamentally correct. What is needed is a demonstration of error on the part of the Greek metaphysical categories/ideas that the early church fathers incorporated into their thought about God and the Bible. In other words, an evaluation of the biblical evidence for each model is required.

Second, proponents of the Open view, like those of the Process view, have also been influenced by Greek thought. Recall the philosophical argument against compatibilism; it claims that the future does not yet exist and that therefore, propositions about future contingents cannot be true. This argument, which articulates *a priori* commitments of Open Theists, was first formulated by Aristotle![37] Thus, those who dismiss divine

---

justice comes from the Greeks and Romans. Thus, to simply point out the influence of Greek thought on our conception of God is to say very little and certainly does not serve as a viable critique.

37.   Aristotle argued that if all affirmations and denials must be either true or false, then nothing happens by chance; there is no contingency. Consider two claims regarding the future:
       John will freely eat a piece of chocolate cheesecake tonight;

and

       John will not freely eat a piece of chocolate cheesecake tonight.

       According to Aristotle, it seems that one must be correct, while the other is false. But if, for instance, the first is true and the second is false, then the first is true necessarily, and there is no contingency in my decision to eat the cheesecake tonight. He further argues that it is of little help to say something like
       John may freely eat a piece of chocolate cheesecake tonight;

or

       John may not freely eat a piece of chocolate cheesecake tonight;

because neither one is true. For, when faced with the decision to eat or not-eat the cheesecake, I will do one or the other. No matter which I do, the statements regarding what I may do are both false. Thus, Aristotle concludes, it seems that the truth of propositions regarding the future (even those thought to refer to contingents like the statements about my eating or not eating the cheesecake) discounts contingency and future events happen necessarily.

       Now, this argument by Aristotle has been a set-up. He has led the reader into a quagmire from which he now intends to lead his followers out. He appeals to experience, noting that there are many events which come about not by necessity, but by the free decisions of men; there are many potentialities. All things, contrary to the argument presented, do not happen of necessity.

       This, however, is not to say that all things do not have to either be or not be. In fact they do; for any given contingent future event, it must either come to pass or not come to pass, although it cannot be said whether it will or not. For example, it is true that I will either eat a piece of chocolate cheesecake, or I will not, and so one of the two propositions regarding what I will do is true. The necessity has to do with the option of eating cheesecake, not with how/what I decide. Thus, one of the options must be true, though it cannot at this time be known which, because neither is true *now*. Aristotle explains, "For one half of the said contradiction must be true and the other half false. But we cannot say which half is which. Though it may be that one is more probable, it cannot be true yet or false. There is evidently, then, no necessity that one should be true, the other false, in the case of affirmations and denials. For the case of those things which as yet are potential, not actually existent, is different from that of things actual. It is as we stated above." Aristotle, *De Interpretatione* ix., in *Aristotle: The Organon I,*

foreknowledge because of its alleged incompatibility with an open future have also been strongly influenced by Greek thought.

In response to the biblical argument, many traditional theologians have pointed out that there is a hermeneutical problem with the Open Theist case. Many passages point to God's unchanging nature, and those that describe God as changing his mind refer to his posture toward the given situation at that time, rather than to his lack of knowledge. These, and other examples cited by Open Theists, will be addressed later.

The Open Theist claim that the traditional conception of God is unloving cannot be sustained, though the tradition has sometimes struggled to reconcile divine love with impassibility. Some evangelical theologians have discarded the concept of divine impassibility and seen divine immutability as a reference to character and being, rather than the totality of who he is.[38] Some have seen these attributes as reflective of man's standing before God, which can change, even while God does not.

None of this should lead to a wholesale rejection of the traditional attributes. The idea that God is personal still coheres with many of them, even those highlighted by Open Theism. For example, Open Theists have failed to establish a logical connection between the doctrine of divine timelessness and an impersonal view of God. Christian theologians have long maintained that, even though God exists apart from time, he nevertheless loves the creation eternally. There is no good reason to reject the possibility of an eternal love or an eternal concern for others. The same thing can be said regarding the doctrine of divine foreknowledge. No logical connection has been demonstrated to exist between the doctrine of divine foreknowledge and a lack of personality on the part of God.

As already noted, Open Theism seems to rely on an *a priori* commitment to the Aristotelian claim that propositions describing future contingents are neither true nor false, but Aristotle's position wrongly allows only two options: Fatalism, or the open future. Theological determinism, for instance, stands as a viable alternative; it is not open because everything is determined by God's will, but it is not fatalistic because everything does not happen by necessity—God could choose to cause things to be other than they in fact are.

Likewise, although many of the proponents of an Open view have surveyed the competing alternatives for reconciling divine foreknowledge and creaturely freedom and found them wanting, the discussion is still quite lively. In fact, many within the Christian tradition, if forced to choose between divine foreknowledge and creaturely freedom, prefer to reject the latter instead of the former. For example, Freddoso writes:

---

trans. Harold P. Cooke, Loeb Classical Library (Cambridge, MA: Harvard University Press, 1938), 141.

38. For example, see Alister E. McGrath, *Christian Theology: An Introduction* (Cambridge: Blackwell, 1994), 213–19.

> Still, I cannot hide my dismay. The likes of Justin Martyr, Tertullian, Origen, Augustine, Anselm, Bonaventure, Aquinas, Scotus, Ockham, Luther, Calvin, Molina, Bañez, Suarez, Arminius, Leibniz, and Edwards surely realized that they could spare themselves a lot of philosophical grief if only they would repudiate divine foreknowledge and with it the traditional understanding of divine providence, according to which every event that transpires in the universe, including every free action, is either knowingly intended or knowingly permitted by God prior to creation. Yet not one of these Christian intellectual heroes so much as entertained such a drastic expedient; to the contrary, the very thought of it would have appalled them. Were they less enlightened than we are about the Christian Faith as it pertains to providence and foreknowledge? Were they, as Hasker intimates (p. 191), the unwitting victims of an over-hellenized theology? (Even Luther and Calvin?!) It verily takes one's breath away to suppose so. Yet Hasker and his co-travellers apparently do suppose so.[39]

Extremely good reasons must be given for rejecting a doctrine that has so long stood at the center of orthodox thought about God. Since good answers to the problem can be given, the Open Theists' claim that God does not have comprehensive foreknowledge must be rejected.

Calvinism

Calvinism is a system of understanding theology most closely associated with the work of John Calvin, and is best known for its approach to understanding God's determining will in providence and salvation.[40] It conceives of divine providence as a function of God's willing all that occurs. In his *Institutes of the Christian Religion*, Calvin hopes to defend his view of divine providence against charges that it makes God the cause of evil. Calvin begins by admitting that God ordains all things, but is careful to point out that the primary concern of God's providential activity is propelling Christians to godliness and defeating evil. He is particularly critical of attempts to evaluate the justice of God's work because humans have no right to call God to account, and ought to respond to God's governance with worship.[41] He also notes that much of God's governance is

---

39.   Alfred J. Freddoso, review of *God, Time and Knowledge*, by William Hasker, *Faith and Philosophy* 8 (1993): 100.

40.   Horton points out that "Calvinism" is something of a misnomer for several reasons, the chief of which is the historical truth that the Reformed Churches emerged across Europe as a result of the work and thought of many persons with much greater diversity of thought than other reform movements of the time. He writes, "Far more than Lutheranism, Reformed theology was a 'team sport,' whose faith and practice were shaped by international cooperation among many figures whose names are now largely forgotten." Michael Horton, *For Calvinism* (Grand Rapids: Zondervan, 2011), 29.

41.   He writes, "No man, therefore, will duly and usefully ponder on the providence of God save he who recollects that he has to do with his own Maker, and the Maker of the world, and in the

mysterious or secret (i.e., his hidden counsels), so that it is right to say that all things happen by his will, though he causes no evil.[42] A proper understanding of providence, Calvin insists, will lead believers to seek out God's good will and follow it. This is in contrast to pagan Fatalism, which views providence as an exemption from guilt for sin or an overbearing force that destroys freedom and leads to despair.

Calvin then seeks to answer what is perhaps the most common objection to his determinist view of providence: the ordination of evil and suffering and the justice of God. Later, in the chapter on the problem of evil, these issues will receive further treatment, refinement, and examination, but here we will confine our examination to Calvin's answers to those who complain that God is unjust if he punishes those who injure others (e.g., murder, assault, or steal) when their actions had to have been ordained by his will, and they are themselves instruments of his providence (e.g., instruments of his justice or punishment, etc.). While Calvin admits that a murderer could not have murdered unless God had willed it, he denies that the murderer serves the will of God by murdering. In order to make this claim, he distinguishes between the motives of the human actors, and the use God makes of their evil intentions. They remain guilty because their sins are a result of their own desires, choices, and actions, and God's holiness is not impugned because he simply utilizes their evil actions for his good purposes.[43] Most Calvinists appeal to the concept of two wills in God, conceived either as declarative and permissive, or revealed and secret, etc., in order to explain how some events may be correctly described as *willed* by God, but not *serving* his will.[44]

Still, Calvin notes, the primary emphasis of Scripture is upon God's special care and provision for his people and his love for believers.[45] Christians will thus recognize God's hand in any good they receive, even if it comes by means of earthly instrumentality (e.g., the work of men); God is given the glory for anything truly positive we enjoy.[46] Similarly, when Christians endure suffering, either as a result of the evil of men or of natural cause, they should recognize that God has willed it for their

---

exercise of the humility which becomes him, manifests both fear and reverence." John Calvin, *Institutes of the Christian Religion* 1.17.2, ed. John T. McNeill, trans. Ford Lewis Battles, 2 vols. (Louisville: Westminster, 1960), 102.

42. He writes, "Therefore, since God claims to himself the right of governing the world, a right unknown to us, let it be our law of modesty and soberness to acquiesce in his supreme authority, regarding his will as our only rule of justice, and the most perfect cause of all things,—not that absolute will, indeed, of which sophists prate, when by profane and impious divorce, they separate his justice from his power, but that universal overruling Providence from which nothing flows that is not right, though the reasons thereof may be concealed." Ibid., 103.

43. Ibid., 1.17.5.

44. Arminians have sometimes criticized these distinctions, but such criticisms are misguided, for any position orthodox on divine foreknowledge and providence must make similar appeals.

45. Ibid., 1.17.6.

46. Ibid., 1.17.7.

good in some way or another. For example, when we are wronged by others, we have an opportunity to learn patience and to exercise humility, grace, and forgiveness; and when disaster strikes, we have an opportunity to exercise self-reflection and, perhaps, repentance. The point, of course, is that God uses even evil and suffering for our good, though we sometimes do not recognize it.[47] Ultimately, Calvin insists, his view of providence has more to do with acknowledging the Lord for his goodness than with deciding how to act in any given situation (God's Word already tells us this). To see God's providence behind all things should result in humility and self-reflection.

Calvinism tends to have a stronger view of divine causation than Open Theism and Middle Knowledge. Calvin is careful to note that God's sovereignty is *not mere permission*, but that he is *active* or ultimately responsible for all things, and appeals to several biblical examples of evil actions that are ascribed to God (e.g., Babylonian invasion of Judah; Jer. 1:15; 7:14; 25:9; 50:25). He writes, "it is more than evident that they babble and talk absurdly who, in place of God's providence, substitute bare permission—as if God sat in a watchtower awaiting chance events, and his judgments thus depended upon human will."[48] So Calvin emphasizes God's activity in persons' sinful actions/hardening of hearts. He objects to the claim that God merely permits sin, and instead argues that God's work is active and in some sense, causative: "it is said that the same Satan 'blinds the minds of unbelievers' (2 Cor. 4:4); but whence does this come, unless the working of error flows from God himself (2 Thess. 2:11), to make those believe lies who refuse to obey the truth?"[49] So God both hands men over to Satan, to a depraved mind, and the like, and deceives them himself. Calvin thus directly claims that God can will the evil of men while also condemning it. The apparent contradiction is due to our limited capacity to apprehend the simplicity of God: "when we do not grasp how God wills to take place what he forbids to be done, let us recall our mental incapacity, and at the same time consider that the light in which God dwells is not without reason called unapproachable (1 Tim. 6:16), because it is overspread with darkness."[50]

In order to illustrate his point, Calvin appeals to an example set forth by Augustine wherein two sons—one good and one bad—have opposing wills regarding their father's imminent death. The good son wills, contrary to God's will, that the father live, while the bad son, consonant with God's ultimate will in the matter, but for selfish and evil reasons, wills that the father die. In this case, the evil son's desire coincides with God's will, and the good son, for good and godly reasons (love of his father) has desires

---

47.   Ibid., 1.17.8.
48.   Ibid., 1.18.1, 231.
49.   Ibid., 1.18.2 , 232.
50.   Ibid., 1.18.3, 233.

contrary to God's will. This example nicely illustrates how someone with evil desires can have a goal that aligns with what God has determined, but it fails to address the more problematic issue of why God's goal for a given situation is what would typically been seen as bad or evil.

Calvin argues that, even though people sin in accordance with God's will, promptings, and governance, they are still justly condemned because when they act sinfully, they do so out of their own selfish and sinful desires. It is not as though they are aware of his secret will (that they sin) and act out of a desire to be obedient; quite the contrary, they act in direct disobedience to God's precepts/commands. He goes on to offer examples: Absalom sleeping with his father's concubines, Shimei cursing David, Jeroboam leading a revolt of the northern kingdom, and Judas betraying Christ, but unfortunately, he never explains *how* God *willing* that they sin does not itself explain what he means by God willing sinful deeds, save vague references to God's *secret will* (or secret inspiration) and God *willingly permitting* sin (an attempt to deny mere permission and replace it with a more active concept, while still abrogating God of responsibility).

I have emphasized Calvinism's difficulty with the problem of divine control and human sin for a number of reasons here. First, it helps the reader distinguish Calvinism's view of providence from those of Middle Knowledge on the one hand, and Theological Fatalism on the other hand. Second, it shows how Calvinism's conception of freedom is used to claim that creatures freely choose their own actions while those actions are willed or determined by God. Third, it illustrates the claims made later in the chapter on the problem of evil regarding Calvinism's difficulty with the problem. Fourth, it enables the reader to see how Calvin himself addresses the criticism of his strong view of divine determination in providence.

Theological Fatalism

As noted earlier, pagan philosophers and theologians struggled with questions of divine control and human freedom as well. One approach to dealing with these issues was to deny that there is any contingency or freedom and to claim that all things happen by necessity. This view came to be called Fatalism, because in much of the early Greek stories, it was the Fates, and not the gods, who determined the future. In some instances, the gods even seem to be subject to Fate (or the Fates), while in others, the supreme God appears exempt from such control.[51]

---

51. In Norse/Germanic mythology, Fate is most closely associated with the nine Valkyries, whose primary role was to mark those mortals who were to die in battle. This determination appears independent from and even beyond the control of the gods, even Odin, though it is often cast in terms of fulfilling the will of the supreme god. In the *Iliad*, Zeus is portrayed as having the ability to circumvent the Fates, but he nevertheless chooses to allow the fate of his son, Sarpedon, to achieve its end; he dies at the hand of Patroclus, and Zeus is left to mourn the loss (at least as much as is fitting for a god to mourn the death of a mortal!). Elsewhere in the same book, we are told of a conversation between Thetis, the goddess mother of Achilles,

Perhaps the most well-known version of Fatalism from the serious philosophy of the ancient Greeks and Romans is that of the Stoics, who emphasized the ethical response one ought to have to the Necessity which is a fundamental aspect of reality. Persons are exhorted to *accept*, or come to terms with Nature's prescriptions; acceptance of one's destiny is the key to happiness and ethical conduct. Of course, the pagan notion of Fatalism, with "the Fates" who spin the web of history and dictate the activities and events of all history, is neither an attraction nor a stumbling block to Christians. However, there is a notion of divine providence among some Christians that is close enough in ideology to warrant the name "Theological Fatalism" and is popular enough to demand comment.

At its most basic, Theological Fatalism is the notion that all things, even the actions of God, happen by necessity. God wills all events and actions, and nothing can thwart his will, but his will is set and could not be otherwise. Some versions have the divine will as the direct cause of each and every action, thought, or event, but such a view is not essential to the model. All that is required is the belief that things could not be other than they are. Many times, this belief is tied to the concept of divine perfection. God's perfection must be manifest in his will and actions, and since he must perform the "best," he really only has one option. All of his actions, thoughts, and will are conceived as flowing directly and unchangingly out of his nature (as perfect).

John Piper, a popular Calvinist pastor/scholar, has expressed views dangerously close to this position when, somewhat jokingly, referring to himself as a *seven-point Calvinist*. Matt Perman explains that Piper's two additional "points" are really just what Piper sees as natural outflows of traditional Calvinism as expounded at the Synod of Dort. They are 1) belief in double-predestination, and 2) that this is the best of all possible worlds. Of course, Calvinists have long disagreed over these issues, but the important point to note here is that Piper's position is often adopted uncritically at the popular level in a way that leads to Theological Fatalism.

Piper's claim that double-predestination—the belief that God predestines some to salvation and Heaven and others to condemnation and Hell—follows from his view of unconditional election and is not of concern to us here, controversial though it may be. The claim that this is the best of all possible worlds is much more problematic. As Perman explains, it is the belief "that God governs the course of history so that, in the long run, his glory will be more fully displayed and his people more

---

and Hephaistos, the blacksmith of the gods, in which she pleads with him to make a new suit of armor and shield for her grief-stricken son after his closest friend, Patroclus, is killed by Hector of the Trojans. Hephaistos agrees to the request, but curiously notes that it will make no difference because it is Achilles' destiny to die at Troy: "Do not fear. Let not these things be a thought in your mind. And I wish that I could hide him away from death and its sorrow at that time when his hard fate comes upon him as surely as there shall be fine armor for him, such as another man out of many men shall wonder at, when he looks on it."

fully satisfied than would have been the case in any other world."[52] In other words, God's purposes and will could not have been equally met or satisfied in any other way. It is not a far leap to the conclusion that God's nature is such that he had to create and had to do so just the way he did; he really had no alternative in the matter.

To be fair, Piper himself has never (at least to my knowledge) made this claim and has even taken steps to distance his own views from that of Theological Fatalism. While holding to the best of all possible worlds doctrine, Piper maintains that God's will is the determining factor in his decisions. For example, in commenting on Exodus 33:19, he claims that God was telling Moses, "I am absolutely self-existent and absolutely self-determining. I exist freely, without cause or control from any other. And I have mercy freely. At the deepest decision of my mercy there is no cause or control or constraint by anything outside of my own will. That is what it means to be God, Yahweh. That is my name and the essence of my glory."[53]

Piper is to be commended for maintaining the freedom of will in God, but it is hard to see how he can do so consistently while claiming that this is the singular best possible world because of God's perfection. Piper would likely argue that there is a perfect union of will and nature in God so that his desires *just are* consistent with what his nature dictates, so that God's freely willing is properly constrained by his perfection. At first glance, this line of argumentation seems both logical and reasonable, but there are good reasons for rejecting it as erroneous and inconsistent with historical Christianity.

Most importantly, it offers an unsophisticated theology because it violates the doctrines of divine aseity, omnipotence, and freedom. God is not self-sufficient because if all his actions are necessary (as an outflow of his necessary nature), then the creation itself becomes necessary (violating the fundamental distinction between God's being and that of creation). If he had to create, then in some ways he is dependent upon the creation. Under Theological Fatalism, we all become necessary beings of sorts.[54] Second, Theological Fatalism is based on the false idea that God's obligation to do the best limits him to only one option. It assumes that there is one "best" option for any given action, but it should be clear that there

---

52. Matt Perman, "What Does Piper Mean When He Says He's a Seven-point Calvinist?," posted January 23, 2006, http://www.desiringgod.org/articles/what-does-piper-mean-when-he-says-hes-a-seven-point-calvinist.

53. John Piper, "The Freedom and Justice of God in Unconditional Election," posted January 12, 2003, http://www.desiringgod.org/messages/the-freedom-and-justice-of-god-in-unconditional-election.

54. Some may wish to point out that the necessity associated with the creation in this view is still of a different sort from the necessity of God. There is not space here to develop an argument for the conclusion, but it would require some kind of principle of transfer of necessity. Still, if both God's existence and actions derive their necessity from his perfection, then the conclusion seems to follow.

could be several equally good options which are the best way for God to achieve his desired ends.

Another theologian sometimes thought to support Fatalism is Martin Luther, largely due to his polemic against freedom. He denied true creaturely freedom on the basis of the connection between divine foreknowledge and omnipotence on the one hand, and on the basis of human sinfulness on the other hand. According to Luther, since God's foreknowledge cannot err, and since God's will is never thwarted, then whatever he foreknows or wills happens of *necessity*. An extended quote will prove illuminating:

> God knows nothing contingently, but…he foresees and purposes and does all things by his immutable, eternal, and infallible will. . . . If he foreknows as he wills, then his will is eternal and unchanging (because it belongs to his nature), and if he wills as he foreknows, then his knowledge is eternal and unchanging (because it belongs to his nature).
>
> From this it follows irrefutably that everything we do, everything that happens, even if it seems to us to happen mutably and contingently, happens in fact nonetheless necessarily and immutably, if you have regard to the will of God. For the will of God is effectual and cannot be hindered . . . moreover it is wise, so that it cannot be deceived. Now if his will is not hindered, nothing can prevent the work itself from being done, in the place, time, manner, and measure that he himself both foresees and wills.[55]

Luther clearly demurs free will, claiming that the whole of Scripture speaks out against it.

Though it is his primary concern, Luther does not stop at the denial of one's ability to perform righteous acts. He further claims that when one tries to act freely, he is asserting himself over against God; the doctrine of free will is a manifestation of the sinful nature and is in direct opposition to God, the gospel, and everything that is holy. Luther writes, "it is at the same time certain that free choice is nothing else but the supreme enemy of righteousness and man's salvation, since there must have been at least a few among the Jews and Gentiles who toiled and strove to the utmost of the power of free choice, yet just by doing so they did nothing but wage war against grace."[56] Free choice, then, is illusory; humans have the freedom to sin, but not the freedom to do good. The human will is enslaved to "sin, death, and Satan, not doing and not capable of doing

---

55.   Martin Luther, *The Bondage of the Will*, trans. P. S. Watson, in *Luther's Works, vol. 33: Career of the Reformer III*, ed. Philip S. Watson (Philadelphia: Fortress, 1972), 37–38. I am indebted to William Lane Craig for this quote. See William Lane Craig, "Middle Knowledge: A Calvinist-Arminian Rapprochement?," in Pinnock, ed., *The Grace of God and the Will of Man*, 142.

56.   Luther, *Bondage of the Will*, 181.

or attempting to do anything but evil."[57] For Luther, the doctrine of free will is not only contrary to Scripture, it is an assertion of the creature over the Creator.[58]

While the concern of Luther for preserving the providence of God is admirable, and while it must be duly noted that his arguments against free will were written primarily in the context of a discussion of salvation by grace, which is not aided by any human works, it is still difficult to imagine that when one chooses to eat a hamburger instead of a slice of pizza, he is devoid of an understanding of righteousness, and is waging war against grace. It is also difficult to imagine that when one asserts that a choice to eat a hamburger instead of a piece of pizza is a free choice of the individual creaturely will, he is unwittingly speaking a doctrine of demons against the Scriptures.

Middle Knowledge

Middle knowledge has long been associated with Arminian theology, though it was first put forth by Catholic writers.[59] Arminianism is often characterized as a polar opposite of Calvinism, but this is not the case. The two are much closer than most think, especially with regard to practical application. More will be said about this later; for now, we should just note that Calvinism and Arminianism represent the orthodox Christian consensus, with Process Theology and Fatalism serving as polar opposites.

In discussions about providence, I have found it helpful to think of the alternate theories as points along a series of sliding scales. Consider the following diagram. Leaving aside problems with proximity to one another and only considering locations of the theories/models relative to the concerns presented, we can see how they compare.

---

57.   Ibid., 206. This inability, Luther contends, is due to original sin. Since the Fall, humanity has been enslaved to sin and therefore, is not free with respect to any actions, except insofar as the tainted will chooses to sin; it is not forced to sin by God. Luther explains, "Original sin itself, therefore, leaves free choice with no capacity to do anything but sin and be damned." Ibid., 203.

58.   He writes, "In a word, since Scripture everywhere preaches Christ by contrast and antithesis, as I have said, putting everything that is without the Spirit of Christ in subjection to Satan, ungodliness, error, darkness, sin, death, and the wrath of God, all the texts that speak of Christ must consequently stand opposed to free choice; and they are innumerable, indeed they are the entire Scripture." Ibid., 218.

59.   There is some debate about the relationship between Molinism and Arminianism; some argue that Arminius was not only aware of Molina's work, but incorporated it into his theology, while others dispute this claim. For the former, see Eef Dekker, "Was Arminius a Molinist?," *Sixteenth Century Journal* 47, no. 2 (Summer 1996): 337–52; and for the latter, see Roger Olson, *Arminian Theology: Myths & Realities* (Downers Grove: IVP, 2006), 194–97; see also William Witt, "Creation, Redemption and Grace in the Theology of Jacob Arminius" (PhD diss., University of Notre Dame, 1993), 363–66.

Less	Direct Divine Control	More
Lesser	Problem of Evil	*Greater*
More	Creaturely (Human) Freedom	*Less*

Process Theology	Open Theism	Arminianism	Calvinism	Theological
(Finite Godism)		(Middle Knowledge)		Fatalism

Process Theology has the least amount of direct divine control. In fact, God is unable to control much of anything. This also means that God cannot be charged with responsibility for evil and suffering. Under the Process view, creatures have the greatest amount of freedom as well. By contrast, Theological Fatalism boasts an extremely high degree of divine causation, which consequently leads to a lesser degree of creaturely freedom. The problem of evil is particularly acute for this model. The other models have varying degrees of the three, depending upon where they fall on the sliding scale. It is my contention that middle knowledge best handles these issues, taken together.

ASSUMPTIONS

Before we begin our study of middle knowledge, some preliminary assumptions should be set forth, as all questions related to Providence cannot be addressed in such a short work. In some cases, the reader may feel frustrated at the brevity of the discussion or may wish for a more detailed examination. To them, I can only apologize and suggest further research.

The Nature of God

Theology Proper is the area of systematics that primarily refers to examination of God's nature and attributes. Thinking about God is at the heart of the theological enterprise, but it has its limitations. Two in particular deserve comment. The first limitation has to do with our finitude and capacity for knowledge. God is infinite and we are finite, and while we desire to know him, we can never fully comprehend him as he is. As Jesus put it, no one has seen the Father except the Son (John 6:46; cf. John 1:18; 1 John 4:12). God is transcendent—beyond the created order—and is therefore, in at least some ways, inaccessible to us. At the same time, he has revealed himself to us, drawn close to us, speaks to us, and condescends for us so that we may know him. In a word, he is immanent. God's transcendence and immanence must both be respected; to overemphasize his transcendence is to view him as completely other and unknowable, and to overemphasize his immanence is to view him as similar to (or worse, equal to) the creation. The second limitation is related, and has to do with the limitations of human language to express divine truth. When we speak of God, we always speak analogously: God's love is both like and unlike our love, God's knowledge is both like and unlike our knowledge, etc. As we investigate how God governs the created order, we must remember these two limitations in order to acknowledge the tentative nature of our conclusions.

Divine Omnipotence

One of the most common errors in the doctrine of God is to overemphasize one attribute to the exclusion of the others. Perhaps the attribute most abused in this way is omnipotence, because it is seen as most clearly defining what it means to be God. When one attempts to think about the nature of God, some view of power usually comes into play, most commonly infinite power.[60] Nevertheless, it is unclear exactly what it means to say that God is all-powerful. At first glance, we may be tempted to say that God can do just anything and no action is beyond his ability. Under this interpretation, to say that there are some limits to what he can do is to deny omnipotence and thus, his deity, but most theologians and philosophers have disagreed with this claim.

There is a whole body of literature devoted to answering the complex philosophical questions related to the meaning of omnipotence. Perhaps the most entertaining engagements on the issue came a number of years ago, when a series of articles that sought to answer the age-old question, "Can God make a rock so heavy that he can't lift it?" were published in scholarly philosophy journals. The question was first raised by an atheist in an attempt to demonstrate that the notion of an all-powerful being is incoherent. The ensuing discussion, while somewhat humorous, helped clarify the meaning of divine omnipotence. It does not mean he can do just anything; there are some limitations to what an omnipotent Being can do, but they are not deficiencies because, in most cases, it simply makes no sense to suppose such actions can be performed.[61]

---

60. The task of natural theology—reflection on the nature of God by consideration of the being of God—typically involves such thoughts. Anselm's famous ontological argument may serve as representative.

61. J. L. Makie first raised the question in the context of discussions over the logical problem of evil. He argued that it makes no sense to suppose that an omnipotent being could make beings that he could not control. Therefore, any appeal to divine limitation in answering the problem of evil denies God's omnipotence and therefore, fails. J. L. Mackie, "Evil and Omnipotence," *Mind* 64, no. 254 (April 1955): 200–212. Several responses were published with varying degrees of nuance. Richard Swinburne, for example, separated the question into two distinct actions. In effect, he argued that God could make just such a rock because he is omnipotent, but then he could also lift the rock because he is omnipotent. For Swinburne, as long as these issues remain in the realm of the theoretical, God's omnipotence is preserved. If God were to actually create such a stone, then his power would be compromised. Swinburne, *The Coherence of Theism*, 157–63. Mele and Smith seem to agree; Alfred R. Mele and M. P. Smith, "The New Paradox of the Stone," *Faith and Philosophy* 5, no. 3 (July 1988): 283–90. Others, such as George Mavrodes, Bernard Mayo, and

This clarification was not a new development in theology. Christians have long held that God possesses infinite power, but have likewise recognized at least some limits to the actions he can perform. The most obvious have to do with God's performing actions inconsistent with his nature. Consider the following statements: "God exists" or "God has always existed" or "God is love," etc. It is abundantly clear that God could not, no matter how much he may desire to do so (and I do not think he would), make any of these statements false. For example, he could not make the first false because he would have to exist in order to do so! Similarly, it is generally agreed that God is by nature, loving. He could not cease to be loving because that is, in part, what it means for him to be who he is. Similar points could be made regarding any of God's essential attributes. So far, so good; what has been said is not particularly controversial.

What is not so clear is how other statements thought to be necessarily true could also be outside of God's ability to make false. Take, for example, a mathematical formula: "1+1=2." On this view, God cannot make this false. Similarly, God cannot make "1+1=5" true. Instead, these propositions are true (or false) by necessity and could not be otherwise. To suppose that God could, by some act of his will, make "1+1=5" true simply makes no sense. The best we can hope for is to change the meaning of the terms—make "1" really refer to "2½," or make "=" really mean "≠," or make "5" really mean "2," or something of that sort. But to retain the current meanings of the terms and still make "1+1=5" true moves beyond rational comprehension.

When I make this point in class, invariably someone complains that I am trying to force God to conform to "human ways of thinking" or to constrain God's ability or power to "human logic and/or math." In response, I point out that the fundamental laws of logic and math are not mere human constructs, but are instead ways of describing reality, and although some aspects of reality could be otherwise, it is clear that some could not (we have already noted that God's existence and nature are necessary aspects of reality). In addition, if God is rational (in any

---

Alvin Plantinga, have suggested that the challenge begins with the assumption that God is not omnipotent. If God were assumed to be omnipotent, then the argument would not make sense because it includes a sort of contradiction built into the expectation—that is, to make a rock so heavy that he can't lift it would require that God perform two contradictory actions—and this is the problem with the requirement. Bernard Mayo, "Mr. Keene on Omnipotence," *Mind* 70 (1961): 249–50; George Mavrodes, "Some Puzzles Concerning Omnipotence," *Philosophical Review* 72 (1963): 221–23; "Necessity, Possibility, and the Stone Which Cannot Be Moved," *Faith and Philosophy* 2, no. 3 (July 1985): 265–71; Alvin Plantinga, *God and Other Minds* (Ithaca: Cornell University Press, 1967), 168–73; see also C. Anthony Anderson, "Divine Omnipotence and Impossible Tasks: An Intensional Analysis," *International Journal for Philosophy of Religion* 15 (1984): 109–24. Still others, like G. B. Keene and Wade Savage, have argued that the double negatives in the requirement cancel each other out and therefore, amount to nothing. G. B. Keene, "A Simpler Solution to the Paradox of Omnipotence," *Mind* 69 (January 1960): 74–75; "Capacity-Limiting Statements," *Mind* 70 (1961): 251–52; C. Wade Savage, "The Paradox of the Stone," *Philosophical Review* 76 (1967): 74–79.

meaningful sense of the term), then the laws of logic and math may be descriptive of his very nature. Consider the fundamental laws of logic. The law of identity says that something is equal to itself ($A=A$). While it seems almost absurd to say such a thing because it is self-evidently true, the point is this: it makes no sense to suggest that anyone, even an omnipotent Being, could make it false or its opposite true (i.e., $A \neq A$). There simply is no way to articulate what it means for the law of identity to be false. The very suggestion that it *could* be false is literally nonsense.

There are even more serious concerns with denying the laws of logic or suggesting that they are contingent (dependent on God). If the fundamental laws of logic do not hold, then all communication and thought becomes meaningless because words cease to have meaning: True≠True, Omnipotence≠Omnipotence, etc., and the implications of this are obvious. If True≠True, then it may be that True=False, but this is ridiculous. When I ask students to explain what they mean when they say that God is not bound by human laws of logic, they simply claim that he can do anything, yet they fail to realize that this claim is itself dependent upon the laws of logic being true, for it depends on words having meaning. In fact, if the laws of logic are viewed as contingent, then skepticism and relativism follow. This unforeseen consequence is disastrous for theology, not to mention ethics, discipleship, communication (including divine revelation), and even love!

If the claim that God is not bound by the laws of logic is so erroneous and injurious, why would anyone make it? Why would so many people have difficulty with the claim that God's ability is constrained by them? Perhaps they have in mind some biblical passages that seem to teach God does have power over necessary truths like mathematical formulae and the laws of logic. For example, Paul writes to the Ephesians, "Now to Him who is able to do *above* and *beyond all* that we ask or *think*—according to the power that works in you—to Him be glory in the church and in Christ Jesus to all generations forever and ever. Amen" (Eph. 3:20–21; HCSB). How can my claim be reconciled with Paul's words here? Does Paul not basically say that divine omnipotence means that God can do things beyond human logic? A close examination of the text will reveal that this is not the case. When Paul notes God's ability to do more than we ask or imagine, he is referring to God's eternal plan of salvation, specifically for the Gentiles.[62]

---

62. Throughout the book of Ephesians, Paul explains the complex relationship between Israel and Gentile believers and how God has reconciled Gentiles to himself through Christ and made them recipients of the covenant promises to Abraham. Earlier in the chapter, Paul refers to the redemption of the Gentiles in the church as a mystery: "The mystery was made known to me by revelation, as I have briefly written above. . . . This was not made known to people in other generations as it is now revealed to His holy apostles and prophets by the Spirit: the Gentiles are co-heirs, members of the same body, and partners of the promise in Christ Jesus through the gospel" (Eph. 3:3, 5–6). Clearly, then, the benediction Paul offers extolling God's ability to work wonders is not meant to refer to a philosophical understanding of the nature of omnipotence, but is instead a song of praise for what God has done in Christ for all humanity.

Two places in Scripture record the rhetorical question, "Is anything too difficult for the Lord?" The implication is, of course, that nothing is beyond God's ability, but in both cases, the reference to God's power has to do with fulfilling his covenant promises: first, to Abraham by seemingly reversing the menopausal process in his wife, Sarah (Gen. 18:14), and second, to Israel by returning the people to the land after the Babylonian captivity (Jer. 32:27). They are not meant to suggest that God can override necessary truths or violate the fundamental laws of logic, even if they do communicate something of the mystery or incomprehensibility of his will and power. One other passage which also appears to teach that God's power enables him to do just anything is found in Christ's words, "With God, all things are possible" (Matt. 19:26). Again, though, the context precludes this interpretation. The words of Jesus here are meant to speak of God's work of grace in salvation. Jesus had just challenged the rich young ruler to sell all his possessions, give them to the poor, and follow him. When he departed, Jesus told his disciples that it is difficult for the rich to enter the kingdom of heaven (easier for a camel to go through the eye of a needle). Their response was to question the possibility of salvation for anyone. It is at this point that Jesus referred to God's power to save (all things are possible). Clearly, then, Jesus's words are meant to refer to salvation. They are not meant to be an exposition on the nature or extent of God's power. Thus, the point stands: It makes no sense to suppose God can make a contradiction true, or make a necessarily false statement true (or vice versa). These issues are very important for the doctrine of middle knowledge, as will become clear.

A similar but perhaps more dangerous error is to set the attributes in opposition to one another. The most common manifestation of this problem is when God's mercy is viewed as tempering, or worse, overwhelming, his justice. To see mercy and justice in this way is ultimately disastrous for one's view of salvation and even atonement. Under this view, the self-sacrifice of God is seen as somehow an unjust act, but merciful nonetheless. Instead, the attributes of God should be seen as working together. Justice, mercy, holiness, wrath, transcendence, immanence, love, etc., are all perfect, infinite, indivisible, and harmonious in God.

Divine Omniscience

Divine omniscience and propositional knowledge
Proponents of middle knowledge make some assumptions about divine omniscience. The first is that God's knowledge may be conceived in terms of propositional knowledge; he has knowledge of propositions or discrete statements of fact. To say that the content of God's knowledge is propositional is not to say that he lacks knowledge of ideas or essences or beings, but simply that he knows the truthfulness or falsity (or *truth values*) of statements of a factual nature. For example, while God knows that I am writing this chapter by hand, we may speak of him knowing

the proposition, "John Laing is writing the Introduction by hand." God's omniscience can thus be thought of as an infinite number of propositions. This is not a particularly controversial idea, though it may seem somewhat strange to those not acquainted with contemporary discussions of divine omniscience among systematic and philosophical theologians.

Logical order of divine thoughts
The second assumption is that God's thoughts may be conceived as having a *logical* order. To say that there is a logical order to divine thoughts is really to say that a dependency relationship exists between some of the propositions of divine thought (due to their content). *Before* God can (or in order for God to) know the meaning of any proposition, he must know the meaning of the terms in the statement. For example, it should be obvious that God knows the proposition, "one plus one equals two (1+1=2)." Such knowledge, though, is logically dependent upon an understanding of the concept of addition, the meaning of one, the meaning of equals, the meaning of two, etc. Thus, it is proper to speak of God's knowledge of "one" being logically prior to his knowledge of "one plus one equals two."

A word of caution is in order here. The language used is meant to protect God's essential omniscience (that God is, by nature, all-knowing). *Logical priority* is used to mean that while a dependency relationship exists between items in the content of God's knowledge, there was never a time when God lacked some knowledge. While God's knowledge of "one" and mathematical concepts is logically prior to his knowledge of "one plus one equals two," there was never a time when God did not know "one plus one equals two." Logical priority and logical dependency should not be confused with temporal priority, even though, in human knowledge, they go together because of our ignorance and finitude (e.g., I had to first learn the concepts of "one" and "two" and addition before I could know that one plus one equals two). Although it may seem strange, the concept of logical priority is not particularly controversial among Christian theologians; most Calvinists and Arminians have used these concepts in discussions of divine decrees.[63]

---

63. Calvinists have typically debated the order of decrees most hotly. Some have maintained that God's election should be primary, and so suggest that the first decree (logically) was to elect some to salvation and condemn some to punishment. Following this decree was the decree to create humans, then the fall of humans into sin, and then the death of Christ for the salvation of men. This position is known as supralapsarianism. Others have seen this as both morally repugnant and illogical and have therefore argued that the decree to create humans had to *precede* (in the logical order of things) the decree of the fall of man or the election of some and the condemnation of others. This approach is known as infralapsarianism or sublapsarianism. The positions taken on this issue and the strengths and weakness of each are not relevant for the discussion here; what is relevant is that the concept of logical priority is one that has come to be seen as conventional in talking about the divine mind, especially with respect to God's creation decisions. As Calvinist John Feinberg writes, "The debate about the order of decrees focuses most precisely on the logical order of the decrees. Although it makes little sense (at least from a Calvinistic perspective) to ask about the temporal order of the divine decrees, one can still ask

For example, it seems obvious that God's decision to create the world the way he did is logically dependent upon his decision to create something. That is, we may say that God's decision to create in general is logically prior to his decision to create a world with green grass or a blue sky, or a world where I exist, etc. This is not to suggest that there was time when God did not know he would create a world with green grass or a blue sky, but it is to say that such knowledge has a dependency relationship with his knowledge that he would create even though he knew all of these truths eternally.

The Nature of Human Freedom

One of the most difficult topics for understanding providence is the nature of human freedom. Two basic models exist: libertarianism and compatibilism. Libertarian freedom refers to the ability to choose between competing alternatives. It is so named because the individual has the *liberty* to choose to perform either of two possible actions; after he chooses, it is proper to say that he had the ability to have chosen other (than he did, in fact, choose). Compatibilist freedom refers to the ability to choose to act in accordance with one's desires. It is so named because it is *compatible* with there being causes internal and/or external to the individual that may be spoken of as being *efficient* for the choice. Put differently, we may say that the individual freely chose the course of action he did, but he could not have done otherwise. Frame explains, "Compatibilist freedom means that even if every act we perform is caused by something outside ourselves (such as natural causes or God), we are still free, for we can still act according to our character and desires."[64]

Proponents of middle knowledge are convinced that libertarianism is correct. There is much to commend it. First, it is the most obvious and common understanding of freedom. Most people think of freedom as the ability to choose between various options and to act without coercion (or at least overwhelming coercion or duress). Most would scoff (at least initially) at the suggestion that a choice could be free, even if so determined that the individual really only had the ability to choose one of the options. For example, we might say that I have the ability to freely order a pizza for dinner tonight. On most accounts, this would mean that I have the ability to either order a pizza or not order a pizza (and could really do either). Few persons (apart from professional philosophers and theologians of a certain stripe, or evolutionary biologists with a penchant for seeing all thoughts and actions as caused by genes) would say that my choice to order a pizza is the result of a chain of causes that may be traced

---

what God logically decreed first, second, and so on to happen." John S. Feinberg, *No One Like Him* (Wheaton. IL: Crossway, 2001), 532.

64. John Frame, *The Doctrine of God: A Theology of Lordship* (Phillipsburg, NJ: Presbyterian & Reformed, 2002), 136.

to the creation of the universe or that my choice is the manifestation of a personality trait that I was born with such that I may be spoken of as having the property, *orders a pizza on August 10, 2015*. Even if such claims are made, most would deny that the choice was genuinely free.

Second, the libertarian view accords well with our lived experiences. Returning to my example of ordering a pizza, it seems that I really do have the ability to choose between ordering and not ordering, and if I order, it still seems that I could have chosen to not order, and vice versa. Many would find odd the claim that my inborn desires (or desires that follow deterministically from the way I was created and the experiences I have had) determined my choice to order the pizza on this particular occasion, but did not determine my choice to order pizza on another, similar occasion, and instead determined my choice to not order a pizza.

One of the most compelling arguments for libertarian freedom has to do with moral responsibility. Most proponents of libertarianism argue that their view of freedom allows for a greater degree of moral responsibility for human choice and action than compatibilism does.[65] A corollary to this is that it also lessens divine responsibility, while compatibilist freedom seems to increase God's responsibility for evil.

Some have also argued that a genuine loving relationship requires libertarian freedom. They claim that truly personal relationships require the ability to hurt one another. In most cases, arguments of this sort point to man's relationship with God, and contend that God's desire is for man to respond to his call with genuine and personal love, and that such responses cannot be caused by God, neither in his creating the individual's personality nor by overriding the individual's will. This argument proves compelling to many—love not given freely is no love at all. However, it is not obviously true and it seems that proof is not possible. Persons either agree with the requirement of libertarian freedom for love or they do not.

Yet, libertarianism is not without its critics. Perhaps the most common complaint against libertarian freedom is that it is incoherent or self-defeating because of its denial of efficient external causation for free decisions. That is, since proponents of libertarian freedom insist that free actions cannot be caused by anything external or internal to the individual, save an exercising of his will, those actions are seen to have no cause, and this seems preposterous! All actions must have a cause which can be noted when explaining the decision.[66] The only Uncaused Cause is God![67] Grudem seems to advocate this critique: "Scripture nowhere says that we

---

65. Some libertarians have argued that compatibilism removes human responsibility and places blame for evil squarely on the shoulders of God, though most do not do so. What is really in mind here is a matter of degree. Libertarianism lessens the degree to which God is responsible for evil.

66. Many of the advocates of this criticism have referred to libertarian freedom as *contra-causal freedom*, a term not used by libertarians due to its erroneous characterization.

67. Of course, this argument makes use of the cosmological argument from causation.

are 'free' in the sense of being outside of God's control or of being able to make decisions that are not caused by anything."[68] Frame makes a similar allegation, equating libertarian choice with causeless choice: "Nor does Scripture indicate that God places any positive value on libertarian freedom (even granting that it exits). . . . One would imagine, then, that Scripture would abound with statements to the effect that causeless free actions by creatures are terribly important to God, that they bring him glory. But Scripture never suggests that God honors causeless choice in any way or even recognizes its existence."[69]

A different manifestation of the same argument is related to the likelihood of one choice over another, the nature of freedom, and the ability of the individual to make any choice whatsoever. According to this version of the argument, libertarian freedom, in its denial of personal preference as the efficient cause of the choice one makes, along with its insistence that the individual could choose either of two alternatives, creates a barrier to the individual's ability to choose. Since both options must be viable alternatives, and the individual's desires cannot be the *cause* of the choice, it is argued, then there cannot be any causal explanation for the choice, except the person *willing*. But on what basis can the person will one course of action over another? It seems that no answer can be given. If no cause can be given, then the choice must be arbitrary or irrational. If the individual uses rationality to choose, then it seems that the lack of reasons will preclude him from making any decision whatsoever! In any case, the result for libertarianism is disastrous—it either leads to inaction or irrationality.[70]

These arguments are misguided because they wrongly assume that libertarian free choices require that, all things being equal, the person is completely indifferent. In fact, Wright refers to libertarian freedom as *liberty of indifference*, but this is not what most libertarians mean by free choice.[71] I know of no proponent of libertarian freedom who claims that for a choice to be free, the individual must have no preference whatsoever. All libertarianism requires is that one's preference does not preclude him from having the ability to choose the other option. Compatibilism argues that one's preferences are determinative so that he does not have the ability to choose either of two options. While there may be some occasions where one really does not care, they are rare and are not the only instances

---

68. Wayne Grudem, *Systematic Theology: An Introduction to Biblical Doctrine* (Grand Rapids: Zondervan, 1994), 331.

69. Frame, *The Doctrine of God*, 140.

70. The well-known thought experiment concerning Buridan's ass, who dies of starvation between two identical piles of hay, is representative. The concept is much older than the fourteenth-century French philosopher from whom it gets its name, and is still used in one form or another today. See, for example, R. K. McGregor Wright, *No Place for Sovereignty: What's Wrong with Freewill Theism* (Downers Grove, IL: InterVarsity, 1996).

71. Ibid., 44.

of free choice. They do show what is wrong with this criticism. Consider the following example: my wife suggests that we watch a movie, and offers two movies that I have seen, neither of which I wish to see again. Both are "chick-flicks": *Howard's End* and *Pride and Prejudice*, and are about the same length. I really do not care which we watch, but my wife wants my help, so I say, "*Howard's End.*" She then indicates that she may prefer *Pride and Prejudice*, and so I say, "fine." As best I can tell, I feel no resentment at our watching *Pride and Prejudice*, except that she asked my advice and then went another way; I really did not care which movie we watched. According to the critique, though, there really must have been something about me, such that I would prefer *Howard's End,* and that is why I initially chose it. If I were really indifferent, we would still be trying to make a decision. But my reaction to the final choice of *Pride and Prejudice* speaks against this very argument; I did not care, but could still choose an option.

Other arguments against libertarianism have also been offered. Some have suggested that it tries to elevate man to the level of God or make man master over God. Similarly, some have suggested that libertarianism requires that man can thwart God's decrees or plans. For example, Frame writes, "Scripture does not explicitly teach the existence of libertarian freedom. There is no passage that can be construed to mean that the human will is *independent of God's plan* and of the rest of the human personality."[72] This, though, is not what libertarian freedom means either. Part of the problem, it seems, is that compatibilism is construed in terms of its compatibility with events being determined, while libertarianism is construed in terms of the ability of the individual. Some of the difficulty of the subject of human freedom may be clarified if libertarianism and compatibilism were spoken of in the same way; e.g., in terms of the origin of the individual's choice. Libertarians argue that the choice one makes, if free, is determined by the individual himself without any external cause. Compatibilists, by contrast, argue that the free choices persons make are determined by the individual as he was made by God. That is, God made the person in such a way that he would have the desires he, in fact, has, and that he can only act in accordance with his desires. Libertarians argue that God made the person with a free will and that individual desires are not based in the way God made the individual. So, at the end of the day, what an individual will choose in any given situation, according to compatibilism, is tied back to God's creating work. For libertarians this is not so, as we shall soon see.

The Nature of Divine Freedom

As should be clear from what has already been said, proponents of middle knowledge are committed to the view that God possesses libertarian freedom. In saying this, I mean to claim that there are choices God

---

72. Frame, *The Doctrine of God*, 140.

can make which could have been otherwise. For example, while God could not perform actions that are unholy, he could have created differently. This is not a particularly controversial claim, as most Calvinists allow that God is libertarianly free with respect to at least *some* choices, even if they fail to use this term. For example, Frame suggests that God could have *not-created* or could have *not-redeemed* humanity; to create and to redeem were free choices he made. While Frame attempts to distinguish God's freedom of choice here from libertarian freedom, he is unsuccessful. He attempts to make this distinction because he thinks libertarianism denies causation, but what he describes is essentially an exercising of libertarian choice: God could really choose between two mutually exclusive courses of action (i.e., create or not-create; redeem or not-redeem) and nothing external or internal to him, save his exercising of his will, causes the choice. Frame writes, "I would say that God's essential attributes and actions are *necessary*, but that his decrees and acts of creation, providence, and redemption are *free*. They are free, not merely in a compatibilist sense, nor at all in a libertarian sense, but in the sense that we know nothing in God's nature that constrains these acts or prevents their opposites."[73]

Amazingly (given Frame's strong Calvinist stance), most Arminians (and thus, proponents of middle knowledge) agree with the basic point Frame hopes to make here—that God freely chooses how he will act with respect to creation, providence, and redemption. Nevertheless, they disagree with Frame's dismissal of libertarian freedom in God. They deem his characterization of libertarian freedom (as anarchist or illogical) erroneous. To be sure, Frame's attempt to create a third category of freedom certainly seems strange, since compatibilist and libertarian freedoms cover the range of meanings of freedom with regard to choice, and his description of the kind of freedom God enjoys is one that most proponents of libertarian freedom endorse.

CONCLUSION

In this chapter, I have attempted to lay out some of the basic presuppositions held by proponents of middle knowledge. First, they hold to belief in meticulous divine providence, which is to say that all things happen within the purview of God's governance. Put differently, they can say that God is in control of all things, even down to the tiniest detail. Second, proponents of middle knowledge are careful to avoid overemphasizing one attribute to the detriment of the others. In saying this, what I was primarily concerned with noting is that they do not view omnipotence as a sort of "anything goes" with respect to divine power; there are still some things that God cannot do, but this does not diminish his power.

---

73. Ibid., 235–36.

The limitations on omnipotence we affirm are only those actions which it makes no sense to suppose God could perform. Third, I noted that much of the discussion surrounding middle knowledge has conceived of divine omniscience in terms of God's knowledge of an infinite number of statements (propositions). Last, I pointed out that proponents of middle knowledge believe in libertarian freedom, over against compatibilist freedom. This means that proponents of middle knowledge believe that creatures, when acting freely, have the ability to choose between competing alternatives and not merely the ability to choose in accordance with the desires they were created to have.

CHAPTER 1

THE DOCTRINE
OF MIDDLE KNOWLEDGE

INTRODUCTION

The doctrine of middle knowledge was first articulated by Jesuit Counter-Reformation theologian Luis Molina in his massive *Concordia Liberi Arbitrii cum Gratiae Donis, Divina Praescientia, Providentia, Praedestinatione, et Reprobatione, ad nonnullos primae partis D. Thome articulos* (henceforth, *Concordia*), a work originally meant to be a commentary on Thomas Aquinas' *Summa Theologica*, but which wound up only addressing the relationship between human freedom and the efficaciousness of God's grace in salvation. The *Concordia* immediately drew criticism from the Dominicans, who feared it came dangerously close to Pelagianism—a fourth-century heresy which claimed that humans did not inherit a corrupt nature from Adam and could therefore earn salvation by their good works—because it maintained that God's grace was made efficacious by the free actions of individuals. This initial criticism grew into a full-fledged controversy within the Roman Catholic Church, and it occupied the thoughts and minds of many leaders for twenty-five years. Interestingly, the controversy was never fully resolved. Middle knowledge (sometimes called "Molinism" for Molina) was Molina's attempt to reconcile God's providence with human freedom.

MIDDLE KNOWLEDGE OR *SCIENTIA MEDIA*

The doctrine of middle knowledge is so called because it is thought to be *in the middle* of the traditional categories of divine thought, natural and free knowledge.[1] When it is said to be *in the middle* of God's natural and

---

1. These were Molina's terms for the epistemological categories handed down by Aquinas. Aquinas preferred the terms *Scientia Simplicis Inteligentia* (Simple Intelligence) and *Scientia Visionis* (Knowledge of Vision). See Thomas Aquinas, *Summa Theolgica* 1.14.9; and Aquinas, *Summa Contra Gentiles* 1.66.4.

free knowledge, two things are meant. First, it has characteristics of both kinds of divine knowledge, similar to a cross between natural knowledge and free knowledge. Second, it comes in between natural and free knowledge in the *logical order* of God's thought *process* regarding creation (if such analogous language may be used of the mind of God). Before these concepts are fleshed out, a brief explanation of natural and free knowledge should be presented.

Natural knowledge refers to the truths God knows by his nature. Since his nature is necessary, He has knowledge of all necessary truths by knowledge of his own nature. Thomas Aquinas conceived of it as God's knowledge of all to which his power extends by virtue of his being Creator and being omniscient.[2] Note that Aquinas did not say that this knowledge comes from God's *creating* or his decision to *create*, but from his nature as the ground of all being.[3] The basic point is this: God's knowledge of all necessary truths is located in his natural knowledge. Necessary truths are of two sorts: 1) metaphysically necessary truths, such as theological absolutes, mathematical formulae, or tautological statements, and 2) statements of possibility. Since the content of natural knowledge is itself necessary, natural knowledge can be described as that part of God's knowledge which could not have been different from what it is. It follows from this that it is independent of his will. Put differently, God has no control over the truth of propositions known by natural knowledge because they are necessarily true. As noted in the introduction, this is not to question his omnipotence or to go awry of good theology.[4]

---

2. Aquinas writes, "But the power of anything can be perfectly known only by knowing to what its power extends. Since therefore the divine power extends to other things by the very fact that it is the first effecting cause of all things, as is clear from what we have said (Q. II, A. 3), God must necessarily know things other than Himself." Thomas Aquinas, *Summa Theologica* I.14.5, trans. Laurence Shapcote, rev. Daniel J. Sullivan, in *Great Books of the Western World*. Vol. 17, *Aquinas* (Chicago: Encyclopedia Britannica, 1990), 79.

3. Aquinas speaks of God's *proper* knowledge of discrete entities, which is to say that God knows things as they are distinct from one another as they have potentiality to exist if He were to create them.

4. We noted that Christians have historically claimed that God cannot perform actions inconsistent with his nature, and it makes no sense to suppose even an omnipotent being could perform the logically impossible. Meaning and rationality depend on the laws of logic holding, and so for "omnipotence" to have any meaning, the laws must be binding. In addition to the laws of logic proper, we also noted that it makes no sense to suppose that God could make mathematical formulae false, since a change in meaning of the terms would be required. The same principles apply to tautological statements. A favorite example in the literature has been the statement, "All bachelors are unmarried." This statement is both obviously true and necessarily true. That is, it could not possibly be wrong because the definitions of the words simply make it true. A bachelor is, by definition, unmarried and there could not be a bachelor who is not unmarried (i.e., who is married). Once a man gets married, he ceases to be a bachelor. Thus, it is no deficiency in God's power for him to lack the ability to make the statement, "All bachelors are unmarried" false. It simply makes no sense to suppose it could be made false.

Free knowledge refers to the truths God knows by knowing his own will. It is his knowledge of those items, persons, or true propositions that he knows will exist because of his knowledge of what he intends to, or will, create. Thus, in one sense, free knowledge comes by his freely exercising his will in creating or controlling events within the created order. The content of this knowledge are truths that refer to what actually exists, existed, or will exist. Aquinas calls this *knowledge of vision* because he conceives of it as directly tied to God's infinity and his observation of all events in eternity.[5]

Since free knowledge comes from God's creative act of will (which is a free decision), it follows that the content of that knowledge is contingent. In other words, because God did not have to create what he did create, any true propositions dependent upon his choice about what to create are contingent (i.e., not necessary). For example, the proposition, "John Laing exists" is true only because God chose to create me. It is a contingent truth because my existence is not necessary. So free knowledge includes only metaphysically contingent truths, or truths that could have been prevented by God if he had chosen to create different situations, different creatures, or to not create at all. God knows the proposition in the example, "John Laing exists," by his free knowledge.

Thus, it is by his free knowledge that God has exhaustive knowledge of the future. As Molina states, it is by his free knowledge that he knows "absolutely and determinately, *without any condition or hypothesis,* which ones from among all the contingent states of affairs were in fact going to obtain and, likewise, which ones were not going to obtain."[6] So free knowledge can be described as both contingent and dependent upon or posterior to, God's will. Flint has set forth the double distinction in divine knowledge in graph format:

	Natural Knowledge	*Free Knowledge*
Truths known are:	(1) Necessary	(1) Contingent
	(2) Independent of God's free will	(2) Dependent on God's free will[7]

---

5. Aquinas writes, "Now a certain difference is to be noted in the consideration of those things that are not actual. For though some of them may not be in act now, still they were, or they will be, and God is said to know all these with the knowledge of vision; for since God's act of understanding, which is His being, is measured by eternity, and since eternity is without succession, comprehending all time, the present glance of God extends over all time, and to all things which exist in any time, as to subjects present to Him." Aquinas, *Summa Theologica* I.14.9 (trans. Shapcote, 83).

6. Luis de Molina, *On Divine Foreknowledge: Part IV of the Concordia*, trans. Alfred J. Freddoso (Ithaca: Cornell University Press, 1988), 52.9, p. 168.

7. Thomas P. Flint, "Two Accounts of Providence," in *Divine and Human Action: Essays on the Metaphysics of Theism*, ed. Thomas V. Morris (Ithaca, NY: Cornell University Press, 1988), 157.

To these two distinctions in divine knowledge, Molina added a third, which incorporated facets of each: *scientia media*, or middle knowledge. Middle knowledge is similar to natural knowledge in that it is prevolitional (prior to God's choice to create) and therefore its truth is independent of God's determining will. It is similar to free knowledge in that the truths that are known are contingent (in this case, dependent on creaturely will). Again, following Flint, the distinctions in divine knowledge can be represented graphically:

	Natural Knowledge	Middle Knowledge	Free Knowledge
Truths known are:	(1) Necessary	(1) Contingent	(1) Contingent
	(2) Independent of God's free will	(2) Independent of God's free will	(2) Dependent on God's free will[8]

The doctrine of middle knowledge proposes that God has knowledge not only of metaphysically necessary truths via natural knowledge, and of truths expressing what He intends to do via free knowledge, but also a third class of propositions which have characteristics of each. The truths known by natural and middle knowledge inform God's decision regarding what he will create by limiting the sorts of worlds he can create (or actualize). Thus, middle knowledge is characterized as *God's prevolitional knowledge of counterfactuals of creaturely freedom*. In order to unpack this mouthful, an examination of counterfactuals needs to be undertaken.

COUNTERFACTUALS

A number of years ago, I attended a high school reunion. It was good to see many of my old buddies from high school, most of whom I had not seen in years. It was interesting to see how our lives had turned out; there were not a few surprises, as is often the case with these sorts of meetings (at my ten-year high school reunion, I won the "Most Changed" award). As we visited, the conversation inevitably turned to our antics while in high school, reminiscing on some of the more humorous events. The conversation also included discussion about the people we used to hang out with, including those we used to date. I began to wonder what happened to my first serious girlfriend, who I will call Susan.

Susan and I dated during my senior year in high school. We were somewhat of an odd couple; she was one of the more outspoken Christians at our school, while I was a self-proclaimed and rather vocal atheist. Despite these differences, we grew very close, but a long-term relationship was not to be. When I graduated, I left for Army Basic Training and knew

---

8. Ibid., 158.

I would have to subsequently move to another state where my father's job had transferred. We talked about long-term possibilities, but while I was at Fort Knox, Susan broke off contact and refused to see me when I returned. She had good reason for breaking up with me, as our relationship violated the dictum against being unequally yoked (2 Cor. 6:14), and thus compromised her commitment to Christ. It was heart-wrenching for me at the time, and I fell into a depression for several months.

It was during this time that I came to saving faith in Jesus Christ. I had attended chapel services while in Basic, and when I moved out to Kansas to attend Kansas University, I encountered an energetic group of young people who loved the Lord. I attended their weekly Bible study and worship, and even bought my own Bible. However, I still did not believe. In a somewhat strange event, I remember praying to God, "Lord, if you exist, help me to believe in you and have faith." I never accepted Jesus during one of their Bible studies or worship services and I eventually broke with the group over a doctrinal issue. Yet I continued to read my Bible, pray and seek God, and faith came. I cannot point to a moment when that faith came (only God truly knows), but it was sometime between May and August 1988, by which time I was a convinced believer.

The discussions with my old high school buddies about the past got me thinking. Such reminiscences, especially with regard to past relationships, naturally lead to thoughts about how our lives have turned out and about how they may have been different. I could not help but wonder what my life would be like if Susan had not broken off contact with me, or if we had married. Would I still be a professor of theology and philosophy at a Southern Baptist seminary? Would I still be a Chaplain in the Army? Would I even be a Christian? None of the answers to these questions are clear or obvious. It may very well be that her breaking up with me at that point in my life was what I needed to come to faith in Christ; then again, perhaps not. I have often thought it was one of the key factors in breaking down my pride so that I might be humble before God, but this does not mean it was *necessary*. Who knows if it was (necessary)? Can such things be known, even by an all-knowing, all-seeing God? The answer to this last question has been the basis of much heated debate in Christian philosophical circles in recent years, as we will see in the next two chapters.

The idea that my life would have turned out a particular way if things had gone differently with Susan is dependent upon belief in what philosophers loosely refer to as "counterfactuals." As the term is used in the literature, a counterfactual is a statement of how things *would definitely* be if things had gone differently. It seems that most people intuitively believe that counterfactuals can be true, that there are some true statements about how things would have been if other things had gone differently from how they did go. Some counterfactuals seem obviously true, such as the following:

If I had married Susan, my daughter Sydney would not have been born.

Since Sydney is a product of my wife Stefana and me, she could not have been the product of my marriage to Susan.[9] Any time we wonder about how things would have turned out differently if some other event had gone differently, we show that we believe in counterfactuals.

There are many types of counterfactuals, but those that are most relevant for our discussion are counterfactuals of creaturely freedom. These are statements about how someone would freely act if things were different. So, for example, the statement

If Susan had continued dating John, he would . . . today;

describes what I would be doing today if I had remained in the dating relationship with Susan. The idea behind this is that many free actions are performed in response to prior circumstances, and when those circumstances do not obtain, there is still a truth about what the individual would have done. Yet counterfactuals of creaturely freedom are not limited to descriptions of events that never occur. Philosophers who discuss these issues commonly refer to all propositions of the form, "If . . . then . . ." as counterfactuals, even if the events described did actually happen. For example, the statement, "If John were to ask Stefana to marry him, she would freely accept" is described as a counterfactual which is true in the actual world. This terminology can be a bit confusing, since the statement is not counter to the facts, but it has become standard in the literature. The idea behind it is this: before God created, there was no actual world, so all if-then statements were counterfactuals *at that time*.[10]

---

9. Some may wish to suggest that we cannot know if this statement is true because, technically speaking, Sydney could still have been born if I had married Susan. After all, I could have had an affair with Stefana, or Susan may have passed away early, leaving me a widower and I could have then met Stefana and been married. However, the basic point of what I was trying to communicate is true, even if the counterfactual needs to be written more precisely. For example, we could write a counterfactual which communicates the same idea as follows:

If I had never met my wife, Stefana, my daughter Sydney would not have been born.

This counterfactual seems not only plausible, but obviously true. While it could still conceivably be false, the point that some counterfactuals can be true still stands. Some perceptive (or nit-picky) readers may still suggest that Sydney could have been born. If I had made a deposit at a sperm bank and Stefana had been inseminated with that deposit, Sydney could have been born. Pushing possible scenarios to the ridiculous, though, does not count against the assertion that counterfactuals can be true, at least at first glance. A counterfactual could be written which discounts all contact between my seed and Stefana's egg and this would preclude the possibility of Sydney's birth.

10. Many of the writers in the area have expressed frustration over the term *counterfactual*, since it is sometimes used in reference to events that are actualized. Kvanvig calls it "misleading" since God uses counterfactuals to bring about the actual world. Jonathan Kvanvig, *The Possibility of an All-Knowing God* (New York: St. Martin's, 1986), 124. Freddoso tries to address the

The contemporary discussion of middle knowledge includes a number of interesting, though somewhat dense principles/ideas. Perhaps the most profitable has been the use of possible worlds semantics in evaluating the truth claims of various counterfactuals. It is to this topic that we now turn.

POSSIBLE WORLDS SEMANTICS

"What if you could travel to parallel worlds, the same year, the same Earth, only different dimensions—a world where the Russians rule America, or where your dreams of becoming a superstar came true, or where San Francisco was a maximum-security prison? My friends and I found the gateway. Now the problem is, finding a way back home." Such were the words used to introduce one of my favorite television shows when I was growing up, *Sliders*. (For the record, I now see it as a bit cheesy, but an interesting concept nonetheless.) It was about four people who are sucked into a wormhole that leads to a parallel universe. They have a portable device for opening such passageways, but can neither control the time it opens nor the destination to which it leads, so they move from one *Earth* to the next (*sliding*), hoping one day to return to their own reality. On each parallel Earth, they discover how things are different from their own world (or their own histories). Sometimes things are vastly different, as in one episode where virtually all humans were extinct, while other times, things are quite similar. Yet, at its most basic, *Sliders* assumes that things *could* have been different from the way they in fact are—that events did not have to occur exactly as they did, or that people could have done things differently.

This assumption seems obvious to most people, and can be described as an existential quantification; it is based on one's experiences. For example, today I left my mobile phone at home, but it seems quite clear that things could have been different (e.g., I could have put it in my pocket and brought it to work). Most persons would not require a proof that I could have done so, but just believe it, probably based on their own, similar experiences. Likewise, most of us do not see ourselves as necessary. While we would all like to think we are important and contribute something of value to the world and mankind, we readily acknowledge that the world would still *exist* (and probably get along just fine) if we had never been born. We take this to be the case from our knowledge of our spheres of influence and from observation of how things progress when

---

problem by preserving the distinction made by Molina between *conditional future contingents, absolute future contingents,* and *conditioned future contingents.* Alfred J. Freddoso, "Introduction," in Molina, *On Divine Foreknowledge,* 22. Lewis also recognizes the difficulty with the term because some are in fact true, but notes that he cannot find another term which conveys what he wishes—*counterfactual* may be too narrow because it seems to exclude constructions with true antecedents, but *subjunctive conditionals* is too broad because it includes futurable statements that are not under consideration. David Lewis, *Counterfactuals* (Cambridge, MA: Harvard University Press, 1973), 3–4.

we are absent from our normal processes (e.g., when we are out sick from work). Of course, we could also reason to the same conclusion through rational thought/argumentation. For example, most theists believe that God is the only necessary being and that he is self-sufficient. Those two beliefs combine to imply that we are not needed for God's well-being; we are contingent. Thus, most of us readily acknowledge that things could have been different. What is not so obvious, but has become somewhat standard language in modern modal logic and in discussions surrounding the doctrine of middle knowledge, is that such belief (that things could have been different) is belief in *possible worlds*.

While in the show *Sliders*, the alternate possible worlds really do exist (put more formally, they have *ontos*, or being) as separate versions of planet Earth with their own histories and geological developments, etc., this is not necessary for the popular possible-worlds-analysis of truth.[11] Rather, the concept of possible worlds can be used as a way of referring to different possibilities and for evaluating their likelihood. A possible world is best understood as a complete set of possible states of affairs, where a state of affairs is a description of any particular situation. For example, *John Laing's writing a book on middle knowledge* is a possible state of affairs that is included in the actual world. Similarly, the state of affairs, *John Laing's never writing a book on middle knowledge* is a possible state of affairs that is not included in the actual world, but is included in some possible worlds.

As already noted, most persons would affirm that there are many ways things could have been different; in fact, there appears to be a virtually infinite number of ways things could have been different, from something as simple as my remembering my mobile phone this morning, to more complex issues like the color of the sky or perhaps even the laws of physics.[12]

---

11. David Lewis, the most prolific author related to the subject, argues that it does, but many philosophers have disputed this claim. According to Lewis, belief that everything is not necessarily so is in actuality the belief that "there exist many entities of a certain description, to wit 'ways things could have been.'" Lewis, *Counterfactuals*, 84. If this assertion is taken at face value, then it can be concluded that anyone who asserts that things could have been different, believes in the existence of entities that might be called *ways things could have been* (or possible worlds). Lewis argues that those who do not wish to take the claim at face value deny it because their presuppositions do not allow for possible worlds: "I do not know of any successful argument that my realism about possible worlds leads to trouble, unless you beg the question by saying that it already *is* trouble." Ibid. By contrast, Kripke has argued for what he calls a stipulative account of possible worlds, seeing them as more than mere sets of propositions, but less than ontological entities; as purely formal items for consideration. Saul Kripke, *Naming and Necessity* (Cambridge, MA: Harvard University Press, 1980). Robert Adams, Alvin Plantinga, William Lycan, and Peter Forrest see possible worlds as merely a complete description of the way things could be. For the purposes of our discussion, we will follow this view.

12. Throughout this chapter, I refer to a virtual infinity regarding the possibilities for the world. Some may wonder why such language is used. After all, the possibilities are either infinite or not. The idea, though, is that there are so many ways things could be different so as to seem infinite even though in actuality, there is, indeed, a finite number of possibilities. One need

As Lewis notes, the set of worlds considered possible is, at least to some extent, relative to one's own opinions about possibility.[13] This is not to say that which worlds are possible is wholly relative, but rather our understanding of which worlds are possible is relative. A lot of thought about possible worlds is derived from individual philosophical opinions regarding how things *could* have been different. It makes sense to believe in the existence of a world where my truck is blue rather than black, or where I weigh three hundred pounds rather than (approximately) 180 pounds, but it does not make sense to believe in the existence of a world where those items deemed *necessary truths* are different.[14] Since the doctrine of middle knowledge proposes that God has knowledge of all possible truths, the modern version of Molinism speaks of God's knowledge of all possible worlds.

There is much technical philosophical jargon and discussion surrounding the possible worlds analysis of truth and many a student has been lost in the nuances of terminology. However, at its most basic, it really only has to do with the nature of possibility and what could have been the case. We will try to present the basic ideas in the philosophical discussion in the following pages, though a complete understanding of the technical arguments is not necessary in order to understand the basic theory of middle knowledge.

Actualization of Worlds

One of the distinctive features of Molinism which makes it such a powerful approach to understanding the relationship between divine providence and human freedom is the claim that God has knowledge of not only all possible worlds, but also of how all possible free creatures would in fact act in all possible circumstances, and that this knowledge is logically prior to and therefore informs, his creative decision. However, it has become common in the philosophical literature on the subject to refer to God's

---

only consider all the possible arrangements of currently existing molecules to get an idea of what is meant—it seems that there is an infinite number of ways the molecules could be arranged before we even consider changing the molecules themselves, or adding new molecules or subtracting molecules. For each arrangement, there is a possible world. However, while this *seems* to allow for an infinite number of possible worlds, in reality there is a finite number of arrangements. The possibilities are also finite because they are composed of finite items. Put differently, anything composed of finite items must be finite, and therefore, the universe and possibilities of universes, are finite. Conversely, anything infinite cannot be composed of finite items (or attributes).

13. Lewis writes, "For instance, I believe that there are worlds where physics is different from the physics of our world, but none where logic and arithmetic are different from the logic and arithmetic of our world. This is nothing but the systematic expression of my naive, pre-philosophical opinion that physics could be different, but not logic or arithmetic." Lewis, *Counterfactuals*, 88.

14. It is interesting to note that Plantinga has defined necessary truths as those laws or propositions which are true in all possible worlds. Alvin Plantinga, *The Nature of Necessity* (Oxford: Clarendon, 1974), 55.

providential activity as *actualizing* states of affairs, rather than *creating worlds*.[15]

This actualizing activity needs further clarification, though, for it is hard to understand how God can actualize worlds where people do what he wishes without impinging on their freedom. Put differently, it is not altogether clear that God can actualize the free actions of creatures.[16] For example, consider the following state of affairs:

> John Laing's ordering a pepperoni pizza tonight.

Surely God, being omnipotent, can actualize this state of affairs (or cause it to obtain). He could force me to pick up the phone, dial the number for Papa John's Pizza, and say, "I would like to order a pepperoni pizza," by overriding my decision-making processes. This would clearly not be a libertarianly free action. There are, however, other ways of understanding God's activity in bringing about my ordering a pepperoni pizza which do not violate my freedom. In an effort to explain this, some philosophers have drawn a distinction between two kinds of actualizing activity: strong and weak actualization.[17]

Strong actualization was represented in the example above, where God actively caused me to call Papa John's Pizza and order a pepperoni pizza.[18] By contrast, weak actualization refers to the bringing about of an event by means of the free actions of another.[19] This concept can be illustrated by

---

15. It is too simplistic and technically incorrect to assert that God creates a world where his will is achieved through the free decisions of creatures. It is seen as semantically improper to say that God created the world because, it must be remembered, that the *world* (in the sense used), is not an object which had a beginning, but rather one of many complete sets of compatible states of affairs which have subsisted in the mind of God for all eternity. Plantinga explains, "We speak of God as *creating* the world; yet if it is α of which we speak, what we say is false. For a thing is created only if there is a time before which it does not exist; and this is patently false of α, as it is of any state of affairs. What God has created are the heavens and the earth and all that they contain; he has not created himself, or numbers, propositions, properties, or states of affairs: these have no beginnings. We can say, however, that God *actualizes* states of affairs; his creative activity results in their being or becoming actual." Ibid., 169.
16. The basic concept of freedom presumed here is that agent acts freely when there is nothing external to that agent which constitutes a determining factor in that action's performance.
17. See Plantinga, *The Nature of Necessity*, 172–73; and Roderick Chisholm, *Person and Object: A Metaphysical Study* (La Salle, IL: Open Court, 1976), 67–69.
18. Flint and Freddoso offer a definition of strong actualization: "Roughly, an agent S strongly actualizes a state of affairs p just when S causally determines p's obtaining, i.e., just when S does something which in conjunction with other operative causal factors constitutes a sufficient causal condition for p's obtaining." Thomas P. Flint and Alfred J. Freddoso, "Maximal Power," in *The Concept of God*, ed. Thomas V. Morris (New York: Oxford University Press, 1987), 139.
19. Flint and Freddoso explain, "In such cases the agent in question, by his actions or omissions, strongly brings it about that another agent S is in situation C, where it is true that if S were in C, then S would freely act in a specified way." Ibid., 140.

an appeal to counterfactuals of creaturely freedom. Suppose the following counterfactual of freedom is true:

> If Pizza Hut had a sale on its Big New Yorker pepperoni pizza for $5 each and John Laing was aware of it, then he would order one (even if he had just eaten dinner).[20]

Armed with this knowledge, God could weakly actualize my ordering a pepperoni pizza tonight by placing me in a situation in which I become aware of the sale.[21] For example, God may cause (strongly actualize) me to drive down a particular road that has a billboard advertising the Big New Yorker sale, or he may cause me to change the channel on my television to a station that is currently airing a commercial for the Pizza Hut promotion. In both cases, God will have strongly actualized a state of affairs he knows will lead to my free decision to order a pepperoni pizza. Thus, God can weakly actualize my ordering a pepperoni pizza without compromising my freedom, at least not with respect to the decision to order the pizza. Of course, these examples are a bit simplistic, for God could use a string of weak actualizations to bring about my ordering a Big New Yorker. That is, it may be possible for God to orchestrate events so that I freely order the pizza without any violations of anyone's freedom.

It should be clear that the distinction of strong and weak actualization is a powerful tool for understanding the relationship between divine providence and human freedom. However, under the Molinist system, there are limitations to the states of affairs God can actualize. For example, God cannot strongly actualize counterfactuals of freedom because the strong actualization destroys the freedom of the actor. God is also limited in the states of affairs he can weakly actualize due to the true counterfactuals of freedom.

Suppose the counterfactual mentioned earlier is true. Suppose that I would order a Big New Yorker pizza if Pizza Hut sold them for $5. In that case, God could bring it about that I freely order one, but he could not bring it about that I freely refrain from ordering one while being aware of the sale.[22] Similarly, if the counterfactual were false, then God could not weakly

---

20. I am painfully aware that Pizza Hut no longer offers the Big New Yorker pizza in most (if any) markets.

21. Of course, there is no guarantee that such a sale will in fact take place. I have assumed that it does in my example, but even so, there is nothing which precludes God from actualizing (either strongly or weakly) the state of affairs, *Pizza Hut's placing the Big New Yorker pepperoni pizza on sale for $5.*

22. In the philosophical language, God can weakly actualize the corresponding state of affairs,

> John Laing's being aware of Pizza Hut's sale on the Big New Yorker pepperoni pizza for $5 each and (freely) ordering one;

but he cannot weakly actualize its opposite, namely

actualize my being aware of the sale and freely ordering a pizza, but he could weakly actualize my being aware of the sale and freely refraining from ordering one. Note that this does not mean that God cannot strongly actualize either state of affairs; he could always override my freedom to force me to order or not order, but then those would be different states of affairs (since my freedom is included in the states of affairs mentioned). It follows from this that since possible worlds are combinations (or sets) of states of affairs, and some states of affairs are unactualizable (or infeasible) for God, then God is limited in terms of which worlds he is able to bring about. In order to help clarify this notion, it has been suggested that possible worlds be organized according to the counterfactuals that are true in them.

Feasibility of Possible Worlds, Creaturely World-Types, and Galaxies

In order to understand how possible worlds may be organized for purposes of examination, several notions require explanation. The first has already been alluded to, and is feasibility. While there is a virtually infinite number of possible worlds, all are not feasible for God to actualize; they are not live options because of the true counterfactuals. For example, if it is true that I would order one pizza from Papa John's if I were aware of a sale, then all possible worlds in which I would not order a pizza or in which I would order more than one pizza if aware of the sale are not feasible. They are logically possible (there is nothing about my ordering two pizzas, for instance, which violates the fundamental laws of logic), but not real options. As we might imagine, there will be a great number of possible worlds that are not feasible. This concept will become more clear as we examine the other two notions.

Thinking about worlds in this way leads to the second notion that needs explanation: creaturely world-types. A creaturely world-type is a complete set of counterfactuals. It includes all compatible truths, including all compatible counterfactuals of freedom. There are many circumstances that any given individual could find himself in, and for each set of circumstances, there is a virtually infinite number of corresponding counterfactuals which are mutually exclusive. Sticking to the example of the pizza sale, consider the state of affairs, *John's seeing a commercial for Papa John's veggie lovers pizza on sale for $5*. On the surface, it may seem that there are only two counterfactual possibilities: that I either order one, or I do not.[23] In one sense, this is true, for it seems that I must do one or the

---

John Laing's being aware of Pizza Hut's sale on the Big New Yorker pepperoni pizza for $5 each and (freely) refraining from ordering one.

23. These two possibilities can be represented by the counterfactuals:

If John were to see a commercial for Papa John's veggie lovers pizza on sale for $5, he would not order one

and

other. However, the counterfactual which states that I will not order one can actually be viewed as representative of a set of counterfactuals of freedom with different consequents. For example, it could include situations where I would not order a pizza at all and instead eat something else (a hamburger, a steak, a PB&J sandwich, etc.) or eat nothing at all, or it could include situations in which I order more than one veggie lovers pizza (two, three, four, etc.). So, for any possible circumstance a free creature may find himself in, there is a virtually infinite number of possible actions he may take which correspond to a virtually infinite number of counterfactuals of freedom. A creaturely world-type will include one counterfactual for each set of circumstances, and for every possible combination of counterfactuals, there is a creaturely world-type described by (or composed of) it. While there will be a virtually infinite number of creaturely world-types, only one will be true (the one which is comprised of the true counterfactuals), and therefore, only possible worlds of that world-type are feasible. Flint explains (assuming T is the true creaturely world-type):

> But God has no control whatsoever over the truth of T; there is no complete creative action God has the power to perform such that, were he to perform it, T would not be true. From this it follows that God has no control over the fact that some T-world is actual. . . . So there are many possible worlds which, given his middle knowledge, God knows he is not in a position to actualize.[24]

This may appear to be a serious deficiency of middle knowledge because it unsatisfactorily limits God's power, but this is not entirely accurate, for each creaturely world-type includes a virtually infinite number of possible worlds. This is due to the fact that the circumstances described by the counterfactuals may or may not be actualized in any given possible world. In other words, you could have many possible worlds which share counterfactuals but which differ with respect to a whole host of factors—who exists, how things are arranged, which situations/circumstances actually obtain, etc. So there really is a virtual infinite number of possible worlds that are feasible for God to actualize, even given the constraints due to the true counterfactuals. This leads to the third notion in organizing possible worlds: galaxies.

The term "galaxy" is used in the philosophical literature to refer to the set of possible worlds in which a particular creaturely world-type holds. So for every world-type (Tn), there exists a corresponding galaxy (Gn) of possible worlds in which the counterfactuals of that world-type are true. Following Flint, we may say that Galaxy 1 ($G1$) is comprised of the set of worlds

---

If John were to see a commercial for Papa John's veggie lovers pizza on sale for $5, he would order one.

24.   Thomas P. Flint, *Divine Providence: The Molinist Account* (Ithaca, NY: Cornell University Press, 1998), 51.

in which World-Type 1 (*T1*) holds, the set of worlds in which World Type
2 (*T2*) holds makes up Galaxy 2 (*G2*), and so forth.[25] If *T1* is the true creaturely world-type, then it follows that all the worlds in *G1* are viable options
for actualization by God. It also follows that every other creaturely world-
type includes at least one false counterfactual, and therefore the galaxies in
which those world types hold must be deemed infeasible.[26]

According to the theory of middle knowledge, God comprehends all
possible worlds by means of his natural knowledge. He then combines this
with his middle knowledge, by which he knows which creaturely world-
type is true and thereby knows which galaxy (or which possible worlds)
is feasible for him to actualize. It is at this point that God, by means of
his free knowledge, or his knowledge of his own will, comes to decide
and know which world will be actual, and which worlds would have been
actual. The combination of these three logical moments in the pre-creative
knowledge of God affords him complete knowledge of the future while
maintaining a significant amount of creaturely freedom. It must be admitted that this way of speaking appears both speculative and confusing to
most, save professional philosophers. Fortunately, a complete grasp of
the ideas of creaturely world-types and galaxies is not essential for a basic

---

25. Ibid. Zagzebski essentially means the same thing when she speaks of galaxies—it is a set of possi-
     ble worlds which are compatible at some level with each other. She writes, "So for each world-
     germ God might have created, there is a set of possible worlds compatible with that world-germ.
     Let us call each such set of worlds a galaxy. . . . So galaxy 1 is the set of worlds compatible with
     world-germ 1, galaxy 2 is the set of worlds compatible with world-germ 2, and so forth." Linda
     Zagzebski, *The Dilemma of Freedom and Foreknowledge* (New York: Oxford University Press,
     1991), 129–30. It must be noted, though, that Zagzebski's *world-germ* should not be equated
     with the concept of *creaturely world-type* described above; they are not the same. A world-germ
     is a more vague notion. It is described by Zagzebski as the foundations of a world, which may
     be compatible with a host of possible worlds. Included in a world-germ are things like laws,
     substances, and even results of direct action by God on those substances, whereas a creaturely
     world-type is strictly made up of (described by) counterfactuals.
          Interestingly, Flint speaks of creaturely world-types being true relative to the worlds they
     describe (or relative to the galaxy of worlds they describe). This is misleading since it has
     already been asserted that only one creaturely world-type is true. Thus, I have chosen to use
     the term "holds" to communicate the relative (indexical) nature of the truth of creaturely
     world-types in relation to the worlds described by them.
26. This may seem to be too deterministic or even impious because of the severe limitations placed
     on God's creative options. However, two points are in order. First, it must be remembered that
     each galaxy is comprised of a virtually infinite number of possible worlds. It is wrong to think
     of God as having an extremely limited selection in reference to the kind of world he can actu-
     alize. In the example above, *G1* includes a great diversity of worlds that God can choose from.
     Second, it must also be remembered that the feasibility of worlds and galaxies is dependent
     on which counterfactuals are true, and that this is contingent. Flint writes, "Even if *T1* is the
     true world-type, it need not have been, for the counterfactuals which constitute it are only
     contingently true. *T2* or *T3* or any other creaturely world-type might have been true instead.
     And, of course, had any of them been true, then the worlds in *G1*, which we are assuming to
     be in fact feasible, would not have been feasible. Feasibility, then, is a contingent feature of a
     world or of a galaxy." Flint, *Divine Providence*, 53.

understanding of middle knowledge (though it is if one is going to wade into the deeper waters of the current debates surrounding truth values of counterfactuals).

Comparative Similarity among Possible Worlds

One of the more controversial aspects of the contemporary discussion of Molinism has been the use of possible worlds in determining the truth of counterfactuals. Robert Stalnaker has suggested that the concept of a possible world can be useful in making the transition from belief conditions to truth conditions for evaluating counterfactuals.[27] He argues that a counterfactual is true in the actual world if and only if it is true in the possible world that is most similar to the actual world.[28] This concept is important for some ways of answering the most common objection to middle knowledge, as will be shown in chapter 2.

Implicit in this assertion is that there is an ordering of possible worlds based on their resemblance to the actual world. Stalnaker notes that it is difficult to determine what the most similar possible world will look like, but asserts that it will only include differences from the actual world that are "required, implicitly or explicitly, by the antecedent."[29] The changes or differences allowed, then, must be such that "the least violence to the correct description and explanation of the actual world" is tolerated.[30] He admits that these are vague notions and that more work needs to be done in this pragmatic area.

Lewis agrees that the whole idea of comparative similarity of possible worlds to the actual world is vague. This is due in part to the fact that the similarity relation depends on which criteria are used for comparison and how weights are assigned to the (almost innumerable) criteria. Yet, Lewis argues, this is no different than any attempt at comparative similarity. He uses the comparison of two cities to a third as an example. Which of the first two is *more* similar to the third depends on which characteristics the individual making the comparison decides to use (landscape, architecture, industry, political climate, population, etc.). This problem does not prevent similarity comparisons from being made because, Lewis

---

27.   Stalnaker begins his discussion by explicating the various ways individuals determine whether they believe a counterfactual to be true or not. He concludes that belief in the truth of a counterfactual is directly correlated to one's understanding of how the truth of that counterfactual will fit with his/her beliefs about the world. He writes, "First, add the antecedent (hypothetically) to your stock of beliefs; second, make whatever adjustments are required to maintain consistency (without modifying the hypothetical belief in the antecedent); finally, consider whether or not the consequent is then true." Robert C. Stalnaker, "A Theory of Conditionals," *American Philosophical Quarterly* (1968): 102.

28.   He writes, "Consider a possible world in which *A* is true, and which otherwise differs minimally from the actual world. *'If A then B'* is true (false) just in case B is true (false) in that *possible world.*" Ibid.

29.   Ibid., 104.

30.   Ibid.

contends, we have a basic conception of what similarity means. He writes, "Somehow, we *do* have a familiar notion of comparative overall similarity, even of comparative similarity of big, complicated, variegated things like whole people, whole cities, or even—I think—whole possible worlds. However mysterious that notion may be, if we can analyze counterfactuals by means of it we will be left with one mystery in place of two."[31]

However, Lewis remains skeptical about arriving at a scientific means of comparing possible worlds (like, for example, a mathematical analysis where values are assigned to varying characteristics and weights added to the different types of characteristics).[32] The interesting thing to note here is that this does not constitute an objection to the supposition that there *is* a closest possible world to the actual world, but only to the belief that we may determine which one it is, such that all rational persons agree. Plantinga has echoed this concern, noting that "we cannot as a rule *discover* the truth value of a counter-factual [*sic*] by asking whether its consequent holds in those worlds most similar to the actual in which its antecedent holds."[33] Yet he moves beyond the subjective nature of comparative similarity to note a problem specific to comparing possible worlds, pointing out that "one measure of similarity between worlds involves the question whether they share their counterfactuals," which we cannot know.[34] In fact, in some cases, shared counterfactuals may weigh more heavily than shared facts in determining similarity.

To illustrate this point, Plantinga offers an example in which he describes a near tragedy for rockclimber Royal Robbins. Robbins almost falls as he reaches Thanksgiving Ledge 2,500 feet up the mountain. However, he regains his composure and goes on to reach the top of the mountain. Plantinga asks us to consider the following counterfactual:

> If Robbins had slipped and fallen at Thanksgiving Ledge, he would have been killed.[35]

Although this proposition may seem obviously true, Plantinga notes that it can be false in a world that is more similar to the actual world [α] in terms

---

31. Lewis, *Counterfactuals*, 92. Plantinga agrees: "We do seem to have an intuitive grasp of this notion—the notion of similarity between states of affairs." Plantinga, *The Nature of Necessity*, 174–75.

32. He writes, "We must resist the temptation. The exact measure thus defined cannot be expected to correspond well to our own opinions about comparative similarity. Some of the similarities and differences most important to us involve idiosyncratic, subtle, *Gestalt* properties. . . . The same goes, I fear, for any humanly possible attempt at a precise definition of comparative similarity of worlds. Not only would we go wrong by giving a precise analysis of an imprecise concept; our precise concept would not fall within—or even near—the permissible range of variations of the ordinary concept." Lewis, *Counterfactuals*, 95.

33. Plantinga, *The Nature of Necessity*, 178.

34. Ibid.

35. Ibid.

of particular facts than another world in which it is true. An extended quote may be helpful:

> Now what happens in the closest worlds in which he falls?[36] Well, there is at least one of these—call it $W/$—in which he falls at t just as he is reaching the Ledge; at the next moment $t+1$ (as close as you please to t) he shows up exactly where is in α at $t+1$; and everything else goes just as it does in α. Would $W/$ not be more similar to the actual world than any in which he hurtles down to the Valley floor, thus depriving American rockclimbing of its most eloquent spokesman?[37]

Plantinga goes on to note that if $W/$ is most similar to α, then the counterfactual is false. However, the problem with the conclusion that $W/$ is most similar to α, is that causal (or natural) laws were ignored.[38] $W/$ clearly does not possess the same causal laws as α, whereas a world in which Robbins falls to the Valley floor does. Thus, it seems that $W/$ is not very similar to α, at least with respect to natural laws. However, Plantinga is quick to point out that a salient feature of causal laws is that they *support* or *entail* counterfactuals. This leads him to conclude that we could just as easily reject $W/$ as most similar on the basis that it lacks some of α's counterfactuals (those supported or entailed by natural laws).

Not all contemporary Molinists have embraced the possible worlds analysis of counterfactuals. Alfred Freddoso, whose critical translation of the relevant sections of the *Concordia* has become the standard in the field, has argued that the connection between the antecedent and consequent of counterfactuals "is not reducible to any logical or, more important, causal connection."[39] This is problematic for the Stalnaker hypothesis because it argues that "the truth-value of a subjunctive conditional p depends asymmetrically on the categorical (including causal) facts about the world at which p is being evaluated, so that until the full range of such categorical facts is in place, the truth-value of p is still indeterminate."[40] This seems to lead to the conclusion that the determination of which world is actual is

---

36. It should be noted that Plantinga has already suggested that there may not be one *closest* world, but rather a family of closest worlds. Although he was working on this assumption, he would later abandon it,, as our discussion will demonstrate. Ibid., 175.

37. Ibid., 177.

38. Plantinga writes, "The answer, or course, is that we are neglecting causal or natural *laws*. Our world α contains a number of these, and they are among its more impressive constituents. In particular, there are some implying (together with the relative antecedent conditions) that anyone who falls unroped and unprotected from a ledge 2500 feet up a verticle cliff, moves with increasing rapidity towards the centre of the earth, finally arriving with considerable impact at its surface. Evidently not all of these laws are present in $W/$, for the latter shares the relevant initial conditions with α but in it Robbins does not fall to the Valley floor—instead, after a brief feint in that direction, he reappears on the cliff." Ibid., 178.

39. Freddoso, "Introduction," 74.

40. Ibid.

prior to which counterfactuals are true, but this is clearly unsatisfactory.[41] Freddoso notes that if this is the case (which he does not seek to prove), then Molinists (who wish to hold on to possible worlds semantics) will have to modify the rules governing possible worlds. Ultimately, Freddoso believes the standard semantics for possible worlds is doomed to failure for other reasons as well and he rejects its use outright.[42]

CONCLUSION

In this chapter, I have presented the doctrine of divine middle knowledge as it is distinguished from natural and free knowledge, and explained its usefulness in solving the dilemma of divine providence and human freedom. Middle knowledge is prevolitional like natural knowledge, but its content is contingent like the content of free knowledge. According to the theory, God knows how all possible people would freely act in all possible situations (counterfactuals of freedom) prior to any act of his will, and uses this knowledge to decide which world to actualize so his will is met. Last, I have delineated the salient features of the contemporary approach to Molinism, explaining how the possible worlds semantics and language of world actualization can be helpful in clarifying the doctrine and its contention that not all possible worlds can be created. I explained the use of the idea of comparative similarity among possible worlds and some of the problems associated with it.

Although Molinism can be a powerful tool in answering some of the toughest theological and philosophical problems associated with theistic belief, it is not without its contemporary detractors. An interesting point about the contemporary discussion is that, although the doctrine of middle knowledge was criticized in Molina's day for giving too much credence to human freedom, it has recently been criticized for coming too close to determinism. The major objections to the contemporary formulation will be considered in the next two chapters.

---

41. This objection was first proposed by Anthony Kenny and is the subject of chapter 3.
42. Freddoso writes, "There are, in any case, independent grounds for having doubts about the standard semantics, for example, its inability to accommodate the intuitively plausible belief that subjunctive conditionals with impossible antecedents may differ from one another in truth-value." Freddoso, "Introduction," 75. See also Alfred J. Freddoso, "Human Nature, Potency and the Incarnation," *Faith and Philosophy* 3, no. 1 (1986): 43–45.

CHAPTER 2

THE GROUNDING OBJECTION

INTRODUCTION

Two types of argument against middle knowledge have been set forth in the contemporary discussion, and both deal with counterfactuals of freedom. The first kind of argument denies that counterfactuals of creaturely freedom can be true, and is the subject of the current chapter. Several versions of the argument have been offered, and each will be examined in turn. The second kind of argument denies that counterfactuals of freedom can be true soon enough to be of any value to God, and will be discussed in chapter 3.

CONDITIONAL EXCLUDED MIDDLE

The first argument that counterfactuals of creaturely freedom cannot be true has come in the form of an attack on the principle of conditional excluded middle (CEM). It is often thought that Molinism is dependent upon the truth of this principle because its proponents have often presented counterfactuals in pairs that appear to be contradictories.[1]

The principle of conditional excluded middle is based on the principle of logic known as the principle of excluded middle, which states that a proposition or its negation must be true. Put more formally, the principle of excluded middle can be expressed as *Either p or ~p*. The principle of conditional excluded middle is this principle applied to conditional, or if-then statements. It can be expressed in formal terms as *Either p→q or p→~q*. For example, in the previous chapter, the contention was made that either

---

1. Adams has pointed out that the pairs usually given are not properly contradictories because only the consequent (of the conditional statement) was negated. Adams writes, "To obtain the contradictory of a conditional proposition is not enough to negate the consequent; one must negate the whole conditional, as was pointed out by Suarez's Dominican opponent, Diego Alvarez." Robert Merrihew Adams, "Middle Knowledge and the Problem of Evil," *American Philosophical Quarterly* 14, no. 2 (April 1977): 110.

If John Laing were to see a commercial for the Big New Yorker pepperoni pizza on sale for $5, he would order at least one;

or

If John Laing were to see a commercial for the Big New Yorker pepperoni pizza on sale for $5, he would not order at least one;

is true. Both cannot be true because the truth of one would mean that the other is false. Similarly, one must be true because any action I could take with respect to ordering a pizza after viewing a commercial is described by the two statements.

Counterexamples to CEM

However, some have questioned the claim that one of the two must be true. David Lewis has employed the possible worlds semantics described in the last chapter in evaluating the principle of conditional excluded middle, and concluded that it does not hold in some cases because there may be possible worlds that are equally close to the actual world that include counterfactuals with the same antecedent, but different consequents.[2] In other words, he claims that there may be two possible (but not actual) worlds (equally similar to the actual world) where I see the commercial and take different actions. This is significant because according to the Stalnaker analysis of possible worlds, a counterfactual is true in the actual world if it holds in the possible world that is most similar to the actual world. In order to clarify his point, Lewis presents two counterfactuals for consideration:

If Verdi and Bizet were compatriots, Bizet would be Italian;

and

If Verdi and Bizet were compatriots, Bizet would not be Italian.

He argues that neither statement is true based on comparative similarity of possible worlds because some worlds in which Bizet is Italian may be no closer to the actual world than some worlds in which Verdi is French.[3] Thus, different worlds in which Verdi and Bizet are compatriots for different reasons may be equally similar to the actual world and thus, neither is true.

---

2. Using the terminology common in the literature, let α stand for the actual world. According to Lewis, there may be a world, β, in which the counterfactual $p \rightarrow q$ holds that is just as close to α as another world, γ, in which the counterfactual $p \rightarrow \sim q$ holds.
3. Lewis, *Counterfactuals*, 80–82.

Molinist Responses

Edward Wierenga has questioned Lewis' conclusion, noting that the indeterminacy of which world is closer to the actual world may be due to a lack of knowledge about the actual world rather than genuine indeterminacy regarding similarity among worlds. For example, Wierenga suggests that it may have been the case that Bizet's ancestors considered moving to Italy, or that Verdi's ancestors wanted to move to France. Knowledge of truths such as these would certainly lend insight into which of the two worlds is closer to the actual world and thus, which of the two counterfactuals is true. It is only because such knowledge is not readily available that we cannot determine which of the two counterfactuals is correct.[4] Kvanvig agrees, noting that this is an epistemological point, not a metaphysical point, "and it is a metaphysical point that needs to be established to show that neither of the two is true."[5]

Kvanvig has also argued that the rejection of the principle of conditional excluded middle may be due more to vagueness in the similarity relation among possible worlds than to the implausibility of the principle itself. Since the standard semantics for evaluating counterfactuals do not account for possible worlds that are equally close to the actual world, any such example will lead to the conclusion that the counterfactuals which hold in those worlds are false.[6]

The problem with Lewis' example does not seem to be so much with the possible worlds semantics, as it does with the type of example given. Even if the standard semantics for evaluating possible worlds is accepted, Lewis' example remains unconvincing as a deterrent for belief in middle knowledge because the counterfactuals presented do not refer to creaturely activity and because there are more variables involved than in

---

4. Edward Wierenga, *The Nature of God: An Inquiry into Divine Attributes* (Ithaca, NY: Cornell University Press, 1989), 135. Thus, Wierenga concludes, "our inability to judge one [of the world where (3) is true or the world where (4) is true] more similar [to α] might reflect our ignorance rather than a fact about the world." Ibid.

5. Kvanvig actually considers a similar example with Reagan and Chernenko. The statements Kvanvig considers are (using his numbering):

    (11) If Reagan and Chernenko had been compatriots, then Reagan would have been Russian;

    and

    (12) If Reagan and Chernenko had been compatriots, then Reagan would not have been Russian.

    He writes, "I do not find examples of this sort especially compelling, for it is easy to confuse whether either (11) or (12) is true with whether and how one might determine which of the two is true." Kvanvig, *The Possibility of an All-Knowing God*, 132.

6. Kvanvig writes, "it might be a consideration of the standard semantics for such conditionals that brings one to the admission that the law is false rather than a consideration of particular examples." Ibid.

counterfactuals of creaturely freedom. In the example given, two kinds of changes (at least) are possible which can make Verdi and Bizet compatriots: Either Bizet could be Italian, or Verdi could be French.[7] Yet in a counterfactual of freedom, only one kind of change is possible. In order to see why, consider an example presented by Molina from 1 Samuel 23 (discussed in detail in chapter 9). Saul was chasing David, who took refuge in the city of Keilah. David was concerned that Saul would attack the city and the inhabitants hand him over, so he consulted God. Molina contended that one of the two counterfactuals,

> If David were to remain in Keilah, Saul would besiege the city;

and

> If David were to remain in Keilah, Saul would not besiege the city;

is true. The truth of the counterfactuals depends on only one difference: Saul's action, and it seems that Saul must respond one way or the other. Plantinga takes it to be self-evident that there is an answer to the question of what an individual would do when faced with a decision to act or not.[8] The counterexample offered by Lewis is not a counterexample to counterfactuals of creaturely freedom and it is this that is required to count against the doctrine of middle knowledge.

Robert Adams believes he has given a counterexample to the principle of conditional excluded middle, even when applied to counterfactuals of creaturely freedom such as those that describe Saul's response to David's remaining in Keilah. He argues that both counterfactuals can be denied by the following being true:

> If David were to remain in Keilah, Saul might or might not besiege the city.

He writes, "I believe the case of what Saul would or might have done if David stayed in Keilah provides a plausible counterexample to the proposed law

---

7. Of course, other options are also possible; they could both be of another nationality, e.g., German, American, etc.
8. He writes, "There is something Curley would have done, had that state of affairs obtained. But I do not know how to produce a conclusive argument for this supposition, in case you are inclined to dispute it. I do think it is the natural view, the one we take in reflecting on our own moral failures and triumphs. Suppose I have applied for a National Science Foundation Fellowship and have asked you to write me a recommendation. I am eager to get the fellowship, but eminently unqualified to carry out the project I have proposed. Realizing that you know this, I act upon the maxim that every man has his price and offer you $500 to write a glowing, if inaccurate, report. You indignantly refuse, and add moral turpitude to my other disqualifications. Later we reflectively discuss what you would have done had you been offered a bribe of $50,000. One thing we would take for granted, I should think, is that there is a right answer here. We may not know what the answer is; but we would reject out of hand, I should think, the suggestion that there simply is none." Plantinga, *The Nature of Necessity*, 180.

of Conditional Excluded Middle."[9] The problem with Adams' example is the same as that of Lewis. It appears to be more a matter of epistemological uncertainty than of metaphysical indeterminacy. It seems obvious that Saul must do one or the other—once David remains, Saul must react, and therefore, there is a true statement which describes what his actions would be if David were to remain in the city.

COUNTERFACTUALS AND DETERMINISM

The second argument that counterfactuals of creaturely freedom cannot be true has been the claim that Molinism is deterministic. Since determinism is incompatible with creaturely freedom, any true counterfactuals are not counterfactuals *of freedom*. We will examine the arguments presented by William Hasker, who has offered three variations.

Counterfactuals, Determinism, and Risk

First, Hasker argues that God must take risks in order to avoid some kind of determinism, and he defines risk in terms of a lack of knowledge on the part of the risk-taker: "God takes risks if he makes decisions that depend for their outcomes on the responses of free creatures in which the decisions themselves are not informed by knowledge of their outcomes."[10] Thus, if God's decisions are guided by comprehensive knowledge of how events will turn out, then he takes no risks. The element of risk is lost because of the combination of God's work in creating and God's knowledge of the counterfactuals of freedom. Hasker writes, "But Molinism shows how God can entirely avoid taking any risks; prior to his decision to create anything or to place any free agent in a situation where she would make a choice, God knows exactly what choice would be made and so he knows, prior to any decisions of his own concerning his actions in creation and providence, exactly what the consequences would be of his making and carrying out any such decision."[11]

Hasker is willing to admit that this is not quite the same as Calvinism because persons are not choosing according to determined desires, but he

---

9. Adams, "Middle Knowledge and the Problem of Evil," 110. Peter van Inwagen has argued that might-counterfactuals are proper contradictories for would-counterfactuals (rather than would-not-counterfactuals). See Peter van Inwagen, "Against Middle Knowledge," *Midwest Studies in Philosophy* 21 (1977): 225–36; see also Peter van Inwagen, *An Essay on Free Will* (Oxford: Clarendon, 1983). Gregory Boyd has applied these principles to his version of Open Theism. See Gregory A. Boyd, "Neo-Molinism and the Infinite Intelligence of God," *Philosophia Christi* 5, no. 1 (2003): 187–204; see also Gregory A. Boyd, "The Open Theism View," in *Divine Foreknowledge: Four Views*, eds. James K. Beilby and Paul Eddy (Downers Grove, IL: IVP, 2001), 13–47. For a critique of Boyd's proposal, see David Werther, "Open Theism and Middle Knowledge: An Appraisal of Gregory Boyd's Neo-Molinism," *Philosophia Christi* 5, no. 1 (2003): 205–15.

10. William Hasker, "The God Who Takes Risks," unpublished paper (1999), 1.

11. William Hasker, "Providence and Evil: Three Theories," *Religious Studies* 28 (March 1992): 95.

argues it is still problematic because those decisions are locked into the plan of God once he creates. Libertarian freedom requires the individual to have the ability to choose either of two (or more) options *at the time she is faced with the decision*, but according to Hasker, Molinism seems to place the decision in the past before creation and therefore, removes all risk.[12] He argues that such a strong view of providence is detrimental to personal devotion and human dignity, and makes God the "archmanipulator, knowing in every case exactly 'which button to push' in order to elicit precisely the desired result from his creatures."[13] God's relationship to humanity in Molinism is similar to that in Calvinism, where humans function like robots and God like a cybergeneticist, and this is problematic for human freedom and divine goodness.[14]

Molinist Responses

How is one to respond to Hasker's argument about God, risk, and creaturely freedom? A moment's reflection should make clear that Hasker has begged the question; he has presupposed that foreknowledge and freedom are incompatible. His definition of risk, coupled with his insistence that God take risks if creatures are to be free, amounts to an *a priori* dismissal of divine foreknowledge if humans are free. If one grants Hasker's presuppositions of the necessity of divine risk for creaturely freedom and the elimination of risk by divine foreknowledge, then all attempts to reconcile the two are defeated from the start. Thus Molinists have questioned at least one of his presuppositions.

Specifically, Hasker's definition of risk need not be accepted. It is dependent upon the knowledge of God, but a different rendering of risk can be located in the freedom of the creatures and the choice of God to create. As David Basinger puts it, Hasker's argument is based on a confusion. He writes:

> Specifically, Hasker is confusing two distinct understandings of what it means for God to be a risk-taker: God is a risk-taker in the sense that he commits himself to a course of action without full knowledge of the

---

12. Hasker argues, "To be sure, it is still the creatures, not God, who determine their own free responses to various situations. But God, in choosing to create them and place them in those situations, knew exactly what their responses would be; he views the future, not as a risk taker seeking to optimize probable outcomes, but as a planner who knowingly accepts and incorporates into his plan exactly those outcomes that in fact occur—though, to be sure, some of them may not be the outcomes he would most prefer. The element of risk is entirely eliminated." William Hasker, *God, Time, and Knowledge* (Ithaca, NY: Cornell University Press, 1989), 21–22.
13. Hasker, "A Philosophical Perspective," 145–46. Hasker suggests that the key difference between the two is that part of the programming was completed by a third party.
14. He writes, "But the robot-master still knows all about that part of the program and is able just as before [Calvinism] to fine-tune the situations that the robot encounters so as to achieve just the desired result. Whether the change from Calvinism to Molinism makes the situation appreciably better in this regard is left for the reader to decide." Ibid., 146.

outcome; and God is a risk-taker in the sense that he adopts certain overall strategies—for example, the granting of significant freedom—which create the potential for the occurrence of events that he wishes would not occur.[15]

There is not risk in the sense that God does not know what is going to happen, but there is risk in the sense that creatures imbued with freedom may choose to do something contrary to God's desires or will, even though it may still fit into his over-arching plan. In this sense, God is limited in what he can do by the counterfactuals of freedom.[16] It is here that risk is located. Since God cannot force all events to abide by his will, there is risk in his very choice/act of creating free creatures. If all risk were eliminated, then all outcomes would *necessarily* be those God most prefers, but middle knowledge makes no such claim and affirms otherwise. Since Hasker's definition of risk fails, so does his argument.

Counterfactuals, Determinism, and Individual Power

The second form of the argument that Molinism leads to determinism is set forth as a philosophical argument against an individual's ability to make counterfactuals true. Hasker asks: "Who or what is it (if anything) that *brings it about* that these propositions are true?" and he concludes that it cannot be the individual.[17] If it is not the individual who makes statements about his actions true, then his actions are not free. To make his case, Hasker presents two contradictory counterfactuals of creaturely freedom for consideration. Each refers to a graduate student named Elizabeth who might be offered a grant that will fund research of a newly discovered tribe in New Guinea. According to the doctrine of middle knowledge, if Elizabeth is offered the grant, she will either accept it or reject it, and a proposition describing which she would do under those

---

15.   David Basinger, *The Case for Freewill Theism: A Philosophical Assessment* (Downers Grove: InterVarsity, 1996), 48; see also, David Basinger, "Middle Knowledge and Divine Control," *International Journal for Philosophy of Religion* 30 (1991): 135.

16.   This was referenced in the previous chapter under the concept of feasibility. Basinger claims that God might be "quite lucky," in that he may be able to have his will accomplished through the free actions of individuals, but then again, he may not. David Basinger, "Divine Control and Human Freedom: Is Middle Knowledge the Answer?," *Journal of the Evangelical Theological Society* 36, no. 1 (March 1993): 61. In fact, two of the major proponents of Hasker's approach to divine providence and co-authors of *The Openness of God* have also rejected his understanding of risk. The first is David Basinger and has already been quoted. The second is John Sanders. See Sanders, *The God Who Risks*, 171–72.

17.   Hasker, *God, Time, and Knowledge*, 39. This argument was first proposed in a journal article. See William Hasker, "A Refutation of Middle Knowledge," *Nous* 20 (1986): 545–57. It should be noted that the concept of *bringing about* was ambiguous at best when Hasker first proposed his argument. However, through the philosophical process of discussion, particularly with Thomas Flint, Hasker has proposed a technical definition of *Bring About*: For some X, S causes it to be the case that X, and $[(X \& H) => Y]$, and $\sim(H => Y)$. See William Hasker, "A New Anti-Molinist Argument," *Religious Studies* 35, no. 3 (September 1999): 291–97.

circumstances, is true.[18] Presumably, she wants to conduct the research and to use the grant to fund it, so we may assume that she would accept it if it were offered. According to Hasker, though, it seems that the only way Elizabeth can make the corresponding counterfactual (*If Elizabeth is offered the grant, she will accept it*) true is to actually accept the grant: "In the case of a genuinely free action, the only way to insure the action's being done is to do it."[19]

However, Hasker argues that according to middle knowledge, this is not the case; it is true independent of her acceptance. In order to see why, Hasker first notes that the counterfactual could be true if Elizabeth accepts the grant or not, depending on the circumstances. Obviously, if Elizabeth were never offered the grant, she would not accept it, but it could still be true that if she were offered the grant, she would accept it. He sets forth two counterfactuals and asks which is true:

> If Elizabeth does not accept the offer, it is because she rejected it;

or

> If Elizabeth does not accept the offer, it is because the offer was never made;

and proposes that possible worlds semantics be used to determine the answer: "Is a world in which Elizabeth received the offer and rejected it more or less similar to the actual world (in which the offer was accepted) than a world in which the offer was neither made nor accepted?"[20] Hasker believes that a world in which she does not accept because it was not made is closer to the actual world than a world in which she does not accept because she rejected it, even though the latter world only differs from the actual world with respect to Elizabeth's acceptance of the offer, whereas the former world differs from the actual world with respect both to the making of the offer and the acceptance. The reason the world in which she does not accept because the offer was never made is closer to the actual world is because the counterfactual, *If Elizabeth were offered the grant, she would accept it;* is true in both of them and is not true in the world in which Elizabeth rejects the offer, and this leads Hasker to conclude that in

---

18.   That is, one of:

> If Elizabeth is offered the grant, then she will accept it;

or

> If Elizabeth is offered the grant, then she will not accept it;

is true.

19.   Hasker, *God, Time, and Knowledge*, 40–41.

20.   Ibid., 43.

determining the relative similarity of possible worlds, counterfactuals of freedom outweigh particular facts.[21]

The upshot of all this is that the original counterfactual is true whether Elizabeth accepts the grant or not, and from this, Hasker argues that Elizabeth does not bring about its truth. He develops a general rule from this argument, stating that the truth of a counterfactual of freedom is not brought about by the agent named in it, and concludes that the agent is not free. In order to demonstrate this point, Hasker employs a power entailment principle (PEP), a principle that states that an agent's possessing the power to perform one kind of action entails that the agent possesses the power to perform another kind of action:

> (PEP)   If it is in A's power to bring it about that P, and "P" entails "Q" and "Q" is false, then it is in A's power to bring it about that Q.[22]

Applied to the example of Elizabeth, the (PEP) requires that Elizabeth's acceptance or rejection of the grant *entails* the truth of the corresponding counterfactual of freedom. In other words, if Elizabeth is offered the grant and accepts it, the corresponding counterfactual must be true, whereas if Elizabeth is offered the grant and rejects it, that counterfactual must be true. This, according to Hasker, is where the problem lies because Elizabeth does not have the power to bring it about that the latter

---

21.   Hasker provides a concrete example which can clarify this contention: Suppose that in the actual world, α, Hasker knocks over an ink bottle and destroyed a poster he was working on. At least two possibilities exist with respect to the ink not spilling:

> (i) If no ink had been spilled, it would have been because Hasker did not knock over the ink bottle;

and

> (ii) If no ink had been spilled, it would have been because Hasker knocked over his ink bottle, but no ink spilled (the bottle miraculously righted itself up before spilling any ink).

Consider two possible-but-not-actual worlds, β and γ. In β, (i) is true, whereas in γ, (ii) is true. Hasker points out that, in factual content, the possibility realized in β is not as close to what actually occurred as the possibility realized in γ. In α, the ink spilled and Hasker knocked over the bottle. In β, no ink spilled and Hasker did not knock over the bottle, and in γ, no ink spilled, but Hasker did knock over the bottle. Yet, Hasker notes, it should be clear that β is indeed closer to α than γ is. This similarity is due to the fact that α and β share a counterfactual that is not true in γ, namely

> (iii) If Hasker were to knock over his ink bottle in such-and-such a way, the bottle would fall over and spill ink on his poster.

The counterfactual represented by (iii) outweighs the fact of Hasker knocking over the ink bottle in determining the relative similarity of possible worlds. See *God, Time, and Knowledge*, 43–45.

22.   Ibid., 49.

counterfactual, namely, *If Elizabeth is offered the grant, she will not accept it;* is true and, according to (PEP), this means that Elizabeth does not have the power to reject the grant, and thus, she is not free with respect to her acceptance or rejection of the grant. Hasker concludes that if there are true counterfactuals which describe how an individual will act, they are not counterfactuals of *freedom*; they are deterministic, and thus, middle knowledge leads to determinism.

Molinist Responses

A number of Molinist responses to Hasker's argument have been offered. We will examine the two most prominent.

Counterfactuals, facts, and relative similarity among worlds
The strongest objection to Hasker's argument has been to question the assertion that counterfactuals of freedom outweigh particular facts in determining the relative similarity of possible worlds. Both Molinists and non-Molinists have noted that, although this may be true in certain cases, it cannot stand as a general rule.[23] Hasker's assertion rests on two premises: first, that counterfactuals of freedom are just as fundamental features of the world as are counterfactuals backed by laws of nature, and second, that counterfactuals backed by laws of nature are more fundamental features of the world than are particular facts.[24] The first is the more controversial and has been defended by Hasker in three ways.

First, he has argued that since God has control over laws of nature but not over counterfactuals of freedom, it follows that counterfactuals based on natural laws are not as fundamental as counterfactuals of creaturely freedom.[25] Second, he has appealed to quantum mechanics in order to

---

23.   For Molinist critiques, see Thomas P. Flint, "Hasker's *God, Time, and Knowledge,*" *Philosophical Studies* 60 (1990): 103–105; Flint, *Divine Providence*, 140–48; William Lane Craig, "Hasker on Divine Knowledge," *Philosophical Studies* 67 (1992): 106–108; Freddoso, "Introduction," 75 n. 96; Wierenga, *The Nature of God*, 155 n. 73. Timothy O'Conner, "The Impossibility of Middle Knowledge," *Philosophical Studies* 66 (1992): 139–66.

24.   Hasker initially claimed that counterfactuals of freedom are more fundamental features of the world than are counterfactuals backed by laws of nature, but revised it to the weaker claim found in the text. See William Hasker, "Middle Knowledge: A Refutation Revisited," *Faith and Philosophy* 12, no. 2 (April 1995): 234 n. 6.

25.   Hasker, *God, Time, and Knowledge*, 45. Flint has correctly questioned the logic employed here. If, as the Molinist claims, counterfactuals of creaturely freedom are contingent (upon the agent's choice), then it does not follow that since God does not have control, they are more fundamental to a world—this simply begs the question. See Flint, "Hasker's *God, Time, and Knowledge,*" 107; and Flint, *Divine Providence*, 142. See also Wierenga, *The Nature of God*, 155 n. 73. Hasker has argued that he did not beg the question because his point is not found in his premises. He does admit that "What is true, however, is that I fail to consider this point (viz., the proponent's claim that agents control the truth of the counterfactuals of freedom) in my discussion of whether counterfactuals of freedom outweigh laws of nature, or vice versa." Hasker, *God, Time, and Knowledge*, 46 n. 43. Hasker concedes that he must grant the Molinist his point regarding human control over counterfactuals of freedom—he cannot

claim that the fundamental laws of nature are indeterministic. This claim leads Hasker to assert that counterfactuals based on laws of nature are *would-probably conditionals* and this means that they are less fundamental features of the world than are counterfactuals of freedom.[26] Third, he

---

expect the Molinist to give this up. This leads him to conclude that "we cannot decide, on the basis of these considerations alone, whether counterfactuals of freedom are more fundamental than laws of nature, or vice versa. If anything, what seems to be suggested is that the two are roughly at a parity. If we wish for a more definitive answer to our question, we must look further." Ibid., 47.

26.   Hasker's contention that the fundamental laws of nature are indeterministic is a rather controversial claim in itself. William Lane Craig has characterized it as "false," noting that quantum mechanics and relativity theory (the two dominant concepts in modern physics) are irreconcilable, and that therefore, "relativistic laws are not probabilistic." Craig, "Hasker on Divine Knowledge," 106, 109–10 n. 32. Hasker's rebuttal has come in the form of a bet: "Craig is certainly right about modern physics. But since, as he says, quantum theory and relativity theory are incompatible, it is certain that both cannot be wholly true. What is needed (but has so far proved exceedingly difficult to provide) is a theory of 'quantum gravity' which combines what is true in both theories. If he is interested, I would be prepared to offer Professor Craig a modest wager on the proposition that the combined theory, when it appears, will preserve the indeterminism of quantum mechanics." Hasker, "Middle Knowledge: A Refutation Revisited," 234 n. 8. These issues are too complex to enter into here, but it must be noted that the Heisenberg Principle seems to indicate that uncertainty resides at the subatomic level, while the very concept of a natural law implies constancy. Hasker notes that quantum indeterminacy generally does not have a visible effect on the behavior of macroscopic objects, and claims that this *perceived* constancy allows us, for practical purposes, to treat counterfactuals based on laws of nature as if they were deterministic. However, he points out that while this is important for our practical use of such conditionals, it does not make "any difference at all to their logical status as would-probably conditionals." Ibid., 225.

   Hasker's argument depends on the division of several classes of conditionals, according to their logical strength. Specifically, he sets forth four classes for consideration: logically necessary conditionals, deterministic causal conditionals, counterfactuals of freedom, and would-probably conditionals. He then proposes a conditional of the general form,

   (i) $p \rightarrow q$,

and asks if (i) is true in the actual world, a, which type of conditional will allow its complement, namely,

   (ii) $p \rightarrow \sim q$,

to be true in the worlds closest to a. Hasker correctly notes that if (i) is logically necessary, then there is no possible world in which (ii) is true, and that if (i) is deterministically causal, then there is no possible world which shares laws of nature with a in which (ii) is true. He also points out that under the Stalnaker–Lewis account of possible worlds, if (i) is a counterfactual of freedom, then (ii) cannot be true in a or in those possible-but-not-actual worlds that are closest to a. Yet, Hasker argues, this is not the case with would-probably conditionals: "But with a would-probably conditional, we can have 'P' true and 'Q' false *in the actual world*, and also in possible worlds as close as you please to the actual world. And this shows, I maintain, that would-probably conditionals should be weighted less heavily than counterfactuals of freedom in determining the similarities of possible worlds." Ibid.

   Hasker's argument has proven less than convincing to Molinists, even if his point regarding indeterminacy of natural laws is granted. The problem with it lies in his move from the claim that the fundamental laws of nature are indeterministic to the assertion

has argued that the Christian belief in miracles can serve as a reason for believing that counterfactuals backed by natural laws are more fundamental to similarity among worlds than are particular facts. Since this argument is the strongest Hasker offers, it shall be examined in some detail.

Hasker contends that since miracles are, by definition, a suspension of natural laws, there are examples of counterfactuals backed by laws of nature that are false in the actual world and in those possible-but-not-actual worlds most similar to the actual world. The same cannot be said for counterfactuals of creaturely freedom. For example, suppose that Hasker is working on a poster and clumsily knocks over his ink bottle, but God miraculously intervenes and causes the bottle to right itself up before spilling any ink.[27] Hasker's immediate response is to laugh out loud in praise to God for his grace in preserving his work. In this case, the counterfactual backed by the fundamental laws of nature

> If Hasker were to knock his ink bottle over in such-and-such a way, the bottle would fall over and spill ink on his poster;

is false in the actual world and in those possible-but-not-actual worlds closest to the actual world, and instead the counterfactual

> If Hasker were to knock his ink bottle over in such-and-such a way, the ink bottle would fall over, but no ink would spill on his poster because the bottle would miraculously right itself up before spilling any ink;

---

that counterfactuals based on those laws are merely would-probably conditionals. This move assumes that all conditionals which are contingent (indeterministic) must be would-probably conditionals—to include counterfactuals of freedom! Thus, Hasker has presupposed either: 1) that counterfactuals of freedom are merely would-probably conditionals (as Adams argues), and therefore are unable to provide God with the information necessary for the Molinist system to work, or 2) that counterfactuals of freedom are deterministic, which is what Hasker is trying to prove! Both Flint and Craig have raised this objection to Hasker's claim. Craig writes, "The determinateness of the counterfactual's truth value is not affected by the determinacy of the causal relations involved. Alethic bivalence is just a different category from causal determinacy.

This is evident in that some Molinists, like Freddoso, would say that even a counterfactual about causally indeterminate events such as

(iii)   If a photon were fired through the aperture at t, it would strike the screen at coordinates $\{x,y\}$

is bivalent and may, for all we know, be true. I think the source of Hasker's confusion may be his conflation of a proposition's *certainty* and its *definiteness*. Definiteness refers to its possession of one of two truth values; certainty does not characterize the proposition itself but is our degree of conviction as to which truth value is has. Thus, (iii) may be utterly uncertain to us, but nonetheless definitely true. In the sense that (iii) is definitely true, the consequent *is* guaranteed on the antecedent, regardless of causal indeterminacy." Craig, "Hasker on Divine Knowledge," 106 (see also 107). See also Flint, *Divine Providence*, 143–44 n. 18.

27.   See n. 21 earlier in this chapter.

is true in the actual world and in those possible-but-not-actual worlds closest to it. Likewise, the counterfactual of freedom

> If Hasker were to knock his ink bottle over and God were to intervene, causing the ink bottle to miraculously right itself up before spilling any ink, Hasker would laugh out loud in praise to God for his grace;

is true in the actual world. The important point of Hasker's argument is that according to the Stalnaker–Lewis semantics, this counterfactual of freedom must also be true in all those possible-but-not-actual worlds closest to the actual world. This, Hasker maintains, proves that counterfactuals of freedom are more fundamental for determining similarity among possible worlds than are counterfactuals backed by laws of nature.

As might be guessed, Molinists have found Hasker's conclusion less than convincing. In order to see why, answer the following question: Is it more like the actual world for Hasker to knock over his ink bottle and it spill, but if it had miraculously righted itself up, he *would have* laughed out loud in praise to God, or for Hasker to knock over his ink bottle and it right itself up, and he go tell his wife of the curious event without laughing out loud? It seems that the first scenario is more similar and more likely. That is, Molinists have argued that a change in the laws of nature (or suspension of them) is more significant than a change in someone's free reaction to a miracle.[28] A situation where the physical events are the same, but the human responses are different, seems more similar than a situation where the physical events *are* different (at least when physical

---

28. I am indebted to Thomas Flint's work in this area. He also provides a counterexample to Hasker's appeal to miracles. Flint asks the reader to suppose that he is making a poster, has a history of knocking over ink bottles and spilling ink, has a forgiving wife who has always bought him more ink, and he knocks over the ink bottle again, but this time his wife refuses to buy more ink. Flint contends that in these circumstances, (call them C), the following two counterfactuals would be true:

    (i)   I am in circumstances C and I knock my ink bottle in such-and-such a way → the bottle of ink falls and the ink spills;

    (ii)   I am in circumstances C and I knock my ink bottle in such-and-such a way → my wife (freely) refuses to buy me more ink.

(i) is a counterfactual based on a law of nature, while (ii) is a counterfactual of freedom. According to Hasker's argument, (ii) is a more fundamental truth about the actual world than (i) is. If Hasker is correct, though, the minimal amount of change required to render (ii) false must be greater than the minimal amount of change required to render (i) false. To put this contention in terms of possible worlds semantics, (i) must have counterexamples in worlds which are closer to α than any of the worlds which contain counterexamples of (ii). Flint notes that since (i) is backed by natural laws, it seems that the easiest way for it to be false is a miracle, which are admittedly few and far between. Yet (ii) could easily have been false, especially given the history of Flint's wife's reactions to his previous spills—all that is required for (ii) to be false is for Flint's wife to act on the same reasons she has repeatedly acted on in the past. See Flint, *Divine Providence*, 145–46.

laws are involved!), but the human responses *would have* been the same. Thus, there is good reason for the Molinist to reject Hasker's conclusion and to instead proclaim that counterfactuals backed by laws of nature are more fundamental features of the world than are counterfactuals of freedom. If this is indeed the case, then Hasker's claim that counterfactuals of freedom outweigh particular facts in determining the relative similarity among possible worlds is to be rejected as well.

Rejection of the power entailment principle

Another objection to Hasker's argument is to question his power entailment principle. A number of philosophers have offered alternate versions of the principle.[29] One of the more intriguing suggestions in this regard has come from Linda Zagzebski. She has suggested that God may have power to bring about some necessary truths, and that this may serve as a counterargument to Hasker's power entailment principles.[30] She reasons that if some necessary truths and their negations can be brought about by *someone*, while other necessary truths and their negations cannot be

---

29.   For example, Basinger has proposed that Hasker's power entailment principle be replaced with:

> (PEP/B) If it is in A's power to bring it about that P, and "P" entails "Q" and "Q" is false, then it is in A's power to act in such a manner that, if she were to act in that fashion, "Q" would be (would always have been) true.

This allows the Molinist to claim that individuals do have power, but in no way does this lead to the conclusion that individuals do not have power over the truth of counterfactuals. David Basinger, "Middle Knowledge and Human Freedom: Some Clarifications," *Faith and Philosophy* 4, no. 3 (July 1987): 330–36. Other Molinists have also taken this approach. William Lane Craig suggests that Flint would offer the following alternative to (PEP):

> (PEP/F) If it is in S's power to bring it about that P, and "P" entails "Q" and "Q" is false, then it is up to S whether it be the case that Q;

based on Flint, "In Defense of Theological Compatibilism," *Faith and Philosophy* 8, no. 2 (April 1991): 237–42. Craig, "Hasker on Divine Knowledge," 92. Craig presents his own alternative as well:

> (PEP/C) If it is in S's power to bring it about that P, and "P" entails "Q" and "Q" is false, and Q is a consequence of P, then it is in S's power to bring it about that Q.

Ibid., 109 n. 9. See also Craig, *Divine Foreknowledge and Human Freedom* (Leiden: E. J. Brill, 1990), 89–90. Hasker's rebuttal is twofold: First, Basinger provides no good reason to reject Hasker's original formulation, save the fact that he does not like its conclusion. Hasker wants an argument which can serve as a defeater. Second, Basinger's replacement is tautological (though true). Hasker writes that the change Basinger introduces "empties the principles of their force," and reduces them to the principle

> (PEP/T) If it is in A's power to bring it about that P, and etc. . . . then it is in A's power to bring it about that P.

William Hasker, "Reply to Basinger on Power Entailment," *Faith and Philosophy* 5, no. 1 (January 1988): 88–89.

30.   Zagzebski, *The Dilemma of Freedom and Foreknowledge*, 110–13.

brought about by anyone, then the power entailment principles fail. For example, she claims that a proposition such as

> If there is a Fall, God sends his Son to redeem the world;

may be seen as a contingent truth that God, by choosing to so act in all possible worlds, can cause to be necessary. She writes:

> God has the power to bring about [the counterfactual] and the power to bring about the negation of [it]. But couldn't God decide to send a redeemer in *any* circumstance in which there is a fall? . . . If so, it would be the case that [the counterfactual] is a necessary truth, true in all possible worlds. And it would be a necessary truth precisely because God decided in a certain way, a way in which he could have decided differently.[31]

Hasker expresses serious doubts about the plausibility of Zagzebski's thesis, largely due to the departure from the standard modal logic that it represents.[32] He notes further that her argument leads to the conclusion that the property of decreeing the counterfactual to be true is an *essential* property of God and therefore, he is unable to cause it to be false.[33]

Zagzebski's response to Hasker is twofold. First, she claims that the alternate modal system she employs is valid, and that the burden of proof for the universality of the power entailment principles is Hasker's.[34]

---

31. Ibid., 111. I have replaced the number in parentheses with "[the counterfactual]" in order to avoid enumerated propositions.

32. Allowing God to choose to make a proposition true necessarily is odd, for although the counterfactual of divine freedom is true because God chooses to send his Son, given a Fall, it is still possible (logically) that he not do so. Thus, the counterfactual may be true in all worlds feasible, given God's desire to send his Son, but it would not thereby be true in all possible worlds.

33. Hasker proposes three principles which show Zagzebski's argument to be questionable:

   (i)   A proposition is necessarily true if and only if it is true in all possible worlds;

   (ii)   A property is essential to an individual if and only if the individual has the property in every possible world in which the individual exists.

   (iii)   God, God states, and God's attributes are included in the possible worlds rather than outside them. (i.e., [*sic*] a possible world is a comprehensive "way things could be" for *everything*, not just for all non-divine things).

   William Hasker, "Zagzebski on Power Entailment," *Faith and Philosophy* 10, no. 2 (April 1993): 251. Hasker notes that either God decrees in every possible world that the counterfactual is true, or he does not. If he does not, then the counterfactual is not necessary and Zagzebski's argument fails, but if he does, then the property of decreeing the counterfactual true is one God possesses in all possible worlds which, according to (ii), means that it is an essential property of God. But, Hasker notes, it is not in God's power to shed one of his essential properties. Thus, Zagzebski's argument fails. Ibid., 252.

34. Linda Zagzebski, "Rejoinder to Hasker," *Faith and Philosophy* 10, no. 2 (April 1993): 257.

Second, she makes the further claim that Hasker has dismissed her modal system *a priori*, and therefore, is wrong to assume that an essential property is not under the control of God:

> The question, though, is not whether God can *shed* one of his essential properties, but whether one of God's essential properties is best explained as the result of his choice, a choice which it is true to say he could have made differently, even though it is also a choice which God makes in all possible worlds—i.e., all worlds possible relative to the actual world. The idea that God wills an essential property of his is not without precedent, and if it is ruled out it cannot simply be on the basis of principles such as (i)-(iii) [in footnote 33], much less on the basis of a stipulation of the meaning of modal concepts.[35]

Zagzebski is surely correct that Hasker has presupposed a modal system that is incompatible with her initial argument, but, in his defense, it is that which most philosophers have come to accept; he is correct to require a defense of her alternate system.[36] In addition, Hasker is surely correct to question her understanding of divine attributes. The suggestion that God wills *his own* essential properties is dubious at best, if not incoherent altogether (even if it is *not* without precedent!). To see why, consider the essential property of God, omnipotence (or more properly, the property of *being all powerful*). Now, it seems that God's ability to *will* is dependent upon (logically posterior to?) his having the power to do or grant whatever it is he wishes to do or grant. In order to grant himself or another being all power, he would first have to be all-powerful, but this is circular. Therefore, it must be concluded that even an omnipotent Being cannot will his own essential properties; they just are.

Zagzebski has also offered a counterexample to the power entailment principle that is based on human power. She proposes a situation in which God decides from all eternity that he will perform a certain action on the hypothesis that a free creature were to act in a particular way in a particular situation. For example, God decides from all eternity that if Zagzebski were to perform action, *A*, he would perform action *B* every time. Suppose she is unaware of *B* and therefore, cannot act in such a way as to *intend* to bring it about that God does *B*. Even though her doing *A* results in God's doing *B*, she does not have the power to bring it about that God does *B*; only God

---

35. Ibid., 258.
36. Another problem with Zagzebski's suggestion has to do with its undercutting of the free will defense (see chapter 9). If a being's always freely acting the same way in a particular circumstance led to truths about that action being necessary (as in this case with God sending his Son if there is a Fall), then it seems a whole host of truths typically thought contingent may actually be necessary, dependent upon how a free being exercises that freedom. The free will defense suggests that it may be the case that whenever Adam is free with respect to eating the forbidden fruit, he chooses to eat, but it is still thought to be contingent because it seems obvious that it is logically possible that he refrain.

has that power, even though it is necessary that God does *B* if Zagzebski does *A*.[37] This example, while interesting, ultimately fails because it depends on the questionable assertion that a contingent truth may be *willed* to be necessary if God were to will it to be the case in all possible worlds. This is fundamentally false and therefore, the example fails.

Thomas Flint has called into question Hasker's use of *bring about* in the power entailment principle. He notes that Hasker must give a definition of *bring about* that will be accepted by the Molinist for both claims in the power entailment principle if it is to succeed.[38] It seems that Hasker has done this, and the power entailment principle should now be accepted by most Molinists.[39]

Counterfactuals, Determinism, and the Causal History of the World

Hasker's third argument that Molinism leads to determinism is similar in form to the second argument. He again utilizes the concept of *bringing about* and the power entailment principle, and argues that Molinism compromises libertarian freedom because the individual named in the counterfactual is unable to bring about the truth of its complement,

---

37. Zagzebski, *The Dilemma of Freedom and Foreknowledge*, 114. In order to show how Zagzebski's example refutes the power entailment principle in the text, I have quoted her at length. Against (PEP1), she writes, "I have the power to bring it about that *I do A* is true, and I have the power to bring it about that *I do A* is false. *I do A* entails *God does B* and *It is not the case that I do A* entails *It is not the case that God does B*. Yet I do not have the power to bring it about that *God does B* is true. The truth of that proposition is brought about by God." Ibid., 113. Against (PEP3) [PEP in the text], she writes, "Suppose that I do not do *A* at *t*. I have the power at *t* to bring it about that *I do A* is true, *I do A* entails *God does B*, *God does B* is false, yet I do not have the power to bring it about that *God does B* is true since, again, it is God who determines that he does *B* if and only if I do *A* and that that is the case necessarily." Ibid., 114.

38. Thomas Flint, "In Defense of Theological Compatibilism," *Faith and Philosophy* 8, no. 2 (April 1991): 237–43. Flint writes, "If two propositions are logically equivalent and I have power over the truth of one of them (i.e., its truth is up to me), then it does seem clear that the truth of the other one is within my power as well; what does not seem clear is that I need to have power in the same sense of 'power' over the second as over the first. Suppose I have causal power over the truth of one of two logically equivalent propositions; is it not sufficient that I have counterfactual power over the other? Is that not enough for me to say that each of them is such that its truth is up to me? Hasker gives us no reason to think not." Ibid., 240. Hasker originally responded by claiming that *bring about* is weaker than causal power, but stronger than counterfactual power; that the ability to *bring about* is just that power which stands between causal and counterfactual power. See Hasker, *God, Time, and Knowledge*, 109 n. 25. Interestingly, Linville has argued that the Molinist rejection of power over the past forces him to redefine Hasker's power entailment principles in terms of counterfactual power, which leads to a rejection of libertarian freedom. See Mark Linville, "Ockhamists and Molinists in Search of a Way Out," *Religious Studies* 31, no. 4 (December 1995): 501–15, esp. 506–7. Flint responded to Hasker by pointing out that there are many senses of *bring about* that stand between these two powers and, after examining no less than twelve of them, he concluded that it is doubtful any can serve Hasker's (PEP) well. See Flint, "Hasker's *God, Time, and Knowledge*," 111–14; see also Flint, *Divine Providence*, 148–57. For Hasker's response, see Hasker, "Response to Thomas Flint," *Philosophical Studies* 60 (1990): 117–26.

39. See n. 29 earlier in this chapter.

and therefore, is not really able to choose between competing courses of action. Essential to Hasker's argument is the claim that since God's knowledge of counterfactuals informs his creative decision, once he actualizes a world, the true counterfactuals of freedom become part of the world's causal history and thus, part of the fixed past. He goes one step further and notes that God's knowledge of the true counterfactuals itself is part of the fixed past as well. Consider a pair of counterfactuals of freedom:

> If John were to ask Stefana to marry him, she would freely accept;

and

> If John were to ask Stefana to marry him, she would freely decline.

If the first is true, then the second must be false. Hasker correctly notes that if Stefana is to freely choose, it must be in her power to decline the proposal of marriage, even if she accepts the offer when it is made. That is, it must be an open possibility that she will not accept. For that to be the case, "the truth or falsity of the counterfactual of freedom in question must also be an open possibility, and so must be the fact that it is *that* counterfactual that God contemplated in making his creative decision rather than some other counterfactual" stating that Stefana would decline.[40] Thus, Stefana's being free with respect to marrying me requires her having the power to bring it about that *Stefana is asked to marry John, and she declines.* However, according to the power entailment principle, this means that it is in her power to bring it about that the counterfactual, *If John were to ask Stefana to marry him, she would freely decline,* is true. This is problematic, according to Hasker, because the truth of its opposite (*If John were to ask Stefana to marry him, she would freely accept*) is part of the causal history of the actual world up to the time the marriage proposal is made.[41] Applied to counterfactuals, Hasker argues, the Molinist must see the true counterfactuals as dependent upon the future actions of free creatures.[42]

---

40. William Hasker, "The Antinomies of Divine Providence," paper presented at the Eastern Division meeting of the American Philosophical Association, Washington, DC, December 1998, 13.

41. This leads Hasker to argue that Molinists have to see counterfactuals of freedom as soft facts about the past, akin to the statement, *John and Stefana Laing were married twenty years before they visited Turkey.* Such a statement is about the past, but its truth is dependent upon future events. It is *soft* because at the time this is being written, its truth is still open; Stefana and I have not yet been married twenty years or visited Turkey. After one or both of these conditions are met, or a condition that is strictly inconsistent with the truth of the statement, then it will either be a hard fact about the past or a false statement.

42. He writes, "So I perform an action such that my performing the action, together with the world's past history, entails the counterfactuals of freedom in question, whereas the world's history by itself does not entail this counterfactual." Hasker, "A New Anti-Molinist Argument," 293.

He thinks that the upshot of this is that the history of the world by itself entails the truth of counterfactuals for at least two reasons. First, he notes that even if one is persuaded that God's past beliefs regarding the future are soft, "this conclusion cannot automatically be extended to cover the counterfactuals of freedom."[43] Second, and more importantly, he contends that middle knowledge is part of the world's history because of the function it serves in informing God's creative decision. Since the past is unalterable, the true counterfactuals cannot be changed.[44] He writes, "Middle knowledge is intimately involved in the process by which the world comes to be as it is; it is causally relevant in the highest degree."[45] Similarly, since God considers which states of affairs would be actualized were he to perform any given comprehensive act of creative will based on his knowledge of which counterfactuals hold in each possible (feasible) world, then it follows that his consideration of the counterfactuals of world-actualization is "an integral part of the divine creative action," and is therefore a part of the actual world's history.[46] If counterfactuals of freedom are a part of the world's history in this way, then the agents named cannot bring about the truth and they are not free. Hasker concludes, "Unless Molinists can present convincing reasons why the divine decision-making is not part of the world's history, the anti-Molinist argument succeeds."[47]

Molinist Responses

Most Molinists have questioned Hasker's presuppositions that if the history of the world entails the truth of a counterfactual, then the agent named in the counterfactual cannot bring about the truth of the consequent, and that the history of the world does indeed entail the truth of counterfactuals. Flint correctly notes that these premises imply determinism, and concludes, "no libertarian wants to think that the fixed history of the world entails an agent's free actions."[48] Most Molinists deny Hasker's point that something which has had causal consequences in the past is

---

43.   Ibid., 294. On hardness and softness of beliefs, see chapter 4.
44.   As Hasker writes, any fact that had causal consequences prior to the present time is embedded in the world's past, and it is "out of the question to suppose that those causal processes could now be made different in any way." Ibid. Hasker assumes the Molinist will agree with him in his contention that the past cannot be altered. In a related article, Hasker claims that the Molinist must hold that *the occurrence or non-occurrence of events that have had a causal influence in the past still remains an open question.* This, Hasker maintains, runs against our prevailing notions about the fixity of the past. Thus, the Moliinist must give up freedom, fixity of the past, or counterfactuals of creaturely freedom. Hasker, "The Antinomies of Divine Providence," 13.
45.   Hasker, "A New Anti-Molinist Argument," 296.
46.   Ibid.
47.   Ibid., 297.
48.   Thomas P. Flint, "A New Anti-anti-Molinist Argument," *Religious Studies* 35, no. 3 (September 1999): 302.

a hard fact about the past.[49] In the end, the differences are essentially of presupposition: Hasker presupposes that something which has had causal consequences in the past is a fixed fact about the past, whereas Molinists have strong reasons for rejecting this thesis.[50]

In addition, most Molinists deny that counterfactuals of freedom are part of the world's past. Hasker has admitted that his argument would fail if the Molinist could prove that the divine decision making is not part of the world's history, and one way to do so is to appeal to divine eternity. If God exists outside of time and he created time concurrently with his actualization of the world, then God's pre-creative reflection is not a part of history. Hasker argues that this misses the point because the actual world was not *created* by God, but has always existed (as a possible world). The counterfactuals of freedom are part of the truths related to that world, and they have always existed as well, so when God decides to actualize one of the virtually infinite possible worlds, he considers each world, including the counterfactuals, true to each. These issues will receive more attention in chapter 4. At this point, it is important to note that Hasker's objection presupposes that the truth of the counterfactuals is guaranteed because of God's decision to create a particular world, that the necessity of the divine will is transferred to the counterfactuals of creaturely freedom at the moment he decides to create, and it is for this reason that their truth is guaranteed. This may not be the case, as will be shown in the discussion of the *grounding objection*.

---

49. For example, Freddoso claims that Peter is free to do something (not deny Jesus) that would bring it about that Jesus never foretold Peter's threefold denial (Matt. 26:34; Mark 14:30; Luke 22:34). Even though Jesus's prediction occurred in the past and had (some sort of) causal consequences (e.g., Peter has a memory of Jesus's prediction), it is still in some way contingent until Peter denies Jesus or the cock crows. However, it should be noted that the infallibility of Jesus would then be suspect. A Christology which assumes that Jesus will not be in error requires that either Peter denies Jesus, or Jesus never predicts that he will. The cock crowing with no denial but a prediction leads to a suspect Christology. Flint writes, "I suspect that most relatively orthodox Christians, regardless of their familiarity with the contemporary contest concerning middle knowledge, would have their doubts about HA [the assumption that something which has had causal consequences in the past is a hard fact about the past] were they to see that it implies, for example, that once Jesus has issued his prophecy about Peter, either Peter's freedom or Jesus's infallibility needs to be sacrificed." Ibid., 304. Hasker responds by noting that Peter's being free in this situation requires that Peter is faced with alternative possible futures: one in which he denies knowing Jesus, and one in which he admits to knowing Jesus. This is not a problem, but Hasker also argues that if Flint is correct, then Peter also has alternative possible pasts: "in one of these pasts, Jesus has *not* predicted that Peter will deny him, and this past is *really possible*, it really could turn out to be the actual past, in spite of the fact that Jesus's prediction is still ringing in Peter's ears. At this point, judgments of plausibility are best left to the reader." William Hasker, "Are Alternative Pasts Plausible? A Reply to Thomas Flint," *Religious Studies* 36, no. 1 (March 2000): 105.

50. Hasker charges that these reasons, though, are "*based on Molinism itself*," and therefore, do not contradict his claim that the principle is "extremely plausible." Ibid., 104. Interestingly, Hasker notes that Flint now accepts the argument as valid.

GROUNDING

The No-Grounds Objection

Probably the most damaging attack on the doctrine of middle knowledge has been the charge that counterfactuals of freedom cannot be true because there is nothing (or no one) which can be pointed to that guarantees their truth. Adams writes, "One reason for doubting the truth of counterfactuals of freedom is that it is hard to see what would ground it."[51] Hasker agrees, asking, "What, if anything, is the *ground* of the truth of the counterfactuals of freedom?"[52]

Grounding and God

It is argued that counterfactuals of creaturely freedom cannot be grounded in God for at least two reasons. First, counterfactuals of freedom cannot be grounded in God because determinism would follow. It seems clear enough that God, as Creator, can by means of his divine will cause an individual to act a certain way, either through direct intervention upon his thought processes, or by creating that person in such a way that *every time* he is in situation, *S*, he will perform action, *A*. However, it seems equally clear that this does not allow for libertarian free will. If an individual is only able to choose that which God determines (understood causally), then that individual is not truly free.[53]

Second, it is also argued that counterfactuals of freedom cannot be grounded in God's will because they are prevolitional. One of the essential claims of middle knowledge is that it is independent of God's will. This claim makes the theory appealing as a means for answering the problem of evil. Therefore, counterfactuals of freedom cannot be grounded in God's will.

Grounding and the individual

It is argued that counterfactuals of creaturely freedom cannot be grounded in the causal activity of individuals in the actual world for at least four reasons: 1) truth of counterfactuals is prior to the individual's existence,

---

51. Robert Merrihew Adams, "An Anti-Molinist Argument," in *Philosophical Perspectives, vol. 5: Philosophy of Religion, 1991,* eds. James E. Tomberlin and Peter Van Inwagen (Atascadero, CA: Ridgeview, 1991), 345.

52. Hasker, *God, Time, and Knowledge,* 29. He is careful to note that this question should be distinguished from the question of how one can know a counterfactual to be true. The former question is metaphysical, while the latter is epistemological. Hasker writes, "The question is not, How can we *know* that a counterfactual of freedom is true? It may be that we cannot know this, except perhaps in a very few cases, and although it is claimed that *God* knows them, it is not clear that the friend of counterfactuals (or any other theist, for that matter) is required to explain *how* it is that God knows what he knows. The question, rather, is What *makes* the counterfactuals true—what is the *ground* of their truth?" Ibid.

53. According to Molina, this does not show that "our choice is free, but only that *God* has the freedom to *use our choice* by moving it indifferently to contrary effects." Molina, *On Divine Foreknowledge,* 136.

2) the existence of the individual is dependent upon God's will, 3) counterfactuals are not always actualized, and 4) character and psychological makeup cannot serve to ground free actions of individual creatures.[54]

The first argument relates to the nature of time and causation. It is assumed that backward causation is impossible; an effect cannot precede its cause. According to the doctrine of middle knowledge, propositions that refer to the free activity of creatures are true prior to the creation of the world and, in fact, inform God's creative decision. As Flint puts it, "So our current activity could cause them to *be* true only if that activity caused them to *have been* true in the past, and thus caused God to *have known* them. And this would be to have the cause come later in time than its effect."[55] Thus, it is not the activity of the individual that causes the counterfactual to be true.

Second, if counterfactuals of creaturely freedom were made true by the activity of those named in the counterfactuals, then they would be dependent upon the will of God. This is due to the fact that the existence of particular individuals is contingent, dependent upon God's decision to create them. Thus, in some sense, their actions are dependent on God's will (at least as far as their possibility of performance). This, however, goes against the spirit of middle knowledge which claims that counterfactuals of freedom are true no matter which possible world God actualizes.

This point is further clarified by the third argument, which notes that there are true counterfactuals of creaturely freedom that refer to persons or events that are never actualized. If the truth of counterfactuals were caused by the activity of the creatures to whom they refer, then those counterfactuals which refer to uninstantiated creatures would not have a truth value because they would have no cause.

Last, counterfactuals of creaturely freedom cannot be grounded in the psychological makeups or characters of the individuals to whom they refer for at least two reasons. First, Flint has argued that one's character develops (at least in part) in relation to the world; as a result of his/her actions.[56] If this is correct, then the first three arguments against the grounding of counterfactuals in the individual are applicable here as well. Second, it seems that if psychological makeup determines actions, then compatibiist freedom follows. Hasker describes the problem with attempting to ground the truth of counterfactuals of creaturely freedom in the psychological makeup of the individuals to whom they refer:

> Are the psychological facts about the agent, together with a description of the situation, plus relevant psychological laws, supposed to *entail* that the agent would respond as indicated? If the answer is yes, then the counterfactual

54.   See Flint, *Divine Providence*, 123–24.
55.   Ibid., 124.
56.   Ibid.

may be *true* but it is not a counterfactual of *freedom*; the agent is not then free in the relevant (libertarian) sense. If on the other hand the answer is no, then how can those psychological facts provide good grounds for the assertion that the agent *definitely would* (as opposed, say, to *very probably would*) respond in that way?[57]

Molinist Responses

Five distinct, yet related responses to the grounding objection have been set forth by the defenders of the doctrine of middle knowledge. First, counterfactuals of freedom do not need to be grounded. Second, the grounding objection involves presuppositions that undermine Molinism from the start. Third, propositions that refer to free actions in the actual future are no better grounded than counterfactuals of freedom, yet their truth is not questioned. Fourth, counterfactuals may be grounded in the other-worldly occurrence of the events to which they refer, and last, counterfactuals could be grounded in the persons to whom they refer, as they exist as ideas in the mind of God.

No need for grounding

Some Molinists have responded to the grounding objection by first demanding an account of what it means for a proposition to be grounded. Plantinga writes, "What grounds the truth of such a proposition as *this piece of chalk is three inches long*? I don't have the space to enter this topic; let me just record that the answers to these questions aren't at all clear."[58] He further argues that there seems to be nothing that *makes* or *causes* counterfactuals of freedom to be true, but this is okay because there is nothing that makes propositions about past actions true, even though they are true. He writes, "Suppose, then, yesterday I freely performed some action *A*. What was or is it that grounded or founded my doing so? I wasn't *caused* to do [so] by anything else; nothing relevant *entails* that I did so. So what grounds the truth of the proposition in question?"[59]

---

57. Hasker, *God, Time, and Knowledge*, 24.

58. Alvin Plantinga, "Replies," in *Alvin Plantinga: Profiles, Vol. 5*, eds. James E. Tomberlin and Peter Van Inwagen (Dordrecht: D. Reidel, 1985), 374.

59. Ibid. In this, he suggests that saying the action of the individual grounds the truth of propositions regarding past events or actions can also be applied to propositions about other kinds of free actions: "Perhaps you will say that what grounds its truth is just that in fact I did *A*. But this isn't much of an answer." Ibid. Jonathan Kvanvig has also expressed frustration with the ambiguity of Adams' demand for grounding. According to Kvanvig, it is sufficient to claim that a proposition which states Saul would attack if David remained in Keilah is true just because if David had stayed in the city, Saul would have attacked. No *grounding* is necessary. Kvanvig writes, "Does this explanation state a *ground* for the truth of (4) [counterfactual regarding Saul's freely attacking on David's remaining]? I should think not; but perhaps it is the only answer that can be given for explaining the ground of the truth of any proposition. Until Adams enlightens us as to what would count as a ground and what would not, it is not clear that the simple explanation above is not all that is needed." Kvanvig, *The Possibility of*

Two comments on this approach are in order. First, it seems that this is less of an answer to the grounding objection, and more of an avoidance of the problem. After all, if an account of what *grounding* means can be given, then this response is of little help to the defender of Molinism. More must be said.[60] Second, some accounting of what grounding means has been offered. Hasker has attempted to offer an explanation of the grounding relation on several occasions, and although he admits that he cannot give a general account of it, he claims there is an intuition behind the grounding objection that states that the obtaining of a contingent conditional state of affairs must be grounded in some categorical state of affairs: "More colloquially, truths about 'what *would be the case . . . if*' must be grounded in truths about what *is in fact* the case."[61] It would seem, then, that the grounding objection merits further comment by Molinists.

However, some Molinists have argued that the burden of proof belongs to the detractors of counterfactuals, and they have neither demonstrated that grounds *cannot* exist nor proven that grounds *must* exist for counterfactuals of freedom to be true. In addition, there are counterfactuals of freedom that seem true, but have no grounding. For example, consider the following counterfactual of divine freedom:

> If Adam and Eve had not sinned, then God would not have driven them from the Garden of Eden.

While we may not *know* that it is true (though it is suggested in the biblical text), it still seems that it must be either true or false, even if ungrounded. At any rate, Plantinga rightly points out that since the grounding objection says that counterfactuals of freedom cannot be true, all the defender

---

an *All-Knowing God*, 135–36. Both Plantinga and Kvanvig maintain that an explanation of the grounding requirement must be given and, if one cannot, then the Molinist is under no obligation to abandon the belief that counterfactuals of creaturely freedom can be true.

60. Even Molinist Thomas Flint has recognized this: "I think few Molinists would feel comfortable responding to the "grounding" objection with nothing more than a plea of Socratic ignorance. The suggestions that counterfactuals of creaturely freedom are true for reasons, and that those reasons ultimately have something to do with the causal activities of free creatures, seem both clear enough and plausible enough for Molinists to feel uneasy about straightforwardly denying them." Flint, *Divine Providence*, 127.

61. Hasker, *God, Time, and Knowledge*, 30. See also Hasker, "The Antinomies of Divine Providence." Hasker further notes that grounds exist for other kinds of conditional propositions and concludes that the request for explanation of the grounds for counterfactuals is not unreasonable. He writes, "Logically necessary conditionals are true in virtue of the laws of logic, plus the logical properties of the concepts involved in those propositions. Metaphysically necessary conditionals are grounded in the same way, and in addition by the essential properties of individuals and kinds of individuals mentioned in the propositions. Laws of nature are true in virtue of the inherent causal powers of the natural entities referred to in the laws. Probabilistic conditionals are true in virtue of the non-deterministic propensities of the entities involved. And finally, a material conditional is true in virtue of the falsity of its antecedent or the truth of its consequent." Hasker, "The Antinomies of Divine Providence," 8–9.

of Molinism need demonstrate is that they are possibly true: "…but surely it is *possible* that it's true. . . . There seem to be true counterfactuals of freedom about God; but what would *ground* the truth of such a counterfactual of freedom?"[62] Plantinga concludes that if counterfactuals of divine freedom can be ungroundedly true, then counterfactuals of creaturely freedom can be as well.[63]

Molinists are right to refuse the burden of proof, but if this is all that is said, then the discussion is at an impasse. As David Hunt puts it, "The differences between the two parties are apparently so deeply rooted that further discussion along these lines is unlikely to lead to any progress."[64] So some have attempted to clarify what it means to say that counterfactuals do not need to be grounded.

For example, David Basinger suggests that true counterfactuals are *brute facts* about a particular world, and invites us to consider a counterfactual of freedom:

> If Bob is free with respect to praying for his brother's safety at 7:00 a.m. on the 31st, he will freely pray for his brother.

According to Basinger, no one is responsible for its truth; neither the actions of Bob nor of God make it true. Rather, it is a basic fact about those

---

62. Plantinga, "Replies," 375.

63. Ibid. William Lane Craig agrees with Plantinga and assumes that Adams' response to the idea of counterfactuals about God would be that in cases where God's moral nature does not entail certain actions, God does not know what he would do were one of his creatures to behave differently. Craig writes, "On Adams's view, God could *decide* how he would act if creatures were to act differently and He could be aware of His decision to so act, but He could not believe that He would in fact so act, since such a belief might be erroneous." Craig, *Divine Foreknowledge and Human Freedom* (Leiden: Brill, 1991), 259. There is reason to doubt Craig's assertion here because counterfactuals of divine freedom are not prevolitional. God's beliefs about how he might act in various situations are informed by his knowledge of his own will. Craig notes that if this hypothetical position were adopted by Adams, it would be difficult to prove wrong apart from an appeal to orthodoxy. Yet Craig does not see such a proof as necessary because it is not up to the Molinist to prove his case, but rather to merely show the plausibility of middle knowledge. He argues that the burden of proof is upon the detractor of Molinism to demonstrate that it is impossible for counterfactuals to be true: "We have good grounds *prima facie* for regarding some counterfactuals of freedom as true and theological grounds for affirming God's knowledge of some such counterfactuals, so even if we cannot answer the question as to what makes counterfactuals true, that does not prove that they *cannot* be true, for it may well be the case that our philosophical analysis is just not yet up to the task of answering this question. The Molinist defense of the compatibility of divine foreknowledge and human freedom requires only that it is possible that such counterfactuals are true and known to God prior to his decree. Adams's questions do not show this account to be impossible." Ibid.

64. David Paul Hunt, "Middle Knowledge: The 'Foreknowledge Defense'," *International Journal for Philosophy of Religion* 28 (1990): 4.

possible worlds in which it is true.[65] This does not detract from Bob's ability to act freely, because the argument to the contrary is based on a subtle confusion. The claim that an individual cannot bring about the truth of a counterfactual is really a claim about the individual's ability to actualize a particular kind of world, but it is God who brings about the actual world in which the individual has the right to act freely, and it is the individual who performs the action in question. Basinger writes:

> But to say that Bob did not by his prayer at 7:00 a.m. on the 31st bring it about that this action will occur as a component in the actual world is not equivalent to saying that Bob did not, given the opportunity to pray at 7:00 a.m. on the 31st in the actual world, act freely. The former is a claim about Bob's control over the actualization of the *actualizable action* in question. The latter is a claim about Bob's ability to perform the action *freely*.[66]

Basinger seems to be saying that the individual is not responsible for the fact that the actual world contains the free act because the counterfactual is a descriptive statement about a particular world. Nevertheless, the individual acts freely.

The allusion Basinger makes to the brute facts about a world in which a given individual freely acts a certain way implies that there is something about the constitution of that individual such that, if placed in certain circumstances, he/she will act in a particular fashion. Richard Gaskin has made a similar argument, noting that this was the position held by Francisco Suarez. Gaskin explains: "Suarez argued that the properties recorded by conditionals of freedom, and which are objects of God's middle knowledge, are primitive. It is simply a base-line fact about a free agent (a *habitudo*, as Suarez calls it) that he would do so-and-so in such-and-such circumstances. There is no prospect of reducing that fact to more fundamental facts—in particular not to facts about the agent's intentions or dispositions."[67]

The answers given by Basinger and Gaskin certainly stand as an improvement over the dismissive responses Molinists have generally given

---

65. Basinger writes, "But who then is responsible for the truth of (7) [the counterfactual about Bob's praying] in the actual world? The answer is that no one is responsible. (7) is true in all actualizable worlds, given our scenario, because it accurately describes what Bob will do if certain conditions obtain. But since God (we are assuming) has no control over what individuals freely do and since hypothetical conditionals are true even if the relevant conditions never obtain, it cannot be said that either God or Bob brings it about that (7) is true. Given the assumed coherence of such hypotheticals, they simply *are* true." David Basinger, "Divine Omniscience and Human Freedom: A 'Middle Knowledge' Perspective," *Faith and Philosophy* 1, no. 3 (July 1984): 300.

66. Ibid., 300–301.

67. Richard Gaskin, "Conditionals of Freedom and Middle Knowledge," *The Philosophical Quarterly* 43, no. 173 (October 1993): 426.

to the grounding objection. However, their notions of brute facts regarding how individuals would freely act are quite vague and may lead to determinism. While they do not believe this to be the case, more must be said.

Hidden assumptions

Some proponents of middle knowledge have argued that the grounding objection contains some hidden assumptions that necessarily lead to a rejection of Molinism. According to Craig, it is wrong to ask what causes counterfactuals to be true because this question "mistakenly assimilates the semantic relation between a true proposition and the corresponding actual state of affairs to the causal relation."[68] Zagzebski agrees, noting that the relation between antecedent and consequent in a true counterfactual is weaker than the relation between a proposition and its logical or causal consequence, which is the relation required by the grounding objection.[69] The point here is that a causal connection does not have to exist between a proposition and the state of affairs to which it properly refers. The proposition is true in virtue of the fact that it accurately describes the *way things are*. Their relation is descriptive, not causal. Similar reasoning applies to counterfactuals. They are true because they accurately describe how things *would have been*.[70] To require a causal explanation beyond the free choice of the individual is to assume libertarianism false.[71]

---

68. Craig, *Divine Foreknowledge and Human Freedom*, 261.
69. Zagzebski writes, "An act can therefore be both logically and causally contingent and related to some circumstance as the consequence is related to the antecedent in a 'would' counterfactual. I have not, of course, said here *what the relation is* that holds between antecedent and consequent in a counterfactual, but only that whatever it is, it is weaker than the relation of logical or causal necessity. Adams need not worry, then, that the freedom of an act expressed as the consequent of a true counterfactual is precluded by lack of logical or causal contingency." Zagzebski, *Dilemma of Freedom and Foreknowledge*, 143.
70. Craig writes, "a counterfactual is true in virtue of the fact that its corresponding counterfactual state of affairs obtains. There is thus a reason why the counterfactual is true; its truth has a ground or is founded, if you will; and that reason or ground is its correspondence with reality. But it is misguided to ask who causes it to be true." Craig, *Divine Foreknowledge and Human Freedom*, 261.
71. In order to demonstrate this, Craig draws an analogy between propositions describing past actions and counterfactuals of freedom. He concludes that the same causal explanation is available to both: they are true because they accurately describe the choice of the individual named in the proposition. Craig posits the following proposition:

    Jones freely chose *x*.

    According to Craig, libertarianism assumes that there is no cause of Jones' choice of *x*, except Jones. To ask for a cause of Jones' choice is "implicitly to deny the very liberty the libertarian assumes." Ibid., 262. The claim that Jones caused his choice is not deterministic because no outside force or external cause makes Jones choose one way, and the claim that there is no cause of Jones' choice is not arbitrary because Jones chooses. Thus, both libertarian freedom and agent causation are preserved. The same logic may be applied to counterfactuals of creaturely freedom. Consider the following counterfactual:

    If Jones were in *C*, he would choose *x*.

Gaskin has also argued that the grounding objection assumes Fatalism, or at least denies libertarianism. Gaskin has produced two separate arguments for this conclusion, although only the first will be examined here.[72] Recall, once again, the example of the principle of conditional excluded middle given from the story of David, King Saul, and the men of Keilah. According to the principle, either

> If David were to remain in Keilah, Saul would (freely) besiege the city.

or

> If David were to remain in Keilah, Saul would not (freely) besiege the city.

is true. Robert Adams questioned this assertion, proposing that

> If David were to remain in Keilah, Saul might or might not besiege the city;

Craig argues that the question of what causes this counterfactual to be true implicitly denies Jones' liberty in the same way that the question of what caused the former proposition to be true does, and the same sort of cause is available to both. The causation is internal to the individual. The former is true because it accurately describes the way things are (i.e. Jones chose x by his own free choice), the latter is true because it accurately describes the way things would be if Jones were in circumstances, C (i.e. he would choose x). Craig writes, "There is no further cause of why Jones would freely choose x if he were in C. To think there must be such is to deny the hypothesis of Jones's freedom. Hence, the question as to what causes the counterfactual state of affairs to obtain is simply misdirected. Given agent causation and liberty of indifference, there is and can be no further cause as to why a state of affairs described in a counterfactual of freedom obtains." Ibid. He is careful to note that this does not mean that the free choices of individuals are random or independent of their wills. Counterfactual states of affairs, then, do not just *happen* to obtain; they do have causes, but the causes are not part of an unending chain of causes, or a chain of causes that must begin with divine activity. Rather, the causes are found in the freedom of the individual to whom the propositions refer. Craig writes, "Notice, *pace* Adams, that this is not to say that such counterfactual states of affairs just *happen* to obtain, as though what an agent would freely do is independent of his choice. Such an allegation is analogous to the compatibilist's charge that if one's choices are not determined by further causes, then they are random happenings like the motion of a subatomic particle. The problem with these claims, once again, is that they implicitly deny agent causation, which counterfactuals of freedom presuppose. . . . Similarly, 'Jones would freely choose x if he were in C' is true for no other reason than that is how Jones would choose; no reason is to be given for why Jones would freely choose that way, nor need Jones exist in order for this proposition to be true." Ibid.

72. The second argument Gaskin has developed is akin to Craig's. Gaskin writes, "I want to suggest that those who argue, on the basis of the approach to the semantics of subjunctive conditionals made popular by David Lewis and Robert Stalnaker, that conditionals of freedom cannot be true, are committed, at least in principle, to adopting a distinctively fatalistic posture in respect of the absolute future." Richard Gaskin, "Middle Knowledge, Fatalism and Comparative Similarity of Worlds," *Religious Studies* 34, no. 2 (May 1998): 190.

can serve as a counterexample to the principle, thus denying both counter-factuals of freedom. Gaskin notes that this approach incorrectly construes "would" in subjunctive conditionals as "could not but" or "would have to," and thereby, assumes Fatalism. As he correctly points out, the truth that Saul might (or might not) besiege the city does nothing to undermine the truth of the counterfactuals; the true counterfactual (that Saul would attack) can concurrently be true with the statement that Saul might not attack, at least if Saul is free.[73]

Antirealism, the future, and divine foreknowledge
One of the most promising responses to the grounding objection has been to note the similarity between contingent propositions that refer to the future and contingent propositions that refer to counterfactual states of affairs. It is argued that propositions that refer to the future are no better grounded at the time they are made than propositions which refer to nonactual states of affairs. Thus, any arguments against the truth of coun-terfactuals based on grounding will also count against the truth of future contingents, and the same kinds of arguments used to justify the truth of future contingents can also be used to justify the truth of counterfac-tual contingents.[74] Thus, both a defensive and offensive argument can be constructed from the similarity of the two kinds of propositions.

For example, Richard Otte asks what makes propositions about future free choices true, and evaluates alternatives based in the ground-ing requirement. The first proposal is that current states of affairs either causally or logically necessitate future free actions. However, Otte notes

---

73.   Gaskin proposes two propositions (following his numbering):

>   (14)   If you had asked me the way, I would have told you.

is a true counterfactual of freedom. Since (14) describes a free action, it is possible that Gaskin could refuse to give directions; he does not have to tell. Thus,

>   (15)   If you had asked me the way, I might not have told you.

is true as well. According to Gaskin, the rejection of (14) because of the acceptance of (15) assumes Fatalism: "If we accepted Lewis' interdefinition of 'might' and 'would,' and if we accepted (15), we would have to reject (14), and *vice versa*. But surely (14) and (15) can be true together. The plain fact is that I *would* have told you, although I was free not to, and so *might* not have done. It seems to me that we use conditionals like (14) and (15) all the time, and regard their joint truth as quite unproblematic. At least, that is so if we are not fatalists." Gaskin, "Conditionals of Freedom and Middle Knowledge," 421. In a footnote on the same page, Gaskin notes that Suarez's Dominican opponent, Diego Alvarez, argued that God cannot know conditionals of freedom apart from his own decree because there is nothing for God to know. Gaskin believes this assertion to be question-begging: "But if it is not supposed that conditionals about what *will* happen are automatically strict, there is no reason why it should be supposed that conditionals about what *would* happen in hypothetical circumstances are automatically strict." Ibid., 421 n. 26.

74.   See Freddoso, "Introduction," 70; and Craig, *Divine Foreknowledge and Human Freedom*, 260.

that this is too deterministic and precludes freedom.[75] Just as counterfactuals of freedom cannot be true due to a necessitating relation between the antecedent and the consequent, so also futurefactuals of freedom cannot be true due to a necessitating relation between present conditions and future actions.[76]

The second proposal is that an agent's character, desires, and intentions make true those propositions that refer to his future actions. However, Otte argues (with Adams) that individuals can act out of character, and therefore, character and desires (or intentions) cannot serve to ground the truth of propositions about future free actions. Just as a counterfactual about what Saul would have done had David remained in Keilah cannot be true based on Saul's character, desires, or intentions, so also a proposition describing my choice to read a book about Seinfeld and philosophy cannot be true based on my character, desires, or intentions. Even though Saul hated David, wanted him dead, had pursued him to the region where Keilah was located, had assembled an army, and had a history of attacking his enemies, he still might have decided to peacefully wait outside the city until David and his men came out, or he might have decided to leave the area, or take any number of other courses of action that do not entail his besieging the city. In the same way, even though I recently bought a book about Seinfeld and philosophy, have read portions of the book regularly for several weeks, enjoy much of the humor of Seinfeld and think the book may be useful in teaching my philosophy courses, and have a tendency to work on projects until they are complete, I might still decide that a better use of my time is to work on this book, or I might watch a movie, or even decide to do something out of character such as go to the local night club, drink some beer, and dance all night. In this, then, the futurefactual seems no better grounded than the counterfactual.

Yet Adams seems to believe that propositions about future free actions can be true and that God knows those which are true.[77] They are true

---

75. Otte also argues that the necessitation relation cannot even ground the truth of propositions which refer to future events that *are* causally necessitated by present states of affairs. This defect is due to the fact that a miracle may occur and the causal connections superseded: "Even if an event is causally necessitated by some present state of affairs, it is possible that a miracle occur, and the event not occur. Hence propositions about future events are not true because they are causally necessitated by present events or states of affairs." Richard Otte, "A Defense of Middle Knowledge," *International Journal for Philosophy of Religion* 21 (1987): 166.

76. Adams sees it as self-evident that a free action cannot be necessitated by present circumstances, and thus, a defense of the connection between a necessitation relation and a lack of freedom is not necessary.

77. Whether Adams believes that God's omniscience includes foreknowledge of free choices of individuals or not is irrelevant to Otte's argument. The point at issue is whether propositions which refer to future free actions of creatures can be true or not, and, if they can, how the truth of those propositions is grounded. It does not matter, at least for Otte's argument to succeed, *how* those truths are known or even *if* those truths are known. Interestingly, it is at this point that David Hunt criticizes Otte. He argues that since many philosophers discount

because they correspond to events and decisions which are actualized, with their grounding located in their correspondence to events that take place. Although Adams believes that counterfactuals have nothing to correspond to because they refer to events and decisions that never take place, Otte disagrees, arguing that a similar correspondence relation can serve to ground counterfactuals of freedom:

> According to this proposal, propositions about future free choices are true because they correspond to what *will* happen, or what *will* be actual at a certain time. But this does not appear to be significantly different from saying that conditionals of freedom are true because they correspond to what *would* happen, or what *would* be actual in certain situations. We cannot explain what it is for propositions about future free choices to be true without talking about what *will* happen. Similarly, we cannot explain what it is for conditionals of freedom to be true without the concept of what *would* happen.[78]

Otte points out that what *will* happen (by free actions) is not necessitated by any present actual state of affairs, and concludes that, in the same way, counterfactuals do not have to have a connection to present states of affairs in order to be true, and although he recognizes that there are differences between the two types of propositions—futurefactuals refer to events which will occur, whereas counterfactuals do not; futurefactuals are verifiable (once the events to which they refer occur), whereas the truth or falsity of counterfactuals cannot be known by humans—he maintains that this difference is inconsequential because propositions about future free actions are true (or false) *prior to* the occurrence of the event.[79] Thus, there are no more grounds for the truth of propositions about future free choices than there are for the truth of counterfactuals of freedom. Since

---

the doctrine of foreknowledge (most notably here, the other chief critic of Molinism, William Hasker), Otte's argument proves unconvincing. Hunt writes, "The most that Otte's argument can do, then, is convict of inconsistency those theists who accept foreknowledge while rejecting middle knowledge." Hunt, "Middle Knowledge: The 'Foreknowledge Defense,'" 6. Hunt's criticism is based on a confusion of the epistemological and metaphysical questions of grounding contingent truth. Although I will later argue that the two questions are necessarily tied together, this is not to say that they are the same thing. Otte's argument, then (if sound), can convict of inconsistency those theists who accept foreknowledge of future free actions while rejecting middle knowledge, but it can also convict of inconsistency those theists who accept that propositions which refer to future free actions can be true while rejecting the truth of counterfactuals of freedom.

78. Otte, "A Defense of Middle Knowledge," 167.
79. Otte writes, "Both [propositions about future free actions and conditionals of freedom] are true in virtue of corresponding to some state of affairs that is neither actual nor is necessitated in any way by what is actual." Ibid.

propositions about future free actions can be true, counterfactuals of freedom can also be true.[80]

David Hunt has questioned this approach by noting the difference in the ontological status of futurefactuals and counterfactuals of freedom. This difference is due to the fact that futurefactuals refer to events that actually occur, and is evident because explanations for how God can know futurefactuals of freedom can be given, while no explanation exists for divine knowledge of counterfactuals. Hunt writes, "foreknowledge is grounded in something that actually happens, and it is the occurrence of that future event that sanctions the foreknowledge of it. In contrast, whatever grounds the truth of counterfactuals of freedom is something other than an actually occurrent event."[81] His point is that counterfactuals of freedom, properly speaking, will never have grounding in the actual world, while futurefactuals of freedom will (in the future-occurrence of the event to which the proposition refers). Thus, even if there is nothing that can be pointed to in the present which grounds the truth of a given proposition, there must be grounding in the actual world.[82]

Hunt agrees with Adams that the heart of the problem lies with the very concept of a true counterfactual of freedom, noting that there "appears to be a *contradiction* at their very heart."[83] He argues that the *would* relation between antecedent and consequent in a counterfactual precludes genuine freedom, but this seems to place Hunt in a precarious position, for it is hard to see how the *will* relation does not have the same effect in a futurefactual of freedom. Consider the following two propositions:

> If John Laing were offered a pizza on January 1, 2019, he would (freely) accept.

---

80. Freddoso develops a similar argument, drawing upon probability theory and metaphysical grounding of propositions which refer to both the future and nonactual states of affairs. While some of Freddoso's claims are doubtful, the value of his discussion is his demonstration that the future occurrence of an event does not make propositions regarding the event true; rather, it shows them to have been true. See Freddoso, "Introduction," 71–74.

81. Hunt, "Middle Knowledge: The 'Foreknowledge Defense,'" 14. Although Otte argues that the ontological status of futurefactuals and counterfactuals are the same when futurefactuals are still future, Hunt is unconvinced. Otte (and Freddoso) notes that futurefactuals of freedom are ungrounded in any current actuals states of affairs, yet they are still considered true. However, Hunt disagrees that this means the grounding of futurefactuals of freedom and counterfactuals of freedom are equally mysterious. He argues that this understanding of futurefactuals of freedom is "exceedinly dubious," and that the fact that the states of affairs that make a futurefactual of freedom true *will be actual* constitutes their truth rather than rendering them mysterious. Ibid., 15.

82. He writes, "Whether a statement requires contemporaneous (or any) grounding in the actual world depends on the kind of statement that it is. If a statement is not of a kind that requires such grounding, it is unclear why its lack should be mysterious. It is not as though actual (contemporaneous) grounding is the only sort available; pastfactuals, like futurefactuals of freedom, have a noncontemporaneous grounding; statements of pure possibility, like counterfactuals of freedom, have a nonactual grounding." Ibid., 16.

83. Ibid., 17.

and

> John Laing will (freely) choose to order pizza on January 1, 2019.

The *would* from the first does not seem to remove the freedom from my decision any more than the *will* from the second does. Thus, if Hunt wants to affirm that God has knowledge of propositions regarding future free decisions (such as what I will do on January 1, 2019), then he cannot use the argument given.[84]

Other-worldly occurrence

Both Thomas Flint and Linda Zagzebski have taken Freddoso's principle regarding the present grounding of propositions to imply that counterfactuals of freedom are grounded in the causal activity of a free agent in another possible world.[85] Zagzebski notes that a comparison can be made

---

84. Hunt does not agree with this point, though, and it illustrates the fundamental difference between proponents of middle knowledge and its detractors. Molinists believe that just as there is a way things will actually turn out, there is a way things would have turned out had circumstances been different. According to Hunt, this assumes too much. A libertarian account of freedom must affirm the truth of:

> A might do y.

and

> A might not do y.

However, counterfactuals of freedom claim that

> Under certain circumstances, A would do y.

which renders the other two false. A futurefactual of freedom such as:

> Under certain circumstances, A will do y.

does not render them false. The difference between futurefactuals and counterfactuals is that futurefactuals can be grounded in the actualization of one particular pathway from the various patterns of future possibilities compatible with the actual past and present, whereas counterfactuals cannot be so grounded. Hunt explains, "the claim that A *would do* y if antecedent condition x were to obtain entails that A do y in *all* the relevantly similar x-worlds, leaving none available for A's pursuit of other options." Hunt, "Middle Knowledge: The 'Foreknowlege Defense,'" 20. The problem with Hunt's argument here, though, is that he neglects to recognize Otte's point regarding the timing of the truth of futurefactuals of freedom. Their truth cannot be grounded in their future-occurrence because the even has not yet occurred.

85. Flint generalizes Freddoso's principle in order to formulate a rule for the grounding of various sorts of propositions, including counterfactuals of freedom. Flint proposes two versions:

> "It X the case (Y) that z" is now grounded iff "z is grounded" X the case (Y).

or

> "It X the case (Y) that z" is now grounded iff it X the case (Y) that "z is now grounded."

According to Flint, then, temporally or modally qualified propositions of the form,

between the grounding of counterfactuals of freedom and the grounding of statements about possible actions. She asserts that one's actions in a possible-but-not-actual world can serve to ground the truth of a statement of possibility in the actual world. For example, the proposition, "It is possible that John Laing goes skydiving" is true because there is a possible world where I go skydiving. She then takes the basic principle (of actions in possible-but-not-actual worlds grounding truths in the actual world) and applies it to counterfactuals following the Stalnaker/Lewis analysis for possible worlds. In doing so, she argues that a person's acts in one possible world that is closer to the actual world than another possible world (where the individual does not so act) can ground the truth of counterfactuals of freedom in much the same way as they can ground the truth of propositions about possibility. For example, consider the counterfactual,

> If John Laing were offered a teaching position at Oxford, he would (freely) accept.

The truth of this statement is grounded in my activity in the possible world where I am offered a teaching position at Oxford and I accept, but only if that possible world is closer to the actual world than another possible world with a similar history, except for my declining the offer. However, she is careful to note that the relationship between the two worlds or between my actions in the possible world and the proposition's truth in the actual world is not causal: "To say I bring about the truth of this proposition in one world by my act in another world is only unacceptable if that relation is thought to be causal. But since the relation between acts and truth is probably not causal anyway, there is no worry that this interpretation of counterfactuals of freedom implies that my act in one world causes something in another."[86]

> It X the case (Y) that z.

are grounded if the present tense proposition z is grounded by the causal activity of a free agent where the temporal or modal operator X and the specifier Y indicate that action takes place. Applied to counterfactuals of creaturely freedom of the form ($c{\to}z$), the rule can be set forth as follows:

> "It *would be* the case (if c were true) that z" is now grounded iff "z is grounded" *would be* the case (if c were true).

Flint, *Divine Providence*, 133–34.

86. Zagzebski, *Dilemma of Foreknowledge and Free Will*, 143. According to Zagzebski, all the possible worlds explanation does is aid in explaining what counterfactual and possibility propositions say—that certain things go on in other possible worlds. The grounding of counterfactuals in other possible worlds should be no more problematic than the grounding of possibility propositions in other possible worlds. As she notes, if it is not problematic in the case of "It is possible that John Laing goes skydiving," then it should not be problematic in the case of counterfactuals (she uses the example of her visiting Antarctica). Ibid.

Adams has criticized this position, and argued that there are at least two reasons why this analysis does not *establish* the possibility of middle knowledge.[87] First, the possible worlds explanation does not really offer an explanation of how counterfactuals can be true. As noted earlier, a great deal of ambiguity exists in determining relative similarity among possible worlds. The criteria used are vague in terms of both content and relative weights. In addition, if counterfactuals of freedom turn out to be weighted more heavily than particular facts about the world, then determinism seems to follow.[88]

---

87. Adams incorrectly attributes the other-worldly answer to Plantinga. See Adams, "Middle Knowledge and the Problem of Evil," 112. Craig notes that Plantinga did not argue that similarity of possible worlds *causes* counterfactuals to be true or *establishes* their truth, but rather only that a feature of similarity is that worlds share counterfactuals. Craig, *Divine Foreknowledge and Human Freedom*, 258.

88. Adams offers an argument similar to Hasker's but without the appeal to miracles. He asks the reader to consider two possible-but-not-actual worlds (based on 1 Samuel 23). In the first,

> If David were to remain in Keilah, Saul would (freely) besiege the city.

is true, while in the second,

> If David were to remain in Keilah, Saul would not (freely) besiege the city;

is true. Suppose further that in both

> If David were to remain in Keilah and Saul besieged the city, the men of Keilah would (freely) surrender David to Saul.

is true and David stays in Keilah. Adams notes that it is not at all clear which of the two is more similar to the actual world when the events following David's decision to stay are considered. In the first world,

> David remains in Keilah, Saul besieges the city, the men of Keilah surrender David to Saul, and David is subsequently killed.

is true, while in the second,

> David remains in Keilah, Saul does not besiege the city, and the subsequent history of David, Saul, Israel and Judah goes very much like it did in the actual world.

is true. Since the second world only differs from the actual world with respect to David's remaining in Keilah (a difference which the first also shares) and to the counterfactual which states Saul would attack if David were to remain being true, while the first differs from the actual with respect to David's remaining in Keilah and Saul besieging the city, the men of Keilah surrendering David, and David being executed, Adams surmises that the second is more similar to the actual world than the first world. This judgment of similarity does not lead him to deny the counterfactual which states that Saul would besiege the city were David to remain. Instead, Adams contends that this problem demonstrates that similarity among worlds as a whole does not allow for judgments on the truth of counterfactuals. Rather, only certain kinds of similarities are relevant for such judgments, but they are not in need of possible worlds semantics for consideration: "Some similarities between the actual world and other possible worlds are relevant to that question [truth of counterfactuals]—for example, similarities and dissimilarities in causal laws and in people's characters. But we have already

Second, Adams and other critics of Molinism have contended that this approach to answering the grounding objection leads to a vicious circle, for it seems to make the truth of counterfactuals of freedom in the actual world dependent upon the truth of one's actions in the possible world closest to the actual world. However, similarity among worlds depends upon the true counterfactuals in them. So there seems to be a real chicken-and-egg dilemma here. As Hasker writes, "The following dilemma seems inescapable: If comparative similarity among possible worlds does *not* provide the grounding for the truth of the counterfactuals of creaturely freedom, then we have been given no answer whatever to the grounding objection. If on the other hand comparative similarity *does* provide such grounding, then the charge of vicious circularity returns in full force."[89] This objection will be examined in the next chapter.

Grounding and the mind of God
A growing number of Molinists have sought to answer the grounding objection by appeal to Molina's own concept of supercomprehension.[90] Molina believed that individuals exist in the mind of God as ideas, even before he created them, and that truths about how they would act in various situations were just true of them. This is similar to Basinger's concept of brute facts about possible worlds, except applied to individuals. It preserves the freedom of the creature better because it does not ground the truth of the counterfactual in the possible world in which it is true, but in the individual (thus, the individual is responsible for the truth of the counterfactual), and draws upon an agent-causal theory of freedom.

CONCLUSION

In this chapter, I presented three versions of an argument against the thesis that counterfactuals of creaturely freedom can be true. First, the argument against the principle of conditional excluded middle was examined and

---

considered and rejected the idea of founding the truth of our crucial conditionals on causal laws or on people's characters." Adams, "Middle Knowledge and the Problem of Evil," 113.

However, in actuality, the first is closer than the second is to the actual world. This means that greater weight has been given to Saul's character, assuming it is this which leads Saul to attack in the first and refrain in the second and which leads the actual world and the first to share the counterfactual stating Saul's intention to attack if David were to remain. According to Adams, this assumes that Saul cannot act out of character: "We have a well-entrenched belief that under many counterfactual conditions many a person *might* have acted out of character, although he probably would not have. If the possible worlds explanation is to be plausible, it must not give such decisiveness to similarities of character and behavior as to be inconsistent with this belief." Ibid.

89.   William Hasker, review of *Divine Providence: The Molinist Account*, by Thomas P. Flint, *Faith and Philosophy* 16, no. 2 (April 1999): 251.

90.   See, for example, my "Molinism and Supercomprehension: Grounding Counterfactual Truth" (PhD diss., Southern Baptist Theological Seminary, 2000).

found wanting. Although counterexamples to CEM can be given, they are far from convincing. Most of them are dependent upon the questionable Stalnaker-Lewis semantics for possible worlds analysis, and even if it is accepted, indeterminacy regarding closeness to the actual world stems more from epistemological uncertainty than from metaphysical indeterminacy and the argument fails.

Second, an argument that claims Molinism leads to determinism was examined in three forms. The first contends that since Molinism eliminates all of God's risk in creating, and risk is required for creaturely freedom, then determinism is the result. I pointed out that this argument simply begs the question. The definitions of determinism and risk used in this argument are doubtful at best, and Molinism allows for a measure of risk in God's decision to create because of the limitations placed upon his creative choice by the counterfactuals of freedom.

The second claims that since the agent named in a counterfactual of creaturely freedom does not cause the counterfactual to be true by his/her action, then the action is not free. I noted that this argument is dependent upon two proposals: 1) the contention that counterfactuals of freedom outweigh particular facts for determining similarity among possible worlds, and 2) the power entailment principle. After examining several Molinist arguments against PEP, I concluded that it should be allowed to stand, but the same cannot be said for the first proposal. There is no good reason for the Molinist to accept it. Even if the laws of nature are indeterministic, and even though miracles do sometimes occur, it still seems to be the case that counterfactuals are not as fundamental features of the world as laws of nature.

The third is the most complex and the most difficult to answer. It is claimed that since counterfactuals inform God's decision about which world to actualize, when the agent named in any given counterfactual is placed in the circumstances described by that counterfactual, he/she cannot do other than what the counterfactual says he/she will do because the truth about the individual's action is part of the fixed, unalterable past (*causal* history of the world). I pointed out that this argument fails because it presupposes determinism and because it ignores the hard/soft fact distinction (discussed in chapter 4). I also argued that the doctrine of divine eternity can undermine its claim that the divine decision-making process is part of the causal history of the world. Finally, I proved that this argument is really another form of the next objection to be examined, the *grounding* objection. The argument that Molinism ends in determinism based on the causal history of the world presupposes that the truth of counterfactuals is somehow tied to God's will via his decision to create.

The third and final argument against the truth of counterfactuals is the *grounding objection*. It is my contention that this objection serves as the basis for all other objections to Molinism. The objection basically states that there is no ground, or guarantee for the truth of counterfactuals of creaturely freedom. Counterfactuals of freedom are not grounded in God because they would then be deterministic, and they are not grounded in the individual to whom they refer because they are true prior to, and irrespective of, the individual's existence and actions, and because they would be deterministic if true based on the individual's psychological makeup.

After setting forth the basic argument, I presented five Molinist responses to it. The first response is that counterfactuals do not need to be grounded, and that a more developed explanation of *grounding* is required before an adequate response can be given. Further, there are many kinds of propositions that are not *grounded* in the required sense, yet are still true. The second Molinist response is to charge the detractors of middle knowledge with begging the question. The requirement for a cause of an individual's free action apart from his/her will necessarily implies some form of determinism, and therefore, the grounding objection assumes libertarianism to be false. The third Molinist response comes in the form of a comparison between contingent propositions about the actual future, and contingent propositions about counterfactual states of affairs. Propositions that refer to the actual future are either true or false now, but there is nothing in the present which guarantees their truth/falsity. In a similar way, propositions that refer to nonactual events are either true or false even though there is nothing that guarantees their truth/falsity. Opponents of middle knowledge who accept foreknowledge run into difficulty here. The fourth Molinist response to the grounding objection has been to suggest that the truth of counterfactuals of creaturely freedom can be grounded in the occurrence of the event/action in the possible-but-not-actual world closest to the actual world. I argued that this thesis should be rejected for at least two reasons: 1) there is too much ambiguity in determining the relative similarity among possible worlds, and 2) this argument leads to a vicious circle because similarity depends on which world is actual, and which world is actual depends on similarity. The vicious circle argument will be discussed in the next chapter, but it should be noted that this answer to the grounding objection, if accepted, gives it teeth. The fifth answer provided by Molinists was to build upon the concept of ungrounded truths as brute fact, but to apply them not to the world, but to the individuals to whom they refer. Persons pre-exist in the mind of God as ideas, and are known by him through his knowledge of their being. This answer, along with the argument that counterfactuals need not be grounded (just as futurefactuals have no grounding at the time of their truth), alleviates the concerns about counterfactuals raised by Molinism's opponents.

CHAPTER 3

THE CIRCULARITY OBJECTION

INTRODUCTION

In the previous chapter, several arguments were considered which purport to prove that counterfactuals of creaturely freedom cannot be true. In this chapter, a different but related argument that attacks the usefulness of middle knowledge for God's creative decision will be examined. It may be properly seen as an extension of the grounding objection, though it is typically treated separately. This argument focuses on the steps in the divine deliberative process regarding God's creative work.

COUNTERFACTUALS OF FREEDOM, TRUTH, AND SIMILARITY AMONG WORLDS

Vicious Circle Argument

The first version of this argument was apparently discovered independently by Anthony Kenny and Robert Adams, who both complain that the possible worlds explanation for the truth of counterfactuals leads to a vicious circle. They point out that Molinism requires counterfactuals of creaturely freedom to be true logically prior to God's decision to create, since they are thought to inform that creative decision. However, they argue that a problem exists because the relevant counterfactuals do not at that time have a truth value or are false, and therefore cannot be known.[1] Kenny writes, "But prior to God's decision to actualize a particular world

---

1. It seems that both Kenny and Adams originally maintained that counterfactuals do not have a truth-value, though Adams changed his position to make the claim that they are all false (at least, counterfactuals of creaturely freedom). See the reprint of his "Middle Knowledge and the Problem of Evil," in *The Virtue of Faith* (Oxford: Oxford University Press, 1987), 91, n. 4. He seems to have changed his position due in large part to interaction with Alvin Plantinga, who has pointed out the strangeness of saying propositions do not have a truth value. As Plantinga writes, "But how could a *proposition* fail to have a truth value? Either things are as it claims they are, in which case it is true, or it's not the case that things are thus, in which case it is false." Plantinga, "Replies," 373. On either count, the argument can proceed. What is relevant is the claim that prior to creating, counterfactuals of creaturely freedom cannot be true.

those counterfactuals cannot yet be known: for their truth-value depends, on Plantinga's own showing, on which world is the actual world."[2] Adams concurs: "On the possible worlds theory, moreover, the truth of the crucial conditionals cannot be settled soon enough to be of use to God."[3] Kenny correctly notes that this objection rests on the belief that counterfactuals are true due to the similarity of the possible world in which they hold to the actual world and proceeds from there. Simply put, which world is actual cannot be determined until God makes his creative decision, and that decision cannot be made until the counterfactuals are known.[4] In order to see this more clearly, consider an example supplied by Adams. He invites us to consider a proposition that God presumably knew prior to his decision to create:

> If God were to create Adam and Eve, there would be more moral good than moral evil in the history of the world.

God uses his middle knowledge of propositions like this to aid his decision regarding which possible world to actualize. More generally, God considers propositions—what Adams calls deliberative conditionals—of the form, "If I did x, y would happen," in determining which possible world to create/actualize. Adams argues that the truth of these kinds of statements cannot be determined prior to the actual world being actualized because it "depends on whether the actual world is more similar to some world in which I do x and y happens than to any world in which I do x and y does not happen."[5] The problem is that similarity to the *actual* world depends on which possible world is actual, which in turn depends in part on whether Adams does x. He concludes that the truth of the proposition regarding relative moral good and evil if God were to create Adam and Eve "will depend on whether God creates Adam and Eve."[6]

This argument is really twofold. It rests on the premise that there is an interdependent relationship among the steps in the divine deliberative process regarding creation, and that counterfactuals cannot be true soon enough to be of use to God in his decision regarding creation. These two claims are tied together, but for purposes of analysis, will be treated separately.

---

2. Anthony Kenny, *The God of the Philosophers* (Oxford: Clarendon, 1979), 70.
3. Adams, "Middle Knowledge and the Problem of Evil," 109–17.
4. Kenny writes, "The problem is that what makes the counterfactual true is not yet there at any stage at which it is undecided which world is the actual world. The very truth-conditions which the possible-world semantics were introduced to supply are absent under the hypothesis that it is undetermined which world the actual world is to be. But if truth-conditions are not fulfilled, the propositions are not true; and if they are not true not even an omniscient being can know them." Kenny, *The God of the Philosophers*, 70.
5. Adams, "Middle Knowledge and the Problem of Evil," 113.
6. Ibid., 114.

First, both Adams and Kenny claim that an interdependent relationship exists between the similarity relation among possible worlds and the truth of counterfactuals. This interdependence seems to lead to a vicious circle; the truth of any given counterfactual in the actual world depends on its truth in the possible-but-not-actual world that is closest to it, but the possible-but-not-actual world that is closest to the actual world is the one which shares counterfactuals with the actual world, and so their truth must be determined prior to the establishment of similarity. This may be made more clear if an example is set forth.

Suppose, with Adams, that it is true that the world would be a better place if God were to create Adam and Eve, and God used his knowledge of this in determining which possible world to actualize. Now consider two possible-but-not-actual worlds that are exactly alike, except that in the first, the counterfactual, *If God were to create Adam and Eve, there would be more moral good than moral evil in the history of the world*, is true, and in the second, it is false. In this case, Adams argues, the counterfactual is true in the actual world if the actual world is more similar to the first possible-but-not-actual world than to the second, but the closeness of either of the two worlds (to the actual world) cannot be established until the truth of the counterfactuals in the actual world is set (which, of course, only occurs at the moment God decides to actualize a particular world or at the moment he actualizes a world). The argument may be diagramed as follows, and the circular nature of Molinism is clear:

Figure 1

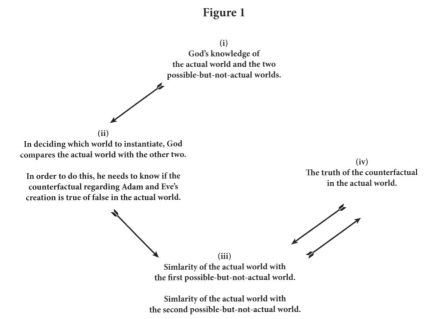

(i)
God's knowledge of
the actual world and the two
possible-but-not-actual worlds.

(ii)
In deciding which world to instantiate, God
compares the actual world with the other two.

In order to do this, he needs to know if the
counterfactual regarding Adam and Eve's
creation is true of false in the actual world.

(iv)
The truth of the counterfactual
in the actual world.

(iii)
Similarity of the actual world with
the first possible-but-not-actual world.

Similarity of the actual world with
the second possible-but-not-actual world.

Second, this argument claims that middle knowledge cannot serve the purpose Molina's system requires because counterfactuals are not true soon enough to inform God's creative decision. According to Kenny and Adams, God's decision about which world to actualize requires information only available *after* he has made his decision about which world to actualize. In other words, a world must be actualized prior to the counterfactuals in that world being true, but the counterfactuals supposedly influence his decision about which world to actualize. An example may clarify the argument.

Assume again that God considered truths such as the aforementioned counterfactual and that he desires a world containing more moral good than moral evil. It follows that the counterfactual (*If God were to create Adam and Eve, there would be more moral good than moral evil in the world*) is true in the actual world. Adams invites the reader to entertain the idea that there is a whole set of worlds that are more similar to a possible-but-not-actual world in which God creates Adam and Eve and there is more moral good than moral evil in the history of the world, than to a second possible-but-not-actual world where God creates Adam and Eve and there is not more moral good than moral evil in the history of the world. Adams maintains that Molinism requires that God compared the worlds of the set with the two possible-but-not-actual worlds in order to aid his decision regarding which world to actualize, and argues that the truth of the counterfactual in the actual world depends on the actual world being a member of that set, but such membership cannot have been established prior to God's decision to actualize the world he did. He claims that this can be seen once we consider another kind of world God could have considered actualizing, a world in which there are no free creatures. Since morality and responsibility are strongly tied to individual freedom (an assumption granted by most Molinists, but not beyond challenge), there seems to be no way to speak of moral good and moral evil in a world where there are no free creatures. If this is the case, then there is no way to determine if it is more similar to the former or latter worlds, and it cannot be a member of the class of worlds considered. In other words, the decision of which world to actualize depends on the worlds' being a member of the desired set, but the world's membership in the set depends on its similarity to the correct possible-but-not-actual world. Some may think that a world containing no free will would result in agnosticism regarding that world's membership in the set. Such a conclusion, though, would be based on the mistaken notion that the complement of the desired counterfactual, *If God were to create Adam and Eve, there would be more moral good than moral evil in the history of the world*; is *If God were to create Adam and Eve, there would be more moral evil than moral good in the history of the world*; and the truth of both of these is indeterminate in such a world. However, the complement of the desired counterfactual is, in actuality, the following: *If God were to create Adam and Eve, there would not be more moral good than moral evil in the history of the world.* This counterfactual would be true in the second possible-but-not-actual world considered, and it would also be true in a world containing no free creatures, for if moral good and moral evil depend on creaturely freedom, then a world which contains no free creatures will have an equal amount of moral good and moral evil, namely none. Adams' argument may be diagramed as follows:

Figure 2

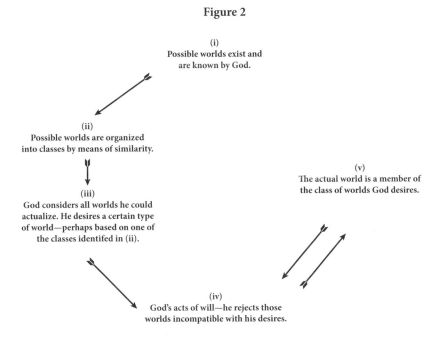

Molinist Responses

At least three responses to this objection are available to the Molinist: 1) deny the use of possible worlds semantics, 2) identify specific flaws in wording or logic in the argument, or 3) clarify misunderstandings of the possible worlds analysis of counterfactuals. All three approaches have been used by Molinists, and each will be briefly examined.

Possible worlds semantics

The argument presented by Adams and Kenny is clearly dependent upon the Stalnaker-Lewis approach to counterfactual analysis. Recall that according to this approach, a counterfactual is true in the actual world if and only if it is true in the possible-but-not-actual world that is most similar to the actual world. Yet, according to Adams and Kenny, similarity cannot be determined until the truth of counterfactuals is known and the truth of counterfactuals cannot be determined until the similarity of worlds is established. As already noted, not all Molinists accept the Stal-naker-Lewis thesis as an adequate explanation of counterfactual logic. If the relation between similarity of worlds and truth is denied, then the objection loses its force.

Logical/wording flaws

Alvin Plantinga has criticized this argument at the point of the *depends on* relation. He notes that the concept of *depends on* must be transitive for the argument to work, but it is not. In order to illustrate his point, he invites the reader to consider an argument which utilizes the same termi-nology, but is clearly false because of an equivocation in the meaning of "*depends on.*" Consider the proposition, "The truth of *The Allies won the Second World War* depends on which world is actual." This should be clear enough, for presumably there is some possible-but-not-actual world where the Allies did not win WWII. Now consider a similar state-ment, but future-directed: "Which world is actual depends on whether I mow my lawn this afternoon." Plantinga claims that, following similar logic to that employed by Adams, it should follow that "The truth of *The Allies won the Second World War* depends on whether I mow my lawn this afternoon."[7]

Linda Zagzebski has argued that Plantinga's response to Adams—that the *depends on* relation between which world is actual and an individual's action is not transitive—misses the point, and that the *depends on* relation need only be asymmetrical. However, her counterexamples and reframing of the circularity objection is not convincing.[8]

Clarification of possible worlds analysis

Probably the most striking problem with the argument presented by Kenny and Adams is that it makes some assumptions about the possible worlds semantics which are not correct. Plantinga correctly notes that underlying this objection is the false assumption that similarity among worlds somehow *causes* or *grounds* the truth of counterfactuals, but this is not how the similarity relation functions in counterfactual logic. Instead, similarity of possible worlds only shows what it means for counterfactuals to be true. Plantinga writes:

> In the same way we can't sensibly *explain necessity as truth in all possible worlds;* nor can we say that *p*'s being true in all possible worlds in [*sic*] what *makes p* necessary. It may still be extremely useful to note the equivalence of *p is necessary* and *p is true in all possible worlds:* it is useful in the way diagrams and definitions are in mathematics; it enables us to see connections,

entertain propositions and resolve questions that could otherwise be seen, entertained and resolved only with the greatest difficulty if at all.[9]

Since similarity among worlds is not what causes counterfactuals to be true, the move from (iv) to (v) in the argument is denied. Rather, (v) is really part of (i). The counterfactuals that are true in the actual world are true prior to God's consideration of the possible worlds; it is part of what God considers. Prior to God's decision to create (and creating!) the actual world is just one among the virtually infinite number of possible worlds being considered. The closest possible-but-not-actual world is only revealed once God creates (as are all possible-but-not-actual worlds because prior to God's creating, they are all merely possible worlds). Relative similarity to the actual world is a function of God's creation decision.[10]

Some Molinists have argued that the actualization of the actual world is progressive and that this removes the force of the objection. For example, William Lane Craig writes, "What this objection fails to appreciate is that parallel to the logical sequence in God's knowledge—natural knowledge, middle knowledge, free knowledge—there is a logical sequence in the instantiation of the actual world as well."[11] Craig argues that it is incorrect to speak of God's actualizing an entire possible world at the first logical moment—God's natural knowledge—though it is true that some aspects of the actual world obtain. At the second logical moment of divine deliberation (middle knowledge), more aspects of the actual world obtain. According to Craig, it is at this moment that "all those states of affairs corresponding to true counterfactuals of creaturely freedom obtain."[12] For example, the state of affairs, *If Adam were offered the forbidden fruit, he would eat*, obtains. At this point, of course, Adam does not exist and God could decide to refrain from creating/instantiating him. It is not until the third logical moment of divine deliberation that the actual world is instantiated by an act of divine will. According to Craig, the force of the *not soon enough* objection has been removed because the premise behind it, namely that counterfactuals must be true before the actual world obtains, has been shown to be false. He writes:

9.   Plantinga, "Replies," 378.
10. All that must be established is that the world to be actualized is one of a particular set, or class, of worlds. Recall the discussion of feasibility in chapter 1. The counterfactual regarding the relative amount of moral good if God were to create Adam and Eve may be true in all worlds God could actualize (that is, in all feasible worlds) and therefore, which specific world is actual does not have to be settled in order for it to be true in the actual world. In other words, the counterfactual may be true in all the possible worlds of a given set and since God only actualizes a world-germ, he does not need to know which world is actual to make his creative decision.
11. Craig, "Hasker on Divine Knowledge," 102.
12. Craig, *Divine Foreknowledge and Human Freedom*, 266.

The upshot of this is that it is not wholly correct to say with Kenny that prior to the divine decree the actual world does not obtain, for certain aspects of it do and other aspects do not. And those states of affairs that do obtain are sufficient for the truth of counterfactuals of creaturely freedom, since the latter correspond with reality as it thus far exists and since possible worlds can be ranked in their similarity to the actual world as thus far instantiated, thus supplying the truth conditions for a possible worlds analysis of the truth of counterfactuals of freedom in terms of degree of shared counterfactuals. Once it is appreciated that there is a logical sequence in the exemplification of the actual world just as much as there is in God's knowledge, then objections to middle knowledge based on counterfactuals' being true "too late" to facilitate such knowledge disappear.[13]

Hasker complains that these answers skirt the force of the objection and return to the grounding objection. He writes, "So we are confronted with this vast array of counterfactuals—probably thousands or even millions for each actual or possible free creature—almost all of which simply are true without any expectation whatever of this fact being given. Is this not a deeply puzzling, even baffling state of affairs?"[14] Hasker is correct to note the close ties between the priority objections and the grounding objections. In fact, it appears that the priority objections reduce down to the grounding objection. Therefore, if an acceptable answer to the grounding objection can be presented, all obstacles to middle knowledge will be removed.

EXPLANATORY PRIORITY, CIRCULARITY, AND DETERMINISM

The second version of this argument has been developed by Robert Adams.[15] Recall that Molinism is based upon the premise that there are several logical steps in God's decision process regarding creation: Necessary truths are logically prior to God's knowledge of counterfactuals of freedom, and the truth values of those counterfactuals are prior to God's knowledge of them. God uses his knowledge of the necessary truths and the true counterfactuals of creaturely freedom in order to decide which possible world to actualize so that he gets what he desires. Flint has characterized Adams' argument as making the claim that the libertarian nature of a person's action requires that it (i.e., the action) be logically prior to the truth of the relevant counterfactual of creaturely freedom

13. Ibid., 267.
14. Hasker, *God, Time, and Knowledge*, 38.
15. See Adams, "An Anti-Molinist Argument," 343–53.

about that action.[16] If this is indeed the argument that Adams is advocating and if he is correct, then the circular nature of the Molinist account of divine foreknowledge and providence, and its viciousness, is readily apparent. It may be diagrammed as follows:

Figure 3

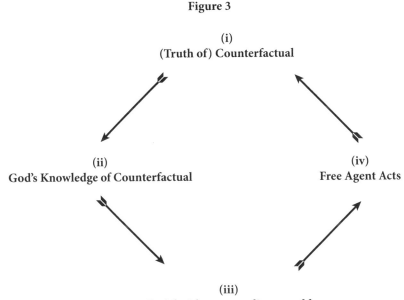

(i)
(Truth of) Counterfactual

(ii)
God's Knowledge of Counterfactual

(iv)
Free Agent Acts

(iii)
God decides to actualize a world
in which a person is in the specified
situation so that he performs the desired action
based on his knowledge of the counterfactual.

Perhaps an example of a deliberative conditional (colloquially, counterfactual of creaturely freedom) known to be true will make the argument more clear. I proposed to Stefana in August, 2001, and she accepted. Thus, the counterfactual, *If John were to propose to Stefana in August, 2001, she would freely accept*; is known to be true, and presumably this information was known to God prior to his decision to actualize any world and it informed/influenced his decision to actualize this world. In other words, God wanted Stefana and I to marry, and he actualized a world in which we would be in a situation where I propose in 2001.[17] Thus, the counterfactual was true logically prior to God's decision about which world to actualize, and prior to any action on my part or on Stefana's part. Yet this

---

16. Flint, *Divine Providence*, 159–62.
17. This is, admittedly, simplistic. After all, it may be that God did not desire a world where Stefana and I marry (though I doubt it), and instead this world met his other desires better than any other world where we do not marry.

characterization of the argument has Adams claiming that it is precisely Stefana's action of accepting my proposal that makes the counterfactual true. Thus, our actions—my proposal and her free acceptance—must be prior to the truth of the relevant counterfactuals and the Molinist system is shown to be circular and therefore, fails.

Figure 4

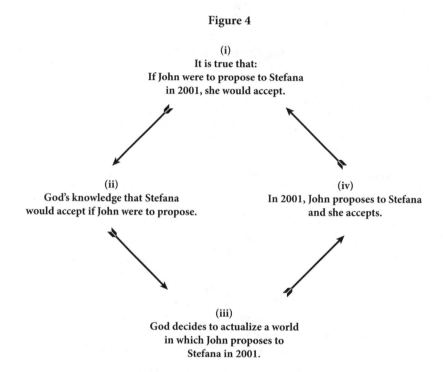

(i)
It is true that:
If John were to propose to Stefana
in 2001, she would accept.

(ii)
God's knowledge that Stefana
would accept if John were to propose.

(iv)
In 2001, John proposes to Stefana
and she accepts.

(iii)
God decides to actualize a world
in which John proposes to
Stefana in 2001.

Flint recognizes that this characterization of the argument includes a step that Adams did not make, namely the move from Stefana's acceptance back to the establishment of the counterfactual, but this move is clearly false according to Molinism. The doctrine of middle knowledge does not require that an action be performed in order for propositions describing that action to be true, but this is precisely the picture of Molinism described. The problem with this interpretation may be seen if a deliberative conditional that is not known to be true is considered. For example, the counterfactual, *If Pius XII had intervened, Hitler would have stopped the deportation of the Jews of Rome to Auschwitz*, may be true, but there is no way for us to know it. Adams seems to hold that Molinism must assert that the counterfactual is false because Pius XII did not intervene. However, Molinism clearly does not lead to this conclusion; in fact, it is based on the claim that conditionals such as this can be true! Herein lies the problem:

Figure 5

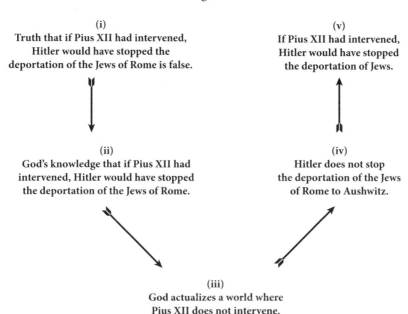

(i)
Truth that if Pius XII had intervened,
Hitler would have stopped the
deportation of the Jews of Rome is false.

(v)
If Pius XII had intervened,
Hitler would have stopped
the deportation of Jews.

(ii)
God's knowledge that if Pius XII had
intervened, Hitler would have stopped
the deportation of the Jews of Rome.

(iv)
Hitler does not stop
the deportation of the Jews
of Rome to Aushwitz.

(iii)
God actualizes a world where
Pius XII does not intervene.

The interesting thing to note about this diagram is that it describes some events which actually occurred. Pius XII did not intervene, and the Jews of Rome were in fact deported, but this does not mean that the counterfactual describing what Hitler would have done had Pius XII intervened is false. In fact, Cornwell believes that it is true, and there is no reason for the Molinist to think him incorrect; there is nothing inherent in the doctrine of middle knowledge that requires the counterfactual to be false due to the events which have actually occurred.[18] Surely this is not the argument Adams presents. Instead, he contends that the free nature of Pius XII's action precludes there being a truth about what he would have done or would do because its being true means that he could not have done otherwise. Put differently, Adams says that counterfactuals are true prior to the action, which renders the course of action certain, but this is contrary to the individual named in the counterfactual having the ability to do otherwise, and therefore, Molinism violates libertarian freedom.

---

18. See John Cornwell, *Hitler's Pope: The Secret History of Pius XII* (New York: Viking, 1999), esp. chapter 7, "The Jews of Rome," 298–318. I am not here suggesting that Cornwell's speculations regarding the actions Hitler would have taken are correct. In fact, I doubt that they are. The point, though, is simply that the Molinist view does not require that the counterfactual stating Hitler would have stopped the deportation if Pius had intervened be false, if Pius XII does not intervene.

While I have attempted to avoid long, protracted arguments with enumerated propositions, I have deemed it necessary to set forth Adams' argument as he originally presented it.[19] This will enable the reader to understand the rather detailed responses by Molinists. Adams' argument proceeds:

(1)   According to Molinism, the truth of all true counterfactuals of freedom about us is explanatorily prior to God's decision to create us.

(2)   God's decision to create us is explanatorily prior to our existence.

(3)   Our existence is explanatorily prior to all of our choices and actions.

(4)   The relation of explanatory priority is transitive.

(5)   Therefore it follows from Molinism (by 1–4) that the truth of all true counterfactuals of freedom about us is explanatorily prior to all of our choices and actions.

(6)   It follows also from Molinism that if I freely do action A in circumstances C, then there is a true counterfactual of freedom F*, which says that if I were in C, then I would (freely) do A.

(7)   Therefore it follows from Molinism that if I freely do A in C, the truth of F* is explanatorily prior to my choosing and acting as I do in C.

(8)   If I freely do A in C, no truth that is strictly inconsistent with my refraining from A in C is explanatorily prior to my choosing and acting as I do in C.

(9)   The truth of F* (which says that if I were in C, then I would do A) is strictly inconsistent with my refraining from A in C.

(10)   If Molinism is true, then if I freely do A in C, F* both is (by 6) and is not (by 7–8) explanatorily prior to my choosing and acting as I do in C.

(11)   Therefore (by 9) if Molinism is true, then I do not freely do A in C.

As should be clear, this critique is similar in nature to Hasker's *counterfactuals as part of the causal history of the world* argument.

Molinist Responses

The most obvious response to Adams' argument here is akin to some offered for the grounding objection. Adams seems to have begged the question of incompatibilism regarding libertarian free will and true counterfactuals of freedom. But this response can seem dismissive, so more should be said. Fortunately, Molinists have offered other answers.

Craig argues that Adams has equivocated in his use of "explanatory priority"; it functions in a different way in (1) from how it functions in (2) and (3). In (2) and (3), explanatory priority seems to refer to the relationship between consequent and condition. Craig illustrates this point by rewording (2) and (3) in order to bring this aspect out:

---

19.   See Adams, "An Anti-Molinist Argument." I have renumbered the propositions here, and in the critiques/responses.

(2a)   If God has not created us, we should not exist;

(3a)   If we were not to exist, we should not make any of our choices and actions.

A moment's reflection will show that this will not work for (1) because

(1a)   According to Molinism, if all true counterfactuals of freedom about us were not true, God would not have decided to create us.

is false. It seems abundantly clear that God may have chosen to create me, even if some counterfactuals about me had been different. This is made especially clear when a counterfactual which has no bearing (so far as I can tell) on the history of the world is considered. The counterfactual, *If John were offered $100,000,000 with no strings attached, he would accept*, is most likely true in the actual world. I do not know it is true, but I do have a high degree of confidence in its truth. At the same time, though, I also feel quite certain that a world where I am offered $100,000,000 with no strings attached is quite distant; I do not foresee any such offers coming my way. If I am correct in this supposition, then it does not seem likely that the counterfactual describing my response to such an offer played a significant role in God's creation decision. What if I really do not know myself as well as I think, and instead, it is true that I would not accept the offer of $100,000,000, even if no strings were attached? What if I am not as worldly as I am inclined to think I am? It does not appear that anything significant follows; this difference would not seem to change anything in God's creative decision, all other things being equal. It follows that, even if the counterfactuals about the creatures God instantiated were different than they in fact are, God still may have chosen to instantiate them. In fact, it seems that there could have been a great many counterfactuals that were different, and God's choice would have remained the same because they would have no impact on the history of the world. Craig believes that the error in Adams' argument is a confusion of reasons and causes. He writes, "Adams's mistake seems to be that he leaps from God's decision in the hierarchy of reasons to God's decision in the hierarchy of causes and by this equivocation tries to make counterfactuals of creaturely freedom explanatorily prior to our free choices."[20]

Flint has also charged Adams with equivocation in his use of *explanatory priority*. The key points in Adams' argument, according to Flint, are (1), (2), (3), (4), and (8). Flint notes that Adams seems to imply that explanatory priority should be understood in terms of causal power.[21]

---

20.   William Lane Craig, "Robert Adams's New Anti-Molinist Argument," *Philosophy and Phenomenological Research* 54, no. 4 (December 1994): 859.

21.   He offers a definition of explanatory priority which captures this element:

(EP/C) x is explanatorily prior to my choices and actions $\equiv$ x is true, and there is no choice or action within my power that would cause it to be the case that x is false.

However, he contends that this understanding of explanatory priority will work for points (1), (2), (3), and (4), but not for (8) because it compromises the doctrine of divine foreknowledge. Thus, a causal analysis of explanatory priority will not work. This is similar to the point made earlier about begging the question.

Next, Flint asks whether explanatory priority can be understood in terms of counterfactual power, and it fares no better.[22] It does not work in (4) because the counterfactual relation is not transitive. If it were, then the upshot of Adams' argument would be that no matter what the individual named in a counterfactual does, the counterfactual will say what it does. This only follows if Adams presupposes that persons do not have counterfactual power over the past. This will be discussed more in the next chapter, but suffice it to say that most Molinists believe that persons have the power to act in such a way that past truths about their free actions would have been different from how they, in fact, were. Thus, Flint concludes that there is no reason for the Molinist to accept the second conjunct of (9).

Flint then considers several other proposals that may serve as definitions of *explanatory priority* for use in Adams' argument, but demonstrates that none are satisfactory.[23] He concludes that it is doubtful any such definition can be given.[24] Thus, he has given the problem back to the detractor of Molinism, but it must also be admitted that no proponents of Molinism

---

I have changed the symbol used to designate this and the other definitions offered by Flint. The definition itself remains unchanged. Flint, *Divine Providence*, 164.

22. Flint's definition of explanatory priority in terms of counterfactual power:

> (EP/CF) x is explanatorily prior to my choices and actions ≡ x is true, and there is no choice or action within my power such that, were I so to choose or so act, x would be false.

Ibid.

23. The proposals are in terms of logical priority, entailment, and contra-causality. They are defined respectively:

> (EP/LP) x is explanatorily prior to my choices and actions ≡ x is true and there is no choice or action z within my power such that my doing z would entail that x is false;
>
> (EP/E) x is explanatorily prior to my choices and actions ≡ x is true and, for any choice or action z within my power, my doing z would entail x;
>
> (EP/CC) x is explanatorily prior to my choices and actions ≡ x is true and I don't have the power to bring it about that x is false.
>
> (EP/LP) fails because it is not transitive, (EP/E) fails because it conflicts with both (1) and (9), and (EP/CC) fails because it is too vague.

See Flint, *Divine Providence*, 169–71.

24. For a more recent attempt to give a definition of *explanatory priority*, see William Hasker, "Explanatory Priority: Transitive and Unequivocal, A Reply to William Craig," *Philosophy and Phenomenological Research* 57, no. 2 (June 1997): 389–93. Hasker proposes the simple definition:

have provided an alternate definition or proven that one *cannot* be given which will work in the argument. In fact, proponents of Molinism must concede that the system employs a conception of priority and that therefore, this problem is one that will continue to be raised by opponents.[25]

(EP/T)   *p* is explanatorily prior to *q* iff *p* must be included in a complete explanation of why *q* obtains.

Hasker correctly points out that (EP/T) is transitive, and uses it to critique Craig's contention noted earlier that explanatory priority functions in a different way in (1) from how it functions in (2) and (3) by an appeal to (1a), (2a), and (3a). Hasker admits that (1a) is false, given (EP/T), but (1) is indeed true because "in deciding to create those persons God did in fact consider all the counterfactuals of freedom that are actually true of them; all of these counterfactuals played a role in the process by which God came to that decision." Ibid., 391.

    Craig has responded, claiming that Hasker's definition is "so generic that we should have to deny its transitivity or so weak that it would not be inimical to human freedom." William Lane Craig, "On Hasker's Defense of Anti-Molinism," *Faith and Philosophy* 15, no. 2 (April 1998): 239. In order to illustrate this, Craig appeals to a rather common event in which each of two persons, Mary and John, attends a party because the other is going. According to Craig, if (EP/T) is transitive, then John attends the party because John attends the party. This statement does not have any meaning and is therefore vacuous. Ibid., 238. Hasker believes that Craig's example is faulty because he doubts that such a decision can be reflexive. Instead, he proposes that, although subtle, the decision of either Mary or John was made in successive stages as the two of them discovered that they both wanted to attend: "Mary's initial signal is followed by John's response, which leads in turn to a response from Mary, and so on. . . . The process may be subtle and complex, but from a causal standpoint it is perfectly straightforward, and there is no violation of asymmetry, as there is in Craig's description." William Hasker, "Anti-Molinism Undefeated!," *Faith and Philosophy* 17, no. 1 (January 2000): 128. It seems to me that Hasker is correct on this score. Flint is also unconvinced by Hasker's definition because he believes that it relies upon the concept of *bring about* which Flint has shown to be problematic. Even if a clear understanding of (EP/T) could be given which is transitive and works for (1), (2) and (3), Flint contends that it would render (8) unacceptable to the Molinist. Flint, *Divine Providence*, 171 n. 12.

25.   It is interesting to note that Adams originally claimed that he was merely employing the concept of priority utilized in formulations of the doctrine of middle knowledge, although he did not attempt to set forth a formal definition of *explanatory priority*. He writes, "The central idea in this argument is that of explanatory priority, or an order of explanation. I think it is roughly the same as the idea that Scholastic philosophers expressed by the term, '*prius ratione*' (prior in reason), but I do not mean to be committed here to any predecessor's version of it. Even if there was no time before God decided to create us, or if God is timeless, God's knowing various things can be explanatorily prior to God's deciding to create us. And it is clear that according to Molinism (as claimed in premise (1)), God's knowledge (and hence the truth) of all the true counterfactuals of freedom about us is prior in the order of explanation to God's deciding to create us, since (by the perfection of God's providence) they were all taken into account in that decision." Adams, "An Anti-Molinist Argument," 347. Flint has attempted to set forth a formal definition of priority as it is used in the Molinist schema:

(EP/M)   *x* is prior to *z* ≡ In either sense (B) [(EP/CP)] or sense (B*) [*x* is prior to my choices and actions ≡ *x* is true, and *necessarily*, there is no choice or action within my power such that, were I so to choose or so to act, *x* would be false.], *x* is prior to God's choices and actions, and *z* is not prior to them.

Flint correctly notes that (EP/M) allows the Molinist to claim that middle knowledge is prior to free knowledge and that natural knowledge is prior to both middle knowledge and free knowledge, claims that are central tenets of Molinism. However, there still seems to be an

CONCLUSION

In this chapter, I have presented a critique of the doctrine of middle knowledge which purports to show that the logical moments in the divine deliberative process required by the Molinist system are incoherent. Two separate, yet closely related versions of the argument were examined, and each was found wanting.

The first version of the argument, offered by both Adams and Kenny, criticizes the possible worlds approach to understanding the truth of counterfactuals. They have argued that the truth of counterfactuals in the actual world is dependent upon which possible-but-not-actual world is closest to the actual world, and which counterfactuals are true in it. However, the closest possible-but-not-actual world to the actual world cannot be determined until the actual world is identified. This fact leads Adams and Kenny to conclude that Molinism is viciously circular. They proclaim that counterfactuals cannot serve the purpose the doctrine of middle knowledge requires of them because counterfactuals are not true soon enough to be of use to God in his decision about which possible world to actualize.

I noted that this version of the *priority objection* relies upon the Molinist acceptance of the Stalnaker-Lewis approach to understanding the truth of counterfactuals. This approach, however, is not inherent in the Molinist system, is not accepted by all Molinists, and has been misconstrued by Adams and Kenny as a causal relationship. The Stalnaker–Lewis approach to the truth of counterfactuals by way of comparative similarity among possible worlds is only meant to be an explanatory tool regarding what it means to say counterfactuals are true much in the same way that truth in all possible worlds is meant to aid in conceiving of the concept of necessary truth. Similarity among worlds does not make or cause counterfactuals to be true.

I also pointed out that this version of the argument assumes that the truth of counterfactuals is grounded in the similarity relation among possible worlds. This answer to the grounding objection, however, was considered and rejected in the previous chapter. Grounding the truth of propositions which hold in the actual world in the occurrence of events in a non-actual world does not seem to be the best solution to the grounding objection. Thus, if a different answer to the grounding objection can be presented, then the vicious circle argument fails.

The second version of the argument has been set forth by Robert Adams and relies heavily upon the concept of *explanatory priority.* According to Adams, since Molinism requires that counterfactuals of

---

irresolvable difficulty: (EP/M) is rather vague, and (B) [(EP/CP)] alone can only make the distinction between prevolitional and postvolitional knowledge; it cannot explain how natural knowledge is prior to middle knowledge. See Flint, *Divine Providence*, 174–76.

creaturely freedom be true (explanatorily) *prior* to the existence of the individuals to whom they refer and, hence, *prior* to the actions they describe, then the freedom of the creatures is removed with respect to the actions described. This loss of freedom is due to the fact that if the counterfactual is true prior to the action, then the individual does not have the power to do otherwise (because if the individual was to do otherwise, the counterfactual would have been false).

It was argued that Adams has made two fatal errors in his critique. First, he has begged the question of the compatibility of truths about future or non-actual actions, and those actions being free. Second, he has equivocated in his use of *explanatory priority*. An interpretation of explanatory priority in terms of causal power presupposes that divine foreknowledge is incompatible with human freedom. An interpretation of explanatory priority in terms of counterfactual power fares no better because it either presupposes that counterfactuals are false (which is what Adams hopes to prove), or it presupposes that the agent named in the counterfactual does not have counterfactual power over the truth of the counterfactual (which is also what Adams hopes to prove). Either way, the argument is suspect because it ends up begging the question. The problem has been handed back to the detractor of Molinism—a satisfactory definition of *explanatory priority* must be given if the argument is to succeed. Since no such definition has been offered, the second version of the *priority* objection fails as well.

CHAPTER 4

DIVINE FOREKNOWLEDGE AND CREATURELY FREE WILL

INTRODUCTION

One of the most cherished doctrines of Christianity is that of divine *omniscience*, and although there has been some debate, the common sense understanding has been that God knows all true propositions, including propositions describing the future.[1] Thus, theologians have maintained that God possesses foreknowledge. However, this belief is not without its problems, for some philosophers have claimed it is incompatible with creaturely freedom. If God knows ahead of time that a person will perform a certain action, then it appears that he must perform that action and thus, does not do so freely. This becomes an acute problem when applied to sinful actions and moral responsibility.

Augustine raises the compatibility issue in his treatise on free will, and casts it in terms of a discussion between himself and a student, Evodius,

---

1. Some theologians have objected to the idea that God's knowledge is propositional in form. William Alston, for example, argues that the Thomistic model of divine knowledge as immediate awareness can be supported by a comparison of human and divine ways of knowing. An appeal to the limitations of human knowledge rather than Thomas' own approach of appealing to the doctrine of divine simplicity, can clarify his point. According to Alston, the propositional character of human knowledge may stem from creaturely limitations. He offers two reasons for this assertion: "First, we cannot grasp any concrete whole in its full concreteness; at most we cognize certain abstract features thereof, which we proceed to formulate in distinct propositions. Second, we need to isolate separate propositions in order to relate them logically, so as to be able to extend our knowledge inferentially." William P. Alston, "Does God Have Beliefs?" *Religious Studies* 22 (1986): 291. Alston goes on to note that, of course, God *can* grasp concrete wholes and necessarily has complete knowledge, so the parcelling of discrete units of thought is not required for him to know or understand something (or everything). This argument, however, should not count against the assertion that God knows true propositions—it is one thing to say that one's cognitive processes operate in such a way that ideas/concepts/facts must be broken down into discrete units (e.g., propositions), and it is another thing to say that one has knowledge of units of this sort. In fact, it seems that a being which has knowledge of complete wholes would necessarily have knowledge of the constituent parts as well.

who asks how it can be the case that God's knowledge (which is perfect) of future sins does not render them necessary and thereby remove human responsibility.[2] Augustine's answer is twofold. First, he argues that God knows the individual's free will *as a free will*. Put differently, the freedom of the action is built into what God knows, and the individual must retain power over his actions if we are to make sense of his having a free will to be known (by God). He writes:

> Thus, we believe both that God has foreknowledge of everything in the future and that nonetheless we will whatever we will. Since God foreknows our will, the very will that he foreknows will be what comes about. There-fore, it will be a will, since it is a will that he foreknows. And it could not be a will unless it were in our power. Therefore, he also foreknows this power. It follows, then, that his foreknowledge does not take away my power; in fact, it is all the more certain that I will have that power, since he whose foreknowledge never errs foreknows that I will have it.[3]

Second, Augustine correctly points out that there is not a causal rela-tionship between God's knowledge and the future event; rather, there is only an explanatory relationship.[4] In other words, God's foreknowledge

---

2. Augustine writes, "Surely this is the problem that is disturbing and puzzling you. How is it that these two propositions are not contradictory and inconsistent: (1) God has foreknowledge of everything in the future; and (2) We sin by the will, not by necessity? For, you say, if God foreknows that someone is going to sin, then it is necessary that he sin. But if it is necessary, the will has no choice about whether to sin; there is an inescapable and fixed necessity. And so you fear that this argument forces us into one of two propositions: either we draw the heretical conclusion that God does not foreknow everything in the future; or, if we cannot accept this conclusion, we must admit that sin happens by necessity and not by will." Augustine, *On Free Choice of the Will*, trans. Thomas Williams (Indianapolis: Hackett, 1993), 3:3, 74.

3. Ibid., 77. Wierenga offers an interesting counter-argument. Consider the claim that:

    (1*) It is not possible that anyone see someone who is invisible.

    A response which is analogous to Augustine's answer here can be constructed. If

    (2*) I see the invisible man;

    is true, then the man I see must be just as I see him, and therefore

    (3*) The invisible man is invisible.

    Wierenga correctly notes that pointing out that (2*) entails (3*) does not demonstrate either that (2*) and (3*) are consistent, or that (1*) is false. In fact, Wierenga argues, even if (2*) entails (3*), it also entails

    (4*) The invisible man is visible;

    which means that (2*) is impossible. Wierenga, *The Nature of God*, 62.

4. This approach was the most common answer to the dilemma of divine foreknowledge and human freedom in the early church. For example, Origen developed an argument along these lines to counter the fatalistic philosophy of the pagan philosopher, Celsus. Origen argued

does not cause the person to sin. The individual sins by his own evil will, choice, desire, and decision, and therefore, he retains responsibility. Augustine explains:

> Unless I am mistaken, you do not force someone to sin just because you foreknow that he is going to sin. Nor does your foreknowledge force him to sin, even if he is undoubtedly going to sin—since otherwise you would not have genuine fore-knowledge. So if your foreknowledge is consistent with his freedom in sinning, so that you foreknow what someone else is going to do by his own will, then God forces no one to sin, even though he foresees those who are going to sin by their own will.[5]

Despite its longevity and popular appeal, this approach has not proven convincing to many contemporary scholars, at least not for answering the problem. For example, in a much-discussed article on the nature of divine omniscience, Nelson Pike claims that it is incoherent. He begins by restating the original problem of the simultaneous existence of divine foreknowledge and creaturely freedom. For clarity, he proposes the example of a man, Jones, who mowed his lawn last Saturday afternoon. Pike argues that if God possesses foreknowledge, then eighty years prior to last Saturday afternoon, God knew that Jones would mow his lawn on Saturday, and if this is the case, then last Saturday afternoon, Jones was not able—it was not *within his power*—to refrain from mowing his lawn, for if last Saturday Jones could really have refrained from mowing his lawn, then Jones had the ability to perform some action, such that, if he were to perform it, God would have held a false belief eighty years earlier, which is impossible if God is omniscient. If Jones cannot refrain from mowing, then his action is not free.[6] Therefore, creaturely freedom and divine foreknowledge are incompatible and one or the other must go.

---

that God foreknows an event because the event will happen, and not vice versa. He wrote, "Celsus thinks that if something has been predicted by some sort of foreknowledge, then it takes place because it was predicted. But we do not grant this. We say that the man who made the prediction was not the cause of the future event, because he foretold that it would happen; but we hold that the future event, which would have taken place even if it had not been prophesied, constitutes the cause of the prediction by the one with foreknowledge." Origen, *Contra Celsum*, trans. Henry Chadwick (1953; repr. Cambridge: Cambridge University Press, 1980), 2:20, 85.

5. Augustine, *On Free Choice of the Will*, trans. Williams, 3:4, 78.
6. Pike summarizes his argument: "If God existed at T, and if God believed at T_1 that Jones would do X at T_2, then if it was within Jones's power at T_2 to refrain from doing X, then (1) it was within Jones's power at T_2 to do something that would have brought it about that God held a false belief at T_1, or (2) it was within Jones's power at T_2 to do something which would have brought it about that God did not hold the belief He held at T_1, or (3) it was within Jones's power at T_2 to do something that would have brought it about that any person who believed at T_1 that Jones would do X at T_2 (one of whom was, by hypothesis, God) held a false belief and thus was not God—that is, that God (who by hypothesis existed at T_1) did not exist at

We have already seen that some groups avoid the problem by denying one of the premises in the argument. Open Theists claim that God does not have comprehensive foreknowledge of the future just because they believe there can be no truths about future free actions. Determinists reject libertarian freedom and instead embrace compatibilist freedom, and in so doing, accept divine foreknowledge and determination, but deny persons the ability to do otherwise. Despite the growing popularity of these answers, many still wish to maintain belief in divine foreknowledge and libertarian human freedom, and argue that the dilemma is only apparent. The two most popular approaches to reconciling these beliefs have been to appeal to divine eternity as timelessness and claim that God's beliefs are outside of time, or to follow Ockham and claim that the necessity of the past does not hold for God's past beliefs. Each will be examined in turn, followed by a discussion of how middle knowledge adds to the discussion.

DIVINE TIMELESSNESS

The doctrine of divine eternity has been held by the church since its inception and actually predates Christianity. It is typically conceived in one of two ways: 1) timelessness, or 2) everlastingness, with the former being the majority position.[7] Some theologians have appealed to divine timelessness as an answer to the incompatibility argument because, if true, then God does not have past beliefs. Since he exists outside of time, his knowledge is not located temporally (yesterday, tomorrow, now, etc.); rather, he knows truths eternally. The upshot of this claim is that God's beliefs about how a free creature will act do not *precede* the creature's actions. Instead, both the divine belief and the creaturely action occur simultaneously in God's frame of reference—or in eternity—and the force of the argument against the compatibility of foreknowledge and freedom fades. Not only is there no causal relation between God's knowledge and the creature's action, but there is not even a before/after relationship between them. This means that God does not really possess *fore*knowledge, and his knowledge of events is not *prior* to their occurrence. So the objection, which relies upon the necessity of the past (beliefs of God), loses its strength. While this solution to the problem is ingenious, it is also based on some rather counterintuitive notions that require further exploration.

T₁," Nelson Pike, "Divine Omniscience and Voluntary Action," *Philosophical Review* 74, no. 1 (January 1965): 34.

7.   Those who hold to the thesis that God's life is eternal in the sense that it transcends the boundaries of time shall be referred to as atemporalists, whereas those who believe God's life is somehow located in time shall be referred to as temporalists.

Traditional Models

While it is often thought that Augustine was the first Christian theologian to make this argument, as already noted, this is not the approach he took.[8] The first theologian to use eternity as a solution to the foreknowledge dilemma was the sixth-century Christian philosopher Boethius. He begins his discussion by maintaining that God's knowledge of the future is certain (to deny it would be impious), and that humans are free because of their capacity for reason, but also admits the difficulty in affirming both.[9] He considers the Augustinian appeal to the lack of causal relationship between the two, but notes that it still seems that a past knowledge of a future event renders that event certain. Boethius sees the key to reconciling foreknowledge and free will as a proper understanding of divine eternity because God's knowledge is a consequence of his eternity.[10] Boethius defines eternity as "a perfect possession all together of an endless life,"

---

8.   Divine timelessness is not an invention of Christian theology. Plato hinted at it, see Plato, *Timaeus*, trans. Francis M. Cornford, ed. Oskar Piest (Indianapolis: Bobbs-Merrill, 1959), 37D–38C, and Plotinus set forth an entire exposition of it. See Plotinus, *The Enneads*, trans. Stephen MacKenna, abr. John Dillon (London: Penguin, 1991), iii.7. Augustine is normally credited with being the first Christian theologian to explicitly argue for the doctrine of divine timelessness, but he did so in order to defend the doctrine of *creatio ex nihilo* (creation out of nothing) and did not apply it to the question of the compatibility of divine foreknowledge and human free will. Augustine's critics charged him with compromising both the immutability and the rationality of God in his assertion of creation out of nothing. First, the immutability of God is called into question because God had to *choose* to create at some point if he created *ex nihilo*. The choice to create is seen as constituting a change in God. The pagan critics believed that God was always engaged in the same act (creation), and thus saved his constancy. Yet for creation to be an everlasting act, matter must also be everlasting (which *ex nihilo* explicitly denies). Hence, creation *ex nihilo* compromises God's immutability because he must begin to do something new. Second, the rationality of God is called into question because God had to choose to create *at some point* if creation is not an everlasting act. Augustine's detractors noted that there seems to be no criteria by which God could decide *when* to create. Dyson notes, "creation *ex nihilo* seems to imply that before he made the world, God had existed for all eternity alone in an empty time, every moment of which was indiscernible from every other." R. W. Dyson, "St. Augustine's Remarks on Time," *The Downside Review* 100 (July 1982): 222. All of the time prior to creation should be exactly alike. Therefore, no time would appear to be preferable for creation as opposed to any other. Thus a rational being would never choose to create.

     Augustine's answer to both of these charges is that God is timeless. The immutability of God is thus preserved against the charges because there was not *a time* in which he chose to create. The choice of God to create is eternal. The rationality of God is preserved because the act of creation was not in time. Rather, time was created concurrently with the universe. There was no sooner or later before God created and, hence, it is an illegitimate question to ask why God created *when* he did. See Augustine, *Confessions* 11.10ff.

9.   Interestingly, Peter van Inwagen has made a similar argument for human libertarian freedom. See Peter van Inwagen, *An Essay on Free Will* (Oxford: Clarendon, 1983), 154–58.

10. Anicius Manlius Severinus Boethius, *The Consolation of Philosophy*, trans. William Anderson (Carbondale, IL: Southern Illinois University Press, 1963). He writes, "Wherefore they which have reason, have freedome to will and nill" (5.2, 107). And again, "But how is it possible, those things should not happen, which are foreseene to be to come?" (5.4, 111).

and claims that it is more glorious than temporal existence, which must "proceedeth from times past, to times to come" and which cannot embrace the total life at once.[11] He argues that God knows future events because he is outside of time and sees all time as an eternal present, or as one simultaneous event. This, according to Boethius, is superior to endless temporal existence for several reasons.[12]

Boethius grounds the eternity of God in divine simplicity (or indivisibility) and infinity. God cannot be in time because all things in time are divisible, whereas God *is* his own essence, singular, without change, without difference, without movement, and without parts. Similarly, all things in time are moving, but God is the Unmoved.[13] Boethius seems to view eternity as a static moment, something to be comprehended in its entirety. By way of analogy, he compares God's view of all of history to human sight, noting that "the present instant of men may well bee compared to that of God in this; that as you see some things in your temporall instant, so he beholdeth all things in his eternall presence."[14] Thus, Boethius seems to propose that a single, static *moment* of eternity encompasses the endless, infinite life of God. This idea is not without its problems, but other theologians expanded upon it.[15]

Thomas Aquinas seeks to defend and develop the conception of eternity set forth by Boethius as the whole life of God. He notes that the use of the word *whole* does not imply that God's life is finite or divisible, but refers to the completeness of that life. Aquinas readily admits that although

---

11. Ibid., 5.6, 116.
12. An endless existence has an innumerable amount of moments, whereas an eternal existence has the full extent of his life. Endless existence encompasses a finite past and a present, but looks forward to the infinite future. Eternal existence encompasses all at once, "to which neither any part to come is absent, nor of that which is past, hath escaped." Ibid. Thus, Boethius points out that the difference between eternal and everlasting is to be found in the relation of the individual (in God's case), or object, to its life. Both affirm an endless life, but eternity refers to the embracing of the whole of existence *at once; in a singular moment.* He writes, "for it is one thing, to bee carried through an endlesse life, which Plato attributed to the world, another thing to embrace the whole presence of an endlesse life together, which is manifestly proper to the Divine mind." Ibid.
13. Ibid.
14. Ibid., 5.6, 117.
15. Robinson notes that this seems to be a contradiction. It is not readily apparent that a single moment can encompass an extended, complex life. However, two options are available. First, the extension implied by an infinite life may not be actual; it is metaphorical or merely apparent. In this interpretation, eternity is metaphysically a singular point. Second, the extension is actual, and thus, the singular moment of eternity is metaphysically extended. Robinson notes that Boethius is unclear as to what he intended here. The first option retains the problem already noted, while the second option seems to simply shift the problem from how a moment can encompass an extended life to how a moment can be extended. Thus, while Boethius has introduced the timelessness answer, he has failed to adequately explain it. Michael Robinson, *Eternity and Freedom: A Critical Analysis of Divine Timelessness as a Solution to the Foreknowledge/Free Will Debate* (New York: University Press of America, 1993), 35–36.

eternity is simultaneously whole, it is sometimes referred to in terms that imply time and succession/division. This is due to the limitations of language. Eternity does not entail succession because there is no before/after or movement in eternity.[16] Aquinas also distinguishes between time and eternity, noting that one difference is that time has a beginning and an end, while eternity does not. This difference is accidental. The fundamental, or absolute difference is found in the fact that eternity is simultaneously whole, whereas time is not; eternity is the measure of permanence, whereas time is the measure of movement and change.[17]

Thus, Aquinas maintains, God has knowledge of all things, including contingent future actualities, because he sees all events as present to him in eternity. He likens God's perspective of creatures and events in time to an individual's observation of several creatures and events on a road from a hilltop. He writes:

> Things reduced to act in time are known by us successively in time. Hence to us they cannot be certain, since as we know future contingent things as such but, they are certain to God alone, whose understanding is in eternity above time; just as he who goes along the road does not see those who come after him, although he who sees the whole road from a height sees at once all travelling by the way. Hence what is known by us must be necessary, even as it is in itself; for what is future contingent in itself cannot be known by us. But what is known by God must be necessary according to the mode in which they are subject to the divine knowledge, as already stated (ANS. I), but not absolutely as considered in their own causes.[18]

Criticisms of the traditional view
Delmas Lewis argues that eternity as timelessness necessitates a tenseless view of time.[19] Since God is essentially omniscient, his view of things must be correct, but if he is timeless and sees things as such, then timelessness

---

16. He defines eternity as, "the apprehension of the uniformity of what is altogether outside of movement." Aquinas, *Summa Theologica* 1.10.1, 41.
17. Ibid., 1.10.4.
18. Ibid., 1.14.13, 88.
19. It should be noted that philosophical discussion of time has led to the delineation of two views of time: 1) A-theory of time, or the tensed view, and 2) B-theory of time, or the tenseless view. The tensed view of time divides it into categories of past, present, and future, whereas the tenseless view simply divides time into before and after relationships. The tensed view of time is often rejected for two key reasons. First, it has been argued that only the past exists. The present only exists as it is past, and the future only exists in the mind as anticipation. Thus, the categories of past, present, and future are seen as dubious. Second, the before and after relationship found in the tenseless view seems to fit better with the relativity of time because the categories of past, present, and future seem to denote absolute simultaneity. Cf. L. Nathan Oaklander, "A Defense of the New Tenseless Theory of Time," *The Philosophical Quarterly* 41, no. 162 (January 1991): 26–38, and L. Nathan Oaklander, "The New Tenseless Theory of Time: A Reply to Smith," *Philosophical Studies* 58, no. 3 (March 1990): 287–92. However, some have

must be the correct view of reality. It follows that time is tenseless with no past, present, or future to speak of, and events can only sit in before and after relationships to one another. The problem is that Boethius, Anselm, and Aquinas all seem to appeal to the tensed view of time to argue *a priori* for a timeless God. This, Lewis points out, is a contradiction.[20] Worse still, he argues that tenseless time destroys human moral responsibility because it does not allow for judgment and forgiveness. He notes that "the only things to which responsibility could be assigned on a tenseless account of persons do not appear to be the sort of things to which responsibility is assignable."[21] Hence, Lewis concludes that the timeless view of God conflicts with Christian views of human responsibility.

Several other criticisms of the timeless model of God have been raised. Davis and Pike have both argued that the work of creation cannot be the work of a being outside of time.[22] The creation of something temporal means that the creation begins to exist at some specific time, *t*. Thus, the creator must perform the act of creating at *t*, which suggests he exists at *t*, and is therefore temporal. Atemporalists have replied that God eternally willed the creation.[23] While it seems that God's willing the creation into existence should be temporally located *at the point of its actualization,* and while the creative act seems to include not only an act of the will of God, but also divine speech and interaction, these considerations are not conclusive. After all, God could eternally will the creation and time into existence and from that point, utilize speech as his mode of creative action. In that case, creating would not *require* time, but might include it at points after time began.

---

argued for the tensed view of time instead; cf. Quentin Smith, "Problems with the New Tenseless Theory of Time," *Philosophical Studies* 52 (November 1987): 371–92.

20. Delmas Lewis, "Eternity, Time and Tenselessness," *Faith and Philosophy* 5, no. 1 (January 1988): 82–83.

21. Ibid., 83.

22. Stephen T. Davis, *Logic and the Nature of God* (Grand Rapids: Eerdmans, 1983). Davis argues that the act of creation seems to require action in time. Even with the eternal willing of the creative act (Aquinas' answer), it would still appear that the act itself must be temporal: "we have on hand no acceptable concept of atemporal causation, i.e. of what it is for a timeless cause to produce a temporal effect" (13). Nelson Pike, *God and Timelessness* (New York: Schocken, 1970): 110.

23. R. L. Sturch, "The Problem of Divine Eternity," *Religious Studies* 10 (December 1974): 489. Sturch notes, "the believer in timeless eternity will presumably hold that the statement means (*a*) that God wishes a universe with a temporal beginning to exist and (*b*) that when God wishes something, that something happens." Ibid. Sturch draws an analogy between God's timeless causation of a temporal creation and the production of a story by an author. The events in the story are temporally located, but the author of the story is not in temporal relationship to the characters in the story. However, such an analogy is limited in its application because of the lack of reciprocity in such a relationship, whereas the creation has a reciprocal relationship with God.

Davis and Pike have also both argued that "a timeless being cannot be the personal, caring, involved God we read about in the Bible."[24] Davis points to the responses of God to people (which implies temporality), and to the work of God which seems to be sequential. He argues that it is difficult to see how a timeless being "can plan or anticipate or remember or respond or punish or warn or forgive. All such acts seem undeniably temporal."[25] Jule Gowen has responded by arguing that God's acts do not necessitate time, because God set up the world in such a way as to not require such temporal interaction.[26] Sturch argues similarly, claiming that the conditional nature of God's decrees allows him to respond temporally even while he exists timelessly. However, Hasker identifies two problems with this idea: 1) If God were timeless, he still could not act after creating; conditionality of decrees is irrelevant, and 2) A timeless existence would afford God knowledge of creaturely actions so that he would not need to make decrees conditional.[27]

Senor has argued that the timeless view of God is incompatible with the incarnation for two reasons: 1) Jesus, who was God incarnate, existed in time and so timelessness cannot be an essential attribute/property of deity, and 2) the incarnation constituted a change in God, which requires time.[28] Both of these points are specific to the second person of the trinity, but Senor argues that since God is a unity, they transfer to God as

---

24. Davis, *Logic and the Nature of God*, 14. If God exists in a static timeless present, then his initial actions are simultaneous with his reactions. This suggests that his reactions are not really a response, and it forces us to seriously reconsider our notions of action itself.

25. Ibid.

26. Jule Gowen, "God and Timelessness: Everlasting or Eternal?" *Sophia* 26 (March 1987): 22. She writes, "God simply sets up the world from all eternity in such a way that certain events will occur at particular times. The conditions sufficient for these events to occur, where those conditions do not include some further act on God's part, are built into the world, so to speak." Ibid.

27. Hasker, *God, Time and Knowledge*, 157.

28. Thomas D. Senor, "Incarnation and Timelessness," *Faith and Philosophy* 7, no. 2 (April 1990): 149–64. Senor argues that since Jesus was a historical figure, then events in his life stand in temporal relation to each other. Thus, Jesus is temporal. The traditional answer (as set forth by Stump and Kretzmann) to this objection is that Christ is temporal is respect to his human nature, and is timeless in respect to his divine nature. Senor responds that this answer smacks of Nestorianism: "So even if it is in virtue of His being human that temporal predicates apply to Him, and it is only in virtue of His being divine that Christ is identical to God the Son, it still follows that Christ is the Son to Whom temporal predicates apply. . . . [I]t would seem that those who use such a maneuver in an attempt to avoid problems with the doctrine of the Incarnation overemphasize the dual nature of Christ and fail to pay enough attention to the unity of His being." Ibid., 154. A related objection to Senor's argument is that an analogous relationship exists with respect to God's relation to space; since Jesus existed in space, God must not be spaceless. Senor anticipated this move, and argues that any being which is ever temporal must always remain temporal. However, a being can be spaceless, become spatially located, and then go back to being spaceless.

a whole.[29] Gunton correctly responds that this is reading too much into the incarnation; it simply proclaims the sanctification of temporality by the eternal.[30]

It has already been argued that the timeless model does not provide an adequate answer to the question of how the temporal can have meaningful interaction with the eternal (if atemporal), but an even greater problem with the timeless model persists. Some believe the timeless model of God suggests that time is not real. Since God's perspective is the correct one, and he sees the future simultaneously with the past, then the traditional temporal distinctions between past, present, and future, as well as the concept of duration, are illusory. Related to this criticism is the charge that the timeless model requires some sort of *backward causation* if simultaneity between the occurrence of an event in eternity with its occurrence in time exists. Simultaneity requires that an event in eternity can be spoken of as occurring *now*. If it can, then God can be conceived of knowing the future *now* in some sense, regardless of what atemporalists claim. The Boethian answer is no help since, if God *sees* an event happening in eternity that is still future in time, then the future has already occurred. Some contemporary philosophers have attempted to refine the concept of timelessness in an effort to alleviate these concerns.

Contemporary Models
Stump and Kretzmann
Eleonore Stump and Norman Kretzmann have sought to explain God's eternity by appeal to the timeless present as *extended*, or possessing *duration*.[31] They argue that this is what Boethius and others meant in their expositions of divine timelessness, and that the interpretation of eternity as an isolated static instant "is a radical distortion of the classic concept."[32] They maintain the traditional view that God's absolute perfection requires that he be an "indivisibly persistent present actuality," and timeless, since temporality implies imperfection.[33]

---

29. Senor admits that not all properties held by one member of the trinity must apply to all, but maintains that temporality is one of them. Still, he offers no definitive argument to this end. Ibid., 161.
30. Colin Gunton, "Time, Eternity and the Doctrine of the Incarnation," *Dialog* 21 (Fall 1982): 263–68. Gunton is right to question Senor's claim, but his answer is not as clear as it could be. The problem with Senor is that language about the Son can be applied to God, but all attributes of the Son are not applied to the Godhead, since he is one person of the Trinity.
31. Eleonore Stump and Norman Kretzmann, "Eternity," *The Journal of Philosophy* 78 (1981): 429–58; repr. Thomas V. Morris, ed., *The Concept of God* (Oxford: Oxford University Press, 1987), 219–52. Citations will come from the reprinted edition.
32. Ibid., 220.
33. Eleonore Stump and Norman Kretzmann, "Eternity, Awareness, and Action," *Faith and Philosophy* 9, no. 4 (October 1992): 463. If one is in time, then his relation to the world is evolving and changing/developing, which suggests imperfection. The idea undergirding the second point is that a perfect life must be possessed perfectly and completely, which is impossible if temporal.

It is the assertion of duration in eternity that makes Stump and Kretzmann's work unique, as timelessness has been traditionally interpreted as denying duration and affirming a static existence. They acknowledge the need for duration in God's existence because he is a living being, noting, "it would be reasonable to think that any mode of existence that could be called a life must involve duration."[34] However, in this admission, they obviously do not mean that timeless duration is the same as temporal duration, and even claim that temporal duration is illusory. They argue that the experience of temporal duration creates the false impression of permanence in the mind of the individual in time. In actuality, past and future do not exist, and the present is a durationless instant (that is, past and future only exist in the mind of the individual, while he exists only in an on-going present that is constantly passing away and in flux). Hence, physical (and temporal) existence is only apparently durational because duration requires beginning and end, and neither exists in the fleeting present. So, they argue, *genuine duration* is fully realized. This is not everlasting duration, but "existence *none* of which is already gone and *none* of which is yet to come—and such fully realized duration must be atemporal duration."[35] Obviously, this understanding of duration challenges everything we think we know of the concept and is therefore open to criticism.

Stump and Kretzmann address two possible objections to their concept of atemporal duration. First, some may argue that a life requires processes which require time. They respond by appeal to Aquinas' view of God as mind; the divine mind can *know*, *will*, and *be* atemporally.[36] Second, some may complain that this technical use of "duration" goes beyond the normal usage of the term. They do not deny this, but rather note that many academic disciplines use words in technical senses that stretch normal usage (e.g., science refers to black *holes*, which are not really holes). If technical language is appropriate for scientific description, surely it is appropriate for theological description. One analogy they utilize references the vast difference between the being of humans and the being of God, and the kind of life humans live and the kind of life God possesses. Human attempts to comprehend the divine life will ultimately fall short because we have no idea of what it would be like to live in anything other than a three-dimensional reality.[37] A second analogy seeks to illustrate the

---

34. Stump and Kretzmann, "Eternity," 223.
35. Ibid., 237.
36. Ibid., 238–39.
37. Stump and Kretzmann, "Eternity, Awareness, and Action," 465. Stump and Kretzmann admit that the technical use of words like *duration* or *present* applied to God can be perplexing. They argue that most criticisms of the timeless model simply do not grasp the vast difference between the mode of human existence and that of divine, and liken human attempts to understand eternal things to "attempts to think themselves up the ladder of being, so to speak: in some respects the theological equivalent of trying to write a story about a person whose mode of existence involves a space with more dimensions than our own" Ibid., 470.

relationship between time and eternity. Stump and Kretzmann posit two parallel lines, one representing temporal time and the other eternity. If the present is represented by light, then on the temporal line, the light will appear as a moving point, going from left (past) to right (future), while the eternal will be a line of light. These analogies do not answer all objections, but they help illustrate the difference between time and eternity. However, the problem of the relationship between events occurring in time and those same events in eternity—the problem of simultaneity—still persists.

For real interaction between the eternal and the temporal, it seems that there must be some kind of simultaneity.[38] Of course, it cannot mean *at the same time* (since there is no time in eternity), but this is not as odd as may first appear. As Stump and Kretzmann correctly point out, even within temporal relationships, simultaneity has to be qualified because of relativity theory; we can only speak of events occurring at the same time within a particular frame of reference. Drawing upon these ideas, they propose the concept of ET-simultaneity:

(ET) For every x and y (where x and y range over entities and events), x and y are ET-simultaneous iff

(i) either x is eternal and y is temporal, or vice versa; and

(ii) for some observer, A, in the unique eternal reference frame, x and y are both present—i.e., either x is eternally present and y is observed as temporally present, or vice versa; and

---

Since, theoretically, it is easier to think *down the ladder*, Stump and Kretzmann appeal to an idea of a lower mode of existence (which they borrowed from Edwin A. Abbott, *Flatland* [1884; repr. New York: New American Library, 1984], chapters 13 and 14) in order to help illustrate the difference between the human and divine modes of existence, and the difficulties of communication across these modes. A one-dimensional world is proposed in which inch-long creatures all exist on a line. The temporal categories of this world are based on the location of the individual on the line. It is also proposed that a human can exist outside the line, and see its totality (beginning to end) all at once. It is presupposed that the human can speak to the inhabitants of this world and they can respond as well. Yet when they try to communicate, the meanings of worlds like *before* and *in front of* are very different. The human thinks she is *in front of* the creatures, but to them, *in front of* refers to the individual who immediately precedes them on the line. To the human, it refers to spatial location, but to the inhabitants of the proposed world, it refers to temporal location. The communication breaks down because there is a different meaning to the temporal terms and the inhabitants of that world have no conception of three-dimensional space. Thus, the three-dimensional concept that the human spoke of appears to be incoherent to those inhabitants. However, it should be noted that although the terms are used to mean different things, they are still being used analogously. Stump and Kretzmann, "Eternity, Awareness, and Action," 471–73.

38.   Stump and Kretzmann, "Eternity," 225.

(iii) for some observer, B, in one of the infinitely many temporal reference frames, x and y are both present—i.e., either x is observed as eternally present and y is temporally present, or vice versa.[39]

While this definition is rather technical, the basic point is straightforward. ET-simultaneity depends on the frame of reference, and events can appear to persons in both the eternal and the temporal frames of reference. Eternity is God's frame of reference while temporality is that of creatures. In the eternal frame of reference, every temporal present is ET-simultaneous, while in the temporal frame of reference, the eternal is simultaneous in one moment. Thus, the life of God is ET-simultaneous with every temporal moment.[40]

Stump and Kretzmann note that some may argue that God could not know temporal realities unless he were temporal. They respond by drawing upon the close connection between space and time on the one hand, and omnipresence and eternality on the other hand. Just as God does not have to be spatially located to know (or interact with) spatial realities, he also does not have to be temporally located to know (or interact with) temporal realities. Such a view of simultaneity between the eternal life of God and temporal reality allows God to interact with the creation while outside of time.

Criticisms of Stump and Kretzmann
A number of criticisms have been raised against Stump and Kretzmann's proposal. The most common is to charge the concept of *timeless duration* with incoherence. As Katherine Rogers points out, this is not mere unimaginability or paradox: "What the charge of incoherence means here is that the very best attempts to explain the *prima faci* paradoxical notion of a timeless extension only succeed in making the concept more opaque, or, at worst, are simply contradiction."[41] She examines the depiction of time and eternity as two parallel lines, and notes that although eternity is seen as a *line* where everything is present, it still has the properties of a point with all the limitations of that concept. In addition, Stump and Kretzmann's proposal has problems of its own: "This seems to run exactly counter to the aim of the circle analogy which was intended to show that an eternal god is wholly and equally present in every possible respect, to each moment of time. The parallel lines analogy inevitably suggests a God who is 'stretched out' some here, some there, some closer, some farther and so is, at least conceptually, divisible, and hence limited and imperfect."[42] To be fair, any diagram meant to depict the life or being of God is subject

---

39. Stump and Kretzmann, "Eternity, Awareness, and Action," 474.
40. Ibid., 475.
41. Katherin A. Rogers, "Eternity Has No Duration," *Religious Studies* 30 (March 1994): 8.
42. Ibid., 9.

to this criticism. Nevertheless, Rogers' more basic point is that the idea of duration necessarily implies divisibility and thus imperfection and finitude. Herbert Nelson points out that the notions of atemporality and duration in Stump and Kretzmann conflict: Atemporality suggests that all events occur at once with no past or future, but duration suggests relationships of *before* and *after*, which naturally imply past, present, and future.[43] He concludes that the very concept is unhelpful and incoherent.[44]

Both Nelson and Rogers conclude that the simple view of timelessness is preferable, arguing that it does not imply a static view of God. Rogers states, "It makes no sense to say that divine timelessness is extended. At this point the safest move might be to settle for the purely negative conclusion that eternity has no duration and say no more."[45] There is some wisdom in this move. It is hard to see why duration is necessary for dynamic personality, especially if the person under consideration is infinite in being and perfection.

Stump and Kretzmann respond that the problem with these accusations is they assume extension and duration require temporality; they have begged the question of the impossibility of atemporal duration. They admit that if duration is understood as movement through time, then the concept *is* incoherent, but defend their use of analogous language for divine existence as sufficient to answer the objection. They are certainly correct that specialized language is acceptable in theology, but stretching terms to the point of abnormal usage is not.[46] The way Stump and Kretzmann use *extension* seems beyond the realm of analogy. For example, it seems that the only conception of duration possible in the English language is that of temporality, and to speak of no change in time *just is* to speak of a moment, not a duration. For an analogy to work, words must have meaning and there must be some sort of similarity in use, but here there is not. Thus, the charge of incoherence stands.

---

43. See J. M. E. McTaggart, *The Nature of Existence*, Vol. 2 (1927; repr. Cambridge: Cambridge University Press, 1968), 13.

44. He writes, "On the one hand, as *enduring* and therefore (by their account) *really* and indeed infinitely extended, the atemporally enduring entity must have stages which *really* lie outside one another in some sense, and thus *not* be all at once (*totá simul*). On the other hand, as *atemporal* and therefore (by their account) *really* existing all at once (*tota simul*), no real constituent can be absent when any other is present." Herbert J. Nelson, "Time(s), eternity, and duration," *International Journal for the Philosophy of Religion* 22, no. 1–2 (1987): 16. Paul Fitzgerald has leveled a similar criticism of atemporal duration, but uses extension as the sticking point. He has pointed out that eternity seems to have both succession and the absence of succession. He argues that all extension requires succession, and succession requires time. Therefore, there cannot be a timeless extension. Paul Fitzgerald, "Stump and Kretzmann on Time and Eternity," *The Journal of Philosophy* 82 (1985): 260–69.

45. Rogers, "Eternity Has No Duration," 14.

46. In fact, too much emphasis upon God's transcendence can lead to abject skepticism regarding our knowledge of him—something Christian theologians and philosophers should seek to avoid.

In addition to these criticisms, the idea of ET-simultaneity itself has also come under attack. Davis argues that Stump and Kretzmann have not really proven anything and have just stated that there can be simultaneity between temporal and eternal events.[47] He also calls into question the coherence of cause/effect relationships in the model because it is difficult to see how a cause can be *simultaneous* with its effect. Thus, he concludes that the idea of ET-simultaneity has added nothing to the discussion but confusion.

Brian Leftow argues that ET-simultaneity ultimately denies causal relations between events in eternity and events in time because it views eternity as simply a frame of reference. This means that events in eternity and time are incommensurable and the hypothesis is unable to explain the relationship between the two.[48] He further complains that it requires four views of simultaneity, several of which are unnecessary, and that it ultimately fails to answer the dilemma of foreknowledge and free will because it makes God's timeless knowledge simultaneous with temporal events. This, he asserts, is no different than viewing divine knowledge as temporal, which was the locus of the problem of Fatalism in the first place.[49]

Leftow

Leftow has proposed his own, somewhat different model of divine timelessness. He criticizes the idea of ET-simultaneity (beyond those already noted) because it places simultaneity in God's observation of events rather than in their actual occurrence. This is due to the *fact* that eternal things cannot exist in time and temporal things cannot exist in eternity. But this is problematic because it seems to imply that if no observers are present, then things are not simultaneous.[50] In addition, a greater error exists. Stump and Kretzmann take temporality and eternality to be locational rather than modal attributes. Under such a viewpoint, two separate (discrete) series of time can be proposed to exist (A and B).[51] If they are temporally

---

47. He writes, "Naturally, just saying that duration is possible in eternity does not make it so." Davis, *Logic and the Nature of God*, 19.

48. Ironically, this is precisely what it was designed to do. He writes, "Thus is seems that for Stump and Kretzmann, if A occurs in eternity and B at some time, no description is available under which they occur at once or do not occur at once within a single reference-frame, and we cannot appeal to causal relations between them to establish their durational order: their relations are just like those of A and B described as occurring in distinct frames of reference. So arguably A and B are durationally incommensurable." Brian Leftow, "Eternity and Simultaneity," *Faith and Philosophy* 8, no. 2 (April 1991): 158.

49. Leftow asserts that ET-simultaneity allows the statement "'God eternally knows that P will do A' is now true" to stand. It can then be asserted that P must do A, and free will is destroyed. Ibid., 158–59.

50. Ibid., 154. Leftow fails to appreciate that an omniscient Being will never fail to observe.

51. Nelson has set forth a view similar to this by postulating two universes. He proposes another universe, Beta, which is not physically, temporally, or spatially related to the universe that exists (Alpha). Since there is no temporal relationship between the two universes, some

separate, then no event in one series of time can have an effect on an event in the other series. Thus, eternity and time cannot be discrete (or separate) because God must be able to affect time. If God exists in the first series, A, then he could not have created the second series, B, as temporally discrete. The creation of B would occur within A, and therefore, eternity and time cannot be discrete and the concept of ET-simultaneity collapses.[52]

Instead, Leftow proposes that events actually occur simultaneously in time and eternity. Basically, he argues that temporal beings can exist in both time and eternity, and that God shares a temporal reference frame with all events. This view does away with the need for ET-simultaneity and is thus simpler. It allows us to speak of God's interaction with temporal events without incurring the problem of his *beginning* to act (even though outside of time), and to explain how his eternal perspective and existence does not repudiate the reality of time and temporal existence. Leftow claims that this is closer to what Boethius *et al.* meant.[53]

---

questions about time cannot be asked (like whether something in Beta is before, simultaneous with, or after, something in Alpha). However, some questions about time can still be asked, but they must be asked from within the universal framework that the question is posed (like if someone in our universe is dead or not). The existence of the other universe, Beta, is not postulated in reference to our time (we cannot say that it *exists* in the sense that it *now exists*). Thus, tenseless verbs are used to refer to things in one universe when the individual speaking is in the other. However, Nelson proposes a new kind of tenseless language to employ when referring to Beta. These statements are to be seen as tenseless in regards to Alpha (our universe), but tensed in regards to Beta: "Such statements are tenseless *only* in the sense that they neither express nor imply any *temporal* relation between these statements and the actions, events, or things referred to in them, or described by them." Nelson, "Time(s), Eternity, and Duration," 7. Nelson suggests that God created both Alpha and Beta, and that God exists outside the frames of reference of both. Thus, God cannot know temporally present facts in either universe ("now"), but he can know the sequences of events within each universe. God's knowledge, under this scheme, must be timeless. If it were not, then God's time would provide a temporal link between Alpha and Beta, and no such link exists. Likewise, God's creative activity cannot be temporally ordered or else a temporal link will again be established. Nelson then drops the existence of Beta, arguing that this proves that timelessness is superior to everlastingness because it allows for the existence of such a universe. However, Stump and Kretzmann have rejected Nelson's concept of two universes because it does not allow for meaningful relationships between the two. Thus, Leftow seems to have misunderstood what Stump and Kretzmann have attempted to do, or they have not adequately explained their position. See Stump and Kretzmann, "Eternity, Awareness, and Action," 470.

52.   Leftow, "Eternity and Simultaneity," 156–57.
53.   The argument can be set forth as follows:
        (1) Since God is spaceless, nothing can move closer to him.
        (2) Change requires motion.
        (3) Therefore, in the world, there is no motion or change relative to God.
        (4) A frame of reference is a system of objects at rest *relative to one another*.
        (5) Based on (3) and (4), God shares a frame of reference with all spatial objects in which nothing changes.
        (6) An event that occurs in one reference frame occurs in all reference frames, including God's.

Leftow notes that some may object to this idea because it seems to require that anything which occurs in eternity be eternal. However, he argues that being temporal and being eternal are mutually exclusive modal properties: "One can say that an entity is temporal iff it is the kind of thing which *can* be located in a series of earlier and later events, states, processes etc., and that an entity is eternal iff it *cannot* be so located."[54] Leftow argues that God cannot be so located because this would require him to be spatially located.

Criticisms of Leftow
Leftow's idea of atemporal duration is subject to the same criticisms of Stump and Kretzmann leveled by Rogers, although his appeal to modal properties escapes some of the other criticisms. He does not fully explain just how an event can occur in both the temporal reference frame and the eternal, and it may require an appeal to mystery.

Leftow opts for a more traditional understanding of God's eternal nature, but his criticisms of Stump and Kretzmann's proposal points to the problem with timelessness as a solution to the problem of divine foreknowledge and human freedom. While the traditional answer to the problem denied that God's knowledge can be temporally located in a before/after relationship with the event known, the same cannot be said of true propositions regarding future free acts. In other words, even if the models of timeless existence are coherent, an appeal to God's timeless existence does not resolve the problems of incompatibility. It just recasts it in terms of true propositions: If it is true *now* that particular persons will perform specific free actions *tomorrow*, then it seems necessary that they perform those actions tomorrow, whether God's knowledge is temporal or atemporal.

OCKHAMISM

One of the most fascinating answers to the dilemma of the compatibility of divine foreknowledge and human freedom was set forth by the fourteenth-century English philosopher/theologian, William of Ockham. Since the publication of Pike's article, Ockham's position has received considerable attention in the philosophical literature.

---

(7) To prevent this from constituting change relative to God, all events must be simultaneous in God's frame of reference.

(8) However, all events cannot be simultaneous in any temporal reference frame.

(9) Therefore, the reference frame God shares with all events must be atemporal. Ibid., 161–64.

54. Ibid., 168.

Ockham's Answer

Ockham began by asserting that future contingents do have truth value and God must know them.[55] While Ockham claimed ignorance about *how* God can know them, he disagreed with the prevailing view, which (following Scotus) claimed that God knows because he willed them *as contingent*.[56] Ockham thought this approach compromises either creaturely freedom or divine certainty: "when something is determined contingently, so that it is still possible that it is not determined and it is possible that it was never determined, then one cannot have certain and infallible cognition based on such a determination."[57]

Ockham's answer to the compatibility problem amounts to a denial of the necessity of God's past beliefs. He draws upon the common sense notion of the asymmetry of the past and the future—the past is seen as fixed, while the future is thought to be open—in order to demonstrate that the supposed conflict between God's past beliefs and future contingency is illusory. He notes that the fixed nature of the past and of truths about the past is not the same as the fixed nature of logically or metaphysically necessary truths.[58] Propositions that were contingent until the conditions were fulfilled have become necessary in the sense that they cannot now be falsified, but this means that the necessity of the past is accidental in

---

55. Craig explains: "It is perhaps in this sense that Ockham often says that God knows which part of a contradiction will be true or false—an expression which copyists often 'corrected' by substituting *est* for *erit* and which the Adams-Kretzmann translation occasionally renders 'is' rather than 'will be' without textual support. For Ockham future contingent propositions *are* determinately true or false because the states of affairs to which they correspond *will* determinately be or not be actually present." William Lane Craig, *The Problem of Divine Foreknowledge and Future Contingents from Aristotle to Suarez* (Leiden: E. J. Brill, 1988), 148.

56. He saw this as part of the divine mystery, and even argued that it is impossible to know how the infinite divine mind works. He wrote, "Therefore I reply to the question that it has to be held without any doubt that God knows all future contingent facts evidently and with certainty. But to explain this evidently, and to express the manner in which He knows all future contingent facts, is impossible for any intellect in this life." William of Ockham, "*Ordinatio*, 31: Q. *unica*. 2.," in *Philosophical Writings: A Selection*, ed. and trans. Philotheus Boehner (Indianapolis: Bobbs-Merrill, 1964), 148.

57. William of Ockham, *Predestination, God's Foreknowledge, and Future Contingents*, trans. Marilyn McCord Adams and Norman Kretzmann, 2nd ed. (Indianapolis: Hackett, 1983), 49. Ockham seemed to think that God's knowledge of future truths is analogous to human intuition: "this intuitive cognition is so perfect and so clear that it is also an evident knowledge of past, future and present facts. Just as our intellect is able to know contingent propositions from our intuitive cognition by which are known not only necessary truth and contingent truth about a present fact, but also which side of a contradiction will be true and which will be false." William of Ockham, "*Ordinatio 31: Q. unica. 2.*," 149.

58. Plantinga correctly notes that the future, properly speaking, is no more alterable than the past. The asymmetry between the past and the future does not consist in the unalterability of the past, yet it is closely related. Plantinga writes, "To alter the future, Paul must do something like this: he must perform some action *A* at a time *t* before 9:21 such that prior to *t* it is true that Paul will walk out at 9:21, but after *t* (after he performs *A*) false that he will." Alvin Plantinga, "On Ockham's Way Out," *Faith and Philosophy* 3, no. 3 (July 1986): 244.

nature, and that some past events are only accidentally necessary. Ockham sees propositions describing God's beliefs about the future as members of this class. The necessity of a proposition is tied to its potency to occur or not-occur and not to its truth or falsity.[59] Thus, Zagzebski correctly concludes that, according to Ockham, the connection of the necessity of the past with potency for the opposite "means that the past determinate truth of such propositions does not fall under the necessity of the past."[60]

Contemporary Formulations

As noted earlier, much of the renewed interest in Ockham's answer to the dilemma is due to a desire to answer Pike's charge that divine foreknowledge necessarily leads to Fatalism. Most contemporary formulations tend to either focus on clarifying the difference between *hard facts* about the past from *soft facts* about the past, and then argue that God's past beliefs are soft, or focus on explicating a definition of *accidental necessity* which will include past events, but not divine knowledge or beliefs.

Hard/soft facts

In one of the earliest published responses to Pike, John Saunders argued that the presumed asymmetry between the past and the future regarding free acts is erroneous, to wit, if individuals can act in such a way as to render the future different, they can also act in such a way as to render the past different. He writes, "Surely there is no more contradiction in saying that one has the power so to act that past situations would be other than in fact they are, than in saying that one has the power so to act that future situations would be other than in fact they are. Of course, we do not so act that either past or future situations are other than they are: but it does not follow from this that we lack the power so to act that they would be other than they are."[61] This is an extraordinary claim, though it is not quite as radical as it may first appear. What Saunders is most concerned to question is Pike's underlying assumption that an individual does not possess the *power* to act so that the past would be different than it in fact is. Saunders argues that whenever an individual can act one way but instead acts another way, he exercises just this power. By way of example, he refers to his own power to write the article at the time he did, or refrain from writing at that time. His writing the article when he did means that his writing stands in a particular relationship with the past, a relationship that would have been different if he had chosen to write the article at a different time

59. Ockham writes, "no matter how true the proposition 'God knows that this side of the contradiction will be true' may be, nevertheless it is possible that this never was true. And in this case there is a possibility of the other side without any succession, because it is possible this proposition should never have been true." William of Ockham, "*Ordinatio 31: Q. unica. 2.*" 149–50.

60. Zagzebski, *Dilemma of Freedom and Foreknowledge*, 68.

61. John Turk Saunders, "Of God and Freedom," *Philosophical Review* 75, no. 2 (April 1966): 221.

(or not at all). Saunders explains, "Although it is true that if I had refrained from writing this paper in 1965, the[n] Caesar's assassination would have been other than it is in that it would not have preceded by 2009 years my writing of this paper, it would be absurd to argue that I therefore did not have it in my power to refrain from writing the paper in 1965."[62]

In a rejoinder to Saunders' article, Pike distinguishes between two types of facts about the past: *soft facts,* and *hard facts.* Hard facts are those that are fully vested in the past, whereas soft facts have a connection to the future. In order to illustrate the difference, Pike asks us to consider the past fact,

Caesar died on the steps of the Senate.

This fact is different in nature from the fact set forth by Saunders, which may be restated as

Caesar died 2009 years before Saunders wrote his article responding to Pike.

According to Pike, the first is a hard fact, while the second is soft.[63] The truth of the first is only dependent upon events having occurred as described in the past, while the truth of the second, at least prior to Saunders' writing, was dependent upon the past event (Caesar dying) and a future event (Saunders writing his article, and his doing so 2009 years after Caesar's death).

Thus, in his influential work on the topic, Plantinga summarizes the Ockhamist position as making a distinction between propositions that are strictly about the past or present, and propositions that seem to be about the past, but are really about the future.[64] He presents two criteria for a fact

---

62. Ibid., 224. For a more popular explanation, see Bruce Reichenbach, "God Limits His Power," in Basinger and Basinger, eds., *Predestination & Free Will,* 110–11.
63. Pike explains, "some facts about the past (for example, facts about Caesar's death) were 'fully accomplished,' 'over-and-done-with, and so forth' [*sic*] in the past (for example in 44 B.C.). These are sometimes called 'hard facts' about the past. The fact that Caesar died on the steps of the Senate is a fact of this sort. On the other hand, some facts about the past are not, relative to a given time, 'fully accomplished,' 'over-and-done-with,' and so forth at that time. The fact that Caesar died 2009 years prior to the writing of Saunders' paper is a fact of this sort." Nelson Pike, "Of God and Freedom: A Rejoinder," *Philosophical Review* 75, no. 3 (July 1966): 370. Pike argues that statements which describe the beliefs of God (or anyone for that matter) *at a given time* are restricted and therefore, *hard facts* about the past. Saunders' counterexample works because he has given an unrestricted principle as representative of Pike's view, even though Pike's principle is restricted; Saunders argument is a *straw man.* Ibid., 371.
64. For example, the proposition, "Paul is seated," is strictly about the present, whereas "Paul was seated," is strictly about the past. However, the proposition, "Eighty years ago, the proposition *Paul will mow his lawn in 1999* was true," is about the past, but it is also about the future—it is a soft fact. So are "Paul correctly believed that the sun will rise on January 1, 2000," and "Eighty years ago, the sentence 'Paul will mow his lawn in 1999' expressed the proposition *Paul will mow his lawn in 1999* and expressed a truth." It should be noted that Plantinga's

to be considered a *hard* fact about the past: 1) genuineness, and 2) strict-ness.[65] For a fact to be *genuine*, it must tell something about the past. For a fact to be *strict*, it must refer only to the past and have no dependence upon the future for its truth.[66] Plantinga notes that the Ockhamist answer to the dilemma is to claim that only hard facts about the past are acciden-tally necessary; put differently, the proposition

> If *p* is about the past, then *p* is necessary;

is false. The argument for incompatibilism (of foreknowledge and free-dom) requires it to be true, so it fails. The issue at hand, of course, is whether propositions that describe God's knowledge of future contin-gents are hard facts or soft facts. Contemporary Ockhamists like Marilyn Adams argue that they are indeed soft, and even suggest that other truths are soft as well.[67] Consider the proposition

> God knew eighty years ago that Paul will mow in 1999.

For the incompatibilist argument to work, the proposition must be a hard fact, but it is not because it depends on Paul's mowing his lawn in the future (Plantinga's article was published in 1986).

Interestingly, it is because of God's essential omniscience that state-ments referring to his past beliefs about future free actions are soft. Consider the proposition,

---

article was published in 1986 and therefore, 1999 was still future. The examples given should be understood in this way. See Plantinga, "On Ockham's Way Out."

65. Plantinga admits that criteria such as these are somewhat ambiguous. He writes, "It may be difficult to give criteria, or (informative) necessary and sufficient conditions for either genu-ineness or strictness; nevertheless we do have at least a partial grasp of these notions." Ibid., 247.

66. Plantinga is careful to note, though, that he is not claiming that a hard fact must not entail *any* propositions about the future: "No doubt *every* proposition about the past, hard fact or not, entails *some* proposition about the future; *Socrates was wise*, for example, entails *It will be true from now on that Socrates was wise*; and *Paul played tennis yesterday* entails *Paul will not play tennis for the first time tomorrow*. What I *am* saying is this: No proposition that entails (18) [God knew eighty years ago that Paul will mow in 1999] is a hard fact about the past, because no such proposition is *strictly* about the past. We may not be able to give a criterion for being strictly about the past; but we do have at least a rough and intuitive grasp of this notion." Ibid., 248.

67. Marilyn Adams has gone so far as to argue that not only are God's beliefs about future contin-gents soft, but so is his existence! According to Adams, a soft fact is a proposition that is at least in part about a time future relative to the time the proposition refers to. She argues that the statement, "God exists essentially" is not a hard fact because it entails that "God exists at t_2," be true, even if it is now t_1 because everlastingness is an essential attribute of God. The point Adams hopes to make, then, is that hard facts are propositions about events that are not future-dependent (do not require the existence of the future), whereas soft facts are proposi-tions about events that require a future.

> Eighty years ago, God believed that Paul will mow in 1999.

If God is not essentially omniscient, then his belief regarding Paul's mowing in 1999 does not entail that Paul mow in 1999, and the proposition describing the belief would thereby be accidentally necessary. The proposition about God's beliefs would then be strictly about the past, and God's belief would be either correct or incorrect, depending upon what Paul does. By extension, statements about (for example) my past beliefs regarding the future are hard and thereby, accidentally necessary. We will have more to say about this later, but the important point here is to note that since God is omniscient and everything he believes is correct, then the proposition about his belief regarding Paul's mowing is logically equivalent to

> Eighty years ago, it was true that Paul will mow in 1999;

and

> There is (i.e., is, was, or will be) such a time as eighty years ago, and Paul will mow in 1999.

Plantinga claims that no one will hold the last statement to be incompatible with Paul's being free with respect to mowing in 1999, except for Fatalists. Thus, the key to understanding Ockhamism is the counterfactual relation of dependency between God's (omniscient) past belief and Paul's future free action:

> But an Ockhamist would also certainly hold that even if God is not *essentially* omniscient, nevertheless his omniscience is counterfactually independent of Paul's actions; that is to say, there isn't anything Paul can do such that if he were to do it then God would not have been or would no longer be omniscient. If Paul were to refrain from mowing his lawn in 1999, therefore, God would not have believed, eighty years ago, that Paul will mow then.[68]

This leads to the second way Ockhamism has been applied in the contemporary discussion: revision of accidental necessity and a proposal that free agents possess *counterfactual power over the past.*

Accidental necessity
A number of contemporary Ockhamists have set forth nuanced definitions of *accidental necessity*, and argued that God's past beliefs about future contingents are not necessary in this way. The most prominent proponents are Alfred Freddoso and Alvin Plantinga. Freddoso begins by

---

68.   Ibid., 250.

noting the tensed nature of all propositions and the standard conception of accidental necessity.[69] Based on the principles of accidental necessity, he notes that most would accept the following rule:

> If p entails q, and p is necessary *per accidens* at t, then no one has the power at or after t to bring it about that q is or will be false.[70]

The question that must be answered is, *which* propositions are necessary *per accidens* at a given moment, t? The most obvious answer seems to be something along the lines of

> If p is true at t, then Pp is necessary *per accidens* at every moment after t, and $\sim Pp$ is impossible *per accidens* at every moment after t.

Yet, Freddoso notes, the Ockhamist will claim that this is false. He explains, "For, according to the Ockhamist, when p is a future-tense proposition true before t, it simply does not follow that in every possible world just like ours prior to t, Pp is true at t and at every moment after t."[71] Instead, Ockhamists claim that contingent propositions regarding the future (true counterfactuals) can be true at a given time, t, and count as part of the world's history only if their present-tense counterparts were already true.[72]

---

69.   Freddoso then sets forth four properties of accidental necessity: first, only logically contingent propositions can be accidentally necessary; second, accidentally necessary propositions are necessary relative to some time (they *become* necessary); third, once a proposition becomes necessary *per accidens*, it remains necessary; and fourth, accidental necessity is closed under entailment.

70.   Alfred J. Freddoso, "Accidental Necessity and Power over the Past," *Pacific Philosophical Quarterly* 63 (1982): 56–58.

71.   Ibid., 59. Freddoso, though, points out that the difficult task faced by the Ockhamist is to explain how two possible worlds can be *just like* one another (share the same histories), but do not have the same futures. Part of the problem here may be the limitations of possible worlds semantics. It seems that Freddoso wants to say that two worlds share the same histories, but do not share counterfactuals. This, however, cannot be correct because under the stipulations given, if p was true prior to t in world α, then at t (in α), p would occur. Similarly, if p was true in β prior to t, then at t (in β), p would occur. Otherwise, p would not have been true. It seems that Freddoso has made the task more difficult by implying that counterfactuals are part of a world's history. For a discussion of counterfactuals and possible worlds, see chapter 3.

72.   Ibid., 60. This is somewhat complicated, so consider the following example offered by Freddoso:

> *David is in Chicago* will be true at t_2;
>
> F(*David is in Chicago at t_2*) was true at every moment prior to t_1.

If any given human has the power at t_1 to make it true at t_1, that *David is in Chicago* will be true at t_2, then that person has the power at t_1 to make it true at t_1 that F(*David is in Chicago at t_2*) was true at every moment prior to t_1.

Freddoso contends that the second proposition is temporally contingent at t_1 since its truth-value at t_1 depends on what will be *presently* true at a future moment (viz., t_2). Thus,

Plantinga also utilizes this approach. He proposes that accidental necessity be defined in terms of the power of agents for purposes of
discussion of theological and logical determinism:

> p is accidentally necessary at t iff p is true at t and it is not possible both that
> p is true at t and that there exists an agent S and an action A such that {1} S
> has the power at t or later to perform A, and {2} if S were to perform A at t
> or later, then p would have been false.[73]

This definition means that neither

> Eighty years ago it was true that Paul would not mow his lawn in 1999;

nor

> God believed eighty years ago that Paul would mow his lawn in 1999;

are accidentally necessary, at least not if God is essentially omniscient and
Paul is libertarianly free, for Paul would have the power to mow or refrain
from mowing in either case.

Plantinga offers two examples in order to clarify these difficult issues:
1) ants moving into Paul's yard, and 2) Newcomb's paradox. First, Plantinga asks the reader to suppose that a colony of ants moved into Paul's
yard last Saturday, and if he mows his lawn this afternoon, they will be
destroyed. However, for some reason, God wants the ants to survive. Thus,
the fact of the matter is that Paul will not mow his lawn this afternoon:

> God, who is essentially omniscient, knew in advance, of course, that Paul
> will not mow his lawn this afternoon; but if he had foreknown instead that
> Paul *would* mow this afternoon, then he would have prevented the ants from
> moving in. . . . But it is within Paul's power to mow this afternoon. There is
> therefore an action he can perform such that if he were to perform it, then
> the proposition
>
> (34) That colony of carpenter ants moved into Paul's yard last Saturday
>
> would have been false.[74]

---

no Ockhamist will reject the last on the basis of the necessity of the second at t_1. He will also
concede that someone may have the power at t_1 to make it true that *David is in Chicago* will be
true at t_2 (by somehow ensuring David's presence in Chicago at that time). Thus, F(*David is in
Chicago at t_2*) may be true before t_2.

73.   Plantinga, "On Ockham's Way Out," 250. He suggests this is reasonable since the definition of
accidental necessity is always used in reference to its impact upon the power of agents anyway.
74.   Ibid., 254.

Of course, this means that (34) is not accidentally necessary even though it seems to be strictly about the past. Plantinga concludes, "So, contrary to what Ockham supposed, not all true propositions strictly about the past—not all hard facts—are accidentally necessary—not, at any rate, in the sense of (31) [his definition of accidental necessity]."[75]

The second example is commonly known as *Newcomb's Paradox*.[76] It refers to an individual who is faced with two boxes in which, eighty years prior, God had placed a sum of money. The individual is told that in box A, there is either $1,000,000 or nothing, and box B contains $1,000. The contents of box A are dependent upon the individual's choice. If he chooses both boxes, then God will know that beforehand and put nothing in box A. If he chooses only one box, then God will have known that and put $1,000,000 in it. According to Plantinga, this puzzle under these conditions entails that there is a proposition, *p*, which is strictly about the past and an action, *A*, that can be performed such that if it were performed, *p* would have been false. Plantinga suggests that if the individual were to choose both boxes, then the proposition,

> There was only $1,000 in the boxes eighty years ago

would be true. However, the individual still retains the power to choose only one box, and if he were to so act, then that proposition would have been false, and instead the proposition,

> There was $1,001,000 in the boxes eighty years ago;

would have been true. Note that both propositions are strictly about the past, yet which is true depends upon the future choice of the individual, and thus, the free individual still has power over their truth. As Plantinga puts it, "hence there is a proposition strictly about the past that is

---

75. Ibid.
76. *Newcomb's Paradox* was originally presented in Robert Nozick, "Newcomb's Problem and Two Principles of Choice," in *Essays in Honor of Carl G. Hampel*, ed. Nicholas Rescher, Synthese Library (Dordrecht: D. Reidel, 1969), 114–46. It was originally posited of a fallible predictor, with both sides receiving support (compatibilists and incompatibilists). For example, see Maya Bar-Hillel and Avishai Margalit, "Newcomb's Paradox Revisited," *British Journal for the Philosophy of Science* 23 (1972): 301; Don Locke, "How to Make a Newcomb Choice," *Analysis* 38 (1978): 21, and Terence Horgan, "Counterfactuals and Newcomb's Problem," *Journal of Philosophy* 78 (1981): 331–56. Craig notes that if the predictor is essentially omniscient (as in Plantinga's example), then freedom is not abrogated. Rather, the choice is then between receiving $1,000,000 and receiving $1,000. All that is eliminated is the possibility that the predictor makes an incorrect prediction and the individual receives $1,001,000. This, however, has no impact on the freedom of the individual (except that it makes the choice much easier—go for box A!). See William Lane Craig, "Nice Soft Facts: Fischer on Foreknowledge," *Religious Studies* 25 (1989): 245 nn. 1–3.

not necessary *per accidens*."[77] Plantinga notes that, using similar reasoning, many other examples could be given. It seems, then, that very few contingent facts about the past are accidentally necessary according to the definition offered by Plantinga.[78] Of particular importance are God's past beliefs about future free actions. The Ockhamist solution suggests that we have counterfactual power over God's past beliefs. Put differently, we have the power to act such that God's past beliefs would have been different than they in fact were. Suppose that I freely write on my blog tonight. In that case, yesterday God believed that I would write on my blog tonight. However, since I have libertarian freedom at the time of my choice/action regarding how to spend my time, I have the power to choose to do something else, for example watch television. If I exercise my freedom in that way, though, God would have always believed that I would watch television. Notice that the language used is careful to avoid saying that I have the power to change God's past beliefs or make God's past beliefs to have been false. The language of Ockhamism is not causal, but descriptive.[79]

Problems with Ockhamism
Two major objections to the Ockhamist solution exist. The first deals with the apparent arbitrary distinction between hard and soft facts that Ockhamism requires, while the second relates to the kind of power individuals supposedly have under Ockhamism. Both objections boast prominent adherents and are formidable, but can be answered.

Arbitrary distinction
A number of philosophers have criticized Ockhamism for its seeming *ad hoc* division of facts into hard and soft categories. For example, Zagzebski complains that contemporary Ockhamists begin with the *a priori* claim that God's past beliefs are soft and then construct "elaborate recursive

---

77. Plantinga, "On Ockham's Way Out," 257.
78. There still are some. For example, I can not now act in such a way that, if I were to so act, then I would never have existed. Likewise, there is no action, A, a human can perform such that, if he were to perform it, then there would never have been any contingent beings. Plantinga concludes, "So the proposition there have been (contingent) agents is accidentally necessary; but it is hard indeed to find any stronger propositions that are both logically and accidentally necessary." Ibid., 257–58.
79. Plantinga believes that accidental necessity of the past should probably be thought of in terms of our inability to *cause* things to have been otherwise. Plantinga's preferred definition of accidental necessity is as follows:

> p is accidentally necessary at t iff p is true at t and it is not possible both that p is true at t and that there exist agents $S_1 ..., S_n$ and actions $A_1 ..., A_n$ such that (1) A_i is basic for S_i, (2) S_i has the power at t or later to perform A_i, and (3) necessarily, if every S_i were to perform A_i at t or later, then p would have been false.

This allows for contingent propositions about the past to be seen as accidentally necessary, while contingent propositions about the future are not. Ibid., 261.

definitions" for hard facts in order to exclude them.[80] She argues that our normal intuitions about the fixity of the past ought not be dismissed just for the sake of providing an answer to the foreknowledge dilemma, but that is what seems to be in play with these arguments. Soft facts, Zagzebski maintains, should seem to be about the past, but upon reflection, are shown to clearly not be, but God's past beliefs, even after much reflection, "still seem to be as past as past gets."[81]

Ultimately, Zagzebski's complaint rests in the fact that Ockhamism requires that the past beliefs of an omniscient, infallible being are soft, while the beliefs of fallible beings are hard, and this seems *ad hoc*: "If both God and Paul's wife believe that Paul will mow the lawn next Saturday, how can God's belief be any less past than hers? God's past belief that *p* is surely a different fact than his essential omniscience, and although the latter assures the truth of the former, it is hard to see how the property of essential omniscience could make the belief weak on pastness."[82] Hasker agrees, claiming that the hard/soft distinction is of little help and proposing his own distinctions in terms of future-indifference instead of agency or power.[83] He argues that statements about God's past beliefs are

---

80. Zagzebski notes that the mere construction of a definition that works does nothing to prove its truth. Zagzebski, *Dilemma of Freedom and Foreknowledge*, 74. Two examples of such philosophical creativity should suffice. Eddy Zemach and David Widerker, in response to Fischer's objection, define hard facts in terms of shared histories of possible worlds and future contingency—a hard fact is future-necessary, whereas a soft fact is future-contingent. Their analysis allows God's past beliefs about future contingents to be soft because God's belief about a future time is inconsistent with time ceasing prior to the time God believes the event will occur. Joshua Hoffman and Gary Rosenkrantz have offered a rather difficult and complicated explication of the hard/soft fact distinction that avoids the problems raised by Fischer. See Eddy Zemach and David Widerker, "Facts, Freedom, and Foreknowledge," *Religious Studies* 23 (1988): 19–28; and Joshua Hoffman and Gary Rosenkrantz, "Hard and Soft Facts," *The Philosophical Review* 93, no. 3 (July 1984): 419–34.

81. Zagzebski, *Dilemma of Freedom and Foreknowledge*, 76. Zagzebski correctly notes that Plantinga's approach, which depends on softness and hardness being closed under strict equivalence, can be used by the opponent of Ockhamism: "A skeptic about the Ockhamist solution need only point out that since *Eighty years ago God believed that Paul will mow his lawn in 1999* is strictly about the past, so is *Paul will mow his lawn in 1999*. So even though Plantinga may be right that if one of these propositions is a soft fact, so is the other, the skeptic is likewise right that if one is a hard fact, so is the other. We are not told why we should take Plantinga's preferred line of reasoning rather than the alternative." Ibid., 81–82. According to Plantinga, the proposition, *Paul will mow his lawn in 1999* is not strictly about the past, but it is equivalent to the proposition, *Eighty years ago God believed that Paul will mow his lawn in 1999*, which thereby cannot be strictly about the past because of the equivalence. Although Zagzebski's basic point should be sustained, the counter-example she offers is not likely. The first proposition hardly seems to be about the past. It would seem, then, that the best approach to refuting Plantinga's claim is to deny the equivalence of the two statements. However, it may prove rather difficult to argue against the entailment relationship that exists between the two statements, given the doctrine of omniscience.

82. Ibid., 84.

83. He writes, "But the main objective in the foreknowledge controversy is to *settle* disagreements about the powers of agents, and it is evident that if the hard fact–soft fact distinction

structurally the same as those about other beings' past beliefs, so if one is hard, then so is the other.[84]

In response, it seems odd that opponents of Ockhamism criticize it for requiring propositions describing human beliefs to be of a different order from propositions describing divine beliefs. Ockham himself believed the two to be in different classes, and confessed his ignorance about how God's mind works, only reluctantly drawing an analogy to human ways of knowing.[85] The key point in Ockhamism is God's essential omniscience and his distinction from creatures. As Plantinga explains, it is the counterfactual relation of dependency between God's omniscient past belief and Paul's future free action that makes it work. He writes, "But the Ockhamist would also certainly hold that even if God is not essentially omniscient, nevertheless his omniscience is couterfactually independent of Paul's actions; that is to say, there isn't anything Paul can do such that if he were to do it then God would not have been or would no longer be omniscient. If Paul were to refrain from mowing his lawn in 1999, therefore, God would not have believed, eighty years ago, that Paul will mow then."[86] It is because God's knowledge is of a fundamentally different sort from human knowledge that his beliefs are accorded a different status.

Ironically, Zagzebski's own approach to addressing the problem of divine foreknowledge and human freedom is based on a Thomistic approach that accentuates the fundamental differences between human and divine knowledge. She draws upon the idea that God knows all truths instantaneously in his own essence and that therefore, there is only one divine state of knowing.[87] Thus, Zagzebski and Ockhamists disagree over the implications of God's essential omniscience for the accidental nature of contingent truths.[88]

---

is *explicated* in terms of powers, then disagreements about what is in our power will simply reappear as differences about the hard fact–soft fact distinction itself." Hasker, *God, Time, and Knowledge*, 81.

84. His conclusion is that if God's past beliefs are always correct and statements of God's past beliefs regarding future actions of creatures are hard, then statements about future free actions (of creatures) are also hard and freedom is abrogated. Ibid., 91–94.

85. Thus, the rich tradition of apophatic theology in the church's history, where the only statements made about God were negative in nature, i.e., what God is not, because positive statements were seen as inadequate to capture the wonder and glory of the divine nature.

86. Plantinga, "On Ockham's Way Out," 250.

87. She explains, "We can then suppose that the difference in contingent truths in different worlds is the difference in what is 'reflected' in God's essence in different worlds. God's knowing all contingent truths is like seeing them through the 'features' of his own essence." The primary object of God's knowledge is his own essence. The contingent truths are secondary objects of his knowledge, and are thereby inessential to God's knowledge, or are accidental. Zagzebski, *Dilemma of Freedom and Foreknowledge*, 90.

88. Similarly, Hasker's argument fails because the Ockhamist is under no obligation to accept Hasker's new definitions of hard and soft facts or his claim that statements about God's past beliefs are future-indifferent (and has good reasons to reject it).

John Martin Fischer argues that the Okhamist distinction between hard and soft facts results in all facts being soft! He claims that, for any given fact, some contingent future event or action can be identified as entailed by it. For example, the current factual proposition,

> John is writing chapter 4;

seems to be a hard fact because it is occurring presently at time, t_1. However, Fischer argues that it entails that at a future time, say t_2,

> John is not just beginning to write chapter 4;

will be true, and this means the current proposition cannot be hard because it requires the future time, t_2. He generalizes this approach to claim that all facts about the past or present depend in some way on the future, and therefore, all facts are soft.[89]

David Widerker correctly points out that Fischer's argument fails because it assumes that since some future truths are entailed by the present fact, their truth requires the existence of the future time.[90] It is true that my current act of writing chapter 4 entails that, in the future, I cannot begin to write chapter 4. Another way of saying this is that it is true that my current act (at t_1) of writing chapter 4 entails that the act,

> John is just beginning to write chapter 4;

does not occur at t_2. However, it should be clear there are several ways that this could be true without my writing chapter 4 at t_1. First, I may simply fail to write at t_2; perhaps I may go to the park, exercise, watch a movie, read a book, etc. Second, I may write at t_2, but work on another chapter or a separate book altogether. Third, I may die before t_2, or perhaps God may decide to stop sustaining my existence prior to or at t_2. More importantly, if all existence were to cease prior to t_2 (and presumably with all existence, time itself), then t_2 would not see my beginning to write chapter 4, though it would still have been true at t_1 that I am writing chapter 4. Unfortunately

---

89. John Martin Fischer, "Freedom and Foreknowledge," *The Philosophical Review* 92, no. 1 (January 1983): 75.

90. David Widerker, "Two Fallacious Objections to Adams' Soft/Hard Fact Distinction," *Philosophical Studies* 57 (September 1989): 103–7.

for Fischer, though, this objection has already been answered.[91] Thus,

---

91.   A third argument against the Ockhamist distinction of facts as hard and soft is related to the
      asymmetry argument, and finds its origins in Fischer. He argues that a *real* soft fact about
      the past is soft because it refers to a relationship of a past set of circumstances which cannot
      be altered, to a future event which is contingent. According to Fischer, God's beliefs about
      the future can be soft only if one state of mind in God can count as two different beliefs. For
      example, the belief that

> (47) At t_2, Clarence will eat an omelet;

if at t_2, Clarence eats an omelet, and the belief that

> (48) At t_2, Clarence will not eat an omelet;

if Clarence does not eat an omelet at t_2, must count as the same mental state in God. Fischer
does not think this is plausible—two different beliefs imply two different mental states.
Fischer, "Freedom and Foreknowledge," 77–78.
      Zemach and Widerker argue that the implausibility is due to the essentialist assumption:

> (49) If some state m has the property of being a belief that p, it has that property *essen-
> tially* (i.e., in all possible worlds).

They note that functionalism can allow for the denial of (49). They claim that human beliefs
consist of the use of symbols which stand for certain states of affairs thought to obtain.
However, if God's thoughts are formed in a radically different way, then it may not be correct
to say that he has beliefs.
      William Alston has presented a similar argument for the conclusion that God does not
have beliefs. According to Alston, if God is to have beliefs, then his knowledge must be propositional because beliefs are *at least* a propositional attitude. He writes, "We have no inkling of
how some psychological state could be a belief without being a belief that p, where p stands for
a sentence that expresses a proposition. Hence a being whose knowledge involves no propositional structure or complexity has no beliefs as part of its knowledge." Alston, "Does God
Have Beliefs?," 291.
      However, Alston also argues that even if God's knowledge is propositional, he still has no
beliefs. He begins by noting that although *believe* is often used in contradistinction to *know*,
the two are not necessarily mutually exclusive; philosophers often use *believe* in a more neutral
sense in which it may or may not count as knowledge. It may seem that belief still does imply
that some of the propositions accepted *may not* count as knowledge, but in the case of God,
no such possibility exists because all of the propositions he accepts must count as knowledge
since he is essentially omniscient. Alston rejects this argument. Just because propositional
"accepts" of humans are referred to as *beliefs* because there is a possibility that they are wrong,
it does not follow that God does not have beliefs. Alston compares this with one's purposes—
just because God never fails to accomplish what he attempts to do does not mean that he has
no purpose. Alston writes, "Thus, even if the divine case does not exhibit the same kind of
contrast between belief and knowledge that we have in the human case, it does not follow that
God does not have beliefs as components of His knowledge." Ibid., 294.
      Alston objects to the idea that *knowledge* equals *true belief plus*. He does not believe that an
adequate addition can be found, and he believes that a stronger definition of knowledge can be
found in the intuitive model in which the knower has an immediate awareness of a fact. This
model, according to Alston, has been the dominant model in the history of theology. Alston
claims that this is a stronger model because the object of knowledge is guaranteed existence,
whereas *true belief plus* does not offer such a guarantee. This argument, though, does not seem
to make sense. Consider the idea of *justified true belief*. This seems to offer just as strong of
a guarantee. It appears that, although he tried to avoid utilizing the traditional dichotomy of

Fischer's objection fails.[92]

Power over the past
The second major objection to Ockhamism is that it makes claims regarding the power of free creatures over the past which cannot be sustained. It is related to the previous objection, and may be developed from the *arbitrary distinction* argument. Consider two propositions:

> Smith correctly believed at t_1 that Clarence will have a cheese omelet at t_2;

and

> God believed at t_1 that Clarence will have a cheese omelet at t_2.

On the Ockhamist account, both are soft facts about the past because their truth is dependent upon Clarence eating a cheese omelet at t_2. However,

---

belief versus knowledge, Alston has done just that. Hasker has responded to Alston, claiming that God does have beliefs and that Alston's preferred view—the propositional intuitive approach—does not appear to be propositional at all. See William Hasker, "Yes, God Has Beliefs!" *Religious Studies* 24 (1988): 385–94.

Zemach and Widerker note that language and symbol use are community dependent, but God is not so constrained. They argue that what is needed is a relational model of beliefs and states of affairs—God's mental state, m, is not *caused* to mean p by the fact that p. Instead, it is in virtue of its being the case that p, that God's mental state m means p. Zemach and Widerker explain: "Thus, the property *is a belief that p* is a relational property m has in virtue of its relation to the fact that p. Therefore, 'God's belief that p' is a non-rigid designator which picks out m in some worlds only." Zemach and Widerker, "Facts, Freedom, and Foreknowledge," 26. This, Zemach and Widerker argue, means that one's ability to bring it about that p means that he has the ability to bring it about that the actual world is (or is not) a p-world. This ability means that he can bring it about that one's token of 'God's belief that p' will (or will not) refer to God's mental state m in one's world. Zemach and Widerker believe that the underlying problem with Fischer's objection is that it assumes that God's mental states can be described non-relationally. This assumption is problematic because it does not adequately address the tension between the essential properties of God and the fact that he responds differently to different circumstances.

92. In response, Fischer complains that Widerker's argument is dependent upon a special definition that allows God's past beliefs about future contingents to be soft, while past beliefs of others regarding those same future contingents are hard, and this, he maintains, is somewhat contrived. He writes, "On (A') [Fischer's reconstruction of how Widerker defines the distinction between hard and soft facts in Adams' argument] a fact such as the fact that God believed at *T1* that Jones would mow his lawn at *T2* (let us call this fact, '*F1*') is a soft fact about *T1*, as stated above. Now, consider the following fact, which is generated by simply counting all the persons who hold the belief at *T1* that Jones will mow his lawn at *T2*: 'Exactly *N* persons believed at *T1* that Jones would mow his lawn at *T2*.' (Let us call this fact, '*F2*'.) I claim that if *F1* is considered a soft fact about *T1*, then *F2* should be considered a soft fact as well. That is, if God is actually one of the *N* believers, then intuitively *F2* should be considered a soft fact about *T1*. But whereas (A') implies that *F1* is a soft fact about *T1*, (A') implies that *F2* is a hard fact about *T1*: *F2* does not entail that time continue after *T1*." John Martin Fischer, "Snapshot Ockhamism," in Tomberlin, ed., *Philosophical Perspectives*, 360.

the initial appearance of similarity is misleading, for there is an important asymmetry between them. Suppose that Clarence does not eat a cheese omelet at t_2. In that case, neither proposition would be correct, but for different reasons. At t_1, Smith would have nevertheless believed that Clarence will have a cheese omelet at t_2, but he would have been wrong. The basic action (i.e., Smith's believing) would have occurred, and therefore, a proposition describing his belief is a hard fact (that is, "Smith believed at t_1 that Clarence will have a cheese omelet at t_2" is a hard fact). The proposition above would only be false because it includes an evaluative statement of Smith's belief (i.e., "correctly"). However, the action described in the second proposition (i.e., God's believing) would not have occurred at all. It seems, then, that Clarence has the power to cause a past event to have not occurred. If creatures do indeed possess power of this sort, one of two things follow: either backward causation is possible (which is doubtful), or creatures possess a power that cannot be utilized (which seems contradictory), and thus, Ockhamism fails.

In response to the first conclusion, we must again note that Ockhamism expressly denies that persons can change the past. The argument above wrongly assumes that God could have held a false belief initially, and have his past belief retroactively changed to reflect truth after the creature acts. Perhaps it is best to see the Ockhamist solution as a corollary to the Augustinian position. Just as the Augustinian response denies a causal connection between God's beliefs and future creaturely actions, so the Ockhamist response denies a causal connection between the creatures' actions and God's past beliefs. This is why the language is so specific: Creatures have the power to act such that God's past beliefs *would have always been different* from what they indeed were, but that is not the same thing as the power to cause God's past beliefs to be different from *what they actually were*. In the first instance, the actuality of beliefs is still set in the past, whereas in the second, the actuality is changed.[93]

A number of philosophers have suggested that Ockhamism ascribes to individuals a power they are unable to exercise, or at least, will not exercise. Even defenders of the principles undergirding the theory seem

---

93. I see the confusion here as analogous to the debates over libertarian freedom. Some opponents of libertarian freedom have objected to it on coherence grounds, noting that it makes no sense to claim that an individual has power to act otherwise because power to do "otherwise" is conceived in relation to the action that has already taken place, but at the time the individual acts, there is no "other" because there is no fact of the matter regarding how the individual acted. So the language of doing "otherwise" is misleading and confusing, and it appears that the same type of confusion exists here. In saying the creature has the power to act so that God's past beliefs would have been "other," we set his beliefs here in opposition to already established beliefs and, so, the idea seems incoherent. However, as noted, the key to Ockhamism is the claim that they would *always* have been different, and, in that case, the actual beliefs he held would have been actual and the beliefs he did hold would not be "other," but would be "actual." Whether this adds clarity or confusion will be left to the reader. It does, however, serve as an *entre* to the second false conclusion noted above.

to admit this. For example, Talbott suggests that freedom requires power over God's past beliefs, including power to bring it about that God held a different belief at a time earlier than one's action, but he adds a parenthetical note that the power is obviously "unexercised."[94] Adams agrees, noting that "no one will in fact exercise such a power."[95] Although neither Talbott nor Adams claims that the power *cannot* be exercised, their statements that it (definitely) *will not* be exercised imply just that.[96]

But is the power really unexerciseable or never exercised? Perhaps not. Recall that Saunders argues that it is exercised every time an individual acts with libertarian freedom. To be sure, the power to *change* the past would be

---

94. Thomas B. Talbott, "On Divine Foreknowledge and Bringing About the Past," *Philosophy and Phenomenological Research* 46, no. 3 (March 1986): 455–56.

95. Marilyn McCord Adams, "Is the Existence of God a 'Hard' Fact?" *Philosophical Review* 76, no. 4 (1967): 496.

96. An example may clarify this point. In an article defending Ockhamism, Alfred Freddoso entertains the objection that the Ockhamist model allows two contradictory propositions to be true at the same time. For example, suppose the proposition,

David will not be in Chicago at t_2;

is true, but David is free and therefore has the power at t_1 to make it false (by going to Chicago at t_2). If David exercises this power, then the proposition,

David is in Chicago at t_2;

is true at t_1, even though the proposition,

David is not in Chicago at t_2;

was true at all times prior to t_2, but this is absurd if not contradictory! Freddoso responds by claiming that the conclusion does not follow. If David exercises that power, then it was *never* true that David is not in Chicago at t_2, because its being true at every moment prior to t_1 "entails only the [*sic*] one will *in fact* make it the case that its negation was true at every moment before 'T' [t_1]. It does not entail that no one has the power to do so." Freddoso, "Accidental Necessity and Power Over the Past," 65. Freddoso's answer, though, seems to lead to the conclusion that David possesses a power that is unexerciseable, for if David were to exercise the power, then the past would never have been what it in fact was. Thus, there seems to be a sense in which the power ascribed to free agents by Ockhamism is a power that *cannot* be exercised because it leads to a vicious circle. If such power were exercised, then the past would have been different than it in fact was, but then the future action of the creature would not be an exercising of power over the past. According to the example above, it is true at t_1 and at all times prior to t_1 that David will not be in Chicago at t_2, but Ockhamism claims that David has the power to perform an action, A, so that it was always false at t_1 and all times prior to t_1. The problem is that if David were to perform A, then the proposition, *David will not be in Chicago at t_2* would have always been false, and instead the proposition, *David will be in Chicago at t_2* would have always been true, and therefore, at t_2, action A would not be an action which is an exercising of David's power over the past because it would be an action consistent with the past truth of the latter proposition. This is due to the fact that at t_1, the former (*David will not be in Chicago at t_2*) was not true, but instead, the latter (*David will be in Chicago at t_2*) was true. Thus, the power over the past spoken of by Ockhamists cannot be exercised. It seems, though, that an unexerciseable power is no power at all, and therefore, the Ockhamist contention that free agents have power over the truth of some accidentally necessary propositions is incoherent.

unexercisable, but if libertarian freedom is a coherent notion, then it seems to entail just the sort of power Ockhamism proposes. Some may complain that this is begging the question, but it is not. It is only guilty of assuming that propositions about the future can be true.[97] At its heart, this objection wrongly assumes a power to alter the past, but this is not the claim of Ockhamism, and so the criticism fails and Ockhamism prevails.[98]

MOLINISM

A number of philosophers—friends and foes alike—have claimed that Molinism offers a solution to the problem of divine foreknowledge and human freedom that is its own, unique solution on a par with that of the Augustinian, Boethian, and Ockhamist solutions; and, to be sure, Molina thought that he had done so in his work. The belief is so pervase that Molinism commended an entire chapter in Zabzebski's and Craig's scholarly books on the topic, among others.[99]

Fischer has persuasively argued that Molinism provides no such separate answer to the dilemma and instead assumes one.[100] His critique amounts to the claim that Molinism has libertarian freedom built into the counterfactuals God uses in determining (and thereby knowing) the future.[101] While he is correct that Molinism does not provide a "nuts-and-bolts" answer to the question of foreknowledge and free will, he overstates the case when he claims that Molinism adds nothing to the discussion.[102] Molinism affirms the substance of each of the three answers already

97. That assumption is based on the notion of bivalence and/or excluded middle: either a future event will happen or it will not happen. If it does, then statements saying it would happen are shown to have been true and those saying it would not happen are shown to have been false.

98. It assumes that the first proposition (*David will not be in Chicago at t_2*) *was true* prior to David's action, and then was made false by David's action, and it assumes the alternate proposition (*David will be in Chicago at t_2*) *was false* until David's action at t_2, and then its status was changed to being true.

99. To be fair to Craig, as will be seen below, he seems to acknowledge that Molinism is dependent upon Ockhamism, though he still defends Molina's attempts at applying middle knowledge to the problem. Those who have made these claims have rarely, if ever, seriously attempted to explain exactly how Molinism does so. For example, Zagzebski's chapter turns into an extended discussion of the truth of counterfactuals and the grounding objection, and Craig's speaks of middle knowledge merely as the fact of God's knowledge of counterfactuals and its value for his providence.

100. John Martin Fischer, "Putting Molinism in its Place," in *Molinism: The Contemporary Debate*, ed. Kenneth Perszyk (Oxford: Oxford University Press, 2012), 208–26.

101. Fischer writes, "Molinism does not stand on a par with the views of Boethius, Aquinas and Ockham, which are indeed attempts to answer the incompatibilist's worries. At best, the theory of middle knowledge explains how God knows about future contingents, given that he can know about them at all (something it does not seek to address)." Ibid., 216.

102. For example, Fischer argues, "it is (again) important to see that Molinism is *not* doing *any* work in replying to the Basic Argument [against incompatibilism]" or again, "Molinism is playing no role in addressing the Basic Argument." Ibid., 217.

discussed, even if it does not utilize all three in answering the dilemma. Allow me to explain.

Molina himself was skeptical of the timelessness answer to the dilemma, as he conceived of it as claiming that events occur in eternity prior to their occurrence in time, and he thought that would destroy their contingency; they would be determined. Fischer is correct that Molina assumed libertarian freedom of creatures and simply built it into his model via counterfactuals of freedom. Some may complain that this simply begs the question of the compatibility of foreknowledge and freedom, and in a sense, they are correct, but it is not problematic, for each of the other answers to foreknowledge and free will also *beg the question* in the same or similar ways. The timelessness answer still asserts that there is a truth about what the agent will do and that, in fact, the agent freely acts in eternity *before* he does so in time. It is the agent's free act in eternity that affords God his foreknowledge of the event.[103] Ockhamism begs the question regarding the contingency of God's past beliefs about future contingents. So the Molinist position can be accused of begging the question but this should not be a cause for concern.

Ironically, underlying this complaint is a question-begging rejection of libertarian freedom (or rejection of there being truths about libertarianly free actions prior to their occurrence). If having libertarian freedom built into the structure of counterfactuals is not allowed, the grounding objection has been assumed, and all talk of determinate truth regarding future free actions must be abandoned, for the same assumptions sit at the heart of the rejection of the divine timelessness and Ockhamist solutions. If Molinism is guilty of the assumption of divine foreknowledge and libertarian freedom, that is okay; both have a strong position in the history of the church. The burden of proof is on the detractors to demonstrate that they are either incoherent notions, or false, or incompatible.[104]

Molinism makes use of the Augustinianism view when speaking of God's middle knowledge of creaturely actions, but not middle knowledge of his own. If God had middle knowledge of his own actions, then he would not be free, but his middle knowledge of creaturely actions does not destroy their freedom. This is not a contradiction, because God's knowledge of others' actions is not causative, while prior knowledge of his own actions would preclude the exercising of his will (or would stand in danger of his being wrong).

---

103. I recognize that modern proponents of the model take great pains to speak of *simultaneity* between events in time and eternity, but the fact remains that if God's knowledge of an event as it occurs in eternity affords him *foreknowledge* (that is, knowledge of an event prior to its occurrence in time), then the event's occurring in eternity prior to its occurring in time is unavoidable.

104. See my paper, "On Molinism, Question Begging, and Foreknowledge of Indeterminates," paper presented at Randomness and Foreknowledge Conference, Dallas, TX, October 25, 2014.

Craig notes that Molina rejected the Ockhamist solution, largely because he saw it as the claim that God has power to change the past or bring about a past that is different from the past that was actual. Yet Craig also points out that Molina's own solution seems to make use of the principles underlying the current understanding of Ockhamism. After all, if the opposite really is able to occur, as Molina himself admits, then it seems clear that God's foreknowledge is able to have been different.[105] This is the point I have made here. All proponents of libertarian freedom who hold to divine foreknowledge must tacitly endorse the principles of Ockhamism. This can be seen in Molina's own answer to the objection that middle knowledge leads to Fatalism because if God foreknows x will happen, then x will happen necessarily because there is no power over the past. Molina maintains that what God now knows cannot be changed, and the future event remains contingent. The future event will obtain as God knows it will obtain, but it could have been otherwise, and if it were otherwise, God would have always known that. Similarly, Molina argues that God's foreknowledge is certain, and a foreknown event will certainly occur, but this does not mean the future event is not able to not-occur. In both of these affirmations, then, Molina suggests counterfactual power over the past.

Molinism also makes use of the timelessness view of divine eternity as a way of explaining logical priority in the divine decision-making process while avoiding the problems associated with temporal priority. Molinists must hold to this view of divine eternity in order to avoid Hasker's claim that God's use of counterfactuals of creaturely freedom are part of the world's causal history and thus, deterministic. God's consideration of the counterfactuals of freedom is not part of the world's history because it is a timeless act.

CONCLUSION

While Craig has surely overstated the case when he concludes "Molina's reconciliation of divine foreknowledge and future contingency is thus a very novel and provocative one," Fischer's claim that Molinism adds nothing to the discussion of divine foreknowledge and human freedom because it depends upon the Ockhamist concept of counterfactual power over the past and upon the Augustinian claim that foreknowledge is not

---

105. Craig writes, "Unfortunately, Molina then confuses the issue by concluding that given what God foreknows, He is not able to bring it about that he knew otherwise. But the question is not whether the retrocausal account is viable; the issue is whether, given the fact that the future event is able not to occur, God's foreknowledge, in virtue of His middle knowledge, is not also able to be different. . . . Should Molina not have held in the same way that God's foreknowledge, in the composed sense (that is, given the content of His middle knowledge), is not able to be otherwise, but that it, in the divided sense (that is, taken in abstraction from middle knowledge), is able to be otherwise?" Craig, *The Problem of Divine Foreknowledge and Future Contingents*, 189.

causative, is surely incorrect.[106] Molinism does add something to our understanding of divine foreknowledge that the others do not have, for it explains how God knows future contingents contingently while retaining divine freedom. Divine timelessness as an explanation of God's knowledge of the future seems to compromise his freedom, and Ockhamism offers no insight into how God knows the actual future. Molinism provides the most robust model of providence that contributes significantly to our understanding of how God may know the future—even a future where creatures sometimes act with libertarian freedom.

---

106. Ibid., 198.

CHAPTER 5

PREDESTINATION AND SALVATION

INTRODUCTION

For evangelical Christians, perhaps more than anyone else, soteriology, or the doctrine of salvation, serves as the primary focus of concern to the faith. For good or ill, most other doctrines—arguably even Theology Proper (doctrine of God) and Christology (doctrine of Christ)—are examined with a view to how they clarify our understanding of salvation. This should not be surprising, since the good news of the Gospel has to do with the salvation effected in Christ.

ATONEMENT

Soteriology involves a number of issues, from questions related to the nature and purpose of the creation generally and humanity specifically, to God's relationship with humanity taken corporately in his kingdom generally and covenants specifically, and taken individually with respect to personal guilt and forgiveness. Central to Christian soteriology is the cross of Christ, and when theologians speak of the cross, they most often mean to refer to atonement theory, or how Christ reconciles man to God. As Stott has said, "All inadequate doctrines of the atonement are due to inadequate doctrines of God and man."[1] There are several atonement theories; the six most prominent will be briefly surveyed in a generally historical order.

Release from Evil Powers/Ransom to Satan

One of the earliest atonement theories emphasized the release believers experience from malevolent powers, conceived either in terms of death (Rom. 5:14; 8:2ff.) and sin (John 8:34; Rom. 7), or the Devil (John 12:31; Eph. 2:2). The theory usually incorporates the language of payment/purchase and redemption (1 Cor. 6:20; Matt. 20:28; Mark 10:45), as well

---

1. John R. W. Stott, *The Cross of Christ* (Downers Grove, IL: IVP, 1986), 109.

as Christ's defeat of those evil powers. It has thus been referred to variously as the *Christus Victor*, Patristic, Classic, or Ransom to Satan theory.

Irenaeus of Lyons (ca. AD 140–202) seems to have been the first to articulate a theory of the atonement. His theory is normally associated with the concept of recapitulation and the principle that *whatever God assumes is saved*.[2] In recapitulation, Christ has reworked those elements that led to the enslavement of humanity to sin, death, and the devil, and has fixed them in the incarnation, releasing humanity from that slavery.[3]

Perhaps the most dominant approach to the theme of release was to conceive of it as a payment or ransom paid to Satan. Gregory of Nyssa is representative of this viewpoint. According to Gregory, humanity sold itself into slavery (to Satan) by giving in to passion and lust, and God's justice requires that he pay a price that Satan is willing to take for its rescue. The ransom paid would have to be more valuable than what was held, and since Christ is more valuable than humanity, if Satan were to take Jesus for men, he would gain. Yet because the Son was incarnate, Satan mistakenly thought he could contain him.[4] Satan is described as a fish, caught when it goes for the bait. His own lust/hunger leads to his destruction. Jesus broke the hold Satan had on him by resurrection from the dead. Thus, Satan lost both humanity and Christ.

This method of saving humanity, Gregory argues, demonstrates God's goodness, wisdom, and justice all at once. He anticipates some of the later objections, noting those who are concerned that God is portrayed as a deceiver make a category error. Instead of questioning the honesty of God, we should examine the justice and wisdom of the action. On both counts, God is found true. The action is just because it is giving Satan both what he is due and the same consideration he gave to humanity (tricked Eve). The action is wise because it is driven by love for humanity.

Satisfaction

The second approach to atonement is most often called the Satisfaction theory. Tertullian (ca. AD 155–225) may have anticipated this theory when

---

2. See, in particular, Irenaeus, *Against Heresies* 18.6–7.

3. This approach to understanding salvation was determinative in the Christological controversies of the fourth and fifth centuries, but was never widely held as the primary way God has saved humanity in Christ.

4. Gregory speculates that Satan could not behold the Son apart from the flesh of Jesus, and this led him to believe he could take the man Jesus as "ransom." He writes, "But it was out of his power to look on the unclouded aspect of God; he must see in Him some portion of that fleshly nature which through sin he had so long held in bondage. Therefore it was that the Deity was invested with the flesh, in order, that is, to secure that he, by looking upon something congenial and kindred to himself, might have no fears in approaching that supereminent power; and might yet by perceiving that power, showing as it did, yet only gradually, more and more splendour in the miracles, deem what was seen an object of desire rather than of fear." Gregory of Nyssa, *The Great Catechism*, in *Nicene and Post-Nicene Fathers*, Second Series, vol. 5: *Gregory of Nyssa: Dogmatic Treatises, etc.* (Peabody, MA: Hendrickson, 1994), 493.

he spoke of the cross as a motivator for ethical conduct and repentance as compensatory toward God.[5] Later, Anselm, the Archbishop of Canterbury (AD 1033–1109), developed the concept of satisfaction more fully. He found the idea of God paying Satan repugnant, as he believed the glory, honor, and power of God preclude him from being beholden to anyone. He also doubted Satan has legitimate power over humanity and thus concluded that payment language in salvation refers to God paying himself.

Anselm's view is based in the idea that all men, in sinning, have failed to give God the honor and glory he deserves.[6] God's holiness and justice require that his offended honor be restored by humanity (who offended it), but no man can do so because all have taken some away, and all honor is due God. In addition, since the creation is in need of redemption, satisfaction must be made by someone greater than all things, because the payment must be greater than what it redeems, but nothing is greater than everything that exists except God. This results in a dilemma: a debt is owed by humans, but only God can satisfy it, and he cannot simply forgive sin without payment because his holiness and justice require that his honor be satisfied. Since it is man that sinned and must make satisfaction, but only God can do so, satisfaction *must* be made by a God-man (*the* God-man). Anselm writes, "If it be necessary, therefore, as it appears, that the heavenly kingdom be made up of men, and this cannot be effected unless the aforesaid satisfaction be made, which none but God can make and none but man ought to make, it is necessary for the God-man to make it."[7]

Moral Influence

Peter Abelard (AD 1079–1142) argued for what has come to be called the Moral Influence theory of the atonement. He claims that the primary attribute of God is love, and that this supreme love is demonstrated in the incarnation and passion of Jesus. This leads to a faith and love response from humanity resulting in reconciliation. This view is best understood as a reaction against Anselm's satisfaction theory. Abelard complained that Anselm's approach does not adequately address the love of God so central to the cross, and instead relies on sheer logic. He also thinks the Satisfaction theory is confused and an offense to God's justice.[8]

---

5. Tertullian appropriated the term, "satisfaction," from Roman law in order to describe the penitent activity: it pays God back for his work in salvation. In other words, Tertullian sees the cross as leading individuals to repent, which serves as a sort of legal transaction in which God is repaid something that he paid on behalf of sinners, or that he lost as a result of sinful activity (it is not clear which Tertullian has in mind).

6. He sees acts of disobedience as fundamentally the result of an improper attitude whereby God is not given the respect due him.

7. Anselm, *Cur Deus Homo* 2.6, in *St. Anselm: Basic Writings*, trans. S. N. Deane, 2nd ed. (La Salle, IL: Open Court, 1962), 259.

8. He complained that it makes no sense to claim that Original Sin requires the death of Christ because the murder of Christ seems to be a greater sin than the sin of Adam. If Adam's eating

So, in answer to the question, "Why did the Son have to die?" Abelard seems to answer, "in order to fully identify with humanity."[9] In Jesus's identification with humanity, an example to be followed was given, but it is the demonstration of divine love that objectively changes our dispositions towards God by a work of the Holy Spirit in our hearts. He elicits a love response to God, and it is *here* that the atonement finds expression: "Wherefore, our redemption through Christ's suffering is that deeper affection in us which not only frees us from slavery to sin, but also wins for us the true liberty of sons of God, so that we do all things out of love rather than fear—love to him who has shown us such grace that no greater can be found, as he himself asserts, saying, 'Greater love than this no man hath, that a man lay down his life for his friends.'"[10] So the Moral Influence theory includes both subjective and objective elements.

Penal Substitution

The view of the atonement most popular among evangelical Christians has been the Penal Substitution theory. At its most basic, the theory sees Christ's death as the means by which the Son took upon himself the punishment of death that humans rightly deserve as a result of their sins. Jesus was punished (penal) in our place (substitution).[11] Demarest rightly describes it:

> According to this view sin, which is primarily a violation of God's law, not his honor, results in the just penalty of death. But in love Jesus Christ, our substitute, in his *life* perfectly fulfilled the law and in *death* bore the just penalty for our sins. Expressed otherwise, on the cross Christ took our place and bore the equivalent punishment for our sins, thereby satisfying the just

---

the forbidden fruit requires the sacrifice of the Son of God, then what penalty can be required for the murder of Jesus, the innocent Son of God? According to Abelard, there is no good answer. More importantly, though, Abelard complains that the requirement of the death of an innocent for the crimes of others is unjust; it speaks against the fairness and goodness of God himself! According to Abelard, Jesus showed us how to live in complete obedience to the Father, and demonstrated God's love for us (in that he condescended to us in the Incarnation), but his death was not compensatory. So when Abelard says that Christ's death is expiatory, he means that in his subjection to death, the Son showed his obedience to the Father and his love for humanity.

9. A fundamental aspect of human existence—of that which we hope to be saved from—is mortality. If Jesus were to not really die, then he would not have fully identified with the human condition, and since it was the Father's will that the Son should do so, obedience to the Father's will required subjection to death on the cross.

10. Peter Abailard, *Exposition of the Epistle to the Romans*, trans. Gerald E. Moffait, *A Scholastic Miscellany: Anselm to Ockham*, ed. Eugene R. Fairweather (Philadelphia: Westminster, 1956), 283–84.

11. The penal substitutionary view is a development of the satisfaction motif. Like the satisfaction theory, it is based on the idea that some form of satisfaction is required by man, but no mere human can pay. Unlike the satisfaction theory, it sees sin primarily as active—a violation of God's law and an affront to his holiness—and this incurs the just wrath of God.

> demands of the law and appeasing God's wrath. As repentant sinners appro-
> priate Christ's vicarious sacrifice by faith, God forgives sins, imputes Christ's
> righteousness, and reconciles the estranged to himself.[12]

Since all persons have sinned and have corrupt natures as a result of the
Fall, all persons stand under condemnation. The Old Testament sacrificial
system points to the means by which the wrath of God is appeased; the
proper punishment for sin is death (Rom. 6:23), and God may be propitiated by the shedding of blood of an innocent in place of the guilty party.
This is exactly what the New Testament claims of Christ (Heb. 9:22). He
died in the place of guilty humanity and averted the wrath of God from
those who are united with him through faith.

John Calvin, who clearly set forth the Penal Substitutionary view,
noted that the transactional nature of the atonement points not only to
an averting of divine wrath in the death of Christ, but also a transfer of
guilt from sinners to Christ, as well as a transfer of his righteousness to
those who trust in him by faith. Calvin also saw significance in the means
of Christ's condemnation: he was condemned as guilty by a human court,
which points to the judicial nature of his death, yet he was proclaimed
innocent by Pilate, which points to the fact that he died in the place of
others. The means of Christ's death is also significant: The cross was cursed
(in the opinion of men and by God's Law), which points to the transfer of
guilt; Christ became sin for sinful humanity (Gal. 3:13).

Calvin is quick to point out that, while the cross removed our guilt,
there is more to salvation than mere forgiveness. The power of death also
had to be defeated since all humans remain in its grasp. Christ conquered
it by first allowing himself to be subject to it and then by resurrecting from
the dead. On the cross, Christ endured the spiritual death that we faced as
a result of sin; he experienced the wrath and judgment of God, but in the
resurrection, he was vindicated, and conquered the physical effects of the
Fall. Calvin rightly notes that death and resurrection cannot be properly
divided in the work of Christ. They are so closely tied, so closely associated, that when one speaks of the death of Christ or of the cross, the
resurrection is included automatically. Calvin ends his discussion with a
summary that is worth quoting at length:

> We see that our whole salvation and all its parts are comprehended in Christ
> (Acts 4:12). We should therefore take care not to derive the least portion
> of it from anywhere else. If we seek salvation, we are taught by the very
> name of Jesus that it is "of him" (1 Cor. 1:30). If we seek any other gifts of
> the Spirit, they will be found in his anointing. If we seek strength, it lies in
> his dominion; if purity, in his conception; if gentleness, it appears in his
> birth. For by his birth he was made like us in all respects (Heb. 2:17) that he

---

12. Bruce Demarest, *The Cross and Salvation* (Wheaton, IL: Crossway, 2006), 158–59.

might learn to feel our pain (cf. Heb. 5:2). If damnation, we seek redemption, it lies in his person; if acquittal, in his condemnation; if remission of the curse, in his cross (Gal. 3:13); if satisfaction, in his sacrifice; if purification, in his blood; if reconciliation, in his descent into hell; if mortification of the flesh, in his tomb; if newness of life, in his resurrection; if immortality, in the same; if inheritance of the Heavenly Kingdom, in his entrance into heaven; if protection, if security, if abundant supply of all blessings, in his Kingdom; if untroubled expectation of judgment, in the power given to him to judge. In short, rich store of every kind of good abounds in him, let us drink our fill from this fountain, and from no other. Some men, not content with him alone, are borne hither and thither from one hope to another; even if they concern themselves chiefly with him, they nevertheless stray from the right way in turning some part of their thinking in another direction. Yet such distrust cannot creep in where men have once for all truly known the abundance of his blessings.[13]

Example

The Example view of the atonement, the idea that Jesus showed humans how to rightly live in proper relationship to God, has been referenced throughout the history of the church, but has always been associated with defective views of Christ, sin, or salvation. For example, the earliest example theory relied upon a Pelagian view of the sin nature, and argued that humans have the capacity to live without sin in order to obtain eternal life. The revival of the Example theory in the post-Reformation era among the followers of Faustus Socinus (i.e., Socinians) incorporated an Arian Christology (view that Jesus was the divine Son of God, but not fully deity like the Father), along with adoptionist elements (view that Jesus was made the Son of God sometime after his birth, usually at his baptism). At their most basic, they reject the sacrificial interpretation of the cross and any objective atonement on the part of God.[14] Emphasis is placed on Jesus's

---

13. Calvin, *Institutes of the Christian Religion* 2.16.19 (trans. Battles, 527–28).

14. The Socinians reacted against the Satisfaction theory of the atonement, calling it "false, erroneous, and exceedingly pernicious." First, they accuse those who hold to satisfaction of poor exegesis, claiming that the Bible makes no mention of such a scheme. Instead, they claim that proponents of Anselm's view string unbiblical inferences together and call it an argument. Second, they challenge the concept of *satisfaction*, arguing that it violates grace; for salvation to be *by grace*, it must be given freely, but if a payment is made, grace is not given freely, and hence, ceases to be grace. Of course, the heretical view of the person of Christ contributes to this conception, for the possibility of the creditor paying the debt himself is not entertained. Thus, the Father's requirement of payment is seen as an abrogation of grace precisely because the payment is made by *another* (i.e., the Son). Third, they claim that the Satisfaction theory is logically flawed on several counts. For example, they question the claim that the death of one can pay for the deaths of many. One eternal death could only pay for one eternal damnation. So, Jesus's death could only pay for one sinner, not all, and if it is argued that all eternal deaths can be paid by Jesus because he is divine and therefore, infinite, a problem arises. For the infinity of the Son to be applied to the payment made, the divinity of the Son had

faithful obedience to the Father, and sinners are reconciled to God by emulating that faith/obedience.

Redemption is reinterpreted as liberation from sin and punishment.[15] Jesus's death is salvific, but not as a payment to the Father in order to satisfy offended honor, avert wrath, or any such thing. Rather, Christ's obedience to God leads to his glorification and exaltation by God, and in the same way, we may also be glorified if we follow his example of love, purity, faithfulness, and piety, *even unto death*. Thus, Example views of the atonement fall short (because they fail to account for human depravity and offer works-based approaches to salvation).

Governmental

The Governmental view of the atonement was developed by Hugo Grotius in defense of the Penal Substitution theory against the Example view of the Socinians, although it has since been viewed as a distinct theory. Grotius' legal training as a jurist greatly influenced his thought. His primary concern is to preserve the justice of God against the attacks of the Socinians and to explore its implications for understanding the cross in light of a penal substitutionary model. Grotius contends that there were two key purposes for the death of Christ: the preservation of divine justice, and the exemption of humans from the punishment for sin. He conceives of God as a benevolent ruler whose primary concern is the administration of justice and law in order to benefit his subjects whom he loves.

Grotius begins by considering the relationship between God's nature and law. Whereas the Penal Substitution theory, at least as advanced by Calvin, views the law as a perfect expression of God's nature such that he must punish sin with death (shedding blood), Grotius argues that only lawfulness is tied to God's nature as just, and any particular expression of law is subject to the divine will. The point that Grotius hopes to make is that the law is not something intrinsic and he is not obligated to it. If

---

to make the payment (i.e., suffer eternal death). The Socinians see the idea of God dying/suffering as incoherent. Similarly, they argue that the Satisfaction theory promotes more love of Christ than of God, for God seems bent on injuring us, while Christ seems to love us, but this is distorted. Fourth, they complain that the Satisfaction theory promotes sin because it claims that future sins are already forgiven, thus removing the disincentive to sin. Last, they charge that the Satisfaction theory improperly conceives of God's attributes in opposition; his mercy and justice seem to war against one another. Ultimately, they claim, these attributes are misconstrued: "For what is that justice, and what too that mercy, which punishes the innocent, and absolves the guilty?," *The Racovian Catechism* 5.8, trans. Thomas Rees (London: Longman, Horst, Rees, Orme & Brown, 1818), 308.

15. So, we may speak of man as captive to sins *themselves* (sin, the world, the devil, and death), and we may speak of God and Christ as the redeemer(s), and we may also speak of the ransom price as Christ (or his soul), but this is not properly a redemption (purchasing): "The only difference lies here, that in this deliverance of us from our sins themselves, no one receives anything under the name of ransom, which must always happen in a redemption properly so called." *Racovian Catechism* 5.8, 314.

the law were intrinsic to God, then he would be mutable and if he were obligated to it, the law would be greater than he. Grotius writes, "The law is not something internal within God, or the will of God itself, but only an effect of that will. It is perfectly certain that the effects of the divine will are mutable. By promulgating a positive law which at some time he may wish to relax God does not signify that he wills anything but what he really does will."[16]

So, Grotuis distinguishes different ways God administers his laws: some are abrogated, some are relaxed, some are immutable. For example, the dietary and ceremonial laws were abrogated, and are no longer binding on Jews, while those promises of God sealed with an oath (e.g., promise to bless Abraham) can never be changed because God is faithful. The principle which states that sinners will be punished with everlasting death can be relaxed (and even abrogated) if God so chooses, and this does not speak against his justice. Still, Grotius argues, any relaxation of penal law has the potential to undermine the authority of the law and the perceived power of the Lawgiver: "It is common to all laws that in relaxing, the authority of the law seems to be diminished in some respects."[17]

The law that sinners should be punished seems to be *naturally* true and, therefore, is not to be relaxed without *very* good reasons, and of course, very good reasons can be given: If all sinners were punished with everlasting punishment, then human reverence, love, and worship of God—along with divine favor of humans—would cease. Very good reasons also exist for executing punishment for sin. First, God wanted to demonstrate how greatly sin displeases him, expressed in wrath. Second, the fear of punishment is an important preventive measure against sin. And third, stability requires consistency; if punishment is threatened but not carried out, anarchy ensues.

Ultimately, God chose to forgive the sins of humanity because of his great love, but the means by which he chose to do so is the way that most clearly demonstrates his nature as just, loving, merciful, and holy. That is, God chose to redeem us because of his love, and he chose the way that would reveal himself most clearly and comprehensively. Grotius writes:

> But because among all his attributes love of the human race is pre-eminent, God was willing, though he could have justly punished the sins of all men with deserved and legitimate punishment, that is, with eternal death, and had reasons for so doing, to spare those who believe in Christ. But since we must be spared either by setting forth, or not setting forth, some example against so many great sins, in his most perfect wisdom he chose that way by

---

16. Hugo Grotius, *A Defence of the Catholic Faith Concerning the Satisfaction of Christ, against Faustus Socinus*, trans. Frank Hugh Foster (Andover, MA: Warren F. Draper, 1889), 75.
17. Ibid., 79.

which he could manifest more of his attributes at once, viz. both clemency and severity, or his hate of sin and care for the preservation of his law.[18]

Grotius summarizes his thought by pointing to the incarnation and crucifixion as the ultimate expression of God's love. We were spared by One who thought (thinks) sin should be punished, so much so, that he gave his only Son for our sins! He writes, "So may we say with emphasis of this divine grace. It is *above* law, because we are not punished; *for* law, because punishment is not omitted; and remission is granted that we may live hereafter *to* the divine law."[19]

Assessment

Increasingly, evangelical scholars are recognizing that most atonement theories have some truth and are not mutually exclusive, but complimentary. For example, Oden writes,

> The satisfaction and Christus Victor themes come closer to being consensual approaches (in the tradition of the [*sic*] Irenaeus, the Cappadocians, Augustine, Anselm, and Calvin) than the others. All four need some corrective voices from the others to form an adequate teaching. They are best viewed as complimentary. The scriptural and ecumenical teaching of atonement requires a good balance of the moral nature of man, moral government of God, the substitution of Christ for us in our place, and the consequent victory of Christ over demonic powers."[20]

Erickson places emphasis upon penal substitution as the overriding theory and sees the others as subordinate, but he does not see them as competitors.[21]

It is probably best to view the different theories as addressing different concerns or answering different questions about how Jesus secured our salvation in the cross. The Release from Evil Powers/*Christus Victor* model speaks to the effect of Jesus's crucifixion and resurrection from a more eschatological focus; it secured the ultimate defeat of the power of sin, evil, and death. The Satisfaction theory speaks to the necessity of the incarnation and the impossibility of a merely human salvation, why works-based approaches to salvation cannot work. The Moral Influence theory speaks to the Christian life, how the cross communicates the immense love of God for humanity and how reflection on who Christ is and what he did should inspire us to love God more and serve him more faithfully. The Example theory invites consideration of Jesus's life and moral teachings so

18. Ibid.,107.
19. Ibid., 110.
20. Thomas C. Oden, *The Word of Life* (San Francisco: HarperCollins, 1989), 414.
21. Millard Erickson, *Christian Theology*, 3rd ed. (Grand Rapids: Baker, 2013), 748–52.

that we may know what faithful obedience looks like. The Penal Substitution model speaks to the mechanics of the crucifixion. It is the primary atonement theory among evangelicals because it most fully addresses the biblical account of how salvation works in the cross. The Governmental theory speaks to broader theological questions than how God secured salvation in the cross, moving instead to questions about whether salvation could have conceivably been different, and to how the nature of God is related to the way salvation works. Thus, one does not have to choose one atonement theory to the exclusion of the others; he can maintain that Christ's death propitiated the wrath of God by paying the penalty for humanity's sin and thus setting men free from the power of sin and death, while also claiming that God could have conceivably effected salvation another way, if he so chose.

Suppose God determined that setting up a formal system wherein forgiveness is effected through the shedding of blood would most fully realize his purposes for creation, whether those purposes were to maximize his glory (perhaps the most popular suggestion) or to most clearly reveal himself to humanity, or to maximize the number of persons saved/ratio of saved to lost, or something similar. Whatever his goal or goals (and they are not necessarily mutually exclusive), it seems that if it/they involved the free decisions of persons, a Molinist analysis makes most sense.[22] Under the Open Theist and Process models, God's choice to save humanity by means of an incarnation, crucifixion, and resurrection may not reach his ultimate goal(s) for the creation.[23] Under determinist

---

22. Presumably under a Molinist interpretation, God would make use of a counterfactual of creaturely freedom very much like the following in order to decide what sort of world to make, who to save, and how to meet his desired ends:

    If God were to create beings in his image and were to invite them to enjoy fellowship with him, they would freely choose to sin and incur his just wrath, and if in these circumstances, God were to choose to establish lawful order whereby sin can only be forgiven by the shedding of blood and he were then to pay the price himself for the sins of humanity by dying on the cross, so that his mercy and justice and holiness were clearly revealed, then the greatest number of humans will freely respond in faith and love to God's offer of salvation.

    In addition, as will be seen in the chapter on science and creation, it also allows God to ensure that his goals are met through those free decisions, while still allowing the theologian to claim that God could have (at least conceivably) chosen to do things another way.

23. First, God cannot know that if he were to create humans, they would Fall. Many Open Theists have suggested that the Fall required God to react in a way that changed directions. Second, the God of Open Theism cannot know that if Christ were to die on the cross and rise from the dead, it would have the desired effect(s). Many Open Theists doubt that the cross was not in God's original plan/purposes for creation. In a particularly illuminating moment, John Sanders suggests that the cross was not in God's original plan and was an adjustment in order to meet the problem of sin. Sanders claims that God willed for Christ to die for humanity and that he was as sure as one can be that the Jewish leadership would have Christ crucified, but there is still an air of uncertainty in God's knowledge regarding atonement, and the death of Jesus on behalf of sinners appears to be an instance of what Sanders elsewhere

models (Calvinist or Fatalist), God's choice to save humanity by means of an incarnation, crucifixion, and resurrection will reach his ultimate goal(s) for the creation, but other problems surface: either God's freedom is compromised or the crucifixion seems capricious.[24]

The Molinist may claim that God could have possibly effected his plan in another way, and that God's plan will meet its ultimate goal. If there is any draw of the Governmental theory for the individual Christian theologian, if he finds something wanting in the claim that God had to save humanity by means of an incarnation due to something inherent in the nature of the way things are (including God's nature), if he believes God chose to save humanity this way but could possibly have done so another way (or not at all), then the Molinist account of soteriology (at least atonement theory) will be most attractive.

SOTERIOLOGY

Most evangelical discussions of soteriology tend to focus on the individual: individual guilt, individual faith, individual forgiveness, and individual destiny for eternity. It has become almost axiomatic to reference the foci of the infamous "five points" [of Calvinism], represented by the acronym, TULIP: (T)otal Depravity, (U)nconditional Election, (L)imited

---

refers to as "Plan B." Sanders makes many references to "Plan B" as a way of speaking of God's dynamic relationship with his plan for the created order, and plan that is in constant revision in response to changing (and unforeseen) circumstances. See for example, Sanders, *The God Who Risks*, 58, 64, 231. Sanders writes, "The more traditional view, that the incarnation was not planned until after God learned (in his foreknowledge) about the Fall, implies that although Christ may *now* be the decisive turning point for human history, he was not so in God's original plan. Hence, a major readjustment in God's purposes must be posited in that the incarnation becomes a *contingent* matter (contra supralapsarianism). My own view is that the incarnation was always planned. Human sin, however, threw up a barrier to the divine project, and God's planned incarnation had to be adapted in order to overcome it." Ibid., 103.

In addition, the Openness interpretation suggests that God could not know that the greatest number of humans will freely respond in faith, and this calls God's rationality into question. If the cross is reactionary and done in some ignorance of the consequences, then it seems unwise, extreme, and kneejerk for him to offer his son as a sacrifice when he has no assurance it will achieve the desired result. Even if he has good reason to think that his sacrifice will achieve the results he desires, we would probably see the offer as premature; after all, we should expect that all other potential salvific actions be attempted first, just in case there were a less costly means by which salvation could be secured.

24. Calvinism sometimes struggles with offering a good answer to the question, "Why did Christ have to die on the cross?" If, on the one hand, the answer given makes appeal to the satisfaction motif and draws upon God's nature and the Fall to argue that the cross was necessary, then God's freedom seems compromised. If, on the other hand, the answer given refers to God's free sovereign choice and appeals to mystery, then the action seems unnecessary. In other words, if God can illicit faith responses in humans by a sheer act of his will without reference to external circumstances, if God creates faith in persons by unilaterally (monergism) regenerating them and irresistibly graciously creating faith in them, then it seems that he should be able to do so without an incarnation and subsequent crucifixion.

Atonement, (I)rresistable Grace, and (P)erseverance of the Saints, even though they are now almost universally acknowledged to be ahistorical (in terms of the Synod of Dordrecht) and somewhat misleading.[25] Still, they nicely raise important issues for consideration. Several of the topics represented in the acronym will be addressed here, primarily with respect to how Molinism may add clarity to the discussion.

Human Depravity

Christian theologians have universally agreed that there were adverse effects of Adam's sin upon all of humanity; when theologians refer to the "Fall," they typically mean to refer to those effects and not merely to Adam's initial sin.[26] While there has been some debate regarding the physical ramifications of the Fall (i.e., whether or not it literally led to the physical deaths of Adam and Eve and their progeny), what has been of particular interest to theologians has been the effects of the Fall upon the spiritual condition of humanity. At the dawn of the Protestant Reformation, Martin Luther and Desiderius Erasmus engaged in a spirited debate over the nature of free will and man's ability, as it were, to respond positively to God's free offer of salvation. As noted in the introduction, Luther doggedly refused human ability to not only earn salvation, but to perform actions deemed "good" or "godly." He argued that sin has so infected man that he always chooses evil and never chooses the good, and that even actions that appear good on the outside, are sinful: "it is plain that no man is brought any nearer to righteousness by his works; and what is more, that no works and no aspirations or endeavors of free choice count for anything in the sight of God, but all are adjudged to be ungodly, unrighteous, and evil . . . if they are not righteous, they are damnable and deserving of wrath."[27]

Likewise, John Calvin argued that man, unaided by God's grace, cannot repent of his sins and believe the gospel. This claim, in and of itself, was not particularly controversial, as even Erasmus admitted as much and all Protestants have agreed, but Calvin and his followers took it to mean that the aid rendered by God enabling men to believe the gospel had to be rebirth. That is, Calvinism argues that persons must be born anew in order

---

25. Stewart does a nice job of tracing the acronym's "shadowy history," and calling its continued use into question. Kenneth Stewart, *Ten Myths About Calvinism: Recovering the Breadth of the Reformed Tradition* (Downers Grove, IL: IVP, 2011), 79. See in particular, chapter 3, "TULIP Is the Yardstick of the Truly Reformed," and the Appendix, "The Earliest Known Reference to the TULIP Acronym." Ibid., 75–96, 291–92. Limited atonement will not be addressed here, largely because it is a contentious issue, even among Calvinists. In fact, there is good reason to think that Calvin himself did not hold to it.

26. The term, "Fall," refers to both Adam's specific act of disobedience in eating the forbidden fruit and the negative effects of that sin upon the creation generally and humanity specifically.

27. Martin Luther, "The Bondage of the Will," in *Martin Luther's Basic Theological Writings*, ed. Timothy F. Lull (Minneapolis: Fortress, 1989), 201.

to believe; faith comes as a result of regeneration. As will be addressed further in the discussion of *ordo salutis* in chapter 9, this belief has proven rather controversial, and a number of Protestant groups (and not a few Catholics) have rejected it. These issues cut to the heart of the doctrine of salvation, by raising questions related to the nature of election, predestination, faith, and reconciliation.

Sovereign Election

The doctrine of election refers to God's choice of a person or group of persons to receive some form of blessing, most importantly, salvation. Closely related to this is the concept of predestination, which refers to God's determination *beforehand* (before the person exists, before his creative act, before any conditions are met) to grant salvation to the individual or group. While it is clear from Scripture that God's election extends to the nation of Israel (cf. Deut. 7:6–8; Isa. 4:8–9; Rom. 11) through Abraham and the various covenants following (Abrahamic, Mosaic, Davidic), most commonly in evangelical circles the concern has to do with particular persons being predestined for salvation prior to their being born. The Bible makes it clear that Christians were elected and predestined for salvation in Christ, and that this election is a pure act of God's graciousness and love (Rom. 9:11–12; Eph. 1:4–6). What is not so clear is whether (or not) non-Christians were elected and predestined for condemnation apart from Christ, and whether (or not) this has any negative consequences for the doctrine of God or one's system of theology and providence. What is also not so clear is the basis of the election of the saved; Calvinists and Molinists often disagree here.

Excursus on reprobation

The question of so-called "double predestination," of whether God predestines some (most) to Hell while predestining some (few) to Heaven has plagued discussions of election from the earliest years of the church. It has often stood as a criticism of Calvinist soteriology because, it is argued, the stronger determining activity of God in one's coming to faith suggests that God's election to salvation is capricious and necessarily entails an election to reprobation, an act that seems more hateful than loving.[28] As Olson writes:

> How is God love if he foreordains many people to Hell for eternity when he could save them because election to salvation is always completely

---

28.   After all, so the argument goes, if God can save all persons and he is by nature loving and gracious, and if saving persons just is an act of grace and love, then it seems that he ought to save all. The fact is that in *choosing* some for salvation, he necessarily *chooses* the others for condemnation, and therefore, Calvinist election results in a double-predestination, a result that is inherently unloving and contrary to the revelation of God in the Bible.

unconditional and has nothing to do with character or choices? How is it that God wants all people to be saved if he determines some specific individuals to be damned? How is it that God has no pleasure in the death of the wicked (Ezek. 18:32) if he foreordains everything, including their reprobation and eternal punishment, for his good pleasure? How is God good if he purposefully withheld from Adam the grace he needed not to fall—knowing that Adam's fall would result in the horrors of sin and evil and innocent suffering of history?[29]

While a more in-depth examination of the issues undergirding these concerns can be found in the next chapter, a few words are in order. First, most Calvinist authors reject the supposition that God is somehow obligated, as a result of his loving and gracious nature, to save all (or any!). Rather, they rightly argue that God's saving any is gracious in itself, and correctly assume that the actions God has taken (and will take) are perfectly reflective of his nature and that some attribute (e.g., holiness) may serve as the basis for a condemnation consistent with his nature. Whatever God's reasons for creating (e.g., maximizing his glory), they are perfectly and mysteriously met in a world where few are saved and many are condemned. As popular Calvinist teacher and apologist R. C. Sproul has said, "I have no idea why God saves some but not all. I don't doubt for a moment that God has the power to save all, but I know that he does not choose to save all. I don't know why. . . . One thing I do know. If it pleases God to save some and not all, there is nothing wrong with that. God is not under obligation to save anybody. If he chooses to save some, that in no way obligates him to save the rest."[30]

Second, many Calvinists have rejected the charge of double predestination on Scriptural grounds. They point out that references to election and "the elect" in the Bible always refer to salvation and the saved; there are no biblical references to election of the reprobate. In addition, they argue, Hell was prepared for Satan and his demons (Matt. 25:41) and not humans, and this speaks to God's purposes in creating humanity (i.e., for fellowship with God). They reconcile God's purposes for some persons

---

29. Roger E. Olson, *Against Calvinism* (Grand Rapids: Zondervan, 2011), 111. The quote comes from a chapter entitled, "Yes to Election; No to Double-Predestination," which includes an extended discussion of criticisms of double-predestination and unconditional election by critics of Calvinism, as well as defenses by Calvinist authors. Ibid., 102–35.

30. R. C. Sproul, *Chosen By God* (Wheaton: Tyndale, 1988), 37. Ironically, most Arminians (and Molinists) agree with Sproul's claim here, taken literally at face value. No one questions the power of God to save all, and no one (orthodox on divine foreknowledge and predestination) denies that God does not choose to save all, and all agree that God is not obligated to save anyone. However, it is clear that when Sproul appeals to divine omnipotence, he means to claim that God *really could* save all, not just make reference to the vastness of God's power. Thus, it is the implications in Sproul's statement with which Arminians take issue, not the factual claims.

being unrealized with his deterministic control by appeal to the concept of passive and active work. God's choice of some for salvation is an active work of grace, while his failure to choose others for salvation is passive; he does not *choose* some for condemnation.

While these clarifications are helpful, they do not escape the full force of the complaint, especially given the Reformed theological framework. It is to be expected that the passages which speak to election would refer to the saved because the focus of the biblical narrative is upon salvation history, and much of the New Testament is epistolary, written to believers who *just are* the elect. Still, some passages do seem to indicate an election to condemnation for some (Rom. 9:22; cf. 9:23–24; 1 Peter 2:8; Jude 4), and so the claim that the Bible never refers to election to condemnation, while technically and literally true, is literarily misleading. In addition, an argument may be constructed which proves double predestination by questioning the active/passive distinction in divine work (as Calvin does). If God's control extends to the very decisions persons make (i.e., he creates faith in those who are saved), then his decision to not give faith to particular persons is an active choice on his part. Similarly, if all history were predetermined before creation, then Hell was created with a view to the final judgment of humanity as well as to that of the Devil and his angels.

Third, it is worth pointing out that the issue of double predestination stands as something of a problem for all positions orthodox on divine foreknowledge and predestination. That is, under Molinist principles, God predestines some (few) for salvation and in so doing (if the argument holds), also predestines some (many) for condemnation. Molinists must also argue that, whatever God's reasons for creating, they are met in a world where few are saved and many are condemned and so they must reckon with the potential implications of double predestination as well. That is, the charge of double predestination, as a critique of the goodness and lovingkindness of God, cannot stand as a pure weakness of the Calvinist presentation of divine election and predestination, over against Arminian conceptions, for most Arminians maintain not only that God foreknew who would be saved, but utilized that knowledge to predestine the elect (and not predestine the non-elect).

Still, as with the problem of evil taken broadly, the difficulties of double predestination are particularly acute for Calvinism, as Molinists can appeal to *feasibility* to argue that God may not have been able to save all (even if his power is sufficient to do so), while Calvinists can make no such claim.[31] Since Molinists can appeal to feasibility and a self-imposed

---

31. They consistently argue that God is able to save all because he is sovereign and *really can* get whatever he wants. Consider the following quotation from Jonathan Edwards. The emphasis is upon God's moral authority to decide whom to save, if any, but it is clear that he also means to communicate that God's omnipotence requires that he have unrestrained ability (save his own nature) to do as he wishes, and so the ratio of saved to lost becomes a perfect reflection of his

limitation upon God's options due to his free choice to create free creatures, they therefore do not have to appeal to another attribute (e.g., holiness) in order to explain reprobation. In many Calvinist presentations,
God's holiness and justice appear to be at odds with his love and mercy
(i.e., God's love and mercy lead him to cause a few to believe and be saved,
while his holiness and justice lead him to leave many in unbelief and be
condemned), while in Molinism, no such bifurcation seems necessary; it
may not have been feasible for God to create a world with a greater ratio
of saved/unsaved or a better balance of good and evil.[32] In Molinism, it is
not God's love and mercy at odds with his holiness and justice, but rather
his desire to save all with their free decisions to reject his offer.[33]

Basis for election

The basis of the election of those who are saved and the relationship
between God's predestining work and his foreknowledge are particularly
contentious issues among Calvinists and Arminians. Calvinists have typically argued that predestination determines foreknowledge. They contend
that God knows the future—and especially who will be saved—because
he determined the future and predestined those persons to be saved.
This means that foreknowledge is logically dependent upon and logically
posterior to predestination. Persons are elected for reasons known only
to God (usually left merely as "his good pleasure" or something similar),
but not on the basis of foreseen merit, foreseen faith, or the like. This position has come to be known popularly as *unconditional election*. While
some detractors of Calvinism have questioned the justice of this doctrine,
Calvinists have emphasized the graciousness of election itself. For example, Boettner writes:

> It may be asked, Why does God save some and not others? But that belongs
> to His secret counsels. Precisely why this man receives, and that man does

---

desires and will. He writes, "When men are fallen, and become sinful, God by his sovereignty
has a right to determine about their redemption as he pleases. He has a right to determine
whenever he will redeem any or no. He might, if he had pleased, have left all to perish, or
might have redeemed all. Or, he may redeem some, and leave others; and if he doth so, he may
take whom he pleases, and leave whom he pleases." Jonathan Edwards, *The Justice of God in
the Damnation of Sinners* 2.3 (Newark, NJ: John Tuttle, 1814), 14.

32. Some may complain that I have been particularly unfair to Calvinism here, and may challenge my claim regarding the opposition of divine holiness/justice and love/mercy. It is true
that most Calvinists would deny this characterization, but it often seems that Calvinists put
greater emphasis on holiness and/or omnipotence, while Arminians place greater emphasis
on love. Both are based on a misguided notion that one attribute is primary, to the denigration
or exclusion of the others.

33. Some may wish to claim that it is God's desire to save all at odds with his choice to create
persons with libertarian freedom and the ability to reject the offer of salvation. I see this as not
substantially different from what I have written, though the statement in the body of the text
places more responsibility upon the creatures.

not receive, when neither deserves to receive, we are not told. That God was pleased to set upon us in this His electing grace, must ever remain for us a matter of adoring wonder.... When we consider, on the one hand, what a heinous thing sin is, together with its desert of punishment, and on the other, what holiness is, together with God's perfect hatred for sin, the marvel is that God could get the consent of His holy nature to save a single sinner.[34]

Arminians have typically argued that foreknowledge serves as the basis for predestination. They argue that God predestines some to be saved based on his knowledge of how they will respond to the work of the Holy Spirit in their lives. This means that predestination is logically dependent upon and logically posterior to divine foreknowledge, and is sometimes called *conditional* election, but it must be emphasized that the conditions upon which election is based are not good works or merit, but rather saving faith effected by a movement of the Holy Spirit upon the individual. John Miley writes, "it is still open for us to maintain that it was on the divine foresight of their free compliance with its required term [faith]. . . it is in such full accord with the Scriptures respecting the actual conditionality of salvation, that it may be successfully maintained."[35]

Molinist soteriology does not require that God elect persons based on foreseen faith, but many Molinists have held to this view. In point of fact, when Arminians say that God elects based on foreseen faith, what most really mean is that God elects based on the counterfactuals of creaturely freedom that refer to individual faith responses persons would have if placed in the right circumstances, and then God predestines them by ensuring they will find themselves in those circumstances where they will believe. This approach allows for an explanation of why all persons do not get saved, even if it is God's desire that they do so. The Molinist can claim

---

34.   Loraine Boettner, *The Reformed Doctrine of Predestination*, (Phillipsburg, NJ: Presbyterian & Reformed, 1932), 96.

35.   John Miley, *Systematic Theology* (New York: Hunt & Eaton, 1893), 2:263. Calvinist Michael Horton argues that the Arminian appeal to conditional election based on foreknowledge does not escape the force of Arminian complaints against Calvinist soteriology: "Many find conditional election (based on foreseen faith) attractive out of a concern to protect God from the charge of injustice. However, mere foreknowledge does not resolve the problem of evil or the final judgment of the lost." Horton, *For Calvinism*, 58. As previously noted, in one sense, Horton is certainly correct; no position orthodox on providence can fully escape the problem of evil, and no position orthodox on election can fully escape the problems of double predestination. However, Horton seems to be addressing the position that has come to be known as *simple foreknowledge*, which denies God has middle knowledge and instead suggests that God uses his knowledge of the *actual future* to guide his providential activity. At risk of grave oversimplification, it may be claimed that such knowledge provides God no help in directing the future; his knowledge of what *will* be the case cannot aid his decisions about what to bring about because what he will bring about is included or built into that knowledge. Since Horton claims that "mere foreknowledge" cannot resolve the problem, he is surely correct. However, middle knowledge can prove useful to God in his decisions about how to guide the future and it can alleviate some of the problems associated with the doctrine of election.

that Peter was really serious and speaking literally when he says that God desires that none should perish and all would come to saving faith (2 Peter 3:9), but also that a world where all accept Christ and are saved may not be a feasible world. Calvinists have historically made similar claims about God's intentions and desires regarding the genuineness of God's offer of salvation to all who hear the gospel, but have been unable to offer much by way of a consistent explanation for why those desires are not met. If election is unconditional and grace is irresistible so that atonement is limited by God's sovereign choice for reasons known only to him, then it seems that if God desired all be saved, then all would be saved, and it also seems that if Jesus only died for the elect, then the offer of salvation to all who hear the gospel is not genuine; the offer is only truly made to the elect. Hoekema appeals to the category of paradox, and suggests that God's work in salvation is not subject to the laws of logic, but such appeals are neither satisfying nor coherent.[36] By contrast, Molinism can consistently claim that God truly desires all be saved, that the offer of salvation to all who hear the gospel is a genuine offer, and that God has predestined only some (i.e., those he knew would respond favorably) to be saved, without appeal to paradox or wholesale mystery.

Effective Grace

The primary complaint against the Molinist approach is that it seems to make the efficaciousness of God's grace dependent upon human free will rather than God's good pleasure or free decision. However, while the complaint has a long history—Molina himself was criticized for it—it is true only of some versions of Molinist soteriology and need not apply to all. Consider the following example.

---

36. In his discussion of the "well-meant gospel call"—that God really means to offer salvation to all hearers of the gospel if they were to repent and believe—Hoekema considers the apparent contradiction between the doctrines of definite election (unconditional election) and limited atonement on the one hand, and a real gospel offer on the other hand. He criticizes those, like Herman Hoeksema, who deny God's desire that all be saved and that a genuine offer is made, as holding to "an overly rationalistic" theology. He appeals to divine transcendence as the answer, but then chalks it up to paradox: "Since the Scriptures teach both eternal election and the well-meant gospel call, we must continue to hold on to both, even though we cannot reconcile these two teachings with our finite minds. We should remember that we cannot lock God up in the prison of human logic. Our theology must maintain the Scriptural paradox." Anthony A. Hoekema, *Saved by Grace* (Grand Rapids: Eerdmans, 1989), 79. It seems that Hoekema has here equated paradox and a lack/violation of the laws of logic, but this leads to a problem. There is no such thing as "human" logic, as a category separate from other forms of logic or from the fundamental laws of logic, upon which all rationality depends. To violate the laws of logic *just is* to be incoherent, and if rationality is an essential attribute of God, then it makes no sense to suppose he can suspend, violate, or work outside of those laws; they are not laws which impose themselves upon him, but rather are expressions of his nature. In addition, as noted already, the two truths are not necessarily opposed/contraries. They may be reconciled by appeal to Molinism.

Suppose there are two persons: John, who accepts Christ and is saved, and Martin, who rejects Christ and is lost. The Molinist can maintain that prior to creating, God saw:

> If I give a certain amount of grace to John to enable him to believe in me, he will believe;

and

> If I give a certain amount of grace to Martin to enable him to believe in me, he will not believe.

In this case, God uses this information to decide which world to actualize, and indeed give John grace so he can believe (and thus effecting John's faith), and to not give Martin grace so he can believe (thus preserving God's sovereignty over salvation without causing Martin's unbelief or preventing Martin from believing) and without it being the case that God withheld the grace that would have enabled Martin to believe. In this case, the grace given to John is efficacious because it will get the result for which it was intended. Martin was not given grace to enable him to believe because, even if he were, he would not believe.

The important point to note here is that under this model, the efficaciousness of God's grace is not dependent upon human response as if the human response "activates" God's grace, or transforms it from general/common grace to efficacious/effectual. God gives efficacious grace to John, and John thus believes. Similarly, this model does not claim that unbelievers are given grace that is meant to be efficacious, but because of their unbelief, it is made ineffectual, as if efficaciousness is "up in the air" until the human either believes (making it efficacious) or does not believe (making it ineffectual). Such a reading is a misrepresentation of the proper logical order of things.

This model thus avoids the common Arminian error of a strong semi-Pelagianism and preserves the sovereignty of God in salvation; salvation is much more dependent upon the work of God not only in Christ's sacrificial death, glorious resurrection, and steadfast mediation, and the Father's gracious declaration of innocence, but also the Holy Spirit's work in empowering fallen man to believe, than upon man's free choice. Too often in Arminian soteriology there is an overemphasis upon prevenient grace (the faith-enabling grace given by the Holy Spirit) and its availability to all persons so that the outcome is a tip of the hat to divine enablement, while the primary concern seems to be with the individual's choice for or against God.[37] The model presented here

---

37. This emphasis was particularly clear in the revivalist preaching of the eighteenth century, and can even be seen among Calvinists of the era. For example, Charles G. Finney, out of concern

allows the Molinist to claim that faith is a free human response to God's call to salvation, but also a gift of God.

Some may complain that this model makes God somehow unfair because he is not depicted as giving all persons an equally good chance at salvation; they may argue that God must give all equal enabling (prevenient) grace for belief in order to preserve his fairness. This may be true of the God of Open Theism, who cannot be sure of the outcome of the granting of grace, but it is not true of the Molinist or Calvinist God. According to Molinism, God's knowledge of all counterfactuals of freedom allows him to know ahead of time that Martin will reject Christ, even if he is given a sufficient amount of prevenient/enabling grace to believe. Thus, even though God does not grant Martin the grace to believe, he is still just in condemning Martin for his unbelief. This is not the case in Open Theism, where God cannot be sure that Martin will not believe if given prevenient grace (and so God would be unjust in condemning Martin without first giving him the grace to believe) and it is not the case in Calvinism, where Martin would believe in given grace (rebirth), so God withholds it so that Martin will not believe and be condemned. In both the Open Theist and Calvinist models, God's fairness seems tenuous.

Regeneration and Faith
Individual Christians' experiences with salvation can differ greatly. Some people hear the gospel and are miraculously saved right then, as if something like a light-switch was turned on in their spirits. When first confronted about their sin or when they first hear of the love God has for them, they are cut to the heart, and respond by repenting and trusting Christ for salvation. Both Calvinism and Arminianism are able to

---

for the waning evangelistic zeal among some Calvinists, offered a series of lectures on how revival may be induced by appeal to the emotions. Ironically, while he meant his concerns to be primarily "in-house," they were picked up by Arminian pastors/evangelists. Finney wrote, "Religion is the work of man. It is something for man to do. It consists in obeying God with and from the heart. It is man's duty. It is true, God induces him to do it." Charles G. Finney, *Lectures on Revivals of Religion*, rev. ed. (1835; New York: Fleming H. Revell, 1868), 9. Finney flatly denies that revival is a miracle, and instead claims that it results from natural means applied properly. In this, it is clear that he means there are things that can be done which facilitate emotional responses (in his words, "excitements") that make people more likely to respond favorably to God's call. Ibid., 12. However, Finney also clearly states that a work of God on the heart of the individual is necessary for salvation: "But means will not produce a revival, we all know, without the blessing of God. No more will grain, when it is sowed, produce a crop without the blessing of God." Ibid., 13. Still, Finney uses the analogy between revival and grain to argue that human means are necessary in evangelization and in setting the conditions for revival, just as they are in planting and growing grain. Ibid., 13–14. Finney's concern to undermine the laissez-faire approach to the gospel by highlighting the human component served to bolster Arminian emphases upon the individual sinner's choice for God, even though Finney did not mean for this to be the case.

adequately explain this phenomenon. A Calvinist interpretation appeals to the regenerating work of the Holy Spirit through the hearing of the gospel as an explanation for the instantaneous faith response in the individual; upon hearing the gospel, the individual is made alive to God's word by the Holy Spirit rebirthing him, and he is then enabled to believe the gospel and given a disposition that wants to trust Christ as Lord and Savior. An Arminian interpretation appeals to prevenient grace and the convicting ministry of the Holy Spirit to claim that the individual is enabled to respond appropriately, and freely chooses to do so, as the Holy Spirit draws him and empowers him.

However, some have an experience of salvation that seems more like a process. My own testimony is like this. God began to draw me unto himself when I was in high school, but I largely refused his promptings. While I can now see that he was softening my hard heart toward the gospel by placing positive examples of Christianity into my life, at the time I simply refused to believe. Over time, and through a series of events, I came to a position where I wanted to believe the gospel and wanted to be a Christian, but I simply could not believe. I was attending Bible studies and worship services, reading the Bible on my own, and meeting with a Christian friend to discuss issues related to faith. Still, as I read the stories of Jesus's miracles—walking on water, casting out demons, healings, etc.—I saw them as fairy stories; they just did not ring true. My friend advised me to continue doing what I was doing, and to start praying and asking God to help me believe. Although it seemed very strange for me, an atheist, to pray, I thought "it can't hurt," and so I began asking God for faith. Over the next several months, I continued to read my Bible, pray, and attend worship, and somewhere along the way, faith came. The point of the story may surprise many readers, for it may seem to have a very strong Calvinist ring to it (since I asked God to give me faith), but in actuality, Calvinism has a very difficult time accounting for my experience.

My testimony includes numerous places where God was calling/drawing me to himself, and where I responded with a measure of faith. Over the course of the year or so when I was a "seeker," God was prompting me to draw closer to him, and in many cases, I did, though I was most certainly not saved. Consider my conversation with my friend about my inability to believe; surely I was not yet reborn, but by agreeing to continue toward faith and by having the desire to move in that direction, I was responding to the work of God in my life in what can only be described as some kind of positive faith (even if not *saving* faith). I responded in faith prior to being saved, and I could even have turned away, and I was on a faith journey that began prior to my rebirth.

Arminianism/Molinism is able to account for this phenomenon by appeal to the concept of prevenient grace. The Holy Spirit calls and draws the individual, and gives him grace that enables him to respond in faith to God's call, though the individual may not fully accept the gospel at this point. Still, the response is positive, appears to be a type of faith, and therefore requires a work of the Holy Spirit upon the individual in order to overcome the sin nature. Calvinism, by contrast, seems ill-equipped to deal with such situations because it either has to argue that the individual is not responding in faith until the moment of salvation, or there is an enabling work of the Spirit prior to salvation akin to the Arminian concept of prevenient grace, but this undermines the entire Calvinist soteriology. Once the requirement for regeneration preceding faith is abandoned, one of the fundamental distinctions between Calvinism and Arminianism is denied.[38]

Most reformed thinkers simply do not address this type of situation, and instead emphasize the immediate nature of regeneration out of a concern to protect the distinction between justification and sanctification, a distinction important for differentiating Protestant theology from Catholic theology.[39] Berkhof seems to hint at a similar situation when he refers to regeneration as a category that normally coincides with conversion, but in some cases may not. He speaks of it being possibly subconscious such that the individual is not aware he has been regenerated. If that is the case, then it may be that I was regenerate before I realized I had faith, but such an interpretation seems to fly in the face of how most reformed theologians (and most Christians generally) speak of faith. Still, Berkhof really seems to be addressing the post-salvation doubts that individuals have, especially when they struggle with sin, not a regeneration of which one is not aware at the time of rebirth.[40]

---

38. The two fundamental distinctions are the relationship between regeneration and faith and the conception of creaturely freedom. Calvinists assert that regeneration must precede faith, while Arminians claim that regeneration is a work of God in response to one's faith. Calvinists hold that free creatures only possess compatibilist freedom, while Arminians claim libertarian freedom for humans and angels.

39. For example, in Berkhof's discussion of regeneration and effectual calling, he argues that regeneration is an instantaneous shift of one's nature, not a gradual work in the soul. He sets his view in opposition to Roman Catholicism and "all semi-Pelagians," who he believes teach some form of "intermediate stage between life and death." Louis Berkhof, *Systematic Theology* (1939; repr. Grand Rapids: Eerdmans, 1993), 468. Berkhof's assumption that Arminians (who he calls "semi-Pelagians") teach an intermediate state or a progressive regeneration is based on his theological presupposition that regeneration is necessary for saving faith. With that as a starting point, he cannot allow for an interpretation of the Holy Spirit's work in salvation that *enables a real faith response* by the individual that is not also salvific. The categories are foreign to his theology.

40. Berkhof writes, "The change may take place without man's being conscious of it momentarily, though this is not the case when regeneration and conversion coincide; and even later on he can perceive it only in its effects. This explains the fact that a Christian may, on the one hand, struggle for a long time with doubts and uncertainties, and can yet, on the other hand, gradually overcome these and rise to the heights of assurance." Ibid., 469. Notice that the example Berkhof uses does not seem to refer to someone who claims to lack faith, but continues to do the things that may lead to faith. Rather, it seems to refer to someone who comes to faith, but then struggles with doubts.

A second problem with the Calvinist claim that regeneration must precede faith and is given via irresistible grace has to do with the ongoing struggle with sin after conversion. In Calvinism, grace is irresistible with respect to salvation; the individual stands in complete opposition to God, lost in his sin until God's spirit regenerates him, thus enabling and causing him to believe in such a way that he cannot refuse. In the mechanics of Calvinist soteriology, it is in the granting of new life and a new nature through regeneration that the individual is compelled to believe the gospel, though not against his will because he has a new will consistent with his new nature as a child of God, and thus, desires to follow Christ.

However, the logic seems to break down when applied to the Christian life, for at some point after regeneration and saving faith, the new nature no longer functions to determine belief in the individual because he can resist and grieve the Holy Spirit. The grace to believe due to regeneration is now resistible for the believer, and he must work to remain in step with the Spirit and to resist the draw of fleshly desires. Of course, the Spirit is actively involved in empowering the individual to do those things necessary—pray, read the Bible, yield himself to the Holy Spirit, etc.—but the point is that in this, the Spirit's work seems very much like prevenient grace in Arminian soteriology. It is a resistible enabling grace and work of the Holy Spirit that relates to the individual trusting the Lord and following him. The only difference is that the Arminian claims that this work of the Spirit can operate on unbelievers and believers, while Calvinists contend it can only work on believers.

It would almost seem that Calvinists should believe in some form of sinless perfectionism after regeneration, since regeneration leads to a new nature that compels faith; one might wonder why it should not also compel faithfulness. Ironically, it has historically been some Arminians who have emphasized the propensity (in believers) for perfection prior to glorification, and some reformed theologians have argued that believers are composites of the old self and the new self, analogous to Jekyll and Hyde.[41] Some, however, reject this interpretation and instead claim that believers are totally and only "new" (Rom. 6:6; 2 Cor. 5:17; Col. 3:9–10; Eph. 4:20–24). For instance, Hoekema argues that the new self still struggles with sin and is in need of continual renewal, growth, and transformation, because he still has a sin nature in addition to a new nature: "Christians are no longer old persons but new persons who are being progressively renewed. They must still battle against sin and will sometimes fall into sin, but they are no longer slaves of sin. In the strength of the Spirit they are now able to resist sin, since for every temptation God will provide a way of escape (1 Cor. 10:13)."[42] Unfortunately, this explanation clears up little, in part because it does not address how God's spirit is able to strengthen

---

41. The analogy to Jekyll and Hyde is from Hoekema, *Saved by Grace*, 204.
42. Ibid., 214.

believers without overwhelming the sin nature, in part because it makes no attempt to reconcile reformed teaching on the necessity of regeneration for belief—which is an irresistible grace—with the resistibility of grace in sanctification, and in part, at least for Hoekema, because sanctification is in some ways equated with regeneration.[43]

The point to be made here is not that Calvinism should lead to perfectionism, or that Calvinism seems to short shrift the Holy Spirit's power in sanctification (compared to his work in regeneration), and it is not meant to suggest that Calvinists make the audacious claim that the grace given to unbelievers is such that they must believe and be faithful, while the grace given to believers is somehow inadequate and ineffectual. Such characterizations are insulting, unhelpful, and misleading. The point to be made here is that it appears that those Calvinists who deny sinless perfectionism after salvation (i.e., most Calvinists) must incorporate something akin to prevenient grace in their model of how the Holy Spirit works in sanctification, and therefore, they have little room to criticize the Arminian concept of prevenient grace, at least conceptually. They may deny such grace is sufficient to move an unbeliever to the point at which he may believe, but they may not deny the coherence or conceptual strength of such grace.

Nevertheless, many Calvinists have been critical of prevenient grace, arguing that it is unbiblical and incoherent. For example, Turretin argues that the concept of a grace that is resistible is problematic on several counts, including the weakness of man, the power of God to meet his own desires, the nature of regeneration and its effect on the human heart, the work of God on the human will, and what he calls "absurdities." By this, he suggests that it makes salvation dependent upon the human sinner rather than God, that those who are saved should not properly thank God (because it was their own doing), that God's foreknowledge would be called into question, and that it makes Satan's influence upon humanity on a par with God's (i.e., neither can determine or sway humanity with any certainty).[44] These characterizations have led to much confusion.

One way of explaining the concept of prevenient grace is to appeal to the story of Adam in the Garden. Evangelicals have been most concerned with the effects of the Fall upon the spiritual condition of humanity, but have shown surprisingly little interest in the pre-Fall spiritual condition of Adam. Questions related to Adam's pre-Fall ability to choose the good, or to trust in God, deserve to be answered. It seems obvious enough that Adam had a kind of freedom that allowed him to choose to sin and bear the responsibility for that sin, but if the doctrine of the Fall, with humanity's collective inheritance of corruption from Adam as a result,

---

43. Hoekema correctly notes the diversity of images for sanctification, and that there is a definitive as well as progressive way of speaking of sanctification. Ibid, 202–9.

44. Francis Turretin, *Institutes of Elenctic Theology*, 3 vols., ed. James T. Dennison, Jr., trans. George Musgrave Giger (Phillipsburg, NJ: Presbyterian & Reformed, 1994), 2:553–54.

is correct, then it stands to reason not only that humans are not inherently sinful (i.e., in virtue of being human), but also that Adam had the capacity to act in faith. It may be the case that Adam's pre-Fall condition can illumine our understanding of humanity's condition when given an enabling grace to believe. That is, prevenient grace may be conceived as bringing the individual to a similar spiritual enablement as Adam prior to the Fall, with one difference: Adam communed with God directly (unmediated) and the creation was not yet subject to sin and death, and he still chose to sin, whereas persons today have the disadvantage of required mediation for their interactions with God, and have viewed sin and corruption as "normal."

Assurance of Salvation and Perseverance of the Saints

One of the perennial problems that pastors often face in the counselor's role has to do with the security of one's eternal destiny in the face of ongoing temptation and struggles with sin, even after he has accepted Christ as Lord and Savior, and thus, been reborn. Martin Luther, even when living the life of a monastic dedicated to God as a result of a miraculous salvation from death, famously struggled with fear of judgment and self-loathing because of his acute sense of his own sins, to the extent that his confessor, Johann Staupitz, once in frustration told him to go and commit a sin worth confessing.[45] He serves as an example of the kind of struggle parishioners can have with the life of faith and holiness; many have an acute sense of guilt for sins committed after rebirth, and rightly so, but often the fear of God that gives rise to the conviction for sins transforms into fear for one's eternal destiny, even despite repeated efforts at repentance. This is when pastors need to offer wise theological counsel that is practical.

The doctrine of perseverance has traditionally been held by those in the reformed tradition over against Catholic theology, which has tended to see such certainty of one's salvation as presumptuous. Interestingly, although the possibility of loss of salvation has come to be associated with Arminianism through the Remonstrants, Arminius himself believed in both perseverance of the saints and assurance of salvation.[46]

---

45. Kittelson describes Luther's conscience as "an unforgiving monster," and notes that Staupitz's care for Luther as a young, struggling monk greatly aided his spiritual care. Luther himself claimed that Staupitz prevented him from sinking into the pits of hell. James M. Kittelson, *Luther the Reformer: The Story of the Man and His Career* (Minneapolis: Augsburg, 1986), 84.

46. He admitted that he was open to being convinced otherwise from the Scriptures and that some passages seem to teach the possibility of apostasy. He wrote, "Though I here openly and ingenuously affirm, I never taught that a true believer can, either totally or finally fall away from the faith, and perish. Yet I will not conceal, that there are passages of Scripture which seem to me to wear this aspect; and those answers to them which I have been permitted to see, are not of such a kind as to approve themselves on all points to my understanding. On the other hand, certain passages are produced for the contrary doctrine [of unconditional perseverance] which are worthy of much consideration." James Arminius, *Arminius Speaks:*

On perseverance, he first noted that the power of the Holy Spirit at work in the believer is sufficient to allow him to overcome sin and the Devil: "So that it is not possible for them [saints], by any of the cunning craftiness or power of Satan, to be either seduced or dragged out of the hands of Christ." He then appealed to the promise of rebirth and the completed nature of that transformation in order to claim certainty once an individual places his faith in Christ.[47] Calvinism has typically appealed to God's determining will as the basis for perseverance. Just as God determined individual faith, so also he will determine that those who are truly reborn will remain faithful to the end. While perseverance is often referred to colloquially as "once saved, always saved," as a doctrine it is less concerned with the permanence of salvation, once completed, and more with the individual believer remaining in the faith. The question of the possibility of one losing his salvation is more a by-product of the assertions made regarding that perseverance.

There are many good reasons—theological and biblical—for accepting the doctrine of perseverance. For example, salvation is referred to as a *promise* given by God and which looks to a future fulfillment (Titus 1:2; 1 John 2:25; Eph. 1:13; Heb. 11:13, 39; James 2:5), and it is *sealed* by God, indicating his ownership (2 Cor. 1:22; Eph. 4:30). In addition, the Holy Spirit is described as an *earnest* or *down payment* on salvation, which guarantees a later realization (2 Cor. 1:22; 5:5; Eph. 1:14), and as an *inheritance* (Eph. 1:18; Col. 3:24; Heb. 9:15; 1 Peter 1:3–4). Christ is described as the *firstfruits* of our salvation, which points to a later harvest (1 Cor. 15:20–23; Rom. 8:23), and our adoption as children of God suggests permanence of the relationship (Rom. 8:15–23; 9:4; Gal. 4:5). Jesus assured believers that no one can snatch his sheep from his hand (John 10:27–29), Paul declares that if God is for us, no one can stand against us (Rom. 8:31–34) and no one can separate us from the love of God in Christ (Rom. 8:35–39), and the book of Hebrews boldly declares that salvation for believers is secure because Jesus has gone through the heavens, was tempted without sin, is God/deity, intercedes for us as the perfect high priest and sacrifice, and will never leave us nor forsake us (Heb. 13:5). The New Testament also suggests that Christians who die in sin can still be saved (e.g., man sleeping with his father's wife, who is handed over to Satan for destruction of the flesh so that his soul will be saved in the end; 1 Cor. 5:5; see also 1 Cor. 11:30; 1 Thess. 4:13; Acts 5). So Calvinists and Arminians can agree on the principle of assurance, though they disagree somewhat on the basis for that assurance.

While Calvinists assert that the only way to ensure perseverance is to place it in the certain and stable *will* of God, a counterfactual analysis applied to the divine deliberative process (i.e., middle knowledge) can

---

Essential Writings on Predestination, Free Will, and the Nature of God, ed. John D. Wagner (Eugene, OR: Wipf & Stock, 2011), 70.
47.   Ibid., 69.

also account for this doctrine. For example, in deciding who to elect, God may not only have considered who would respond with appropriate faith if given prevenient/enabling grace, but also who would remain faithful to the end, given the Holy Spirit's work. That is, God may have considered truths such as

> If I were to grant John grace to enable him to believe the gospel and he were to do so, and I were to continue to move in him, transforming him into the image of Christ, he would freely remain in the faith.

and

> When John sins and I convict him of that sin, he will freely repent and return to me in faith.

So an Arminian analysis predicated on middle knowledge can also affirm perseverance, but with one difference: it can account for the situations in which persons are reborn, but fall away from the faith and die in their sins. It will still maintain that those individuals are ultimately saved, but it has an explanation for how persons may have been pulled away by sin. By contrast, Calvinism struggles with explaining this problem.[48] In the previous section, the work of the Holy Spirit in one's progressively coming to faith was discussed. It was argued that Arminianism's appeal to prevenient grace allowed for a real faith response of individuals, even before salvation. It was also shown that Calvinism struggles to explain why regeneration compels faith for salvific purposes, but does not compel faithfulness for sanctification purposes, and herein lies the problem. Again, it seems that Christians who have been regenerated and given a new nature, such that

---

48. Keathley does a fine job of discussing the difficulty for modern Calvinists, especially those in American evangelicalism, where Edwards' theology is so influential. In addressing this problem, Keathley writes, "At this point a number of compatibilists decide to be inconsistent with their advocacy of determinism by affirming that believers have a limited ability to choose to the contrary. R. C. Sproul, Sr. and Robert Peterson both affirm that the redeemed regain a measure of the freedom of integrity. Sproul Sr. explicitly depends on Augustine rather than Edwards when he declares that the regenerate regain what Adam lost, i.e., the simultaneous abilities to sin and to not sin." Kenneth Keathley, *Salvation and Sovereignty: A Molinist Approach* (Nashville: Broadman & Holman, 2010), 90. He notes further that Sproul goes on to actually affirm synergism in sanctification! Other Calvinists (e.g., Piper, Tiessen), though, appeal to the two wills in God (e.g., revealed vs. secret, etc.), in order to argue that God simply withholds sufficient grace from believers for holiness (presumably in his secret/permissive will, he has a purpose for their sin). Keathley rightly questions this move because of what it seems to assert about God: "Let me be clear: I believe that there is much about God's ultimate will we do not know, and that God often works through the evil deeds of humans (Gen. 50:10; Isa. 10:5–15; Acts 2:23). However, I do not believe that when a Christian commits a specific sin it is because God inscrutably withholds sufficient grace. The Bible teaches that, while we may not achieve sinless perfection in this age, victory over any particular sin is always a real prospect for the believer (Gal 5:16)." Ibid.

they naturally want to believe and trust in Christ (as in a Calvinist soteriology), would never fall away, and appeals to two natures seems unable to fully account for both phenomena: a compelling new nature with respect to salvation, and struggling old and new natures with respect to the life of faith. By contrast, Molinism offers an explanation for why believers fall away, because the individual is not compelled to belief by the granting of a new nature, and the counterfactuals of freedom may also include the sins of Christians post-conversion. Consider the following counterfactual:

> If I were to grant John grace to enable him to believe the gospel and he were to do so, and I were to continue to move in him, transforming him into the image of Christ, he would struggle with sin, but ultimately return to the faith

Given libertarian freedom and feasible worlds, Molinism can suggest that it may be the case that some Christians could not have been saved and remain true to the faith throughout their lives after receiving salvation; the counterfactuals of freedom just may not allow it. Calvinism can make no such claim, as it is always the case that God can give an individual the grace to overcome sin. He simply chooses to not do so, for reasons known only to him. So Molinism is able to account for the ongoing believer's struggle with sin in a way that preserves God's sovereignty and goodness, something Calvinism struggles to offer without appeal to mystery or paradox. Molinism is also able to offer assurance of salvation in the same way Calvinism is able to provide security and assurance to the Christian struggling with sin and the fear of damnation.

Open Theism and Process Theology, by contrast, can offer no such assurance or security, for presumably God cannot know if persons will remain faithful, has no way of assuring it without overriding their freedom, and would not do so. Of course, according to Open Theism, God could conceivably force Christians to remain faithful, but such an appeal is unattractive to most Open Theists, and runs against the grain of the whole system.

DISCIPLESHIP, SPIRITUAL GROWTH, AND SPIRITUAL GIFTS

The Christian faith has always been grounded in both corporate worship and individual piety. Growth in the faith—growing closer to God—is dependent upon the individual Christian being disciplined in both of these areas and upon the Holy Spirit's gracious transformative work in the individual, changing his very constitution. Although we believe persons are fundamentally changed at the moment of justification and rebirth, from being a child of darkness and Adam and a slave to sin, to being a child of light and God and a slave to righteousness, we also acknowledge that the Bible speaks of a process following regeneration that is described as *being made into the image of Christ* (2 Cor. 3:18; cf., Eph. 4:13; 2 Peter 3:18; 1 John 3:2).

Just as salvation is dependent upon God's gracious work in the individual such that salvation is solely his from start to finish and he alone is worthy of praise, so also spiritual growth is dependent upon God's gracious work in the individual such that sanctification is solely his from start to finish and he alone is worthy of praise. Just as it is not possible for humans to be good enough to earn their salvation, so also it is not possible for unregenerate humans to purify and sanctify themselves and it is not possible for humans to be good and grow in the faith. Salvation and sanctification both require an initiating work of the Holy Spirit upon the individual, an empowering work of the Holy Spirit upon the individual to respond in faith, and a transformative work of the Holy Spirit in response to the faith.

Still, the Bible does seem to indicate that one's spiritual growth is in some way dependent upon his faith response such that he is responsible for his faith and/or lack of faith. The constant admonishment of the New Testament authors is for Christians to "walk in the light" (Ps. 56:13; 89:15; Isa. 2:5; John 8:12; 1 John 1:7), "walk by the spirit" (Gal. 5:16, 25), "live by faith, not sight" (2 Cor. 5:7; cf., Hab. 2:4; Rom. 1:17; Gal. 2:20; 3:11–12; Heb. 10:38), "be filled with the spirit" (Eph. 5:18), and the like. The very concept of spiritual disciplines that one can practice and that can be a means of entry into a deeper spiritual life suggests a responsibility of the individual for his own spiritual growth.[49] Bible study, Meditation, fasting, silence, solitude, etc., all entail a conscious decision to act, and seem to include the ability to not-act.[50]

The responsibility believers have for their own spiritual condition can also be seen in the New Testament warnings against negative responses to life and the ministry of the Holy Spirit. While it was argued that there are good reasons to hold to the doctrine of perseverance, it also must be admitted that there are many passages, particularly in the book of Hebrews, that warn against falling away (Heb. 2:1–4; 3:7–19; 5:11–6:18; 10:26–38; 12:3, 14–17, 25–29). The admonishments to the readers to remain faithful give instruction for what they may do in order to strengthen their positions, but also suggest that it is, in some way, up to them to refrain from losing heart, losing faith, and falling away.

This responsibility can also be seen in the biblical teaching on believers' control over their spiritual gifts. Unlike the pagan religions of the

---

49. Richard Foster even suggests that unbelievers can practice the spiritual disciplines if they have a desire to seek God. It should also be noted, though, that Foster places great emphasis upon the inward attitude, over against the outward action. That is, while the disciplines are surely practices and are an outward work of the individual seeking spiritual growth, the key to the disciplines' effectiveness is the Godward eye of the practitioner and (more importantly) the work of the Holy Spirit upon the individual. Otherwise, his efforts are a chasing after the wind. Richard Foster, *Celebration of Discipline: The Path to Spiritual Growth* (San Francisco: Harper, 1978, 1998), 2.

50. Of course, this is not absolute, as the philosophical debate over free will and responsibility has a long pedigree and has been addressed elsewhere in this volume.

ancient Near East, which were often characterized by ecstatic experiences with a loss of one's faculties, as seen in the antics of the prophets of Baal and Ashtoreth at Carmel (1 Kings 18), biblical prophets retained control over their faculties. Paul's instruction concerning tongues, prophecy, and orderly worship is especially revealing (1 Cor. 14; esp. vv. 26–33). One should only exercise the gift of tongues if there is another present who can interpret the message for the good of the congregation; otherwise, he is to restrain himself. When persons prophesy in church, they are to take turns and do so in an orderly and controlled manner, suggesting power of the individual over the use of the gift. And if the gifts of healing and miracles are represented by Peter and John in their encounter with the blind man and his subsequent healing, then it appears that the gifts are controlled by the individual believer.[51] Similarly, the true prophets of Israel spoke of their own volition, chose the words to speak, and seemingly had the ability to refuse to speak (even if they sometimes spoke of being compelled; e.g., Jer. 20:9). This control that the biblical prophets maintained over their exercise of prophecy is to be contrasted with the pagan oracles, who often emptied themselves in order to be possessed by the deity, utilized drugs in order to enter a trancelike state, and were essentially uninvolved in the production and articulation of the prophetic word.[52] As noted in chapter seven on biblical inspiration,

---

51. There are some examples where it may be thought that the gifts manifested themselves apart from an exercise of an individual's will (e.g., the possibility of Peter's shadow healing the sick and lame, Acts 5:15, Cornelius' household speaking in tongues, Acts 10:44–46, etc.), but they can be answered. For example, there is no indication that Peter's shadow actually healed anyone, and we are not given enough information about the way the gift of tongues manifested itself at Cornelius' house.

52. It was characteristic of pagan prophets to release control of their mental faculties in order to be controlled by the deity. In discussing pagan oracles, Sheppard and Herbrechtsmeier write, "The behavior of these divine spokesmen is often thought to have been ecstatic, frenzied, or abnormal in some way, which reflected their possession by the deity (and the absence of personal ego) at the time of transmission." Gerald T. Sheppard and William E. Herbrechtsmeier, "Prophecy: An Overview," in *The Encyclopedia of Religion*, ed. Mircea Eliade (New York: Simon & Schuster Macmillan, 1995), 12:8. See also Mircea Eliade, *Shamanism: Archaic Techniques of Ecstasy*, trans. Willard R. Trask (Trenton, NJ: Princeton University Press, 1964). This release sometimes involved drug use. There is a somewhat spirited debate regarding the possibility of intoxication as a result of noxious fumes at the Delphic Oracle in ancient Greece. For a positive argument, see Henry A. Spiller, John R. Hale, and Jelle Zeilinga de Boer, "The Delphic Oracle: A Multidisciplinary Defense of the Gaseous Vent Theory," *Clinical Toxicology* 40, no. 2 (2002): 189–96. For critical evaluations of their work, see J. Foster and Daryn Lehoux, "The Delphic Oracle and the Ethylene-Intoxication Hypothesis," *Clinical Toxicology* 45, no. 1 (2007): 85–89; and Daryn Lehoux, "Drugs and the Delphic Oracle," *Classical World* 10, no. 1 (2007): 41–56. In his confrontation with the prophets of Baal and Ashtoreth, Elijah notes the ecstatic nature of the pagan ritual in which they cut themselves and called out uncontrollably (1 Kings 18). By contrast, the depiction of prophecy in Israel was one in which the prophet retained control of his body, actions, and words. For instance, Ezekiel was instructed by God to refrain from mourning his wife's death as a sign-act for Israel (Ezek. 24:16–18). The obvious implication is that he could have mourned her because he had control of his emotions and actions.

such control distinguishes the verbal/plenary view of inspiration from dictation theories, and biblical prophecy from paganism. Such control seems best explained by libertarian freedom, and God's use of such free actions in his overall plan for humanity is best explained by appeal to middle knowledge.

CONCLUSION

In this chapter, the value of Molinism for an evangelical conception of salvation was considered. After surveying atonement theories, Molinism was shown to better handle questions related to God's purposes and plan in effecting salvation through Christ's death on the cross and resurrection from the dead. It also was shown that Molinism best handles the balancing of God's sovereign election and his fairness/justice. It can account for the gracious granting of salvation due to the human response of faith, and can best explain how divine enablement to believe can be reconciled with the human requirement to trust God while avoiding Pelagian-sounding language of merit.

Molinism was also shown to have the conceptual tools necessary for explaining the on-going experience of salvation in the lives of believers, as well as the spiritual struggle to remain faithful. Molinism is able to maintain a strong view of divine sovereignty over all aspects of salvation, from regeneration to glorification, while offering plausible explanations for phenomena of the spiritual life as diverse as backsliding, practice of spiritual disciplines, and the exercising of spiritual gifts. Subsequent chapters will address some of these practical concerns in more detail.

MIDDLE KNOWLEDGE AND THE PROBLEM OF EVIL

INTRODUCTION

The immense amount of suffering and evil in the world is perhaps the greatest barrier to belief in God. In this chapter, I will argue that Molinism is most effective in answering the most prominent problems of evil. Michael Peterson has helpfully divided the problem of evil into theoretical and existential dimensions.[1] While the majority of focus on the subject has been on the theoretical dimension, and that will comprise the bulk of this chapter, we ought to be mindful of the spiritual dimension of unbelief.[2] More will be said about the pastoral implications of these issues later in the chapter.

THE PROBLEM OF EVIL

The intellectual challenge that evil poses to belief in God has been summarized by David Hume. After cataloging the evil of this world and the suffering of all persons, Hume charges that the fact of evil makes traditional theism incoherent:

> And is it possible, Cleanthes, said Philo, that after all these reflections, and infinitely more, which might be suggested, you can still persevere in your anthropomorphism, and assert the moral attributes of the deity, his justice,

---

1. Michael L. Peterson, ed., *The Problem of Evil: Selected Readings*, Library of Religious Philosophy 8 (Notre Dame, IN: University of Notre Dame Press, 1992), 3.
2. It would be a mistake to ignore the way that the problem of evil affects one's attitudes toward God and theistic belief, one's spiritual development, one's psychological well-being, that is, one's *faith*. So even as we examine the problem of evil and seek to offer answers to this seeming intractable intellectual barrier to faith, let us remember that spiritual forces are at work and that mere philosophical refutation of the objections to faith may win the argument, but lose the person. John D. Laing, "The New Atheism: Lessons for Evangelicals," *Southwestern Journal of Theology* 54, no. 1 (Fall 2011): 13–28.

benevolence, mercy, and rectitude, to be of the same nature with these
virtues in human creatures? His power we allow is infinite: Whatever he
wills is executed: But neither man nor any other animal is happy: Therefore
he does not will their happiness. His wisdom is infinite: He is never mistaken
in choosing the means to any end: But the course of nature tends not to
human or animal felicity: Therefore it is not established for that purpose.
Through the whole compass of human knowledge, there are no inferences
more certain and infallible than these. In what respect, then, do his benevolence and mercy resemble the benevolence and mercy of men?

Epicurus's old questions are yet unanswered. Is he willing to prevent evil, but
not able? then is he impotent. Is he able, but not willing? then is he malevolent. Is he both able and willing? whence then is evil?[3]

This quote nicely raises a number of issues of concern in the problem of
evil. Hume lays out the logical problem of evil at the end with his unanswered questions of Epicurus: either God is not omnipotent, God is not
good, or evil does not exist. Since evil clearly exists, the proper object of
skepticism should be obvious. Hume also questions appeals to the limits
of human knowledge and speech (mystery or anthropomorphism) as
means for deflecting difficult theological questions. If we cannot speak
analogously of God such that our conceptions of goodness and evil do
not stand, then talk about God becomes meaningless. Additionally, Hume
uses the brutishness of nature, along with the basic concept of divine providence, to call traditional theistic belief into question. These are all themes
that will be examined throughout this chapter.

Hume was neither the first nor the last to struggle with the problem,
and Christians of all ages have sought to reconcile God's seeming inaction in the face of evil with his goodness and power. There are typically
two ways to approach the topic: apologetically or theologically; and while
they are not mutually exclusive, they are distinct. The apologetic approach
is to defend the goodness, power, providence, and/or existence of God
against the charge that evil calls one or all into question, and is thus more
limited in scope and focus. A *defense* is an argument designed to refute
a case against God/traditional theism on the basis of evil and may only
seek to undermine one aspect of the case. The theological approach is to
explain why God allows evil to occur and how it fits into his larger providential plan and a larger theological system. It is thus broader is scope
and focus. A *theodicy* is a framework for reconciling traditional beliefs
about God and the existence of evil. It is common to divide theodicies into
two categories: free will theodicies and greater good theodicies, sometimes known as Augustinian and Irenaean respectively, presumably due

---

3. David Hume, *Dialogues Concerning Natural Religion*, Part X, ed. Martin Bell (New York: Penguin, 1990), 108–9.

to their somewhat vague associations with the patristic apologist-theologians. Free will theodicies appeal to creaturely freedom (either human or angelic) as the explanation for evil's origins, while greater good theodicies appeal to some benefit that arises as a result of evil. Even though standard, the division is artificial, for the creaturely free will functions as a greater good within free will theodicies. That is, all theodicies appeal to some kind of greater good, taken either as a direct result of any given instance of evil, or as a basis for the conditions that ultimately lead to some evils.

LOGICAL PROBLEM OF EVIL

Some atheists have argued that there is a logical contradiction in the belief in the simultaneous existence of God and evil. The logical problem of evil has been set forth by many over the years, but the thinker whose work has generated the most discussion recently is J. L. Mackie. In his groundbreaking article, "Evil and Omnipotence," Mackie asserts that theists may only hold to their beliefs through an "extreme rejection of reason" because of the contradictory nature of the simultaneous truth of the propositions, *God is omnipotent; God is wholly good;* and *evil exists.*[4] According to Mackie, it is obvious that a good being will eliminate evil as far as it can and there are no limits to what an omnipotent being can do. Therefore, a wholly good and omnipotent being (like God) would eliminate evil if he were to exist. Since evil exists, there must be no such being.[5] The existence of evil stands in direct contradiction to the existence of God, and it is therefore illogical to believe in God.

Mackie goes on to look at attempts to answer the problem, with restrictions on omnipotence and denials of evil being the primary means. While Mackie admits that these could answer the problem, he is skeptical of their consistency. For example, there is a rich tradition in Christian theology of denying the *existence* of evil and instead seeing it as a *privation of the good.*[6] However, Mackie notes, most inconsistently see privation of the good as itself an evil.[7] He also admits that omnipotence does not mean the ability to do just anything (conceivable), but argues that most theists

4. J. L. Mackie, "Evil and Omnipotence," *Mind* 64, no. 254 (April 1965): 200.
5. Mackie does not make this the conclusion of his argument as he lays it out; rather, he simply concludes that such a being's existence is incompatible with evil's existence, though he assumes that most will agree that evil exists. Ibid., 201.
6. The idea was first clearly articulated by Augustine of Hippo. The popular contemporary explanation draws upon an analogy between good/evil and light/dark. Just as darkness is merely an absence of light and not something positive itself, so also evil is an absence of good.
7. The denial of the existence of evil by seeing it as a privation of the good was never meant to be a denial that there are acts which have the property of *being evil*. Rather, it was meant to deny the claim that since God created all things, he created evil. Evil is not a created *thing*, with *ontos*, but instead is the denial of *ontos*. The property of *being evil* is similar to the property of *lacking good*.

conceive of omnipotence as constrained only by logical possibility (and perhaps divine nature). This constraint does not help, for if it is *possible* for God to create a world with no evil or suffering (and there seems to be no reason to think it impossible), then he ought to have done so.

Mackie considers several other possibilities for answering the argument and rejects each.[8] Of particular interest for what follows are his comments on the appeal to creaturely freedom as the solution. Mackie correctly notes that for such an appeal to work, the theist must argue that a world where creatures are free but sometimes commit evil, is better than a world where creatures are not free and always do good. However, he has two problems with this suggestion. The first, which he does not explore in depth, is that he is skeptical of libertarian creaturely freedom.[9] The second is that he thinks it sets up a false dichotomy: "God was not, then, faced with a choice between making innocent automata and making beings who, in acting freely, would sometimes go wrong: there was open to him the obviously better possibility of making beings who would act freely but always go right. Clearly, his failure to avail himself of this possibility is inconsistent with his being both omnipotent and wholly good."[10] So, Mackie argues, there are good reasons for thinking that God could have created a world where free agents never do evil and that his goodness obligates him to do so. Since the world is not so, God must not exist.

---

8. Mackie first considers the argument that evil is a necessary corollary of good and rightly rejects it. First, he notes that those theists who believe God is not subject to the laws of logic because of his omnipotence could not sue the arguments. Second, though, the problem with the argument is that it fails to see good and evil as qualities or intrinsic features of things or people. Mackie then considers the claim that evil is a necessary means to good. The problem with this suggestion, Mackie correctly notes, is that it can only work if God is subject to causal laws, but most theists claim that God is in control of, or created the causal laws. Additionally, it suggests that God somehow needs evil. The third argument Mackie considers is the claim that a universe with some evil is better than a universe with no evil. He notes that this claim is usually supported in one of two ways: it may be claimed that a contrast enhances the beauty/goodness of any particular, such that without evil, there would be no way to enhance the good, or it may be claimed that progress is preferable to stasis, and that evil is necessary to the ability to progress. Mackie notes that such a solution does not adequately address all the different types of evil or the magnitude of evil. In addition to these considerations, though, at least the former suggests that God's perfect goodness could not be recognized as such without the existence of evil, which means that infinite goodness is somehow inadequate. For a discussion of the second, see the chapter on evolution. Last, Mackie considers the appeal to free will as the explanation for evil, as discussed above.

9. Mackie does argue that if freedom is not compatibilistic, if free acts do not follow deterministically from an individual's character, then it/they must be *random*. In fact, it is his failure to take agent-causal freedom seriously that is Mackie's fatal flaw. Interestingly, it also shows how Mackie's argument is particularly difficult for Calvinist thinkers, who have to assert that God *could* have made persons such that they always do the good, but purposely chose to not do so.

10. Mackie, "Evil and Omnipotence," 209. Pike agrees, arguing that if it is logically possible that free agents not-sin, then God could bring about a world where there is no sin. Nelson Pike, "Plantinga on the Free Will Defense: A Reply," *The Journal of Philosophy* 63, no. 4 (1966): 93–104.

Molinism and the Free Will Defense/Free Will Theodicy

The dominant answer to the logical problem of evil has been Alvin Plantinga's free will defense. The free will defense claims that it is possible God could not have created a world where creatures are free and there is no evil, and he was obligated to create a world where creatures are free because worlds with free creatures (even with evil) are better than worlds without free creatures. A word or two of clarification is in order here.

First, it is presupposed that God is obliged to do the best, but this is not to say that the actual world is the best of all possible worlds, but only that it is among the possible worlds that best meet his goals/purposes for creating. While some theologians claim to know why God chose to create, usually conceived in terms of maximizing his glory or maximizing the number of souls saved, it is hard to have a high degree of confidence in such suggestions, since the Bible never directly addresses God's goals or purposes in creating.[11] If he had multiple purposes for creating, then it stands to reason that there could have been several outcomes that equally meet those purposes and several avenues to each of the desirable outcomes.[12]

In order to see why, consider an admittedly oversimplified example from mathematics. Suppose that we are given a task to produce an equation where the sum is equal to ten. We are given no further instructions or information, except to try to produce the best equation. What would

---

11. Often the discussion of God's purpose in creating reduces to a discussion of God's decrees, understood as having the maximizing of his glory as their basis. For example, the Westminster Catechism states, "The decrees of God are His eternal purpose, according to the counsel of His will, whereby for His own glory he has foreordained whatsoever comes to pass." *Westminster Shorter Catechism*, 7. Williams rightly cautions against such bold pronouncements regarding God's purposes, noting that the only clear answer in Scripture to the question of why God created is that he willed it: "*That* He did it, and then *how* He did it are both stated, but *why* He did it is totally undeclared. Hence, one must exercise much restraint in proceeding further to posit the reason or purpose." J. Rodman Williams, *Renewal Theology* (Grand Rapids: Zondervan, 1996), 115.

There is no reason to think that God only has one purpose for creating. While it is certainly plausible that maximizing his glory and the number of souls saved are both concerns that influenced his decision to create, there could easily be other factors at play as well (e.g., express his love, express his aesthetic nature, etc.). Just as humans often have multiple reasons or goals for acting, so also could God. There is also no reason to think that divine simplicity, if true, must apply to God's purposes, goals, or desires, so that there cannot be a multiplicity of them. It is meant to serve as a means of conceiving of the infinite being of God and the relations of the attributes. Under simplicity, it is still appropriate to differentiate attributes one from another, even while acknowledging their unity in him. Similarly, the multiple purposes or goals God may have for creating may be in harmony in him, but distinguishable nonetheless.

12. Drawing upon the terminology introduced earlier, we may say that there could be several possible worlds that satisfy God's desires or purposes equally well. Even if God does have a single overarching goal, such as maximizing his glory or maximizing the expression of his love, there is no good reason to think that it could only be arrived at by means of a single avenue; there could still be several possible worlds that best meet his goal, several world histories that result in a maximum amount of God's glory revealed.

such an equation look like? A number of ideas come to mind: 10+0; 5+5; 1+1+8; 3+7; 6.72+3.28; etc., and while an argument could possibly be constructed to defend the elegance of the first two as superior to the others, it would hardly be convincing and would still leave us without a means to adjudicate between the two as "best."[13] The point is that there is a virtually infinite number of equations that satisfy the requirement without there being a best among them. Nevertheless, there is also an infinite number of equations that do not meet the requirement at all, namely all equations that do not express a sum equal to ten (e.g., 5+2; 12+7; 12–2; –25+50; 5*2; 1,000,000+9,743; etc.). The analogy to possible worlds and God's creative activity, given his desires/will, should be clear. If God has goals and desires in creating, then there are a number of possible worlds that fall short, and there is a class of possible worlds that equally meet those goals and desires but arrive at the product differently.[14] It seems clear enough that God would be obligated to actualize one of those possible worlds that best meets his purpose(s), if he chose to create.

Second, while the language of obligation suggests an infringement upon God's aseity (self-sufficiency) and freedom, a moment's reflection will reveal that this is not the case. The nature of the obligation has to do with the kind of world God could actualize if he were to choose to create, but he could refrain from creating; nothing internal or external to him

---

13. One may try to argue that "10+0" and "5+5" are more elegant due to the ease of the addition or the repetition of numbers or the symmetry in the equations or the like, but given the parameters of the instructions, it would be hard to defend.

14. Robert Adams wrote a provocative piece on the question of God's obligation to create the best. The bulk of his article is focused on the question of to whom God would be so obliged. God could not be obligated to the nonexistent creatures who would inhabit the best world, because an obligation only exists when both parties exist in relationship one to another. Similarly, Adams notes, a creature who does not exist should not complain about his own circumstances (even if unpleasant)—that he suffers because he is not in the best possible world—because if God were to create the best possible world, that creature may not exist. Adams then moves to consider the Christian notion of grace, and suggests that it could be used to explain why an all-powerful, all-good God may choose to create a world less than the best, for it is more gracious to love a lesser being than to love the best possible being. Of particular interest is Adams' suggestion, at the beginning of the article, that it makes no sense to suppose there can be a best possible world because more goodness can always be added. He writes, "I do not in fact see any good reason to believe that there is a best among possible worlds. Why can't it be that for every possible world there is another that is better?" Robert Merrihew Adams, "Must God Create the Best?" *Philosophical Review* 81, no. 3 (1972): 317. David Basinger has argued that there are sets of worlds that meet God's purposes, and other sets that do not. However, he argues that the obligation that God has in creating extends to individual persons. David Basinger, "In What Sense Must God Be Omnibenevolent?," *International Journal for Philosophy of Religion* 14, no. 1 (1983): 3–15. Hasker has questioned Basinger's claims, arguing that a less meticulous view of providence affords God greater freedom in his creation decisions, and allows for the possibility of gratuitous evil. William Hasker, "Must God Do His Best?," *International Journal for Philosophy of Religion* 16 (1984): 213–33. For Basinger's response, see David Basinger, "In What Sense Must God Do His Best: A Response to Hasker," *International Journal for Philosophy of Religion* 18 (1985): 161–64.

compels him to create. The creative aspect of his nature can be realized/expressed within Godself.[15] Just as God's decision to create is a libertarianly free act such that he can choose to create or not-create, so also his decision about which of the specific possible worlds he will actualize among the class of worlds that meet his purposes is a free choice. So the obligation in no way detracts from God's freedom, aseity, or sovereignty. The purposes for creating, the decision to create, and the choice of possible worlds to actualize are all expressions of his free and sovereign will.

Third, the language of possibility is not incidental. As noted earlier, the requirements for a defense are much more narrow than those for a theodicy. Thus, the free will defense need not prove that it *is the case* that God could not create a world where creatures are free and there is no evil. It need not even show that it is more likely than not.[16] All the free will defense must do is show it is *possibly* true, that these ideas do not violate the fundamental laws of logic.

Fourth, the claim that a world with free creatures may be better than a world without free creatures requires explication. A number of philosophers and theologians have pointed to human (creaturely) free will as the greater good that justifies God's inaction in the face of horrendous evil. Free will is not typically seen as the good itself, but rather as a necessary constituent of the good, which is variously seen as the human capacity to love (understood as necessarily freely given), or the human responsibility for and to others (understood as necessitating the capacity to both benefit and harm others), or as more broad characteristics such as morality, aesthetics, or self-expression/creativity (all thought to be based in human freedom).[17] The point is that each of these goods is grounded in freedom and, so it is claimed, not only requires that humans be free, but also justifies the allowance of evil.

For example, take love: It is claimed that a truly loving relationship must have reciprocity, and to be meaningful, it must be an expression of one's freely developed affections for the other. It is assumed that most of us would find little satisfaction, at least in the long-term, in being the recipient of a coerced love like that described in fairy tales of love potions or love spells. Such "love" seems contrived, artificial, not true. If one of God's purposes

---

15. Some may wonder how such dynamic creativity may find expression in an infinite, static Being. I would suggest that it is here where Trinitarian theology may prove especially valuable. The triune God is dynamic in his relations within himself, and that dynamism can serve as an explanatory tool for dynamism in other areas of his life.

16. Of course, if we could prove it to be the case, or show it to be likely, that would strengthen the case of the apology against the logical argument from evil because it would form the basis of a theodicy to answer the emotive/evidential argument from evil.

17. Swinburne argues for human responsibility in relationship, while Plantinga vacillates between the capacity to love and morality. Richard Swinburne, *The Existence of God* (Oxford: Oxford University Press, 1979, rev. 1991), 188–89; Plaintinga, *God, Freedom, and Evil* (Grand Rapids: Eerdmans, 1974), 9–11, 45–49.

for creating was to maximize the number of persons in loving relationship with him, then to meet that purpose, he would have to create a world where humans are free, even if it means the potential for great evil and suffering, and even if he knows ahead of time that many will not respond in love. As long as his creative act meets its purposes, and its purposes are of greater worth/good than the resulting evil, then God is justified.

Who could know that creating a world with free creatures who have the potential to love or hate and do good or evil would better meet God's desires? The answer, not surprisingly, is the God of Molinism. A God with middle knowledge would know all the outcomes of the free actions of creatures, including the free responses of other creatures to those actions, on down the chains of causation and relational responses in the history of the world. Neither the God of Open Theism nor, in some sense, the God of Calvinism can make that claim.

The God of Open Theism cannot be assured that the freedom enjoyed by creatures would result in an overall surplus of good; it may be the case that the amount of evil in the world would overwhelm the good. If God only has present and past knowledge, then at the moment he creates, he knows his own intentions to create humans with a capacity for love, and he hopes they will realize their potential for good in their actions. However, without knowledge of counterfactuals of freedom, he simply cannot know whether humans will use their freedom for evil or good. He can override their freedom, but that is another matter and arguably, would reduce the relative amount of good to below that of evil (perhaps overriding creaturely freedom would itself be an evil, something God would not do). The God of Calvinism can certainly know that humanity will use its freedom for ultimate good; in fact, he can guarantee it, since he can determine the free decisions of his creatures. However, the free will defense is compromised because its claim that it is possible God could not create a world with free creatures who do not sin is thereby removed. If God can determine free creaturely actions, then he can make creatures freely choose to always do good. The compatibilist must explain why God did not determine all creaturely actions to be good; God seems responsible for creaturely evil and a different theodicy is required. By contrast, the Molinist can claim that God can know good will come about by creaturely freedom, and that God may not have been able to create a world where creatures are free but never sin.

Take the second claim first. Consider the story of humanity's fall: the Garden, Adam, Eve, the serpent, the Tree of the Knowledge of Good and Evil, and the forbidden fruit. Presumably, Adam was free with respect to eating the fruit such that both of the following counterfactuals of freedom are possibly true:

> If Adam is free with respect to eating the forbidden fruit and is offered the fruit by Eve, he will freely accept and eat;

and

> If Adam is free with respect to eating the forbidden fruit and is offered the
> fruit by Eve, he will freely refuse and refrain from eating.

Under typical Calvinist principles, both are live options for God, since the
locus of Adam's decision to eat or not is found in his desires, which are determined by the way he is constituted (in creation by God).[18] Thus, God could
have created Adam so he would freely refuse the offer and refrain from
eating, and he could create Adam so he would freely accept and eat. The
situation is more complex under Molinist principles, for while there *could*
be situations where Adam refuses the offer and fasts, they do not necessarily
exist. It could be that every time Adam is offered the fruit, he always (freely)
accepts and eats. If this were to be the case, then God only has two options
(with Adam): 1) create Adam free and allow sin to enter the world, or 2)
create Adam without freedom and prevent sin from entering the world. The
point here is that a world where Adam is free and does not sin is not a live
option for God (it is not *feasible*, even though *possible*).[19]

Some may wonder what would *make* Adam always choose to eat when
offered the forbidden fruit, if it is possible he not-sin. While the question,
as worded, is somewhat loaded because it suggests a force or entity outside
the individual causing his choices—it is Adam's own willing that determines his choice—the following principle has been suggested by Plantinga
as explanatory: perhaps Adam suffers from *transworld depravity*, a malady
described by the individual's doing at least one morally bad act in every
possible world in which he exists.[20] Of course, if transworld depravity is

---

18.   Here, I am assuming that the truth of counterfactuals of creaturely freedom in a Calvinist
      system is based on the divine will and known by God's free knowledge. This seems to be
      what Calvin himself thought and what the reformed opponents of Arminius at Dort thought.
      However, some Calvinists, following Edwardsian arguments and logic, have claimed that
      counterfactuals of creaturely freedom are known by God's natural knowledge and are, thus,
      necessarily true. This suggestion is fraught with difficulty, but is usually augmented by the
      claim that a corollary with the opposite antecedent is also true and therefore, while both are
      true necessarily (because of possibility), which is actual is still based on God's will and both
      are live options for God prior to his act of will.

19.   The perceptive reader will note that the reference to the specific individual Adam and the
      specific instance of the eating of the forbidden fruit in the Garden when offered by Eve must
      serve as a paradigmatic case in the argument. It could be the case that every world where
      creatures (like Adam) are free (like in the case of the Garden and offer of fruit), some creature
      goes wrong with respect to sin; the specific case of Adam can be universalized to apply to any
      person and even all persons.

20.   More formally, "An *essence E suffers from transworld depravity* if and only if for every world *W*
      such that *E* contains the properties *is significantly free in W* and *always does what is right in W*,
      there is an action *A* and a maximal world segment *S'* such that

      > *S'* includes *E's being instantiated* and *E's instantiations's being free with respect to A* and
      > *A's being morally significant for E's instantiation*,

possible for one, then it is possible for all. That is, it is possible that all persons God could create (or in the philosophical language, all *individual creaturely essences God could instantiate*) suffer from transworld depravity, and if that were the case, then God could not create a world where creatures are free and there is no sin. As Plantinga puts it, "if every essence suffers from transworld depravity, then no matter which essences God instantiates, the resulting persons, if free with respect to morally significant actions, would always perform at least some wrong actions. . . . Under these conditions God could have created a world containing no moral evil only by creating one without significantly free persons."[21] If creaturely freedom is necessary to meet God's purposes in creating, then if God creates, he must create a world where there is sin. If such a situation is *possible*, then there is no *logical* contradiction in believing that God exists and evil occurs. Since there is no good reason to think it impossible, the free will defense answers the logical problem of evil utilizing the Molinist concept of feasibility.[22]

Now take the first claim, that God can know good will come about by means of creaturely freedom, or that God can be assured that his desires/purposes in creating will be met even though he cannot determine the truths of counterfactuals of creaturely freedom. Molinism's theodicy rests in this claim, but Open Theism has no such guarantee. In order to see why, consider the following story.

When I was in college, I had a friend named Tim who told our Sunday School class of the death of his mother when he was a child. Although he noted that it had been a very hurtful experience for him, he also believed that it was this event that eventually led him to salvation in Christ. God used the loss to bring him to a point emotionally and spiritually where he acknowledged his need for God and forgiveness in Christ. The story implies that there are free responses Tim made to his mother's death. Thus, the following propositions capture the story:

> As a direct result of his mother's death, Tim's disposition toward God changed so that he was now more sensitive to God's call to salvation;

> S' is included in W but includes neither E's *instantiation's performing* A nor E's *instantiation's refraining from* A

and

> If S' were actual, then the instantiation of E would have gone wrong with respect to A.

Plantinga, *God, Freedom, and Evil*, 52–3; propositional numbering has been removed.
21. Plantinga, *God, Freedom, and Evil*, 53.
22. Some may question the theological tenability of transworld depravity applied to Adam, since depravity became a problem as a result of the Fall. This is a valid concern, but the concept of transworld depravity is simply an example of the kind of condition that could explain the issue of Adam's choice to sin every time he is free. He wouldn't necessarily have to suffer from it; he may simply choose to sin every time he is free and that is that.

> God, knowing Tim's changed disposition, called him to salvation;

and

> Tim responded in faith to God's call.[23]

Interestingly, though, these points, even if true, cannot stand alone and allow the theodicy to work.

Kenneth Perszyk has noted that greater good theodicies that depend on free human response (as in the example) require God possess middle knowledge.[24] For the greater good theodicy to work, God must know beforehand that good would come from a particular evil event. Otherwise, there is no guarantee that he can get the result he desires. Thus, God must have known that Tim would respond in faith if God were to call him to salvation upon the death of his mother. Moreover, God must have known that this was the best way (or one of the best ways) for Tim to come to faith.[25] In other words, God knew

> If his mother were to die when he was x years old, Tim would be more sensitive to God's call to salvation;

and

> If God were to call Tim to salvation, Tim would respond in faith;

and

> There is no other way for this change in Tim to take place that will require less evil;

prior to the death of Tim's mother. Much more could be said of this example, but the important point is that it demonstrates that the only way God can ensure a greater good (based in free actions) will result from any given

---

23. Some may read this example and fear that it borders on Pelagianism. However, other examples can be given which are not directly tied to salvation. For example, there may be a person who, after traveling to Cambodia and viewing the immense suffering there as a result of a lack of food, comes back to America and begins a relief organization which feeds literally millions. For a discussion of human response in belief and salvation, see chapters 5 and 9.

24. Kenneth Perszyk, "Stump's Theodicy of Redemptive Suffering and Molinism," *Religious Studies* 25, no. 2 (June 1999): 191–211.

25. It is always assumed that God will use the least amount of evil to bring about the greatest amount of good. I have used the term "best" to denote this assumption. However, it may be the case that there are two ways to bring about the same good that entail the same amount of evil.

evil is for him to possess middle knowledge.[26] The God of Open Theism could not know Tim would respond in faith; he might guess it to be true, or think it true, but could not *know* it and could not guarantee the greater good (Tim's faith) would result.[27]

PROBABILISTIC PROBLEMS OF EVIL

The dominant strategy for questioning the existence of God based on evil has been to claim that it is unlikely that an all-loving, all-good, all-powerful being exists, given evil, conceived either in terms of the *amount* or the *nature* of evil in the world. There is a whole family of arguments of this sort. Many suggest that it is more probable that God not-exist than exist, given the evil in the world, so that atheism is the appropriate response to reflection on these issues. However, others make the more modest claims, that reflection on probabilities should lead to agnosticism or can at least establish the rationality of atheism.

Quantitative Argument
The first type of argument simply points to the amount of evil in the world. It agrees that the logical problem of evil fails under the free will defense, but claims that God is not absolved of guilt. Proponents argue that while it is conceivable that creaturely freedom might lead to some evil in the world and *could* constitute a greater good that would lead God to allow some evils, it is nevertheless doubtful of all evil in the world. The massive quantity of evil and suffering in the world outweighs the supposed good of creaturely freedom, and therefore speaks against God's goodness and/or his existence.

This type of argument is sometimes called the emotive problem of evil because of the emotional appeal it enjoys. Stephen Davis summarizes its claims: "If I were God (meaning all powerful and good creator), I would create a better world than this one. I certainly wouldn't create a world with cancer, atomic bombs, child abuse, famine, etc. I would

---

26. Some may find it troubling because they fear it suggests God killed Tim's mother so he could be saved, but this misses the point of the story and fails to appreciate the complexities involved in God's governance of the world post-Fall.

27. A final note about the free will defense. One the one hand, anyone can use it as a response to the logical problem of evil because of its nature *as a defense*. This means that even those who disagree with libertarian creaturely freedom may use it, so long as they grant that such freedom is *possible* and not fundamentally incoherent. Since most philosophers have affirmed libertarian freedom in humans (or at least its possibility), the problem has generally come to be seen as effectively answered. However, for those who question the coherence of libertarian freedom, the free will defense is neither a viable option for response nor a persuasive answer to the logical problem of evil. In that case, a different approach is needed, usually an appeal to another *greater good*. Additionally, even though the free will defense enjoys widespread acceptance, it is of limited use; it only defends theism against the specific charge of incoherence and does not really address the larger problem of evil, and it is to this that we now turn.

create a world without these things. Therefore, it does not seem that the Christian God created this world."[28] The argument assumes that this is not among the best possible worlds; God could have done better, and if he exists, he should have done so. As Rowe puts it, "I'm sure it strikes most of us as just plain reasonable to think that if there were an omnipotent, omniscient being, then a bit more activity on his part would have made the world somewhat better."[29]

This argument has significant emotional appeal, but suffers from a severe lack of precision. One of the most common approaches to answering this objection is to simply question the supposed knowledge of the objector: On what grounds can such an assertion be made? How can the objector claim to know what an omniscient, omnibenevolent, omnipotent being would or should do? For example, Davis writes:

> I have not the vaguest idea what sort of world I would create given the stated conditions, nor do I believe anyone else does. Of course, my general aim would be to create a world with the best possible balance of good over evil. Would eliminating cancer or free moral agents achieve this end? I just don't know, and I do not believe anyone else does either. Of course it is *possible* that if I knew all relevant facts I would create a world much different than this one. But it is also *possible* that I would create a world as much like this one as I could. I just don't know enough to say, and neither does anyone else, in my opinion. And I fail to see any argument here that renders the first more probable than the second.[30]

Of course, this alludes to the greater good thesis; perhaps God has his reasons for allowing the evil he has, and we simply aren't privy to them.

Another approach to answering the objection is to question its lack of specific quantification. The complaint states that God would not allow the amount of evil there is (if he were to exist), but it fails to note how much he would/could allow (if he were to exist), and this failure is deadly for the objection. At the end of the day, most atheistic objectors simply cannot quantify an amount of evil that is acceptable, and the answer invariably devolves into the logical problem of evil. Consider the words of Sam Harris:

> Somewhere in the world a man has abducted a little girl. Soon he will rape, torture, and kill her. If an atrocity of this kind is not occurring at precisely this moment, it will happen in a few hours, or days at most. Such is the confidence we can draw from the statistical laws that govern the lives of six

28.   Stephen T. Davis, "Free Will and Evil," in *Encountering Evil: Live Options in Theodicy*, ed. Stephen T. Davis (Atlanta: John Knox, 1981), 76.

29.   William Rowe, "Ruminations about Evil," in Tomberlin, ed., *Philosophical Perspectives*, 74.

30.   Davis, "Free Will and Evil," 76–77.

billion human beings. The same statistics also suggest that this girl's parents believe—as you believe—that an all-powerful and all-loving God is watching over them and their family. Are they right to believe this? Is it *good* that they believe this? No. . . . An atheist is a person who believes that the murder of a single little girl—even once in a million years—casts doubt upon the idea of a benevolent God.[31]

Harris' point is clear: there is no amount of evil or suffering that is compatible with the existence of God. One instance nullifies rational belief in God. This, then, is our point: the emotive problem of evil is often just a restatement of the logical problem of evil and answered by appeal to the free will defense and theodicy. If the objector claims that some amount of evil is compatible with belief in an omnipotent, omniscient, omnibenevolent God, then he must justify his claim that the current amount is unsatisfactory, while some other amount would be satisfactory. If he cannot (without simple personal appeal/subjectivism), then his position is untenable.

It has sometimes been suggested that God could have used his middle knowledge to arrange things in such a way that free persons would always act rightly. He could have refrained from actualizing those persons who would use their freedom to sin, for instance. This suggestion, of course, only works if something like transworld depravity cannot be true. Still, some have argued that he could pursue a providential strategy in which he only allows persons to act freely when he knows they will perform good works, and override their freedom when they will do evil.

This may be what Mackie had in mind. However, as Perszyk has rightly pointed out, part of the initial attraction of this suggestion is that we typically think of the problem of evil in terms of specific examples with what he calls "thin" antecedents, or counterfactuals that are considered discretely. But when we consider the interrelationships of persons and events in any given possible world, and see that things are much more complex, and that sometimes the initial conditions of one good-resulting counterfactual would require a bad event, or a good-resulting counterfactual may naturally become the initial conditions for a bad-resulting counterfactual, we see that things are more complex than the simple question of why a particular instance of evil occurred or why God failed to prevent a particular tragedy. The complexity of human freedom, relationships, and psychological development, along with the interrelatedness of events in the world and the influences of the past upon the present and future, make such determinations—what God could have changed in order to prevent evil and make for a better world—virtually impossible.[32] In addition, it must be remembered that

31. Sam Harris, *Letter to a Christian Nation* (New York: Vintage, 2006), 50–51, 52.
32. Kenneth J. Perszyk, "Free Will Defense with and without Molinism," *International Journal for Philosophy of Religion* 43 (1998): 38–39. This is not to say that an infinite and omniscient

creaturely freedom itself is a good that may outweigh any given evil. Thus, we would not want a world where creaturely freedom is constantly overridden in order to prevent evil. After all, it is unclear how much divine intervention would be required and how much freedom would remain, if any, in a world where God overrides human freedom in order to prevent every freely performed evil action. It is likewise unclear if some goods would be prevented from coming about. This raises the question of the possibility and impact of supposed gratuitous evil.

Argument from Gratuitous Evil

The strongest probabilistic argument against God's existence draws upon the concept of gratuitous evil and is often referred to as the evidential problem of evil. William Rowe has famously presented this argument.[33] He begins by claiming that we have reason to believe there are instances of intense suffering that could have been prevented without thereby losing some greater good or permitting some evil equally bad or worse. These presumed instances are known as *gratuitous* evil because they seem to serve no greater purpose (i.e., they are not necessary constituent parts to some greater purpose/good). Rowe then notes that most theists grant that an omniscient, wholly good being would prevent the occurrence of intense suffering if he could do so without losing some greater good or permitting some evil equally bad or worse, but this leads to a problem. If God should prevent gratuitous evil, but he hasn't, then his goodness, power, or existence is in doubt.

Rowe correctly notes that those who disagree with the conclusion will probably challenge the claim that there are instances of gratuitous evil. He admits that it cannot be proved beyond all doubt, but suggests there are rational grounds for believing it, and offers examples of what he thinks are clear cases of gratuitous evil. The first involves the suffering

---

Being could not know, but rather that we have no way of knowing how events are related one to another. Our ignorance puts us in a position of inability to make judgments about which evils should have been prevented and which should have been permitted. It may be the case that the evil prevented today would have served as a constraint on some future greater evil perpetrated by others.

33. Edward Madden and Peter Hare were also among the early proponents of the evidential argument from gratuitous evil. They write, "If God is unlimited in power and goodness, why is there so much prima facie gratuitous evil in the world? If he is unlimited in power he should be able to remove unnecessary evil, and if he is unlimited in goodness he should want to remove it; but he does not. Apparently he is limited either in power or goodness, or does not exist at all." Edward H. Madden and Peter H. Hare, *Evil and the Concept of God* (Springfield, IL: Charles H. Thomas, 1968), 3. Their work generated much discussion, and they have responded to a number of their critics. For example, see Edward H. Madden and Peter H. Hare, "Evil and Inconclusiveness," *Sophia* 11, no. 1 (April 1972): 8–12; Edward H. Madden and Peter H. Hare, "Evil and Unlimited Power," *Review of Metaphysics* 20, no. 2 (1966): 278–89.

and eventual death of a non-human animal, presumably due to its inno-cence of moral wrongdoing.[34]

> Suppose in some distant forest lightning strikes a dead tree, resulting in a forest fire. In the fire a fawn is trapped, horribly burned, and lies in terrible agony for several days before death relieves its suffering. So far as we can see, the fawn's intense suffering is pointless. For there dos not appear to be any greater good such that the prevention of the fawn's suffering would require either the loss of that good or the occurrence of an evil equally bad or worse. Nor does there seem to be any equally bad or worse evil so connected to the fawn's suffering that it would have had to occur had the fawn's suffer-ing been prevented. Could an omnipotent, omniscient being have prevented the fawn's apparently pointless suffering? The answer is obvious, as even the theist will insist. An omnipotent, omniscient being could have easily prevented the fawn from being horribly burned, or, given the burning, could have spared the fawn the intense suffering by quickly ending its life, rather than allowing the fawn to lie in terribly agony for several days. Since the fawn's intense suffering was preventable and, so far as we can see, point-less, doesn't it appear that premise (1) of the argument is true, that there do exist instances of intense suffering which an omnipotent, omniscient being could have prevented without thereby losing some greater good or permit-ting some evil equally bad or worse. . . . Is it reasonable to believe that there is some greater good so intimately connected to that suffering that even an omnipotent, omniscient being could have obtained that good without permitting that suffering or some evil at least as bad? It certainly does not appear reasonable to believe this.[35]

Rowe argues that even if there is some sort of good explanation for the specific case of the fawn, it is unlikely that equally viable explanations are available for all instances of suffering in the history of the world.[36]

---

34. It has become increasingly fashionable for philosophers to speak of the problem of animal pain as being particularly problematic for theism. The arguments are varied, but typically focus on either the supposed innocence of the victim, the idea being that animals do not sin, or on the lack of reflective cognition of the victim, the idea being that animals cannot learn and grow from suffering like humans can learn and grow. Theists have responded with refined theodicies. See Michael Murray, *Nature Red in Tooth and Claw: Theism and the Prob-lem of Animal Suffering* (New York: Oxford University Press, 2011); Nicola Hoggard Creegan, *Animal Suffering and the Problem of Evil* (New York: Oxford University Press, 2013); Trent Dougherty, *The Problem of Animal Pain: A Theodicy for All Creatures Great and Small* (New York: Palgrave Macmillan, 2014).
35. William Rowe, "The Problem of Evil and Some Varieties of Atheism," *American Philosophical Quarterly* 16, no. 4 (October 1979): 337.
36. Ibid. Rowe writes, "It seems quite unlikely that *all* the instances of intense suffering occurring daily in our world are intimately related to the occurrence of greater goods or the preven-tion of evils at least as bad; and even more unlikely, should they somehow all be so related, that an omnipotent, omniscient Being could not have achieved at least some of those goods

The point is that the theist has to provide a reasonable explanation for why each and every instance of evil and suffering occurred and was not prevented by God.

The second example involves the brutal rape, beating, and strangulation of a five-year old little girl, borrowed from an article by Bruce Russell. In the article, Russell notes that if God exists, nothing happens which he should have prevented, but argues that events God should have prevented have indeed happened, and concludes that God does not exist. He draws an analogy between the demands of morality upon humans and God; if morality demands action on the part of humans in a particular case, Russell infers, then it demands at least as much action on the part of God. If a human agent would have been expected to prevent some evil, surely God can reasonably be expected to have prevented it as well, but he has not:

> The example I have in mind that supports (9) [Something has happened that any human moral agent should have prevented if he knew about it and could have prevented it without serious risk to himself or others] involves a little girl in Flint, Michigan who was severely beaten, raped, and then strangled to death early on New Year's Day of 1986. The girl's mother was living with her boyfriend, another man who was unemployed, her two children, and her 9-month old infant fathered by the boyfriend. On New Year's Eve all three adults were drinking at a bar near the woman's home. The boyfriend had been taking drugs and drinking heavily. He was asked to leave the bar at 8:00 p.m. After several reappearances he finally stayed away for good at about 9:30 p.m. The woman and the unemployed man remained at the bar until 2:00 a.m. at which time the woman went home and the man to a party at a neighbor's home. Perhaps out of jealousy, the boyfriend attacked the woman when she walked into the house. Her brother was there and broke up the fight by hitting the boyfriend who was passed out and slumped over a table when the brother left. Later the boyfriend attacked the woman again, and this time she knocked him unconscious. After checking the children, she went to bed. Later the woman's 5-year old girl went downstairs to go to the bathroom. The unemployed man returned from the party at 3:45 a.m. and found the 5-year old dead. She had been raped, severely beaten over most of her body and strangled to death by the boyfriend.[37]

Russell argues that any reasonable person would expect another human to intervene and help the little girl, if he could do so, and that a similar

---

(or prevented some of those evils) without permitting the instances of intense suffering that are supposedly related to them. In the light of our experience and knowledge of the variety and scale of human and animal suffering in our world, the idea that none of this suffering could have been prevented by an omnipotent being without thereby losing a greater good or permitting an evil at least as bad seems an extraordinary absurd idea, quite beyond our belief." Ibid., 337–38.

37.   Bruce Russell, "The Persistent Problem of Evil," *Faith and Philosophy* 6, no. 2 (April 1989): 123.

expectation is proper to God. Since God did not intervene, then he must not exist (at least not as traditionally conceived, morally good, omnipotent, and omniscient). Russell considers and rejects several counterarguments. For example, he dismisses the claim that the analogy does not work because God's relationship to creatures is different from that of humans to one another such that it is morally permissible for him to fail to act when it would not be morally permissible for us to fail to act.[38] He argues further that any possible benefit from the child's horrific death cannot justify her suffering at the hands of her mother's boyfriend.[39] Both examples pose a problem of explanation for theists.

Skeptical Theism

Most Christian responses to the evidential problem express some kind of skepticism about gratuitous evil. For example, Plantinga appeals to epistemological uncertainty and notes that just because many evils *appear* to be pointless, we do not thereby have probabilistic reasons for accepting gratuitous evil. To do so, we have to assume that either God would make his reasons for permitting evil clear to us, or that we know many evils are pointless.[40] Neither assumption should be granted by the theist; there are many truths about God and his ways that we don't know and there are many instances in the Bible where seemingly pointless suffering was revealed to have had a good purpose. Wykstra argues similarly, appealing to the vast difference between divine and human knowledge by means of an analogy to human parents and infant children. Just as infants do not understand the good purposes their parents have for allowing them to suffer pain (and we would not expect them to), so also

---

38. He writes, "While it is possible that God's special relationship to his creatures makes it morally permissible for him, but not for any of us, to allow the brutal murder of a 5-year old girl, it is not plausible to think it does. It has been said that God's relationship to his creatures is like that of a parent to his child. But surely that special relationship would not justify God in permitting the brutal murder of the 5-year old since it would not have been permissible of the mother of the child in Flint to have failed to prevent the killing of her child (even by another of her children) because she was its parent. If anything, the special relationship of parent to child would make the duty to prevent the child's brutal murder even more stringent, rather than removing the obligation altogether." Ibid., 124.

39. Russell finds it difficult to believe that there could be any real benefit from the suffering, for the girl or the mother, or the boyfriend, but even if such a suggestion were plausible, he finds it difficult to believe that such intense suffering was a necessary constituent part of that benefit. In consideration of possible *benefits* of the little girl's death, Russell writes, "It is good that a person in need of a vital organ should receive it but it would be wrong to allow a young child to die in order to procure the needed organ. It is also good that the boyfriend or others had the opportunity to develop themselves morally and spiritually, but it would also be wrong to afford them that opportunity if providing it means that a little girl will have to suffer terribly. . . . It seems impermissible to let someone suffer as much as the little girl in Flint did in order to provide someone else with opportunities that will benefit him." Ibid., 127–28.

40. Alvin Plantinga, "Epistemic Probability and Evil," *Archivio Di Filosofia* LVI (1988): 557–84, cited in Rowe, "Ruminations about Evil," 69–88.

humans should not expect to understand the good purposes God may have for allowing them to suffer pain.[41]

Alston takes the argument a step further, suggesting that the evidential argument can only be held by one who is omniscient: "to be justified in such a claim [that there are instances of gratuitous evil] one must be justified in excluding all the live possibilities for what the claim denies to exist [morally sufficient reasons for the given evil]."[42] It is hard to believe that anyone can honestly claim to have reflectively considered all of the potential reasons an omniscient and omnipotent being might have for permitting any given instance of evil and found them all wanting. Such consideration does not even seem possible.

Contra *skeptical theism*
Responses to skeptical theism generally take three forms: incredulity, stronger arguments for gratuitous evil, or challenges to the skepticism it uses because it is problematic for other beliefs. Russell suggests that the gratuitous nature of some evils is self-evident to all rational beings, while Wachterhauser claims that it is immoral to say that some evils are not gratuitous.[43] Rowe charges that Plantinga's response to his original argument is based on a false dichotomy. Plantinga argued that Rowe's claim that there are apparently many cases of pointless evil reduces to either: *it is apparent that certain evils are pointless* or *it is not apparent that certain evils have a point*. The first, Rowe argues, is a stronger claim than he made, while the second is weaker. Instead, the claim that many cases of evil are apparently pointless is that "there is something about them and the situation in which they occur that makes it reasonable

41. Stephen Wykstra, "The Humean Obstacle to Evidential Arguments from Suffering: On Avoiding the Evils of 'Appearance,'" *International Journal for Philosophy of Religion* 16 (1984): 73–93.

42. William P. Alston, "The Inductive Argument from Evil and the Human Cognitive Condition," in Tomberlin, ed., *Philosophical Perspectives*, 36.

43. See, for example, Russell, "The Persistent Problem of Evil"; and Bruce Russell, "Defenseless," in *The Evidential Argument from Evil*, ed. Daniel Howard-Snyder (Bloomington: Indiana University, 1996), 193–205; Brice Wachterhauser, "The Problem of Evil and Moral Skepticism," *International Journal for Philosophy of Religion* 17 (1985): 172. Madden takes a similar approach in his critique of what he calls the "ultimate harmony theodicy," namely, a version of the greater good theodicy that says each evil directly contributes to a good. Madden argues that claims for how particularly horrendous evils are in actuality contributing to good, strain credulity. He writes, "I once mentioned Buchenwald as an example of great moral evil. But it was not really an evil, someone suggested, because it had helped immeasurably in solving the problem of population explosion. I confess that I was greatly agitated: I offered to shovel the speaker into my furnace as an added good. The important point here is this: if one holds the ultimate harmony view and honestly goes into detail trying to discover the ultimate good, he gets really bizarre results." Edward H. Madden, "The Many Faces of Evil," *Philosophy and Phenomenological Research* 24, no. 4 (1964): 487. Madden is correct in both his assessment and his irritation with his debate partner, but it does not follow that no greater good may be reasonably suggested. The problem here has to do with assigning a direct resultant good that is greater than its corresponding evil.

for us to believe that they are pointless."[44] He goes on to note that in the cases of the fawn dying in the forest fire and the rape and murder of the little girl, there can be no overarching good (conceivable) that would justify God's permitting them. While surely emotional, these arguments do not really engage skeptical theism and only restate the original complaints! Only those who already agree with the evidential argument will find them convincing.

Some have engaged the arguments of skeptical theists. For example, McBrayer has questioned Wykstra's use of the parent–child/God–human analogy, expressing doubt that it leads where Wykstra takes it. He argues that the good that follows from suffering should be apparent because loving parents always try to help their children see the good that results from their pain.[45] McBrayer is correct in principle, but he has largely missed the point: The value in communicating the resultant good is directly proportional to the sufferer's ability to apprehend the explanation. At ten years old, my daughter Sydney can understand my explanation for why she needs to get a vaccination, but when she was an infant, I did not bother trying to explain. Instead, I merely sought to provide comfort to her after the shot was administered. If she had never progressed intellectually beyond infancy, then, even at ten, I would not explain why she had to endure the pain of a shot. I would not be obligated to do so and it would be fruitless for me to try. It is presumptuous to assume we could understand the explanation (for evil) if it were given.

Building upon these notions, Durston has appealed to the interrelatedness of events to question gratuitous evil. He argues that our ignorance of how future events are related to past events and of all the ramifications of any given act (or its omission) must leave us uncertain about the status of any given evil as gratuitous or not. For example, an evil perpetrated against someone today may lead him to raise his children differently from how he would otherwise have, thus changing the course of those children's lives. They, in turn, could grow up to affect many others, and so forth. The further into the future considered, the larger the potential good impact of that singular evil act.[46] So the compounding

---

44. Rowe, "Ruminations about Evil," 71–72.
45. Justin McBrayer, "Evidential Arguments from Evil and the 'Seeability' of Compensating Goods," *Auslegung* 27, no. 1 (Winter/Spring 2004): 17–22; see also Justin McBrayer, "CORNEA and Inductive Evidence," *Faith and Philosophy* 26, no. 1 (2009): 77–86.
46. Durston writes, "A single event in the past may at the time appear to be morally insignificant but lead to events of great moral significance decades, centuries, or even millennia later. Similarly, events occurring in the present appear to generate an exponentially increasing number of consequences stretching toward the end of history which, for this argument, is placed at the end of the physical universe." Kirk Durston, "The Complexity of History and Evil: A Reply to Trakakis," *Religious Studies* 42 (2006): 87–88.

of effects, what Durston calls the complexity of history, calls into question all claims about the pointlessness of any evil.[47]

Durston's proposal may be correct, but it is not without potential problems. First, it could be seen as endorsing a deterministic view of history,
wherein the future follows causally and necessarily from the past, with
freedom and contingency removed. While such a view is consistent with
Durston's presentation, it hardly follows from it, and he appears to support
libertarian freedom. The Molinist view of providence is not only compatible with the compounding complexity view, but it makes sense of it.
Middle knowledge explains God's ability to ensure good eventually results
from the free decisions of persons because he can see how all possible
future generations of persons would respond in all situations that could
arise from the occurrence of all possible events today. Second, Trakakis
has argued that Durston is mistaken in his claim that moral appraisals
of current events must account for future impacts. After all, he argues,
charitable acts rendered today may rightly be deemed morally praiseworthy even though we do not know the potential future impact (including
some possible negative results).[48] Trakakis is surely correct in principle,
though he fails to consider the distinction between divine and human
in morality judgments. Judgments of human actions can only take into
account the immediate and foreseeable consequences while judgment of
divine action includes other considerations; we do not know all the consequences of our actions so that our moral praiseworthiness or blameworthiness is restricted to the morality of what we could foresee, along with
the morality of the action itself taken discreetly, but God does know all
the consequences of all potential actions so that his moral praiseworthiness or blameworthiness is expanded to include all consequences of the
actions taken or not taken.[49] Third, one may call into question Durston's

---

47. Kirk Durston, "The Consequential Complexity of History and Gratuitous Evil," *Religious Stud-
ies* 36 (2000): 65–80; Durston, "The Complexity of History and Evil," 87–99; Kirk Durston,
"The Failure of Type–4 Arguments from Evil, in the Face of the Consequential Complexity of
History," *Philo* 8, no. 2 (2006): 109–22.

48. Nick Trakakis, "Evil and the Complexity of History: A Response to Durston," *Religious Studies*
39 (2003): 451–58.

49. As Durston rightly points out, humans are simply unable to calculate the relative moral impact
of actions taken today with respect to future consequences. God, however, could. He writes,
"In order to compare the actual history with an alternate history, we must have knowledge
of an unknown number of consequences stretching to the end of history so that we can sum
the intrinsic moral value of each consequence to calculate A. Secondly, we must look at the
proposed, better alternative event and perform the same summing of all the intrinsic moral
values of the different set of consequences stretching to the end of the alternate history to
calculate B. It is only then that we are in a position to compare the two net moral values and
justify our conclusion that God should have, or should not have, permitted the instance of
evil being examined. . . . Unfortunately, the knowledge that we do have regarding the consequences stretching to the end of actual history is miniscule in comparison to what we do not
know." Durston, "The Complexity of History and Evil," 88–89.

claim that the further into the future one considers, the greater the impact of any given event. It could be the case that one's actions have a profound effect on those persons immediately affected, but as the story of the events are passed from generation to generation, the collective memory becomes more and more clouded until the effective impact of the original act(s) is nil. This, of course, is an accurate representation of a great many events and actions in which we participate, even our lives. After our deaths, most of us fall into relative obscurity until we are eventually forgotten. However, this fact (if true) does nothing to negate the fact that some events/actions that seem obscure, unimportant, or pointless, may indeed have an aggregate impact that is significant, and not only significant, but of a differing ethical value from the morality of the event/action at the time of occurrence. Thus, Durston's argument stands up to scrutiny.

Some critics of skeptical theism argue that it opens a Pandora's box of sorts; if our inability to know leads to such widespread skepticism about our ability to make judgments regarding evil, then it seems that we should be skeptical about a whole host of beliefs: of the past, of morality, of aspects of the external world, of certain theological propositions, or even of our belief-forming mechanisms themselves.[50] For example, Russell has argued that if we cannot have confidence in our belief that some evils are pointless, then we cannot have confidence in our beliefs that God did not create the world five minutes ago and made it appear to be older.[51] Howard-Snyder and O'Leary-Hawthorne have claimed that similar reasoning could be used to undermine confidence in quantum indeterminacy, which they take as established fact.[52]

Arguments of this sort have answers readily available. First, it is possible that we are wrong in our beliefs about the physical world; many evangelical Christians doubt the age of the Earth as propounded by most in the scientific community, and many—theologians and scientists alike—believe that when all the facts are in, quantum indeterminacy will be proved wrong. Second, as Bergmann rightly points out, skepticism regarding our ability to know God's ways (with respect to his use of evil to bring about good) is different from skepticism regarding our belief that the world really is as it appears. The two types of belief are not on par.[53] For

50. For the undermining of morality argument, see Scott Aikin and Brian Ribeiro, "Skeptical Theism, Moral Skepticism, and Divine Commands," *International Journal for the Study of Skepticism* 3 (2003): 77–96.

51. Russell, "Defenseless," 193–205.

52. John O'Leary-Hawthorne and Daniel Howard-Snyder, "God Schmod and Gratuitous Evil," *Philosophy and Phenomenological Research* 53, no. 4 (December 1993): 861–74.

53. Michael Bergmann, "Skeptical Theism and Rowe's New Evidential Argument from Evil," *Nous* 35, no. 2 (2001): 290–91. I do not here mean to imply that young-earth creationism is *the same as*, or on an intellectual par with Russell's example of a 5-minute old earth. I do, however, mean to say that the *appearance of age* argument, often employed by young-earth creationists (inconsistently along with catastrophism) makes use of similar reasoning. God *could* have created the

beliefs regarding secular truths (i.e., truths regarding nonreligious reality, like the material processes of the physical universe), the skeptical theist can draw upon the same reasons for his beliefs that a non-theist uses and need not be skeptical. Beaudoin agrees, but raises an important consideration for the discussion: the use of divine revelation for belief formation.[54] The problem here, if it is a problem, is that there seems to be no way of forming common ground between the theist and the non-theist upon which to adjudicate theological claims/beliefs. On the one hand, the non-theist views the theist's appeal to divine revelation as justification for his beliefs as an obvious instance of circular reasoning. On the other hand, the theist sees the non-theist's critique of the faith based on human standards of reasonability as idolatry. For each, the method of the other is unacceptable. Systematic theologians have long argued for the self-justifying nature of religious beliefs, and they have of late been joined by a number of philosophers as well, and many atheistic philosophers assume there is a standard of reason that may be applied to all inquiry (e.g., empiricism), even into the nature of religious belief.[55] All of this may suggest something of an impasse in the discussion, which will be discussed below.

Some critics of skeptical theism take it even further; both Parsons and Piper argue that skeptical theism actually leads to agnosticism! As Parsons writes in reference to William Lane Craig's claim that we cannot assign probabilities to God's having sufficient reasons for permitting horrendous

---

world five minutes ago and given it the appearance of age, just as he could have created the world 6,000 or 14,000 years ago and given it the appearance of age. In both cases, we would not know any better (at least if he programmed our minds to have memories beyond five minutes past as part of the appearance of age). Of course, most of us do not believe it to be the case that God created just five minutes ago, so on the one hand, Russell's argument needs no answer because we can grant his point while denying its problematic status, while on the other hand, most of us doubt the claim so that some sort of answer ought to be given regarding the basis of our beliefs. Obviously, those who believe in a young earth and appeal to some kind of appearance of age argument do so on the basis of what they believe the Scripture to have revealed about God's actions and the history of humanity. See also Michael Bergmann and Michael Rea, "In Defense of Sceptical Theism: A Reply to Almeida and Oppy," *Australasian Journal of Philosophy* 83, no. 2 (June 2005): 241–51. For a response, see Michael Almeida and Graham Oppy, "Evidential Arguments from Evil and Skeptical Theism," *Philo* 8, no. 2 (Winter 2005): 84–94.

54. John Beaudoin, "Skepticism and the Skeptical Theist," *Faith and Philosophy* 22, no. 1 (January 2005): 42–56.

55. Since systematic theology is the exploration of the meaning of the faith we hold, it is legitimate to presuppose the existence of God and his having revealed himself to humanity in, for instance, the Bible. A growing number of Christian philosophers have argued that belief in God is properly basic and therefore, in need of no justifying argument or proof in order to be rationally/responsibly held. See, for example, Alvin Plantinga, *Warranted Christian Belief* (Oxford: Oxford University Press, 2000); and Alvin Plantinga and Nicholas Wolterstorff, eds., *Faith and Rationality: Reason and Belief in God* (Notre Dame, IN: University of Notre Dame Press, 1983); Most notably, William Alston has suggested that the self-justifying aspects of divine revelation are similar to the self-justifying aspects of sense perception. See William Alston, *Perceiving God: The Epistemology of Religious Experience* (Ithaca, NY: Cornell University Press, 1993).

evils, "But this statement entails that no one can know whether the above proposition (P) [i.e., God has morally sufficient reasons for permitting all of the evils that actually occur] is even probably true. The upshot is that Craig seems to have left us in a position of agnosticism about (P), and so agnosticism about God's existence."[56] Piper develops a similar argument by turning the skepticism of knowledge of gratuitous evil upon knowledge of pure goodness. In effect, he argues that the kind of skepticism appealed to by skeptical theism leads to a lack of confidence in apprehension of goodness itself, as well as God's relation to goodness. After all, if it is possible that our cognitive capacity "is such that we cannot discern certain higher goods which somehow entail the evil we experience as gratuitous; it seems also possible that it is such that we perceive things to be good which in fact are not goods in relation to—as entailed in some way by—certain unknown higher goods."[57] Piper goes on to claim that theism requires confidence in one's ability to adjudicate moral hierarchies. More than this, though, Piper turns Alston's own words against him: if God's being and ways are so mysterious that one cannot know how seemingly gratuitous evil can be used by him for greater good (though presumably it is), then it seems he also cannot know much about God's goodness or those attributes that make him worthy of worship. As Piper writes, "Consequently, it is entirely possible that positive or even probable pronouncements concerning a great many of the claims about the nature of the divine are beyond our epistemic rights."[58]

These claims are overstated. After all, no skeptical theists have claimed absolute ignorance about God and his ways, and there is a rich tradition in Christian theology of emphasizing the transcendence of God. The Scriptures speak of his otherness, and it is appropriate for Christian theologians to draw upon this truth when reflecting upon his work and ways. Rather than seeing the appeal to skeptical theism as an answer to the evidential argument, it is probably best to view it as a caveat to keep in mind: God is mysterious, his ways are above ours, and he sometimes uses evils to bring about his plans, often in ways that those who suffered could never have foreseen apart from divine revelation. To use it as a defeater for the evidential argument is to expect too much from it.[59]

---

56.   Keith Parsons, "Evil and the Unknown Purpose Defense: Remarks Addressed to Theodore Drange's Nonbelief & Evil," *Philo* 8, no. 2 (Fall/Winter 2005): 165 (160–68). cf. William Lane Craig, "God on Trial: Craig Answers Parsons," *Dallas Morning News* (June 13, 1998), 3G.

57.   Mark Piper, "Why Theists Cannot Accept Skeptical Theism," *Sophia* 47, no. 2 (July 2008): 136–37.

58.   Piper, "Why Theists Cannot Accept Skeptical Theism," 139. cf. Alston, "The Inductive Argument from Evil," 97–125.

59.   Claiming ignorance regarding God's purposes or reasons for permitting evils does not say that one cannot reasonably believe none exist. As Parsons rightly points out, atheological arguments from evil are rational and show nonbelief to be a rational position. Parsons, "Evil and the Unknown Purpose Defense," 160–68. It is so because of the seeming obvious nature of

God's transcendence does not release him from moral obligation. As Schlesinger has said, we should "apply as far as possible human ethical standards in our appraisal of Divine conduct" because "we have no other notions of good and bad except those appertaining to human situations."[60] This is not to say that God should be judged by human standards or subject to human modes of thinking. Rather, it is to acknowledge that God is the standard by which we measure and know goodness, rightness, justice, etc., and to rely on his revelation of himself in Scripture as perfectly good. If my theological construct results in a view of God that conflicts with what we know of goodness or justice, then there is good reason to not only question my beliefs about goodness and justice, but also my theology. One or both is probably in error.

While skeptical theists have correctly pointed out that the evidential argument begs the question of the existence of gratuitous evil, it should be noted that the skeptical theist response begs the question of the nonexistence of gratuitous evil. As Rowe points out, if one were to follow skeptical theistic principles to their logical conclusion, no amount of evil can speak against God's existence.[61]

Christianity/Theism and Gratuitous Evil

An increasing number of theists are convinced that there are instances of gratuitous evil and argue that it does not speak against God's existence or goodness.[62] As MacGregor writes, "this seems a far more fruitful path

---

gratuitous evil; it is so obvious that many atheologians take it to be axiomatic and offer little by way of argument or proof.

60. George Schlesinger, "Omnipotence and Evil: An Incoherent Problem," *Sophia* 4, no. 3 (1965): 21; George Schlesinger, "The Problem of Evil and the Problem of Suffering," *American Philosophical Quarterly* 1, no. 3 (July 1964): 244.

61. Rowe writes, "For, to repeat their constant refrain, since we don't know that the goods we know of are representative of the goods that are, we cannot know that it is even likely that there are no goods that justify God in permitting whatever amount of apparently pointless, horrific evil there might occur in our world. Indeed, if human life were nothing more than a series of agonizing moments from birth to death, their position would still require them to say that we cannot reasonably infer that it is even likely that God does not exist. But surely such a view is unreasonable, if not absurd." William Rowe, "Skeptical Theism: A Response to Bergmann," *Nous* 35 (2001): 298.

62. Michael Peterson, William Hasker, Kirk MacGregor, Bruce Little, to name a few. Peter van Inwagen has taken a somewhat unique approach. Like those who agree that there is gratuitous evil, he argues that instances of gratuitous evil do nothing to speak against the existence of God. However, he does not necessarily grant that there are such instances. Instead, he argues that the evidential argument from gratuitous evil leads to something of an infinite regress, similar to the quantitative arguments, such that they eventually require that God prevent all evil. See Peter van Inwagen, "The Argument from Particular Horrendous Evils," *Proceedings of the American Catholic Philosophical Association* 74 (2000): 65–80; see also Peter van Inwagen, "The Magnitude, Duration, and Distribution of Evil: A Theodicy," *Philosophical Topics* 16 (1988): 167–68. However, all are not so convinced. For an interesting critique of van Inwagen's argument (or at least his conclusion that gratuitous evil is therefore compatible with God's existence because God is under no obligation to reduce suffering), see Nick Trakakis, "God,

for Christian theists to take in terms of apologetic tactics, since it neither places upon theistic shoulders the overwhelming burden of proof of showing that none of the world's evils is gratuitous in the face of powerful intuition and evidence to the contrary, nor does it ask hearers of theistic arguments to abandon their cognitive insight that gratuitous evil exists."[63] Little concurs, arguing that the greater good theodicy is fraught with problems, from suggesting evil is necessary to the good, to the ends justifying the means, to undercutting social justice, to creating difficulty for intercessory prayer (why pray for evil to be abated if it always leads to a greater good?), to the relativizing of the concept of the good, to lacking objective criteria for measuring good over against the evil, to placing limits on God.[64] Both agree that the existence of gratuitous evil is self-evidently true.[65]

Beyond this, though, some have argued for the necessity of gratuitous evil, or at least that it serves a vital role in human history and God's plan. For example, Hasker argues that if God were to prevent all gratuitous evil as a matter of necessity, then morality would be undermined. He concludes that God's existence and gratuitous evil are not mutually exclusive; the existence of one does not necessitate the nonexistence of the other.[66] MacGregor argues that evil is necessary to the created order because of its contingency and inherent imperfection; since only God is perfect, only He contains/exhibits no evil.[67] He goes on to argue that libertarian freedom logically requires that persons have the ability to commit evil, and this means that

---

Gratuitous Evil, and van Inwagen's Attempt to Reconcile the Two," *Ars Disputandi* 3, no. 1 (2003): 288–97.

63. Kirk MacGregor, "The Existence and Irrelevance of Gratuitous Evil," *Philosophia Christi* 14, no. 1 (2012): 173.

64. Bruce A. Little, *A Creation-Order Theodicy: God and Gratuitous Evil* (Lanham, MD: University Press of America, 2005), 115–24. Others have also argued that greater good theodicies follow a generally utilitarian ethic (e.g., ends justify the means). See R. Z. Friedman, "Evil and Moral Agency," *Philosophy of Religion* 24 (1988): 6–17. Little sees his own creation-order theodicy as superior to greater good theodicies: "this theodicy removes the burden of proof required by Greater-Good theodicies to demonstrate that the good always obtains—an almost impossible task." Little, *A Creation-Order Theodicy*, x. As the reader may guess, I am not sympathetic to this approach because, as argued, all Christian positions must appeal to a greater good of some sort. Little is no different.

65. In fact, MacGregor argues that belief that at least some evils are gratuitous is properly basic for some persons and thus, in need of no justifying argumentation. Whether or not this is the case, the point to be made here is that several Christian thinkers, along with their atheist counterparts, think it obvious that some evils are gratuitous.

66. William Hasker, "The Necessity of Gratuitous Evil," *Faith and Philosophy* 9, no. 1 (January 1992): 23–44. O'Connor questions the success of Hasker's endeavor to show there is no conflict between the existence of God and gratuitous evil. David O'Connor, "Hasker on Gratuitous Natural Evil," *Faith and Philosophy* 12, no. 3 (July 1995): 380–92. See also William Hasker, "O'Connor on Gratuitous Natural Evil," *Faith and Philosophy* 14, no. 3 (July 1997): 388–94.

67. He writes, "if God chose to create anything at all, evil would necessarily come into existence, not because God created or caused it, but because whatever God created would not be God." MacGregor, "The Existence and Irrelevance of Gratuitous Evil," 174. MacGregor concludes that since created beings can only display perfection nonessentially with the aid of God, then

God is "under the logical constraint of being unable to stop creatures either from choosing anything on the moral spectrum or from carrying out those choices."[68] Included in that spectrum, of course, are acts of gratuitous evil (MacGregor uses the Holocaust as an example).

In addition, MacGregor argues that the Bible supports belief in gratuitous evil. He draws upon Jesus's interpretations of the deaths of the Galileans at the hands of Pilate and of the persons crushed when the tower of Siloam toppled over (Luke 13:1–5). MacGregor writes, "In contradistinction to the Greater-Good Defense, Jesus discloses no overarching divine purpose, such as punishment for sin, for these atrocities, but insinuates their pointless character, testifying to the reality of human depravity and the absence of security beyond the present moment."[69] It is true that Jesus chastised those present for their belief that they were not as deserving of death as those killed, but it could be argued that the point Jesus was making had less to do with the pointlessness of the evil and suffering, and more to do with God's patience, longsuffering, and grace to those who were not so killed. His exhortation to repent and his warning that they too may die if they do not, seems to support this interpretation. Still the principle of the sun shining and the rain falling on both the righteous and unrighteous equally (Matt. 5:45) speaks of the corporate nature of some blessing and suffering, and may suggest that some suffering, taken individually, has no greater purpose and is instead a by-product of other events which have a greater purpose.[70]

There are some very good reasons for questioning the arguments presented by Hasker and MacGregor against the greater good theodicies and for the necessity of gratuitous evil. First, as Chrzan and Inman have both rightly noted, Hasker and MacGregor (and Little and Peterson) do rely on the concept of a *greater good* that justifies God's permission of horrendous evils.[71] For Hasker, the greater good is the sustainment of

---

"gratuitous evil is ontologically inescapable for contingent being every bit as much as perfection is essential to Necessary Being." Ibid.

68. MacGregor, "The Existence and Irrelevance of Gratuitous Evil," 174–5. MacGregor does allow that the constraint is one that God is under voluntarily by his choice to create beings with libertarian freedom.

69. Ibid., 172.

70. The context of Jesus's words here is one of exhortation to love one's enemies. Thus, his reference to the sun shining on the unrighteous in addition to the righteous and the rain falling on the righteous in addition to the righteous really has to do with human solidarity and union. That is, Jesus seems most concerned to communicate the truth that our enemies are really not all that different from ourselves.

71. Keith Chrzan, "Necessary Gratuitous Evil: An Oxymoron Revisited," *Faith and Philosophy* 11, no. 1 (January 1994): 134–37. Chrzan, commenting on Hasker's argument, writes, "If an evil is justified because morality is undermined in its absence, it is odd to construe that evil as gratuitous; preventing the undermining of morality seems like a pretty great good." Ibid., 135. Ross Inman, "Gratuitous Evil Unmotivated: A Reply to Kirk R. MacGregor," *Philosophia Christi* 15, no. 2 (2013): 435–45. Inman notes that MacGregor's view of gratuitous evil is ambiguous. He

morality in the created order, for MacGregor, it is the optimization of the ratio of saved to lost, for Little, it is the power of moral choice, and for Peterson, it is the freedom of creatures and love. So there is something of an equivocation on the notion of gratuitous evil here. More will be said of this below. Second, MacGregor's claim that evil is necessary in virtue of the finitude and contingency of the created order is doubtful and based on a confusion of evil with contingency. It also leads to the dubious conclusion that there would, of necessity, be evil in Heaven/the eternal state (since it is created; Rev. 21), and raises serious concerns for an orthodox understanding of Christology (the man Jesus was finite/contingent, yet without sin/evil). Third, while it is true that God voluntarily chose to create beings with libertarian freedom, there is no good reason to suppose that God is thereby under some sort of logical constraint regarding his intervention activity. He could still intervene to prevent some evils and, in those cases, the creature's action(s) would not be free, but that is not to say libertarian freedom would be eliminated altogether. Still, it does raise an important question (or series of questions) in the debate over gratuitous evil: what sort of program of intervention is expected of God, given his omnibenevolence? MacGregor hints at the correct answer here; the evils do not achieve the greater good and instead the divine responses to the evil do so.

While the necessity of gratuitous evil is questionable, there can be no doubt that a number of significantly evil acts are perpetrated, and that there is intense suffering in this life. Suppose there are gratuitous evils, however, that may be defined. Suppose there are gratuitous evils understood as evils that, *in themselves*, contribute nothing to any good. Suppose there are evils that may be properly described as *pure loss*. Can such evils be reconciled with Christianity generally, and if so, can they be reconciled with a view of providence that is specific? It seems that the answer to both questions is, "Yes," contrary to what many have claimed.

Molinism and gratuitous evil

It is my contention that middle knowledge allows Christians to hold that God is providential over the details of life and that there could be acts, instances, or events that are pure loss.[72] However, one caveat must be acknowledged at the beginning: the argument will still depend on a form of greater good theodicy, so if this is seen as disallowing gratuitous evil, then there is no gratuitous evil. This is the nature of the impasse alluded to

---

distinguishes between *token-gratuitous* and *type-gratuitous* evil events, the difference being that the former refers to the specific evil occurrence itself as not being necessary for a specific greater good, while the latter is more broad and refers to the specific evil or one equal or greater not being necessary for a greater good. He charges that MacGregor seems to only allow for the weaker token version in his defense of theism, but uses the stronger type version in his attack on the greater good theodicy.

72.   For a helpful discussion of relevant issues, see Kenneth J. Perszyk, "Molinism and Theodicy," *International Journal for Philosophy of Religion* 44 (1998): 163–84.

earlier. Chrzan argues that gratuitous evil, by definition, allows no theodicy because its being gratuitous *just is* its defiance of any defense. Thus, no appeal to any greater good can serve to justify the evil under consideration, if truly gratuitous.[73] Chrzan is thus critical of efforts to reconcile God's existence and providence with gratuitous evil.[74] Unfortunately, as Hasker points out, such a definition begs the question and stifles all discussion and creative theological reflection on the issue.[75] In order to see why, consider Keith Yandell's suggestion that a best world (if there is such a thing) may contain gratuitous evil, and Chrzan's response. Yandell's point is that a world that best meets God's desired end state may include evils that do not specifically contribute to a greater good.[76] Chrzan charges Yandell with a severe lack of understanding of gratuitous evil, or at least an equivocation. He writes:

> The definition of a best possible world implies that any change to that world would yield a less excellent world. The definition of a gratuitous evil, however, implies that eliminating it results in a better state of affairs, not a worse or even neutral one: a world with gratuitous evil would be even better without it and hence could not itself be the best possible world. Therefore it is incoherent that the best possible world contain a gratuitous evil; if a world contains a gratuitous evil it is not the best possible world and if the best possible world contains an evil, that evil is not gratuitous.[77]

Chrzan fails on two fronts. First, he fails to take seriously the notion of feasibility and how it functions in a Molinist theodicy. Second, as noted, he begs the question. He defines gratuitous evil in such a way as to make it *a priori* at odds with God's existence, and then states categorically that there are gratuitous evils (and obviously so). To dispute this, Chrzan claims, is to remain in one's ivory tower, rather than to walk the halls of a children's hospital.[78]

73. He writes, "The concept of gratuitousness is thus essentially dependent for its specifics upon the precise formulation of the given theodicy. Obviously, a demonstrably gratuitous evil falsifies its respective theodicy by counter-example." Keith Chrzan, "When Is a Gratuitous Evil Really Gratuitous?," *Philosophy of Religion* 24 (1988): 87. An updated version of the same paper was also published under the same title in the Australian journal, *Sophia* 30, no. 2–3 (1992): 23–9.

74. Chrzan, "Necessary Gratuitous Evil: An Oxymoron Revisited."

75. William Hasker, "Chrzan on Necessary Gratuitous Evil," *Faith and Philosophy* 12, no. 3 (July 1995): 425. See also the debate between Hasker and Rhoda. Alan R. Rhoda, "Gratuitous Evil and Divine Providence," *Religious Studies* 46 (2010): 281–302; William Hasker, "Defining 'Gratuitous Evil': A Response to Alan R. Rhoda," *Religious Studies* 46 (2010): 303–9.

76. Keith Yandell, "Gratuitous Evil and Divine Existence," *Religious Studies* 25 (1989): 15–30. Of course, he makes a much broader point than this, along similar lines to skeptical theism, to wit, no good reasons have been given for thinking there are gratuitous evils.

77. Keith Chrzan, "God and Gratuitous Evil: A Reply to Yandell," *Religious Studies* 27 (1991): 100.

78. Ibid., 102.

The concept of feasible worlds is important here, because it allows for the following principle: some events, acts, and the like, are a part of a given possible world's total construction, but do not contribute to any goods in that world. If this principle can be true, and there seems no reason to think it cannot, then we can see how Molinism can reconcile divine providence with gratuitous evil. A possible world that best meets God's purposes for creating could nevertheless contain events that do not directly contribute to a greater good. Rather, they are by-products of the events in the world, and the world results in God's plan being met. Even Mackie admits that there may be a way around the problem of gratuitous evil, and he sees it as somehow tied to the free will defense:

> It is plain that this is the only solution of the problem of evil that has any chance of succeeding. This defense alone allows the theist to admit that there are some real and unabsorbed evils, some items which the world would, from however broad and ultimate a perspective, be better without (so that this is not the best of all possible worlds), and yet at the same time to detach their occurrence from God, to show them as not having been chosen by God, who none the less seems to have been given a reason, compatible with his complete goodness and omnipotence, and perhaps with his omniscience too, for bringing about the state of affairs from which they arise and for allowing them to occur.[79]

HASKER ON MOLINISM AND EVIL

Somewhat ironically, William Hasker has argued that Molinism actually exacerbates the problem of evil, or at least does nothing to escape it. The high degree of providential control afforded God by middle knowledge presents problems for his goodness because of the immense amount of suffering and evil in the world. On the one hand, Hasker grants that Molinism is technically better off than Calvinism in reference to the problem of evil (since God's decisions are constrained by the counterfactuals of freedom), but on the other hand, he sees the difference as minimal. At times, he seems to suggest that Molinism and Calvinism are two sides of the same coin in this regard.[80] Hasker claims that the Molinist must believe that every instance of evil is permitted by God because it leads to

79. J. L. Mackie, *The Miracle of Theism* (Oxford: Clarendon, 1982), 155–56.
80. William Hasker, "The God Who Takes Risks," unpublished paper (1999), 8. Others have argued similarly. For example, Greg Welty has argued that Calvinists and Molinists are really in the same boat with regard to the problem of evil and sin. Greg Welty, "Molinist Gunslingers: God and the Authorship of Sin," paper presented at Evangelical Theological Society, November 2011. Welty argues that Molinism has to make use of the same strategies as Calvinism in order to escape the charge that God is the author of sin (e.g., paradox, inscrutability, etc.). While he is surely correct that the two systems follow parallel strategies generally speaking (i.e., appeal to an ultimate greater good), he is mistaken in his claim that they therefore are

a greater good that God could not have brought about without its occurrence. This means that God "specifically planned the Holocaust, Saddam Hussein's invasion of Kuwait, the ethnic cleansing in Bosnia—and on and on."[81] He finds this both appalling and unbelievable:

> Without going into the matter at length, doesn't it strain one's credulity almost beyond limits to believe that none of the evils mentioned—or a thousand more that could have been added—could have been prevented without creating an even greater evil, or without losing some good that is great enough to outweigh those truly horrendous evils? Yet this is what the Molinist must affirm, unless he is content to say that God has deliberately arranged for these horrible evils to occur *without* there being any outweighing good that compensates for them.[82]

Ultimately, Hasker argues, those who hold to a no-risk view of providence (which he ascribes to Molinism just as much as Calvinism) cannot escape the conclusion that God is the cause of sin, suffering, and evil.[83]

Molinist Response

As should be clear, Molinists are not convinced by this argument, but neither are many critics of Molinism.[84] Hasker has surely overstated the case when he proclaims that Molinism is just as badly off as determinism, and he has blurred the lines between the different views of providence so that he impugns Open Theism as well.[85] In order to see why, consider the Holocaust.

---

basically no different on the issue. Molinism offers better explanatory options for releasing God of blame.

81. Hasker, "A Philosophical Perspective," 146.

82. Ibid., 147.

83. Hasker is not unaware of the distinction between primary and secondary causes, or the idea of God's permissive versus declarative wills. However, Hasker believes that these distinctions cannot assuage the conclusion that "evil actions are the necessary consequence of causes that were deliberately created by God with full knowledge of what their results would be." Thus, he concludes that it is incoherent for a proponent of the no-risk view to deny that God is the cause of sin. Hasker, "The God Who Takes Risks," 9.

84. For example, see Jerry L. Walls, "Is Molinism as Bad as Calvinism?" *Faith and Philosophy* 7, no. 1 (1990): 85–98.

85. William Hasker, "How Good/Bad Is Middle Knowledge? A Reply to Basinger," *International Journal for Philosophy of Religion* 33 (1993): 113. Hasker notes, correctly, that middle knowledge does not necessarily afford God quite as much power as Craig seems to indicate. At the same time, Hasker gives Craig a rather charitable (and I think correct) reading. He writes, "I suggest, then, that Craig's statement should be interpreted along the following lines: While God cannot obtain just any result he desires, the creative options open to him include a feasible world which he takes as his end in the sense that he *fully endorses* the actualization of this particular world—and, he then achieves its actualization by the appropriate creative actions." Ibid.

Hasker charges the God of Molinism with responsibility for evil because he planned it when he considered the possible worlds, knew of the outcomes, and still actualized this one. Yet it seems that the God of Open Theism also bears significant responsibility and must employ a greater good theodicy, for he knew the thoughts of Hitler as he wrote *Mein Kampf*, and the thoughts of the publisher who released it, and the more than 6 million people who bought copies. He could have caused Hitler to have writer's block or all the publishers to look upon *Mein Kampf* with disdain, or he could have illumined the minds of the German people to the evils of Hitler's ideas. The God of Open Theism knew the minds of the German people on July 31, 1932, the day that the National Socialist Party became the largest party in the *Reichstag* with 230 seats. Surely he could have persuaded or caused those who thought their vote wouldn't matter to go to the polls in order to prevent the Nazis from taking control or he could have changed the minds of some who voted for the National Socialist candidates. The God of Open Theism knew the mind of Paul von Hindenburg on January 30, 1933, at the moment he used his constitutional authority to appoint Hitler Chancellor of Germany, and he did not intervene. If the reply is that God did not know Hitler's becoming Chancellor would eventually lead to the Holocaust, we must respond in utter amazement! God knew Hitler's mind and his plans. Surely God could see what the leaders of several German newspapers and what the leader of the Catholic Party could see! Thus, the God of Open Theism could have prevented Hitler's rise to power in an infinite number of ways, but he did not. The Open Theist may respond by noting that these are general trends, but not specific acts of evil and, therefore, God is released of responsibility, but such reasoning is flawed.[86]

In the midst of suffering, a God who knows what is happening (has present knowledge), is able to intervene, but does not, is hardly better than

---

86. A more specific example—the slaughter of an estimated 33,771 Jews at Babi Yar, a ravine near Kiev, Ukraine on September 29 and 30, 1941—will make this clear. According to Hasker, the God of the Molinist is guilty because he knew beforehand that the German soldiers were going to do this, given the opportunity, and he created a world in which they would be given the opportunity. Thus, the Molinist must asssert that, in the end, there is a greater good that will come out of this. While this characterization is questionable, the important point is that the God of Open Theism cannot escape this charge either because he knew the minds of the German *Einsatzkommandos* that September 29th morning. He knew their intentions, but did nothing to help the Jews. He could have prevented their arrival at Babi Yar, or he could have warned the Jews in a dream, or any number of things, yet he did nothing. It may be asked of the Open Theist why God did nothing. It seems that the only answer that can be given, short of "I don't know," is that God is merciful and wise—there must be a reason that is beyond our ability to comprehend and, given God's infinite goodness, it must be a good reason. That is, God had good reason to think a greater good would ultimately result from his failure to intervene. Interestingly, while the God of Open Theism can only *hope* that good will come of it (ultimately), the God of Molinism can *know* good will ultimately come of it, or of a world containing these evils.

a God who knew what was going to happen beforehand, and permitted it because that suffering somehow fits into his divine plan. A plea of prior ignorance does not abdicate God of responsibility at the time evil is being perpetrated. Thus, Jews who survived the Holocaust cry out against God, not for his providence or his plan, but for his inaction:[87]

> I'm an honest man, I've never stolen, I've never cheated! I've never humili-
> ated anyone! I have done only good, not He. He has done me nothing but
> harm. And now, now you want me to feel sorry for Him? Where was He
> when. ...[88]

> I—Berish, Jewish innkeeper at Shamgorod—accuse Him of hostility, cruelty
> and indifference. Either He dislikes His chosen people or He doesn't care
> about them—period! But then, why has He chosen us—why not someone
> else, for a change? Either He knows what's happening to us, or He doesn't
> wish to know! In both cases He is . . . He is . . . guilty! (*Pause. Loud and clear.*)
> Yes, guilty![89]

Hasker and other Open Theists may complain that this argument is unfair because it is less of a philosophical argument and more of an emotional appeal, and their complaint would not be unfounded, but this is how Hasker's argument against Molinism functions. If Hasker's argument speaks against Molinism, then this argument speaks against Open Theism. Of course, as demonstrated, middle knowledge has a way of absolving God of much guilt while still maintaining a strong view of providence.

CONCLUSION

In this chapter, the most prominent problems of evil have been discussed. The logical problem of evil, which claims that it is incoherent to believe that an omnipotent, omniscient, and omnibenevolent God exists, given the existence or occurrence of evil, was presented. The most common response to the logical problem, the free will defense, was explained and shown to depend on Molinist principles. Several probabilistic problems of evil were also discussed, from quantitative approaches that ulti-mately reduce to the logical problem, to emotive approaches that rely

---

87. For an interesting dialogue between Richard Rubenstein, author of *After Auschwitz: Radical Theology and Contemporary Judaism* and proponent of the view that since God abandoned the Jews, he should be abandoned by them, and Elie Wiesel, author of *The Trial of God* and *Night*, and proponent of the view that although God did not help during the Holocaust, Jews should still serve him, see "Richard L. Rubenstein and Elie Wiesel: An Exchange," in *Holo-caust: Religious & Philosophical Implications*, ed. John K. Roth and Michael Berenbaum (St. Paul: Paragon House, 1989.

88. Elie Wiesel, *The Trial of God*, trans. by Marion Wiesel (New York: Schocken, 1979), 88.

89. Ibid., 125.

on emotional appeals, to evidential approaches that appeal to gratuitous evil and God's inaction as evidence for atheism. Many theists have questioned the assumptions behind the evidential argument, namely that we may know what God should have done, and that there are instances of gratuitous evil. However, even if a type of gratuitous evil is allowed, a Molinist approach can make sense of how evils that do not themselves directly contribute to a greater good can fit in God's plan. Open Theism and Calvinism cannot make the same claim. Even though Molinism boasts meticulous providence, it does not require that God specifically desired or caused all events, including instances of evil, but it does allow that nothing happens contrary to his foreordination.

One issue not addressed, but often discussed in this context, is that of natural evil. Theologians often make a distinction between moral evil and natural evil. Both are seen as problematic for theistic belief, and appeals to natural evil are often made by atheologians in response to free will theodicies. Free will may explain moral evil and suffering caused by others, but it cannot account for suffering wrought by cataclysmic events and natural disasters. Thousands of persons die each year as a result of earthquakes, tsunami, hurricanes, tornados, mudslides, etc., and God does nothing to prevent such evil; in addition, these evils are the result of the very creation he made (and proclaimed good). Thus, some see natural evil as presenting a more difficult problem for theism. However, Christianity has ready answers, if the assumptions underlying the argument are even granted. The argument assumes there is such a thing as natural evil, but there is good reason to reject it as a category or classification. After all, a natural disaster is only viewed as evil or a disaster if it negatively affects someone's life. Otherwise, it is an innocuous natural event. In fact, such events are sometimes seen as natural wonders and sources of aesthetic pleasure. Volcanic eruptions can be stunningly beautiful, and the sheer power of an avalanche can lead observers to wonder at the enormity of the Earth and her Creator. Sometimes the processes that lead to disaster are the very same processes that regulate and produce life on the Earth as well.[90] For example, volcanic soil has many nutrients that make it exceptionally productive for agrarian use, thus attracting many settlers. The point is that calling naturally occurring phenomena evil is questionable and the whole discussion of natural evil spurious.

In addition, Christian theology may appeal to the Fall as an explanation for natural evil. The Bible suggests that the entire created order was

---

90. These ideas are touched upon in the chapter on evolution. Van Inwagen argues that, for all we know, the complexity of the world may require laws of nature just like those we see in the actual world so that any feasible world with those complexities will have the same kinds of pain associated with evolution and biological life. See Peter van Inwagen, "The Problem of Evil, the Problem of Air, and the Problem of Silence," in Tomberlin, ed., *Philosophical Perspectives*, 135–65. See also Paul Draper, "Pain and Pleasure: An Evidential Problem for Theists," *Nous* 23 (1989): 331–50.

adversely affected by the fall of humanity. Death and suffering entered the cosmos as a result. Of course, the Bible also proclaims freedom for the creation through the salvation of humanity (Rom. 8) and a reordering of the natural order at the *eschaton* (Rev. 21 and 22). For these reasons, the problem of natural evil was not discussed in this chapter, though the concepts of the Fall and the *eschaton* will be briefly addressed later.

Another issue not discussed in detail here is the various biblical reasons for why God allows evil and suffering, all of which contribute to a more full theodicy. Evil and suffering are sometimes portrayed as means to testing humanity that can lead to blessing (e.g., Job), or to revealing God's power and glory (e.g., the man born blind referred to in John 9), or to punishing humanity for disobedience to God's commands and unfaithfulness to his covenant (e.g., the Babylonian invasion of Judah referenced in Habakkuk), or to influencing persons to repent of sin (e.g., Hezekiah's illness and impending death thwarted by his contrite spirit, 2 Kings 20:1–21; 2 Chron. 32:24–26; Isa. 37:21–39:8; Jer. 26:18–19). In each of these cases, divine knowledge of counterfactuals of freedom are at least implied. In the case of Job, God had to know that something like the following was true:

> If Job were to lose his sons and daughters as a result of strong winds collapsing the house in which they were gathered, he would freely refrain from cursing God and would instead freely proclaim, "the LORD gives and the LORD takes away; blessed be the name of the LORD" (Job 1:21),

Similar counterfactuals would have to be known for each of the disasters Job experienced and the final result of the story. God knew that Job would hold steadfast in his faith despite his dire circumstances, despite the urging of his wife to curse God and die, and despite the antagonism of his companions. God also knew [spoiler alert!] that Job would respond in humility and contrition by repenting in dust and ashes once he moved from *hearing about God* to *seeing God* himself (Job 42:5–6). In order for God's purpose to bless Job to be realized, God had to have knowledge of how Job would respond to his suffering.[91]

In the story of the man born blind, Jesus's disciples, following the apparent conventional wisdom of the day (despite the moral of Job's story), asked whose sin caused the man's malady, his or his parents'. Jesus claims that the man's blindness existed so that God's work through Christ could be displayed in his life (John 9:3–5). Jesus then proceeded to heal the man, who subsequently had a confrontation with the Pharisees and was banned from the synagogue because of his testimony about Christ (compare 9:22

---

91. This is not to say that God's intention to test and bless Job offer a full explanation for his suffering. The natural disaster that led to the loss of his children may itself have numerous levels of explanation not included in the biblical narrative: Satan, naturally occurring phenomena, divine judgment for their evident sinful lifestyles, etc.

and 9:34). For God's purpose here to be manifest, he had to know several counterfactuals of freedom. For example, the glory revealed in the man seems to be tied not only to his healing, but also to his proclamation/testimony as he confronted the religious leaders. Thus, God had to know,

> If Jesus were to heal this particular man of blindness and he were threatened by the Pharisees and synagogue leaders with excommunication for his proclamation of Christ, he would freely refuse to recant his confession.

In addition, some in the community were probably moved to faith by the man's healing. While they are described as amazed, curious, and in some cases, incredulous (John 9:8–12), they wanted to know more about the healer Christ. If some came to believe in Christ, then the following counterfactual is implied:

> If Jesus were to heal the man born blind, some of the man's neighbors would ask about his healing and eventually place their faith in Christ.

The revelation of Christ through the man's suffering makes most sense if God has knowledge of counterfactuals of freedom, and faith is a free response to Christ. If God simply imparts faith to individuals, then it is hard to see why the suffering and subsequent healing was necessary. If God could not guarantee that some persons would believe, then he is taking a huge risk in allowing the man's suffering.[92]

Similarly, God's answer to Habakkuk's complaints suggests divine knowledge of counterfactuals of creaturely freedom. Habakkuk complained to God about his inaction in the face of gross sin in Judah. Habakkuk could not understand why the immorality that bothered him so much did not disturb God, but God's answer is that he will raise up the Babylonians, a ruthless and godless people, to judge Judah (Hab. 1:5–11) and then judge them for the invasion of Judah (Hab. 2:4ff.). He can do so justly because the Babylonians invade not by God's prompting against their wills, but rather by their own evil desires. Thus, God declares them "guilty" (Hab. 1:11). Such a series of events only makes sense if something like the following were true and known by God:

> If Judah were steeped in gross immorality and the Babylonians were in a position to invade Judah, they would freely choose to invade.

---

92. Some may wonder why the man had to suffer from blindness for so long in order to accomplish God's revelatory purposes here. A good case could be made for the definitive nature of the healing miracle here. Just as Lazarus needed to be dead for some time in order to avoid any accusation of trickery (i.e., the charge that he was not really dead), so also a man blind from birth is definitively and demonstrably infirmed. Adults may fake a handicap in order to take advantage of the charity of strangers (for example), but children would not do so. Many in the crowd apparently knew the many from birth and could confirm his blindness and his identity.

God can weakly actualize the Babylonian invasion of Judah by ensuring the Babylonians were in a position to invade Judah, given Judah's sinful state. If God does not know a counterfactual such as that noted above, he cannot ensure that the Babylonians invade Judah of their own free will. If God causes the Babylonians to want to invade Judah so that they could not have developed alternate desires, then it is difficult to see how he may justly hold them blameworthy for their sinful actions in the conquest of Judah.

The story of Hezekiah's illness, repentance, and the subsequent salvation of Israel from Assyria (for the time being) suggests counterfactual knowledge on God's part. Hezekiah was smitten with an illness, and Isaiah was told to go and tell him to get his house in order because he is about to die. After Hezekiah repents, God grants him another fifteen years to live, and promises to defend the city against Assyria. For reasons known only to him, God decided to tie the fate of the nation to the faith of the king, such that if Hezekiah were to repent, God would save Israel, but if Hezekiah did not repent, God would hand Israel over to the Assyrians. Thus, God's plans for Israel were dependent upon his knowing a counterfactual similar in form to the following:

> If Hezekiah were confronted by Isaiah with his sin, he would freely repent.

If God had caused Hezekiah's repentance, then it seems odd for the prophet to attribute the salvation of the nation to Hezekiah's attitude and faith. If God did not know that Hezekiah would repent, then he could not be assured that Israel's salvation would have the same effect it did.

Holocaust

Any discussion of the problem of evil after the twentieth century must include comment on genocides and there is no more horrific and difficult example than the Holocaust. In such discussion, care must be taken to communicate compassion and love, to engender sympathy and empathy for those victimized, and to seek truth via a method that refuses to depersonalize what took place. In what follows, I will offer an explanation of the Holocaust via the Molinist view of providence, and will try to take seriously the words of David Novak who, in chastising some of his fellow Jews for suggesting something similar to what I present below, offered the following warning: "As long as even one direct survivor of the Holocaust is still alive among us, it is abusive in the extreme to suggest that his or her family and friends had to die because of something they or someone else did, or because they were means to an end. . . . Accordingly, we may not present any explanation of the Holocaust that the mourners and orphans could not possibly accept."[93] Novak is understandably and rightly

---

93. David Novak, "Arguing Israel and the Holocaust," *First Things* 109 (January 2001): 13; also
     available   online   at   http://www.firstthings.com/article/2001/01/arguing-israel-and-the-

concerned for the psychological, emotional, and spiritual well-being of the survivors. He hopes to ensure that discussion of the Holocaust never becomes a cold, detached analysis that forgets the destruction wrought upon real people, and for that concern, he is to be commended. Still, to say that it is illegitimate to offer any explanation the mourners cannot accept is incoherent, for survivors have interpreted the implications of their wartime experiences quite differently one from another. Some have taken the Holocaust as definitive proof that God does not exist and have concluded that atheism is true. Others expressed anger at God, rejected him in their lives, but refused to disavow his existence. Still others have somehow found a renewed faith in God and vitality in worship. Surely those of the latter group offer an explanation that those of the former could not accept, and vice versa.[94] Perhaps Novak's point is that the Holocaust is too fresh, too recent for discussion. Perhaps he means that analysis is not open to those who did not suffer, for they (we) have not earned the right to speak to the issue, and perhaps he is correct in this. Perhaps I have no right to offer philosophical reflection on the meaning of such a hell-on-earth as Auschwitz from my armchair in my comfortable suburban home. I accept that criticism as a valid perspective. Still, I have a responsibility to deal with the hard question of the Holocaust, and to put my faith to the

---

holocaust. Novak primarily discusses two Jewish interpretations of the relationship between the Holocaust and the founding of the modern state of Israel and characterizes them both as messianic in nature. He rejects what he sees as the pietistic Judaism (apocalyptic messianism) that see the Holocaust as punishment for Judaism's assimilation in the modern, secular world and as necessary to make the Jews worthy of a nation-state to call their own. He similarly rejects the religio-nationalist approach (historic messianism) that sees the salvation of the Jews in the establishment of Israel (and the Holocaust formative in that establishment). He characterizes both interpretations as "verbal abuse" akin to that of Job's acquaintances who condemn him, even as they seek to provide comfort. It is without doubt that the analogy fits for the first group, and it is certainly true that the second group has a profoundly misplaced trust and hope, but it is hard to see how the analogy really works for the second group, for the argument makes no suggestion that those who suffered in the Holocaust in any way deserved the pain they endured. Rather, it simply seeks to offer a historical interpretation of the events in the aftermath of World War II, and to add meaning to the great suffering of the Jews. Such an endeavor, even if in error, can hardly be characterized as abusive, even if some of the victims do not agree with its focus or conclusion(s).

94. Most famously, Richard Rubenstein has chosen atheism, and Elie Wiesel has chosen silence. In a now-famous dialogue between the two, Rubenstein writes, "I have often stated that the idea that a God worthy of human adoration could have inflicted Auschwitz on what was allegedly his people is obscene. . . . If the God of the Covenant exists, at Auschwitz my people stood under the most fearsome curse that God has ever inflicted. If the God of history does not exist, then the Cosmos is ultimately absurd in origin and meaningless in purpose. . . . I have elected to accept what Camus has rightly called the courage of the absurd, the courage to live in a meaningless, purposeless Cosmos rather than believe in a God who inflicts Auschwitz on his people." Richard L. Rubenstein, "Some Perspectives on Religious Faith after Auschwitz," in Roth and Berenbaum, eds., *Holocaust*, 355. See also Richard L. Rubenstein, *After Auschwitz: Radical Theology and Contemporary Judaism* (Indianapolis: Bobbs-Merrill, 1966; 2nd ed., Baltimore: Johns Hopkins University Press, 1992). For Wiesel, see the discussion earlier in this chapter.

test. It is therefore in a spirit of love, compassion, sympathy, empathy, and humility that I offer the following analysis.

The suggestion has been that there can be no overriding good that justifies the cruel, systematic extermination of more than 6 million of Europe's Jews. The Holocaust was so barbaric, so contrary to Western civilization's concepts of propriety in war as to create what Rubenstein and Roth, following Kren, call a "historical crisis" that calls into question our understanding of society and its continuity with the past.[95] Taken individually, it would be exceedingly difficult (if not impossible) to argue or prove that each and every death or instance of suffering was necessary for whatever overriding good one may identify as the beneficial result. Even taken as a whole, it is quite difficult to make a case for a greater good that *justifies* all of the deaths, and our ignorance of such justifying reasons has already been noted. However, some good or goods that came about as a result of the Holocaust may be identified even if somewhat or even highly speculative, and if correct, it/they may indeed serve as justifying *goods* for God's permission of that evil.

For example, it is sometimes thought that one result of the immense suffering of the Jews in World War II is the founding of the modern Jewish state of Israel, though most Jewish historians today deny a strong connection between the Holocaust and Israel's establishment.[96] While their concerns are valid, and there has always been a connection between the Jews and the land (since Abraham), there are still good reasons to think that the Holocaust created conditions that intensified the need for an identifiably Jewish political state in the modern era.[97] Of course, questions

---

95. Richard L. Rubenstein and John K. Roth, *Approaches to Auschwitz: The Holocaust and Its Legacy* (Atlanta: John Knox, 1987), 340; George M. Kren and Leon Rappoport, *The Holocaust and the Crisis of Human Behavior* (New York: Holms & Meier, 1980), 13.

96. As evidence, they typically first emphasize the historic connection of the Jewish people to the land of Palestine, and then point to the modern Zionist movement's political successes like the Balfour Declaration of 1917 and the Palestine Mandate of 1922, which predate the rise of Nazism and Hitler's Final Solution. Many fear that too close a connection between the Holocaust and the founding of Israel will mistakenly give Hitler credit for Israel (something no one would want to suggest). As Novak writes, "If there were any such causal relation [between the Holocaust and the founding of Israel] then it would seem we would have to 'thank' the Holocaust in one way or another for the blessing of the State of Israel." David Novak, "Arguing Israel and the Holocaust," 14.

97. Many survivors of the concentration and death camps simply had no homeland to which they could return, and the arguments for the need of a homeland long made by the leaders of the Zionist movement were validated as a result. The successes of the Zionist movement were arguably slow in coming until after the war. Even then, the British were reluctant to truly cede control of the land to the Jews for an independent state. For example, in reference to the Holocaust and its impact upon the founding of the Israeli state, the provisional council of state for Israel, under the leadership of David Ben-Gurion (who was to become Israel's first Prime Minister), wrote in its official declaration of statehood for Israel, "The catastrophe which recently befell the Jewish people—the massacre of millions of Jews in Europe— was another clear demonstration of the urgency of solving the problem of its homelessness

remain. To say it was a result of the Holocaust is not to say that it would not have come about without a holocaust. Many assert Israel would have still been founded without a holocaust, while others believe it would have not. Suppose for argument's sake that it would not have been founded. This fact alone still does not, in itself, justify the Holocaust. What would still need to be true is that the founding of Israel was worth 6 million lives, perhaps more precisely each of the specific 6 million lives lost in the Holocaust. I suspect that, taken from the perspective of the individuals killed and their families, the cost was too high.[98] Thus, the issue of Israel as the greater good resulting from the Holocaust is unclear.

---

by re-establishing in Eretz-Israel the Jewish State." "Declaration of the Establishment of the State of Israel," *Official Gazette* 1, Iyar 5, 5708 [May 14, 1948], available at http://www.mfa. gov.il/mfa/foreignpolicy/peace/guide/pages/declaration%20of%20establishment%20of%20 state%20of%20israel.aspx, accessed July 9, 2014. American President Harry Truman also suggested a link between the two in a speech given for the Conference of the National Jewish Welfare Board in October, 1952. Noting that the defeat of Nazi Germany revealed the full scope of Hitler's Final Solution and that the Jews in the displaced persons camps did not wish to leave the camps, he wrote, "I sent Earl G. Harrison, former Commissioner of Immigration and Naturalization, to look over the camps and give me a report. He told me that the vast majority of the Jewish displaced persons felt their future would be secure only in Palestine. On Mr. Harrison's recommendation, I asked the Government of Great Britain to make available immediately 100,000 entry permits into Palestine. . . . The Jewish Agency for Palestine went ahead with plans to partition Palestine and to proclaim the State of Israel. I am proud of my part in the creation of this new state." Harry S. Truman, "Speech before the National Jewish Welfare Board," October 17, 1952, http://www.jewishvirtuallibrary.org/jsource/US-Israel/ truman_Israel3.html, accessed July 9, 2014. So there are some who believe that the modern state of Israel came about in some way as a result of the Holocaust.

98.   To be sure, some of the Jews killed in WWII would have willingly given their lives for a free Israelite nation in the land of Palestine. Some died fighting as freedom fighters, and it is a safe bet that some who died in concentration camps would have been willing to give their lives for the promise of a free people of Israel in the holy land. However, it is also a safe bet that some would not have been so willing to give their lives or the lives of their children. Still, one's willingness to die for a cause (or not die for a cause) does not determine the worthiness (or unworthiness) of the cause; it only shows the worthiness relative to the opinion or perspective of that individual. The point is that evaluation of the greater good cannot depend, at least not solely, on the perspective of the person(s) wronged. So we are back to the question of whether the founding of the nation of Israel was worth 6 million lives, generally. The answer to this question is not straightforward. It seems clear enough that the blessing of a free nation is worth *some* lives, even innocent lives. The loss of innocent life for the benefit of a good cause is, by definition, martyrdom, and we honor martyrs because we acknowledge their deaths' contribution to the honored good. We acknowledge the martyr's murder as an evil act, but we also thank God for the martyr because of the benefit to humanity of his/her death. So, in principle, the death of some (even innocent) persons for the benefit of a free nation or for a nation dedicated to God may be serving a greater good. The question of the quantity—6 million, a staggering number—is difficult to answer because there is no comparable example in terms of wars for independence. The only comparable numbers of persons lost were at the hands of despotic dictators, and so the question must remain unanswered and we must defer to the mind of God for a proper evaluation. We simply cannot judge the relative good over the history of the world of any given instance of evil.

As noted earlier, the problem with most understandings of greater good theodicies is that they require a one-to-one correspondence between the evils and goods. Each evil must be outweighed by a specific good resulting from the evil. The Molinist approach does not require such a correspondence and instead offers a more complex answer to a very complex problem.[99] However, the argument above still requires a correspondence of sorts—the 6 million deaths must be outweighed by the good of the direct result (e.g., the founding of Israel)—for the evil to be justified. The Molinist approach does not require such a correspondence. It could be that while the founding of Israel is a good that results from the Holocaust, it does not, in itself, justify the Holocaust. It may be that the Holocaust is simply a part of the history of the world, which, despite the great suffering its history includes, is one of the best feasible worlds God could actualize for his purposes in creating. This is all the Molinist picture requires, and it allows us to claim that the Holocaust was not necessary, was not God's desire, and did not necessarily lead to a greater good, but it also allows us to still speak of God's providence even in the midst of such evil and suffering, and to speak of all things working for God's purposes (in creation).

Pastoral Implications

There is one aspect to these issues that has not been addressed, but deserves mention. In the Introduction, it was noted that there is a reciprocal relationship between the amount of providential control and the severity of the problem of evil. This contention was neither presented in argument form nor defended. It was simply stated as a matter of fact, and while most would probably agree, there is at least one way in which it may not be an absolute truth. What I have in mind here are the implications for pastoral theology and ministry of these issues. Simply put, there are some who find comfort in the fact that God is in control, even in the aftermath of great tragedy. In the midst of pain and suffering, some find no solace in being told that the source of their pain is meaningless, inexplicable, or beyond God's ability to affect. Rather, they find peace in the search for meaning; they want to know that their child's death, or their parents' divorce, or the loss of income, etc., fits into God's plan, even if it is not now known how. By contrast, there are others who find the idea of God being in control of all things, even horrendous evils, to be blasphemous and exceedingly

---

99. Kenneth Perszyk has noted the primary problem with generalized theodicies that seek to justify God's goodness in the light of all the evil in the world by some sort of general appeal to free will, God's plan, or some other greater good, without seeking to address specifics. He writes, "Global good theodicies (which claim e.g. that [this] is the best possible world, or that the unobstructed exercise of significant creaturely freedom justifies all evil, moral and perhaps even natural, etc.) look insensitive if not inhuman; a God who permits the horrors allegedly justified by these theodicies looks downright callous if not perverse, a far cry from the loving, caring God of the tradition. Fear, not trust, would appear to be the most appropriate attitude to such a being." Perszyk, "Molinism and Theodicy," 164.

troubling in spirit. No matter what model of providence one puts forth, someone will be offended or upset at the implications for the problem of evil. However, the goal is to deal most fairly with the biblical material and to present an understanding of God's governance that takes seriously the reality of evil, God's goodness and love for humanity, and human moral responsibility. While no model of providence is without problems, the Molinist model offers the best approach to understanding and reconciling these biblical truths.

CHAPTER 7

INERRANCY AND INSPIRATION

INTRODUCTION

"If we can't trust the words of this Book, then we can't trust anything!" The simple country preacher held aloft his well-worn copy of the King James Bible as he sought to strengthen the faith of his congregants and spur them on to lives grounded in God's Word. His sentiments resonate with many Christians, especially when questions of doctrine and faith are at stake. There is, perhaps, no more distinctive doctrine for evangelicals than the doctrine of biblical inerrancy. This is not to suggest that no others hold to this position— surely the official position of the Roman Catholic Church, for example, affirms the truth of the Scriptures—but it is to say that the doctrine of inerrancy has been the hallmark of the evangelical movement since its inception. Belief in both the primacy of biblical authority/sufficiency of Scripture and the trustworthiness of the very words of the Bible is what distinguishes evangelicalism from Catholicism with its emphasis upon tradition or doctrine as revelation on the one hand, and from Liberal Protestantism with its emphasis on experience as primary on the other hand. In this chapter, I will argue that middle knowledge best accounts for biblical inerrancy and the doctrines that undergird it.

Doctrine of Revelation
The doctrine of revelation refers to God's making himself and his ways/ plans known to humanity through various means. It has become common to speak of general and special revelation, with the former being understood as truths about God available to all persons through rational reflection, the work of the human conscience, and observation of the natural realm, and the latter being understood as truths about God that have been made available to select persons or groups by means of specific acts of God in space and time or through visions and/or dreams. Natural theology seeks to attain knowledge of God by means of general revelation, while systematic theology makes use of both general and special revelation. It is widely held among evangelicals that general revelation is sufficient for condemnation

by affording humans knowledge of God's existence, holiness, power, love, justice, mercy, and the like, as well as their own sinfulness and failure to meet his righteous requirements. It is also commonly held that special revelation is necessary for salvation because explicit knowledge of Jesus Christ cannot be attained without it.[1] Avery Dulles has helpfully laid out the various approaches to the doctrine of revelation in the church.[2]

The first model sees *doctrine* as revelation. It is characteristic of Catholic neo-Scholasticism, as represented by Hermann Diekmann, in which the official dogma of the Magisterium is seen as on equal footing with the Scripture. While Dulles places both Protestant neo-Fundamentalism and Evangelicalism, with their emphasis upon propositional revelation, in this category, he is mistaken. It is true that some Protestants appear to treat the doctrines they hold as of comparable authority to Scripture, but this is due to the belief that they are properly based on and derived from the Scripture. Doctrinal authority stands in proportion to its accuracy in explaining the meaning of the Bible. Since Protestants have no infallible authority for interpreting the Scripture, they cannot properly see doctrine as revelation.[3]

The next model sees revelation as *history*, though it has rather diverse manifestations. On the one hand, the biblical theology movement, represented by C. H. Dodd and Oscar Cullman, among others, looks to the acts of God in history as revelation. Proponents of this view typically claim that there are levels of clarity in the revelation, depending on the content of the acts; those acts in the life of ancient Israel and in the life, death

---

1. The second claim is the more controversial of the two. It is based on the assertion that salvation is only available to those who specifically place their faith in Christ, and that ignorance of the gospel provides no protection from God's righteous condemnation, at least for those whose minds are functioning properly.

2. Avery Dulles, *Models of Revelation* (New York: Doubleday, 1983; rev. Maryknoll, NY: Orbis, 1992). I will loosely follow his approach, though diverge at points, especially with regard to what Dulles would surely see as minor differences within a larger family, but which are areas of great concern among Protestant evangelicals. Dulles outlines five major models of revelation.

3. It is true that some fundamentalist groups speak as though their doctrines are revelation, but their confidence in the propriety of their biblical interpretation should not be confused with the doctrinal claim that their doctrine itself is divinely inspired, is the revelation itself, and is therefore equal to Scripture in authority and status. However, closely related to these concepts is the Protestant Charismatic belief in the modern-day spiritual gift of prophecy. It is often conceived as very much the same sort of phenomenon as Old Testament prophecy. The prophet speaks forth the very words of God so that the words themselves are accorded the status of divine revelation. While in practice most who claim the gift of prophecy use it largely for exhortation and encouragement, there is nothing which precludes its use for presentation of new doctrinal teaching. In that case, it would fall within this category. There is a severe lack of clarity on these issues within conservative Protestant circles. Many evangelicals believe the spiritual gift of prophecy ceased at the death of the Apostles, though there is significant debate over the issue. Similarly, it is not uncommon to find proponents of the continuance of the spiritual gift of prophecy who are nevertheless uneasy with the implications of calling it revelation.

and resurrection of Christ are most illuminating. On the other hand, the universal history approach, represented by Wolfhart Pannenberg, sees God's more general guidance of all history as revelation. In both cases, it is what God does and not what he says, that is revelatory.

The third model claims that one's *experience* is revelatory. The experience can either be a specific personal experience of the holy, or more commonly, the universal religious experience of all persons. Friedrich Schleiermacher, father of modern theological liberalism, is representative of this view with his claims that all persons have an innate sense of ultimate dependence upon something outside of themselves and that this serves as the basis for all religious knowledge. It is similar enough to Dulles' fifth category—revelation as *self-awareness*—for them to be treated together. In this view, revelation is conceived as an affective desire to contribute to the *telos* or purpose of the cosmos, which is grounded in God's creative work. In both cases, the experience or affectation are somewhat general in nature and the revelation is nonverbal in form.

The fourth model, what Dulles calls "dialectical presence," may also be termed the *neo-orthodox* model. It appeals to the personal encounter one has with the Word of God found in Scripture. The Word may be understood as the literally risen and ascended Christ (Barth) or the cosmic Christ preached in the earliest kerygma of the church (Bultmann). In both cases, it is the encounter itself that is the revelation, and it comes about by means of worship, prayer, preaching, and Bible reading. As one engages in these spiritual disciplines, Christ comes to him in personal encounter.

The last model, one that Dulles does not recognize as a separate category, is revelation as *Scripture*. This is the model that most evangelicals affirm, for it claims that the Scripture itself, and not its propositional content, is the revelation. Whereas the neo-orthodox position claims that the Bible serves as a vehicle to the revelation, this position claims that the Bible is itself the revelation. This view has an interdependent relationship with the doctrine of biblical inspiration. Since the Bible is seen as the revelation, its inspiration must be seen as encompassing a certain type of work of God, and since the Bible is inspired by God, it is the revelation of his mind, character, plans and purposes.

Doctrine of Biblical Inspiration

The doctrine of biblical inspiration refers to the origination of Scripture. It seeks to explain how the Bible can be written by men but understood to be the Word of God, and it typically assumes a supernatural element, whereby the Holy Spirit moves the human authors to produce the holy writ. It should be distinguished from the concept of illumination, which refers to the process by which the Holy Spirit enables persons to understand Scripture. While all Christian theologians agree that inspiration distinguishes the Bible from other literature as the Word of God, there is little agreement about what that means and about the nature and extent of the Holy Spirit's work in inspiration. Those disagreements have given rise to a surprisingly wide variety of theories of inspiration.

So-called *natural* inspiration effectively denies any supernatural element in the composition of Scripture, save the idea of God as the motivating force behind the entirely human endeavor of inscripturation. This is not to say that just anyone could have penned the Scripture or that the view makes God's existence superfluous. Rather, it claims that the authors of the Bible had an extraordinary perception of eternal truth, especially given their historical and cultural situatedness. Still, the Holy Spirit is not seen as actively involved in the writing of Scripture, and it is the ability of the authors to see into the spiritual realm which is key. The biblical writers may be spoken of as "inspired" in much the same way other great writers (e.g., Homer, Shakespeare, Keats, Longfellow, etc.) are inspired. Thus, the view can be reconciled with belief in the supernatural, though it does not require such belief.

Mystical views of inspiration include a more direct supernatural work of God, but it has less to do with the actual composition of the Scripture, and more to do with the writers or readers of Scripture. The *illumination* theory of inspiration suggests that the biblical authors received a personal revelation from God as they reflected upon him or prayed to him for understanding. The revelation gave them a newfound love for God and a deeper and more profound understanding of his nature and ways, and they wrote the Bible in response to that revelatory event. In this way, the writing of Scripture is a wholly human endeavor, but the experience that gave rise to that work is from God. The *neo-orthodox* theory of inspiration, drawing largely from the work of Karl Barth, is the view that inspiration is largely a work of the Holy Spirit upon the reader of Scripture and the text itself. Proponents of this view speak of the Bible *becoming* the Word of God to the reader as he encounters the risen Christ, who is the living Word of God. Thus, the Holy Spirit uses the Bible to bring persons into existential encounter with Christ; it is a means to an end, and inspiration refers to the mystical encounter one experiences through the vehicle of Scripture. In both cases, inspiration is strongly tied to the human experience of God, and the Bible is seen as a product of human effort tangentially tied to that experience.

Dynamic theories of inspiration typically begin with the claim that the Bible contains the Word of God, but is not itself wholly identified with God's Word. They seem to be largely the result of attempts to speak of the Bible as both supernatural and human in origin, and to reconcile the findings of modern science and biblical criticism with that belief. Many who hold to some variation of this view claim that the Bible is completely true in its doctrinal teachings, but not necessarily in its scientific or historical assertions. There are three broad approaches to understanding dynamic inspiration: conceptual inspiration, degree inspiration, and partial inspiration. *Conceptual* inspiration is the view that God gave the authors of

Scripture notions, ideas, and/or concepts that they then attempted to express in their own words. The words of Scripture come from the human authors, while the basic ideas come from God. In this way, then, the whole may be spoken of as both divine and human, with the human giving rise to the details (and potential errors). *Degree* inspiration arose from the conviction that not all parts of the biblical story are equally important for the church. It claims that the whole is inspired, but in varying degrees, depending on the value and purpose of a given passage. Typically, those passages that speak to doctrinal truth, especially with regard to salvation, are thought to be of greater importance, and thereby attest to a higher degree of inspiration, than those that, for instance, are only of historical concern (e.g., the number of soldiers who took the field in a particular battle). Thus, some portions of Scripture attest to a high degree of inspiration, while others only to a low degree. This view did not make sense to some, who saw in it an inconsistency with the doctrine of God as truthful and infallible—whatever God inspired must be true—and so they rejected it in favor of partial inspiration, since they believed that the Bible does contain errors. *Partial* inspiration is the view that only parts of the Bible are inspired, while others are not. Proponents of this position, in a way similar to proponents of degree inspiration, tend to see the passages that speak to doctrinal matters as more important than others, and thereby use doctrinal density as the interpretive key when attempting to identify those passages that are inspired over against those that are not.

The theories surveyed thus far are those that have typically been rejected by evangelicals because they allow for error and seem to place too great an emphasis upon the human element and not enough on the divine. It should also be noted that, although the theories have been discussed separately from one another, they need not be so conceived; there is often much overlap in the way inspiration is understood among adherents of these views. For example, William Abraham has drawn comparisons between divine inspiration and human inspiration that seem to include both dynamic and mystical approaches. His use of the student-teacher relationship as analogous to the prophet-deity relationship simultaneously suggests conceptual or degree inspiration on the one hand, since the teacher inspires the student while the work remains the product solely of the student, and illumination inspiration on the other hand, since the focus is primarily upon the student not as producer, but as receptor.[4] In fact, Abraham is critical of what he sees as the unbalanced emphasis upon

---

4. Abraham writes, "since the students will vary in ability, temperament, and interests, and since the intensity of their relationship [with the teacher] may also vary, it is perfectly in order to speak of degrees of inspiration. There is no guarantee that inspiration will be uniform, flat, or even in its effects." The reason, Abraham goes on to say, is because the effectiveness of inspiration is as dependent upon the one inspired as it is on the one inspiring. William Abraham, *The Divine Inspiration of Holy Scripture* (New York: Oxford University Press, 1981), 63.

divine speaking in evangelical theories of inspiration, to the detriment of what he refers to as a fuller view of inspiration that incorporates reference to the act upon the writers and the acts of the writers (i.e., they were inspired in their writing).[5]

Nevertheless, the greatest concern for evangelicals has been the doctrine of biblical inerrancy, and this has led most to adhere to either dictation theories of inspiration, or the more popular verbal/plenary inspiration.

Dictation theories were more popular in the pre-modern era and have mostly fallen out of favor in scholarly circles. Their characteristic feature is to view the human writers and/or speakers/prophets as passive tools of the deity. This passivity is often seen as necessary in order to ensure that the end-product is divine in nature. The presupposition that the writing must be partitioned out or assigned to either the human or divine agency is shared with the dynamic views: where the dynamic views place too great an emphasis upon the human role in the production of Scripture, dictation theories place too much emphasis upon the divine.

There are good reasons, both textually and theologically (as well as historically), for rejecting dictation theories in favor of verbal plenary inspiration. First, there are many places in the Bible where the authors refer to themselves in the first person and engage in personal interaction (which make no sense if God is the only one speaking and the human author is just a passive instrument). Similarly, the biblical authors often indicate that they conducted research in the writing of Scripture (Luke is a prime example; see Luke 1:1–3). Second, it was the pagan prophets who, in their ecstatic experiences, would empty their minds and give control to the deity, while the biblical prophets retained their faculties (compare the prophets of Baal and Ashtoreth on Carmel, who seemingly lost their wits and in a frenzy, cut themselves, 1 Kings 18, with Isaiah, Jeremiah, and any other of the OT prophets, who spoke forth Yahweh's words, while showing forth their own thoughts and personalities). Third, dictation theories do not adequately address the range of writing styles, emphases, and vocabularies extant in the biblical text. They simply cannot account for the vast differences among the biblical books. The Bible is both consistent and inconsistent—consistent in message, but inconsistent in form. Dictation theories are inadequate for explaining this phenomenon, while the verbal/plenary theory is able to make sense of the data.

---

5. Abraham writes, "Any responsible and coherent account of inspiration must at least begin with the possibility that there is as much difference between divine inspiration and divine speaking as there is between human inspiration and human speaking. It must consider as a live option that divine inspiration is a basic act or activity of God that is not reducible to other divine acts or activity. It must not be confused with other activity of God, whether this be the creative activity of god or the speaking activity of God." Ibid., 67.

By far, the majority position among evangelicals on biblical inspiration has been *verbal/plenary* inspiration. It claims that the totality of the Scripture (plenary) is inspired by God, and that inspiration refers to the very words themselves (verbal) and not just the concepts. According to the theory, the human authors used their own words (which reflect their distinctive concerns, personalities, vocabularies, and the like) and the Holy Spirit guided the whole process so that the words chosen were/are the very words of God. Proponents of verbal/plenary inspiration typically appeal to the concept of divine concurrence, claiming that God agrees (*concurs*) with human actions in his providential activity, but also that the human authors and God were *concurrently* working in the penning of the biblical text. Carl Henry has nicely summarized this position in eight statements: 1) The text of Scripture is divinely inspired as an objective deposit of language; 2) Inspiration does not violate, but is wholly consistent with the humanity of the writers; 3) The prophets remain fallible; 4) Divine inspiration is a unique and special work of God for the Scriptures; 5) God revealed information beyond the reach of the natural resources of all human beings; 6) God is the ultimate author of Scripture; 7) The whole of Scripture is inspired and there are not degrees of inspiration; and 8) Inspiration is the historic position of the church.[6]

Doctrine of Biblical Inerrancy

The doctrine of biblical inerrancy refers to the truthfulness of Scripture and is inextricably tied to the doctrine of verbal/plenary inspiration. The argument is straightforward: since God is truthful and cannot lie (Num. 23:19; Titus 1:2; cf. Rom. 3:4), then whatever he inspires must be true. Note that as a doctrine, inerrancy is more than the bare claim that the text of Scripture is true, but also affirms that it is true *necessarily* and could not have errors because it is uniquely inspired.[7] There has been much controversy over these concepts, and biblical inerrancy has undergone much refinement as a result. It is now almost universally acknowledged that it only apples to the original manuscripts (*autographa*, the manuscripts actually written by the apostles and prophets), even though we can have confidence in the reliability of the manuscripts that subsist today. The reason it only applies to the original manuscripts is due to the fact that inspiration applies to the original writing, not copying, and that the meaning of inerrancy is tied to inspiration.[8]

---

6. See Carl F. H. Henry, *God, Revelation, and Authority*, 6 vols. (Waco, TX: Word, 1976; repr. Wheaton, IL: Crossway, 1999), 4:144–61. Henry writes, "The Spirit of God made full use of the human capacities of the chosen writers so that their writings reflect psychological, biographical, and even sociohistorical differences." Ibid., 4:148–49.

7. And so the doctrinal statement of the Evangelical Theological Society states, "The Bible alone, and the Bible in its entirety, is the Word of God written and is therefore inerrant in the autographs." See any issue of *JETS* for a copy, or www.etsjets.org.

8. Concern over alleged errors in the Bible, along with distaste for the theological disputes over inerrancy, has led some to favor the use of the term, "infallibility." While the term's

MIDDLE KNOWLEDGE, BIBLICAL INERRANCY, AND THE PROBLEM OF LIBERTARIAN FREEDOM

Evangelicals have long seen at least one of the distinctives of their theology to be a commitment to biblical inerrancy grounded in verbal/plenary inspiration. The concept of the dual authorship of Scripture is foundational to this theory such that the words of Scripture are viewed as both the words of God himself and the words of the human authors.[9] Theologians have wrestled with how to explain this duality in a way that does justice to both the human and divine elements. Some have appealed to analogies to the incarnation, but this does less to *explain* such a view and serves more to *defend* the view against charges of incoherence by other Christian scholars. In the remainder of this chapter, I will argue that middle knowledge can aid in explaining an evangelical view of divine inspiration without sacrificing truthfulness, contrary to charges by its contemporary compatibilist critics.

Middle Knowledge, Divine Inspiration, and Inscripturation

William Lane Craig has argued that the application of the doctrine of middle knowledge to the understanding of divine inspiration is obvious. God can weakly actualize the situations in which the authors of Scripture will compose their books, using the words God wants. In saying this, he means that God can bring about their writing by ensuring that the situation(s) in which they would infallibly write obtain. Craig explains:

---

definition makes clear it is a synonym for "inerrancy," it is not so used in theological discourse. Rather, infallibility has come to mean that the Bible is consistent, trustworthy, and not misleading with respect to doctrinal teaching and content, but may include errors of other sorts. Not surprisingly, this approach has met with criticism by proponents of inerrancy. The drafters of the Chicago Statement on Biblical Inerrancy specifically addressed appeals to infallibility over against inerrancy in articles eleven and twelve: "We deny that it is possible for the Bible to be at the same time infallible and errant in its assertions. Infallibility and inerrancy may be distinguished, but not separated"; and "We deny that Biblical infallibility and inerrancy are limited to spiritual, religious, or redemptive themes, exclusive of assertions in the fields of history and science." "Chicago Statement on Biblical Inerrancy," articles 11 and 12.

9. One of the most influential evangelical thinkers on this topic, Carl F. H. Henry, has argued that primacy should be given to divine authorship, to the extent that it is not really appropriate to speak, as I have above, of *dual authorship*. He writes, "while it is not quite correct to speak of a dual authorship or of a divine-human co-authorship of Scripture, the sacred writers were more than simply divine amanuenses, penmen, or secretaries; they themselves, on occasion, had amanuenses of their own. . . . The Holy Spirit's inspiration of the chosen writers involves a special confluence of the divine and human." Henry, *God, Revelation and Authority*, 4:142. Still, the language of dual authorship pervades evangelical theology. As Donald Bloesch has written, "The paradox is that Scripture is the Word of God as well as the words of mortals. It is both a human witness to God and God's witness to himself. The Scriptures have a dual authorship." Donald G. Bloesch, *Holy Scripture: Revelation, Inspiration & Interpretation* (Downers Grove, IL: IVP, 1994), 87.

The Epistle to the Romans, for example, is truly the work of Paul, who freely wrote it and whose personality and idiosyncrasies are reflected therein. The style is his because he is the author. The words are his, for he freely chose them. The argument and reasoning are the reflection of his own mind, for no one dictated the premises to him. Neither did God *dictate levicula* like the greetings ("Greet Asyncritus, Phlegon, Hermes," etc.); these are spontaneous salutations which God knew Paul would deliver under such circumstances; so also the interjection of his amanuensis Tertius (Rom. 16.22). Paul's full range of emotions, his memory lapses (I Cor. 1.14–16), his personal asides (Gal. 6.11) are all authentic products of human consciousness. God knew what Paul would freely write in the various circumstances in which he found himself and weakly actualized the writing of the Pauline corpus.[10]

Despite Craig's confident assertions, some critics of middle knowledge have questioned if its application to biblical inspiration is sufficient to ensure that the words of Scripture really are without error. For example, John Feinberg has claimed that compatibilist freedom is required to make sense of the words of Peter regarding the writing of Scripture, and to avoid a dictation theory of inspiration (see 2 Peter 1:20–21). He argues that the language Peter uses of the biblical writers being "carried along" (*pheromenoi*) suggests a strong superintendence of the Holy Spirit which can only be explained by either a compatibilist freedom or dictation theory of inspiration.[11] Similarly, Bruce Ware has suggested that the doctrine of inerrancy requires a compatibilist view of freedom in order to work.[12] Commenting on Craig's article, he writes, "I have often wondered, when considering his proposal, if God could succeed with a one hundred percent success rate on Scripture using middle knowledge, why don't we see that kind of record reflected more in other aspects of his governance of the world (e.g., how many people, throughout the world today, have responded to his offer of salvation)?"[13] It is a good question, though the way it has been stated may create more confusion than clarity.

It seems to me that Ware has really raised two distinct concerns with middle knowledge. First, he questions whether middle knowledge really

---

10. William Lane Craig, "'Men Moved By the Holy Spirit Spoke from God' (2 Peter 1:21): A Middle Knowledge Perspective on Biblical Inspiration," *Philosophia Christi* 2, no. 1.1 (1999): 72–73.

11. Feinberg writes, "Given the details of this passage, we must accept either a dictation theory, which says God dictated exactly what the writers wrote, or a theory of inspiration consistent with compatibilism, which allows both God and the writer to be active in the process so as to guarantee that what God wanted was written." John Feinberg, "God Ordains All Things," in Basinger and Basinger, eds., *Predestination & Free Will*, 35.

12. While not stated, he clearly assumes the principle of dual authorship and rejects the dictation theory of inspiration, as the problem he raises assumes that the human author is an active participant in the composition of the text.

13. Bruce A. Ware, *God's Greater Glory: The Exalted God of Scripture and the Christian Faith* (Wheaton, IL: Crossway, 2004), 25.

preserves the concept of the dual authorship of Scripture. He doubts that God's use of middle knowledge in inscripturation really affords him the title of "Author" of the text, and therefore doubts it can result in an inerrant product. Second, he argues that middle knowledge fails to protect both libertarian creaturely freedom and divine providence, and complains that the latter suffers as a result. Specifically, Ware points to the vast number of persons who do not accept Christ as Lord and Savior and are consequently condemned, and argues that if middle knowledge really worked, those persons would freely respond to God's call and be saved.[14] He sees this as evidence of the general failure of middle knowledge, at least on a libertarian conception of creaturely freedom. I will address the second argument first.

Ware's appeal to the number of lost persons really shifts the discussion from the issue of inspiration to that of predestination, and for various reasons, the analogy fails. First, it assumes that predestination and inspiration are equal with regard to God's work, but this may not be the case. That is, it may be that God has good reasons for choosing to refrain from overriding human freedom with regard to salvation while possibly doing so with regard to inspiration (or at least leaving the possibility open). Second, it assumes that the proponent of middle knowledge is committed to the idea that faith is a purely free human response, but this is not necessarily so. Evangelical Molinists may have good reasons for viewing saving faith as a result of divine influence of God's spirit in the heart and mind of the individual, convincing him of the truth of the gospel. Third, Ware seems to assume that Molinism claims that salvation of particular persons is God's sole or primary purpose for creating, and although many Arminians have advocated this position, there is nothing in Molinism that *requires* such a belief. Fourth, in some ways, Ware's argument fails to fully appreciate that the power of middle knowledge is in the fact that it allows that all possible worlds may not be feasible (even while critiquing it on this basis!). So it may be that God could not create a world that better meets his purposes where more people are saved. It could be that God did not have to override the freedom of the human authors of Scripture in order to ensure that they wrote the words he wished, but in order for more people to be saved, he would need to. This is certainly possible, and in fact, I think it is quite likely the way things are, but if I were proven to be wrong in this belief, it would not thereby prove Molinism wrong. Put differently, it may be that all the worlds where persons are free and the authors of Scripture write infallibly include vast numbers of persons who reject the gospel. Thus, the use of the vast number of persons condemned is unhelpful in the discussion, for it only muddies the water.

---

14.   There is a hidden assumption here that the proponents of middle knowledge have claimed that God can get just whatever results he wishes through libertarianly free actions when he uses his middle knowledge to decide which world to actualize.

However, even without such a reference, Ware's underlying concern is certainly a legitimate one, and this brings us back to his original complaint: that the principles of middle knowledge, coupled with libertarian freedom, preclude God from ensuring an inerrant product. The substance of Ware's objection seems to be this: If God's ability is constrained by the true counterfactuals such that there are vast numbers of possible worlds that he cannot actualize, then it seems quite possible that he could not actualize a world where the authors of Scripture do not make an error (or where the authors of Scripture freely write the very words he wishes).

In a very real sense, Ware's concern is perfectly justified. Under Molinist principles, one must admit that it is possible that God could not have actualized a world where the authors of Scripture freely write the very words he wished. Ware points out that while the notion of feasibility is a strength of Molinism for answering the problem of evil, it is a liability for understanding biblical inspiration. Consider the following admittedly basic and somewhat generic pair of counterfactuals of creaturely freedom:

> If Paul were in prison and the Holy Spirit were to inspire him in a particular way, Paul would freely choose the exact words God wished to have written to Philemon;

and

> If Paul were in prison and the Holy Spirit were to inspire him in a particular way, Paul would freely choose words that are not the words God wished to have written to Philemon.

If the first were true, then we can see how God could ensure the inerrancy of the product of Paul's writing, but under Molinist principles, there is no guarantee that the first and not the second would be true. If the second were true, then God would either have to actualize a different world where Paul freely chooses the words he wishes (assuming such a world is available), or he would have to use a different person to write to Philemon, or he would have to override Paul's freedom in order to cause him to use the desired words. So God's ability regarding world-actualization is constrained by the true counterfactuals of creaturely freedom, and this constraint could result in his inability to bring about Paul's freely writing Philemon without error. And so, Ware concludes, a middle knowledge approach to inscripturation cannot guarantee inerrancy, and by this, I take him to mean that it cannot guarantee verbal plenary inspiration. However, there are at least three avenues of response for the Molinist.

First, it should be clear that just because it is possible that God could not so guarantee inerrancy, does not mean it is the way things are. It is also quite possible (and most evangelical Molinists would claim that it is the case!) that the counterfactuals of creaturely freedom regarding which words the authors would choose to write were such that God was able to ensure that each human author chose the exact words he wished. Flint seems to take this tack in his discussion of Molinism and papal infallibility. He simply assumes that there will be at least one option where a candidate speaks unerringly when speaking *ex cathedra* if elected pope.[15] But Ware's point is just this: Molinism, on libertarian freedom, can make no such assumption. It could be the case that there is no feasible world where the candidate for the papacy, if elected, always speaks accurately and truthfully when speaking *ex cathedra*.

It seems to me that both Ware and Flint have erred here. Ware presents the situation as if libertarianism necessarily precludes such a world from being feasible, while Flint presents it as if such a world must be feasible, and both are wrong. Such a world could be feasible, but it is not necessarily so. Underlying Ware's assumption is really his rejection of the truth of counterfactuals of libertarian creaturely freedom, and his endorsement of the grounding objection. Underlying Flint's assumption is either a confusion of possibility and feasibility [doubtful], or a faith commitment that says God would not lead the church to claim the doctrine of infallibility (or in our case, inerrancy and verbal/plenary inspiration) if it were not feasible [more likely]; since the church has put forth the doctrine, it must have been feasible and it must be the case. This seems to beg the question, and while an appropriate move in theology, may not be satisfying to some. I would guess that this argument would not hold much weight in discussion or debate with any critic of papal infallibility. However, as noted in the introductory comments to this chapter, the assumption of verbal plenary inspiration and inerrancy is a common feature of evangelical theology, and so this move should not be problematic for critics of Molinism from the evangelical tradition.

Second, Ware seems to assume that God could not, in certain circumstances, override the human authors' freedom on particular words and still preserve the human element, but this is incorrect. As noted earlier, the Molinist can appeal to divine control; he can claim that, if the writers of Scripture were to libertarianly choose a word that God found objectionable, and there were not ways for him to, for lack of a better term, manipulate the situation so that the author would choose an acceptable word, God could override human freedom and force the author to pen the word he desired. In this case, the occasional word may not be of the human author's choosing, but the majority still would. I am loath

---

15. Flint writes, "Though they [defenders of papal infallibility] may well grant that there are possible worlds with fallible popes, they would insist that such worlds would have different histories from our own.... In a world where the doctrine has been proclaimed, though, there simply is no possibility of a papal *ex cathedra* error. . . . What confidence could one have that this isn't one of those possible worlds in which the pope goes awry?" Thomas P. Flint, "Middle Knowledge and the Doctrine of Infallibility," in Tomberlin, ed., *Philosophical Perspectives*, 385.

to put a number on it, but just for consideration, suppose that ninety-nine percentof the words were freely chosen by the human authors and one percent of the word choice required direct divine intervention. In a case such as this, it seems that even the most skilled biblical critics would have difficulty determining which words were the human author's own and which were not. Why could God not intervene here or there to prevent the human author from writing the wrong word? Why couldn't the proponent of middle knowledge appeal to compatibilist freedom as a possible option for the occasional word (if needed)? It seems that he can. This theory, though, should not be overemphasized, for it is only something to which an evangelical Molinist could appeal; it is not a view to which Molinists typically subscribe. In fact, Flint rightly cautions in the use of such an approach: a view which claims God must control pronouncements every time one is made in order for them to be infallible, ironically enough, undermines God's omnipotence. Flint writes, "Not only does such a view seem somewhat implausible, but it also at least appears rather demeaning both to God and to the pope to suggest that the only way God can infallibly guide his church is by playing Edgar Bergen to the pope's Charlie McCarthy."[16] Interestingly (and, I think, to Ware's chagrin), it also seems to confirm Neo-orthodox objections to inerrancy and verbal/plenary inspiration, for example, that of Karl Barth: "the prophets and apostles as such, even in their office, even in their function as witnesses, even in the act of writing down their witness, were real, historical men as we are, and therefore sinful in their action, and capable and actually guilty of error in their spoken and written word."[17] He continued to argue that, although the sinfulness and fallibility of the human authors of Scripture make it a fallible product, complete accuracy is not necessary: "To the bold postulate, that if their word is to be the Word of God they must be inerrant in every word, we oppose the even bolder assertion, that according to the scriptural witness about man, which applies to them too, they can be at fault in any word, and have been at fault in every word, and yet according to the same scriptural witness, being justified and sanctified by grace alone, they have still spoken the Word of God in their fallible and erring human word."[18]

As perplexing as Barth's words are here, they are clear about one thing: the doctrine of total depravity makes it such that the Bible, understood as a human product, must be both fallible and errant.[19] Ware's argument

---

16.   Flint, *Divine Providence*, 184.
17.   Karl Barth, *Church Dogmatics* I.2, *Doctrine of the Word of God*, trans. G. T. Thomson and Harold Knight, ed. Geoffrey W. Bromiley and Thomas F. Torrance (Edinburgh: T. & T. Clark, 1956), §19.2.4, 529.
18.   Ibid., 529–30.
19.   It is unclear whether Barth sees human finitude and fallibility as equally problematic as human depravity, as a contributing factor to human failings, or irrelevant to the issue. Here, his concern seems to be the idea that everything fallen persons do is tainted with sin so that

seems to follow much the same line of thought, though he does not claim, as Barth, that fallible humans must err, which is the critical flaw in the argument.[20] Obviously, human finitude and fallibility, along with depravity, do not make biblical inerrancy impossible, especially if divine inspiration is conceived as some kind of special empowering by God upon the author of Scripture in writing. I think Ware would agree, so his skepticism regarding God's ability to ensure inerrancy given libertarian freedom is somewhat perplexing. The reason seems to be tied to the next two points.

Third, Ware assumes that verbal/plenary inspiration requires that there was only one way for things to be worded; that there is one best way for ideas to be articulated. This assumption accords well with Ware's Calvinist theology with its commitment to compatibilist creaturely freedom, and also seems to fit quite nicely with the language used to describe verbal/plenary inspiration. Nevertheless, evangelical proponents of middle knowledge have good reason for questioning this belief.

In his consideration of the moderate Calvinist position which claims that God ordered a chain of causes which will result in the authors of Scripture choosing the words they desire, words which coincide with the words God wanted, Craig complains that it effectively results in a dictation theory.[21] He even suggests that compatibilist freedom completely compromises the human component in Scripture and "turns the authors of Scripture into robots."[22] While I agree with Craig that compatibilist freedom is not the best account and instead prefer libertarian freedom, and while I agree with Craig that middle knowledge better explains dual authorship, I think his characterization of the traditional reformed position is overstated. In fact, it seems that both Craig and Ware have, in a somewhat

---

even the pronouncements of a prophet or the writings of an apostle would be so infected and thereby, contain sin or error.

20. Evangelicals have long pointed out the fallacy in the logic: just because fallible humans can err, it does not follow that they must. In fact, it can be proven that, in many cases, fallible humans do not err. For example, while I am a fallible human, prone to many mistakes—my wife can attest to this better than just about anyone—and while I am certainly less godly than the authors of Scripture, I can still write a true and inerrant proposition (inerrant understood in its less theologically loaded meaning of simply, "without error): "$1 + 1 = 2$." My writing true propositions requires no special sanctification, no special divine enablement, no intervention, and no overriding of my human faculties, and this was just one example of a virtually infinite number of propositions I can write: "I believe I was born in Montreal, Quebec," "My daughters' names are Sydney and Sophia," "If one stands outside in the rain, he is likely to get wet," and the like.

21. Craig writes, "Given Calvin's strong views on divine providence, the answer would seem to be that a very rigid determinism is in place whereby God, through the use of all causes under His control shapes the biblical author like clay in such a way that he writes what God has predetermined. But this is worse than secretarial dictation; it is, in fact, strict mechanical dictation, for man has been reduced to the level of a machine. God's causally determining Paul to write his Epistle to the Romans is incompatible with Paul's freely writing that epistle, on any plausible account of freedom." Craig, "Men Moved by the Holy Spirit," 63.

22. Ibid., 66.

ironic turn, made the same assumption regarding these issues, but with opposite effects. Both assume that the key issue at hand is the account of freedom held; Ware assumes that libertarian freedom cannot ensure divine authorship, and Craig assumes that compatibilist freedom cannot ensure human authorship. Both are wrong.

Proponents of compatibilist freedom typically argue that God has made people such that they have the desires they have, but those desires are not directly caused by God, as if they are implanted by him into the minds of the individuals. Rather, they develop in the minds of persons as they interact with the world and have a variety of experiences, as they grow intellectually, and as their personalities develop throughout their lives. On most accounts, Calvinists argue that all possibilities are open to God in that he is able to guide the circumstances of each individual's life so that the person will develop the specific desires God wants him to and freely perform the specific actions God desires. In this (admittedly rough and basic) description, God is able to have exactly the details he desires while compatibilistically free agents perform those actions they desire and choose. Analogous to the development of desires is the development of vocabulary and thus, free word choice. This, then, is the moderate Calvinist explanation of verbal/plenary inspiration. For example, Warfield, who Craig quotes, explains: "If God wished to give His people a series of letters like Paul's He prepared a Paul [to] write those, and the Paul He brought to the task was a Paul who spontaneously would write just such letters."[23] It is this view, or something very much like it, to which Ware appeals. Thus, Craig has unfairly characterized this position as equivalent to mechanical dictation. In fact, Warfield was among the strongest critics of the dictation theory and a pioneer in the evangelical understanding and articulation of verbal plenary inspiration.

However, Craig has hit on an important point, one which Calvinists have failed to adequately address and one which middle knowledge is better equipped to handle. The Calvinist position incurs at least one of the problems with which dictation theories are afflicted. Just as dictation theories are ill-equipped to explain the origin and purposes of variances in author style and grammatical errors, so also the compatibilist approach seems unable to give a full account of them. Whereas dictation theories cannot explain *how* they came to be and *why* God chose to include them, Calvinist views can answer the former but not the latter. That is, compatibilism can explain how it is that the Scripture includes these items—persons developed in such a way so as to acquire the knowledge, experience, vocabularies, and grammatical abilities they did—but cannot offer much by way of explanation for their purpose(s). It struggles to explain why it best suites God's purposes that these persons with these abilities

---

23. Benjamin B. Warfield, "Biblical Idea of Inspiration," in *Inspiration and Authority of the Bible*, ed. Samuel G. Craig (Philadelphia: Presbyterian & Reformed, 1970), 154–55.

and these limitations write the specific words they wrote in the specific styles they chose. The best answer available to the compatibilist, I suspect, is some sort of appeal to mystery or God's good pleasure.[24]

In other words, the Calvinist position, grounded in compatibilist freedom, must argue that the unique vocabularies and writing styles of the human authors, to include grammatical and stylistic errors, were specifically purposed by God, that they were preferable to any of the virtually infinite other options available and that, somehow (mysteriously), they best contribute to the accomplishment of God's purpose(s) in creation. The difficulty here is that this is not really an answer to the question of why God did so; it is simply an assertion that he did! At one level, this is okay because faith-based assertions in theological discourse and appeals to mystery are not completely out of bounds. At another level, this is problematic, for the question of why such items have been included in the Scriptures seems to be a valid question. The criticisms of inerrancy and verbal/plenary inspiration of Scripture are well-documented, and they stem from questions regarding God's purposes for such inclusion. The problem can be stated clearly: If God wanted to reveal himself by means of a divine document—and it is a fair assumption that he did—why would he purposely and intentionally add such items? Are we to think that the inclusion of grammatical errors and unique styles in writing among the various authors would lead persons to believe it to have a divine origin? It seems that items of this sort have caused more difficulty than faith and I don't think we want to, with Origen, claim that such offenses were included in order to point us to the deeper, allegorical meaning because the literal meaning is simply untenable! Think what you want about Bart Ehrman, but he seems brutally honest when he notes the shift in his own thought about the Bible from "the fully inspired, inerrant word of God" to a purely human product (as a result of his own discovery of textual oddities of the sort mentioned):

> The Bible began to appear to me as a very human book. Just as human scribes had copied, and changed, the texts of scripture, so too had human authors

---

24. There is here, of course, an analogy to the so-called "Problem of Evil." Calvinists have to argue that God could have reduced evil, but chose not to. One the one hand, Calvinsits seem committed to the thesis that God could do just anything, as they are exceedingly uncomfortable with Molinist restrictions on what God can do (apart from restrictions due to his nature or logic). So it seems that they suggest that God could, for example, maximize his glory with no humans sinning. On the other hand, Calvinists have consistently maintained that the evil in this world, down to the specifics, are just as they are because they contribute to God's purposes and good pleasure for this world. So, it seems that they suggest that God could not, for example, maximize his glory with no one sinning. Let's suppose that the latter is the more correct Calvinist position and that the former is a mischaracterization. The implications for biblical inspiration are not inconsequential. Each and every word included in the canonical books are the best words God could have chosen for his revelation.

originally written the texts of scripture. . . . It was written by different human authors at different times and in different places to address different needs . . . they had their own perspectives, their own beliefs, their own views, their own needs, their own desires, their own understandings, their own theologies; and these perspectives, beliefs, views, needs, desires, understandings, and theologies informed everything they said. . . . Each author . . . needs to be read for what he . . . has to say, not assuming that what he says is the same, or conformable to, or consistent with what every other author has to say. The Bible, at the end of the day, is a very human book.[25]

How, then, is the compatibilist approach different from the middle knowledge position? The Molinist, committed to a libertarian view of freedom, also argues that the unique vocabularies and writing styles of the human authors, to include grammatical and stylistic errors, were specifically purposed by God. In saying this, we mean that they were the options that were available to God that best contribute to the accomplishment of his purpose(s) in creation. The difference between the two has to do with the options available to God. In the Calvinist view, all possibilities are live options, and in the Molinist view, the live options are constrained by the true counterfactuals of creaturely freedom.

This means that for the Molinist, while it may be true that there was only one way for some of the more technical passages to be worded, it is unclear that it is a requirement for all words of all passages. Craig hints at this issue when he admits that under a middle knowledge perspective, Paul's letters may be said to include items that God did not necessarily desire to be included. This, however, should not be seen as an admission that there could be errors; only that some of the words may have been incidental [neutral]. That is, it may be the case that God does not care which of two synonyms a particular biblical author may choose. Craig writes,

> Perhaps some features of Paul's letters are a matter of indifference to God: maybe it would not have mattered to God whether Paul greeted Phlegon or not; perhaps God would have been just as pleased had Paul worded some things differently; perhaps the Scripture need not have been just as it is to accomplish God's purposes. We cannot know. But we can confess that Scripture as it does stand is God-breathed and therefore authoritative. The Bible says what God wanted to say and communicates His message of salvation to mankind.[26]

While this concept may not be particularly troubling to some Christians, it may be disturbing to others, as it could appear to suggest that God had

---

25. Bart D. Ehrman, *Misquoting Jesus: The Story Behind Who Changed the Bible and Why* (San Francisco: HarperOne, 2007), 11–12.
26. Craig, "Men Moved by the Holy Spirit," 73.

to settle for something which was less than desirable, or that God is not concerned with details, and so we may wish to ask if Craig must make such an admission or allowance. That is, does Molinism require that its adherents hold to a position similar to Craig's here? I think not. As already noted, it just may have been the case that one of the feasible options was a world where the biblical writers, when inspired by the Holy Spirit, just would write the very words God intended they write, and this of their own free will, and the Molinist can, in an admittedly question-begging manner, assert that it was the case. Some may find such an appeal to be unsatisfying and no better than the compatibilist account because it does not really deal with the issues just noted and may, therefore, fall back on Craig's suggestion regarding divine indifference about some wording. But is such a position tenable for evangelicals? Does it compromise essential elements of verbal/plenary inspiration, as Ware and others suggest?

At first glance it may appear to, as it can give the impression that it is in effect saying that the words of Scripture themselves are not inspired or that only the ideas are inspired. Such a claim would be fatal, as the biblical passages which are typically appealed to by proponents of verbal/plenary inspiration (2 Tim. 3:16–18; 2 Peter 1:20–21) certainly suggest divine control down to the very words, and the theory of verbal/plenary inspiration claims that the words themselves are inspired, and this over against the claim that only the ideas were inspired. Harold Lindsell rightly notes that a written work must express ideas in words, and if it is to be true, those words must be the correct words to communicate those ideas: "Thoughts, when committed to writing, must be put into words. And if the words are congruent with the ideas, the words no less than the thoughts take on great importance. Words have specific meanings. To suppose that thoughts are inspired but the words that express them are not, is to do violence to the thoughts."[27]

Central to the traditional notion of verbal/plenary inspiration is the theological notion of *concursus*. It may be that Ware is concerned that a middle knowledge interpretation of biblical inspiration undermines this concept. B. B. Warfield describes its function in an evangelical theology of biblical inspiration: "The Spirit is not to be conceived as standing outside of the human powers employed for the effect in view, ready to supplement any inadequacies they may show and to supply any defects they may manifest, but as working confluently in, with and by them, elevating them, directing them, controlling them, energizing them, so that, as His instruments, they rise above themselves and under His inspiration do His work and reach His aim."[28] Such language is clearly at odds with a middle knowledge application to biblical inspiration, and seems to confirm Ware's

---

27. Harold Lindsell, *Battle for the Bible* (Grand Rapids: Zondervan, 1978), 33.
28. Benjamin B. Warfield, "Revelation," in *International Standard Bible Encyclopedia*, ed. James Orr, 4 vols. (Grand Rapids: Eerdmans, 1939), 4:2580a.

and Feinberg's positions, but as important as Warfield has been in articulating and defending the concepts underlying the evangelical notion of verbal/plenary inspiration, this does not settle the matter, as some may initially suppose.

Confusion over the meaning and method of verbal/plenary inspiration abounds, and it is often difficult to distinguish the position of its advocates from dictation theories. Even none other than Carl Henry has noted that the language sometimes used by proponents is misleading and unhelpful. Somewhat surprisingly, he criticizes the wording of certain articles in the Chicago Statement on Biblical Inerrancy as suggesting dictation. He writes:

> The "Chicago Statement on Biblical Inerrancy," approved by associates of the International Council on Biblical Inerrancy in October 1978, subject to future revision, strenuously disavows dictation, but unfortunately in some passages suggests divine causation of each and every word choice. Scripture is said to be "wholly and verbally God-given" ("A Short Statement," #4); moreover, we read of God "causing these writers to use the very words that He chose" (Article VIII) (see Supplementary Note, Chapter 8). The emphasis on the connection of thought and words, both in propositional revelation and in verbal inspiration, is somewhat obscured.[29]

So clarification on the meaning of verbal/plenary inspiration suggests that both the ideas and the words are important and must be described as inspired, and therefore, as the very words of God, but the description of God's role in the determination of the words should avoid language related to (direct) causation, for the words are also those of the human authors.

Thus, the question persists: can one remain true to the verbal/plenary inspiration while also claiming that some of the words could have been other than they are? It seems that he can, but caution is needed in how such a claim is expressed. Consider the following by evangelical luminary, Donald Bloesch, who calls upon the concept of divine transcendence as a means of upholding the worth of Scripture as the Word of God, while acknowledging its limits as words of man:

> Their [authors of Scripture] language about God and his works is not univocal but symbolic or analogical. Inspiration means that the authors were guided to choose words that correspond with God's Word. But we are not to conclude that they are identical with God's Word, for no human language can encompass or exhaust the unsurpassable reality of divine knowledge and wisdom. God's wisdom and love infinitely transcend all human knowledge and formulation (Job 5:9; Ps 145:3; Rom 11:33; 1 Cor 2:9; Eph 3:18–19).[30]

---

29.   Henry, *God, Revelation and Authority*, 4:141.
30.   Bloesch, *Holy Scripture*, 121.

Hermeneutical theory can be helpful here. It may be that the Molinist can appeal to the concepts of synonymous usage and semantic ranges to address the question of wording. Moises Silva, in the popular hermeneutics text coauthored with Walter Kaiser, warns against overemphasis upon specific word choice in one's interpretive method. While he admits that in some cases, slight differences in synonyms can be used to communicate particular emphases of authors and he admonishes would-be biblical interpreters to investigate the significance of the choice of one word over another, he also reminds them that, in many cases, word choice has more to do with writing style than a desire to communicate a subtle theological truth. He writes:

> We can never forget, however, that writers often use a diverse vocabulary for simple reasons of style, such as a desire to avoid repetition. In those cases, we may say that the differences among the words are "neutralized" by the context. Even when an author makes a lexical choice for semantic (rather than stylistic) reasons, it does not follow that our interpretation stands or falls on our ability to determine precisely why one word was chosen rather than another. After all, people normally communicate, not by uttering isolated words, but by speaking whole sentences. Important as words are, what really matters, then, is how those words have been combined by the speaker.[31]

Perhaps an example will make the point more clearly. When I was finishing my doctoral work, my supervisory professor and I sat down to discuss the dissertation chapters I had submitted. After noting some larger issues that I still needed to address, he asked me about my use of the word, "recognize," at a particular point in the Introduction, and then launched into a five-minute discourse on the loaded nature of the word in philosophical discourse, especially in Platonic epistemology, and asked if I could flesh out more fully how I was incorporating the concept into my overall argument. Of course, the answer was that I was not, and had merely used the word as a synonym for "know" or "come to realize" for variety in wording. I was not making any deep philosophical point and thought that "recognize" could convey the same point just as well as a number of other words. I changed the word. However, the fact still remains that often, numerous different words can communicate the same point and that, while precision in terminology is important, each and every word need not be seen as especially significant (unless the author makes a point of it). Such overemphasis upon exactness can appear gnostic in tendency.[32] Insistence that

---

31. Walter Kaiser, Jr. and Moises Silva, *Introduction to Biblical Hermeneutics*, 2nd ed. (Grand Rapids: Zondervan, 2007), 61.

32. *Gnosticism* refers to the movement found in many religions of the ancient Near East that saw salvation as grounded in some form of special knowledge, usually hidden to outsiders. It made

God inspired the biblical authors to use the words they did because those words were the absolute best they could use and that Scripture had to be worded the way it was in order to communicate what it does, may actually violate this principle. That is, it is a commonly held hermeneutical principle that the biblical interpreter should not insist on a technical meaning for each and every word. Words may be used synonymously and, in some cases, may be used with deliberate ambiguity. This suggests that other words could just as easily have been substituted without doing violence to the message. As Osborne notes, it is important that the biblical interpreter not "read into the text greater precision than it has, a problem especially apt to occur in overexegeting synonymity or antonymity."[33] If the product can allow for such semantic range, it seems justified to suppose that the production could as well. That is, the rules/principles which hold for evangelical hermeneutics suggest that word choice, at least in some instances, could have been other than it was and nothing would be lost from meaning. If this is the case, then Craig's assertion regarding divine indifference may stand as not violating verbal/plenary inspiration. Of course, more discussion, dialogue, and debate is needed, and care must be taken to preserve the divine nature of the product and the distinctive concerns of those forebears who fought the battle for the Bible, but it seems that this position falls within the evangelical camp. This means that Ware's final assumption also fails, and his criticism of Molinism's ability to preserve divine authorship in inspiration and inerrancy also fails.

Possible Concerns/Objections

There is one issue that needs to be addressed before closing this chapter. The reader may have further concerns about the middle knowledge approach to inspiration offered here because it seems too laissez-faire to be a robust doctrine of divine authorship. After all, one could see the model of inspiration advocated as akin to deistic providence, with God setting up the initial conditions and then letting things play out according to the true counterfactuals, but this would be a mistaken interpretation. To be sure, a modern-day Deist could make use of middle knowledge in order to strengthen his own position, but Molinism is not inherently deistic, and the allure of Molinism has been to present a particularly strong view of providence while retaining free will. Evangelical Molinists will agree with Gordon Lewis' three principles regarding the interplay of human and divine in the writing of Scripture: (1) the human authors' unique perspectives were prepared by divine providence (upbringing, education, situatedness, etc.); (2) the human authors' teachings originated with God; and

---

its way into the early Christian church and developed a reading of the biblical text in a way to uncover the hidden truths of God.

33.   Grant R. Osborne, *The Hermeneutical Spiral* (Downers Grove, IL: IVP, 1991), 88.

(3) the human authors' research and writing were conducted under super-natural supervision.[34]

It seems to me that this objection is based on the same line of thinking as the grounding objection, noted in chapter 2. It assumes that the only type of inspiring work available to God is either overpowering the prophets completely, or choosing persons who will, of their own accord and apart from any work of God, decide to write the very words that God wanted, but this is obviously false. Recall the representative counterfactual utilized earlier:

> If Paul were in prison and the Holy Spirit were to inspire him in a particular way, Paul would freely choose the exact words God wished to have written to Philemon.

It has, built into its structure, two important features: the active, inspiring work of the Holy Spirit, and the freedom of word choice of the author (Paul). In this alone, then, the model escapes the objection raised, even if it may seem like the Molinist is begging the question. However, as already noted, there is no good reason to think that counterfactuals of this form couldn't be true, and there are intuitive reasons for thinking they could.

Still, the objector may complain that no real explanation of inspiration has been offered; only a vague reference to the "particular way" the Holy Spirit "inspires" the author has been given. This is a valid complaint. The Holy Spirit's moving of the prophets and apostles to write is admittedly mysterious and may, at times, take the form of conceptual inspiration, and at other times, take the form of dictation, just so long as in both instances, the particular words chosen meet with divine approval and accurately communicate truth without any error. In most cases, though, the inspiring work is a supernatural movement upon the mind, heart, and/or spirit of the prophet in order to select the exact word or one among the approved range/group of words that God desires. For lack of a better term, it probably has many features of persuasion, but without the problems of Process or Open Theism and the propensity for divine error in those systems.

CONCLUSION

Which position best accounts for what we see in Scripture and what we believe about the Scripture as divine revelation and humanly authored?

---

34. Gordon Lewis, "The Human Authorship of Inspired Scripture," in *Inerrancy*, ed. Norman Geisler (Grand Rapids: Baker, 1980). Lewis writes, "The supernatural aspect of inspiration is not dictation apart from human means, but the extraordinary use of human means such as research (Luke 1:1–4), memory (of events in Christ's life), and judgment (1 Cor. 7:25), so that what was written conformed to God's mind on the subject and did not teach error of fact, doctrine or judgment." Ibid., 256.

Which is more problematic: the potential for God not getting the exact words he desires under Molinist principles, or concerns regarding the rationality of God's choice to include authorial oddities under compatibilist principles? I trust I have demonstrated that the complaints raised against Molinism can be answered and that reservations regarding its compatibility with a thoroughgoing evangelical notion of biblical inspiration can be set aside. By contrast, the problems noted for the compatibilist approach to biblical inspiration cannot be so easily dismissed, and therefore, the Molinist account appears to best explain divine inspiration/dual authorship.

Still, much of the discussion has depended upon philosophical and speculative theology, and because of this approach, the perceptive evangelical may feel somewhat cheated; after all, solid evangelical theological method begins with the text of Scripture and responsible exegesis. This cannot be denied, and while philosophy of religion and speculative theology can serve to aid developmental theology, at the end of the day, we must acknowledge that the ways of God are mysterious and beyond our comprehension. While the doctrine of middle knowledge may be helpful in explaining how the text can be written by God while retaining the distinctive emphases, language, concerns, and the like, of the human authors, we must agree with Bromiley, who proclaims, "The inspiration of Scripture is genuinely the work of the sovereign Spirit, whose operation cannot finally be subjected to human analysis, repudiation or control, but who remains the internal Master of that which he himself has given, guaranteeing its authenticity, and declaring its message with quickening and compelling power."[35] An appeal to mystery may be somewhat unsatisfying to the stern philosopher, but it is a staple to the humble worshiper in his quest of *faith seeking understanding*. May we always have the attitude of the latter and eschew our tendencies toward the former when they conflict.

35.   Geoffrey W. Bromiley, "The Church Doctrine of Inspiration," in *Revelation and the Bible: Contemporary Evangelical Thought*, ed. Carl F. H. Henry (Grand Rapids: Baker, 1958), 217.

CHAPTER 8

SCIENCE AND THEOLOGY

INTRODUCTION

The doctrine of creation is intimately connected to the doctrine of Providence. After all, it is over the created order that God exercises his governance, and the choice of an omniscient Being to create in the first instance suggests that he had a plan that he will guide to completion.[1] Christians have long believed that God's choice to create (and all the details contained therein) was not accidental, and that therefore, each item in the created order, each process, each event in its history, was in some sense planned and fits into God's plan. Thus, study of the natural world has implications for the doctrine of providence.

SCIENCE AND THEOLOGY

Science and Theology both make claims about the natural world, about natural processes and development, about how things have come to be the way they are, and about the ultimate end to which the universe is moving. Theologically, this has to do with the doctrines of creation, eschatology, and providence, and scientifically, it has to do with cosmology, physics, and biology, among others. The relationship between science and religion is unclear and lends itself well to controversy or hostility on the one hand, and collaboration or mutual strengthening on the other hand. In his Gifford Lectures delivered in 1989 at the University of Aberdeen, Ian Barbour helpfully set forth the four most common ways of understanding the relationship between the two: 1) Conflict, 2) Independence, 3) Dialogue, and 4) Integration.[2] He initially presents the categories as if neatly defined, but it is clear that the lines between them are much more porous than normally thought.

---

1. It is for this reason that many systematic theology textbooks place the doctrine of creation under the doctrine of providence or alongside the doctrine of providence under the doctrine of God.
2. His first series of lectures were published by Harper Collins: Ian Barbour, *Religion in an Age of Science* (San Francisco: Harper Collins, 1990).

Under the heading of "Conflict," Barbour places both scientific materialism and biblical literalism, and notes that neither group really takes the
claims of the other particularly seriously. Ratzsch agrees: "the less actual
contact of competing ideas there is, the easier it is for favorite ideas—on
both sides—to be credited within their respective camps with a status they
really do not deserve. Indeed, each side can see the case as so utterly closed
that the very existence of opponents generates near bafflement."[3]

According to Barbour, scientific materialism makes both metaphysical and epistemological claims, namely that matter and energy are all
there is, and the only appropriate approach to knowledge attainment is
the scientific method. Everything is explainable by physical laws. By way
of example, he points to sociobiologist Edward O. Wilson, who argues
that social sciences and humanities will eventually be understood as sub-
disciplines of biology, where human behavior, belief, and thought are
reduced to neurology with no room for psycho-spiritual explanation.
Barbour's discussion of biblical literalism is less clear because he offers
no examples of religious who discount science as a means to knowledge.[4]
He points out incidents of conflict between particular interpretations of
the Bible and the prevailing scientific view of the day (e.g., the Galileo
affair, the ongoing battle between Darwinism and scientific creationism),
but offers no specific statements denying science. In fact, he would be hard
pressed to find anyone who makes such statements.[5] Many evangelicals
have expressed concern that the methodological naturalism presumed
in scientific work may lead to metaphysical naturalism, but this does not
automatically result in conflict between science and religion.[6]

---

3. Del Ratzsch, *The Battle of Beginnings: Why Neither Side Is Winning the Creation-Evolution
    Debate* (Downers Grove, IL: IVP, 1996), 9. He continues: "The attempts of both sides to achieve
    quick victory by decreeing that the other side fails to meet some favorite philosophical defini-
    tion of science are nearly without exception unsuccessful." Ibid., 11. For example, a favorite
    argument by anti-evolutionists is to utilize a Popperian criterion for science (i.e., falsifiability)
    and argue that Darwinism fails, but that is but one way of defining the heart of science.

4. For example, Henry Morris, in the preface to a book written as a grammar-school textbook
    (published in both public school and general editions), writes, "The latter book [public school
    edition] deals with all the important aspects of the creation-evolution question from a strictly
    scientific point of view, attempting to evaluate the physical evidence from the relevant scientific
    fields without reference to the Bible or other religious literature. It demonstrates that the real
    evidences dealing with origins and ancient history support creationism rather than evolution-
    ism." Henry Morris, *Scientific Creationism*, 2nd ed. (Green Forest, AR: Master Books, 1985), iv.

5. Those he most likely has in mind—proponents of creation science who read the biblical
    account of creation literally and therefore believe the Earth is about six thousand years old
    and Darwinism false—do not disparage the scientific method or eschew the work of scientists.
    While many are scientists themselves, they admittedly and unapologetically give primacy to
    the biblical text, but this is not an eschewing of science.

6. While there are legitimate reasons for concern, Ratzsch notes, a naturalistic method does not
    require a naturalistic metaphysic. One can follow a naturalistic approach to the study of nature
    without committing himself to the view that nature is all that there is to Reality. Even though the
    evolution model may incorporate naturalistic processes and may work well with a naturalistic

Barbour appeals to neo-orthodoxy and existentialism as two repre-
sentatives of the "Independence" model, wherein science and religion
are viewed as distinct approaches to truth with their own discrete areas
of concern. Typical dichotomies include depictions of science as objective, religion as subjective; science as public, religion as private; science
focused on *how-questions*, religion focused on *why-questions*; science as
quantitative, religion as transcendent or symbolic; and the like. John Polkinghorne, world-renowned physicist and Anglican priest, sees science
and religion as complimentary in knowledge attainment, but he also sees
them as addressing different questions.[7] He sees science as more focused
and limited in scope than religion because it asks questions of function or
composition and not of meaning, purpose, or significance.[8]

---

metaphysic, it does not imply or require one. Ratzsch writes, "But the fact that the evolution
model is inherently contrary to the creation *model* and that biological evolutionary theory is
perhaps absolutely indispensable to the evolution model does not by itself suggest in the slight-
est that there is any logical tension between theism and the biological theory of evolution. That
two worldviews are mutually inconsistent as *wholes* does not imply that every specific part of
each must be inconsistent with the other." Ratzsch, *Battle of Beginnings,* 182. Ratzsch explains
what he means by "evolution *model*" and "creation *model*": "If we understand the evolution
model to be, basically, that the cosmos is self-existent and the creation model to be, basically,
that the cosmos is not self-existent, then . . . those two options do, pretty clearly, about cover
it—they are exhaustive. And they are mutually exclusive—only one can be true." Ibid. While
this way of putting things may add more confusion than clarity to the discussion, the basic
point is that one who believes in God may still seek a natural explanation for natural phenomena. In discussing intelligent design complaints about methodological naturalism in science,
Pennock points out that there are no similar intelligent design complaints about other spheres
where naturalism is the drive: "Science is godless in the same way that plumbing is godless.
. . . Surely it is unreasonable to complain of a 'priesthood' of plumbers who only consider
naturalistic explanations of stopped drains and do not consider the 'alternate hypothesis' that
the origin of the backed-up toilet was the design of an intervening malicious spirit." Robert
Pennock, *Tower of Babel: The Evidence against the New Creationism* (Cambridge, MA: MIT
Press, 1999), 282. Pennock is a bit unfair here because Christian philosophers of science have
only complained that sometimes naturalistic explanations are seen as the only viable means to
knowledge attainment. In addition, as intelligent design proponents have pointed out, there
is an element of hypocrisy in assigning scientific status to the search for extraterrestrial life
while rejecting that status to the hypothesis of an intelligent designer. Both make assumptions
about intelligence undergirding observed patterns in the natural world. William Dembski has
made this argument on several occasions, often by appeal to the SETI program (depicted in the
movie, *Contact*). See, for example, William Dembski, *No Free Lunch* (Lanham, MD: Rowman
& Littlefield, 2002), 6–7. See also William Dembski, *The Design Inference: Eliminating Chance
through Small Probabilities* (Cambridge: Cambridge University Press, 1998), 26–32.

7. He writes, "I am very convinced of the unity of knowledge. There is one world of human
    experience and human understanding that we are trying to come to grips with. If we are to
    understand that world, we need the insights both of science and religion, and of a number of
    other forms of rational human inquiry as well. Therefore, I see science and religion as being
    complementary and not conflicting." John Polkinghorne, *Serious Talk: Science and Religion in
    Dialogue* (Valley Forge, PA: Trinity Press International, 1995), 1.

8. So the two areas of inquiry both seek after truth from different perspectives, asking differ-
    ent questions, and may be conceived as existing along something of a continuum. He writes,
    "Science and theology lie at opposite ends of a spectrum of rational human enquiry into

The differences between "Dialogue" and "Integration" appear more a matter of degree than substance. Both positions see overlap between scientific and religious inquiry, and both believe knowledge may be gained through either or both approaches to investigation. "Dialogue" seems more tentative while "Integration" seems more optimistic about what science and religion can contribute to one another and to a comprehensive worldview. As Barbour puts it, dialogue has more to do with "indirect interactions" involving "boundary questions and methods" in the fields of science and religion, while integration refers to more direct relationships where scientific theories influence religious beliefs or both "contribute to the formulation of a coherent worldview or a systematic metaphysics."[9] While Barbour clearly prefers these interactive models to that of separation and conflict, his application of the model does not seem substantially different from that of conflict. He allows only a one-way influence in the integration (his favored) model: science may influence religious beliefs, but not vice versa, as he characterizes models that allow religion to influence scientific beliefs as conflict. This suggests that Barbour gives primacy to science rather than allowing for true mutuality and integration. The fluidity of all these models show that the reconciliation of scientific and religious interpretations of the natural world is more difficult than typically thought, and most persons make earnest attempts to integrate both areas into their total view of the world (in varying degrees of success). Evangelicals are no exception. Even though we have absolute fidelity to biblical truth, we acknowledge tentativeness not only in our scientific findings, but also many of our biblical interpretations.

There are numerous approaches to the doctrine of creation held by evangelicals and several models for understanding God's activity in creation. Only a few will be mentioned here, and the interested reader may find more detailed analysis and a more nuanced discussion of the relevant issues in a number of other sources.[10] Although they are often discussed as disparate models, it is best to view them as residing along a continuum, with immediate creation in the recent past at one end, and evolutionary creation over millions of years (theistic evolution) at the other end. Each model attempts to deal faithfully with biblical data and scientific findings.

---

reality. At the scientific end is the realm of impersonal experience; at the theological end is the realm of the experience of the transpersonal. In between lie the realms of human personal encounter with reality, which are the subjects of disciplines such as aesthetics and ethics. The whole spectrum of enquiry makes up the rich many-stranded texture of human knowledge, surveying the encounter with the multi-leveled reality of the one world of human experience. Ultimately, all these insightful disciplines must find their mutual reconciliation and integration with each other." John Polkinghorne, *Science & Theology: An Introduction* (Minneapolis: Fortress, 1998), 128.

9.   Barbour, *Religion in an Age of Science*, 16.

10.   One particularly helpful and accessible book on the topic is Mark F. Rooker and Kenneth D. Keathley, *40 Questions about Creation & Evolution* (Grand Rapids: Kregel, 2014).

Immediate creation, often referred to as young-earth creationism or special creation, is the belief that God created by means of pure supernatural act to bring creatures into existence in some kind of full-formed state. It is most commonly conceived of as God literally speaking creatures into existence according to species, and is often associated with belief in a young universe, typically 6,000–14,000 years old. The Genesis account of creation is thought to be a literal comprehensive description of God's creative work, and the genealogies found in the book are used to date that work. While it is a popular view among conservative Christians, many have still found it unconvincing.

Some have accepted the scientific consensus on the age of the Earth, but also found the young-earth reading of Genesis creation convincing. In an effort to reconcile an old Earth with a literal six 24-hour-day creative work of God, these theologians offered a compromise position known as the Gap theory. The Gap theory proposes that God created the universe and planets millions of years ago but that original creation fell into chaos and disrepair (most often thought to be a result of Satan's fall). This creation is described in Genesis 1:1. Beginning in verse 2 of chapter 1, the writer of Genesis describes God's reordering of the cosmos for the creation of new living beings, culminating in the creation of humanity in his image. The gap theory allows that God created humanity and animals in the way described in the creation account (i.e., immediate special creation in the recent past), but also that death and destruction preceded the Fall, and that the Earth existed long before humanity.

A number of evangelicals have not seen a need to interpret the creation accounts in Genesis quite so literally, but still wish to hold to a strong account of divine work in the creative process. Progressive creation is a popular way of reconciling a concrete, direct work of God in creation with a long creative process for the universe and living creatures. It is sometimes associated with the Day-Age theory, which suggests that the days of the Genesis creation account were not twenty-four-hour periods, but rather were longer, unspecified periods of time, normally thousands of years each.[11] The important point to note for progressive creation, though, is that it conceives God's creative work, at least in terms of speciation (or bringing about new species) as a special, interventionist work of God (described in Genesis as speaking).

Some Christians have seen the Genesis account as having many literary features that make a literal reading tenuous, and have therefore seen the mechanics of God's creative work best described by the work of scientists. Theistic evolution is the view that God created by means of

11.   While in its early years the Day-Age theory divided cosmic history into six even parts (the seventh day being the present age or more commonly, the future), most modern proponents do not see a need for the days to be of equal length and instead view them as corresponding roughly to geological ages.

evolutionary processes such as those described by Neo-Darwinism. It holds to an old Earth, and suggests that God has guided genetic mutations to give rise to new species, but views that guidance as more persuasive and less interventionist in nature. Whereas in progressive creation, God may insert new genetic information or even directly and immediately create a new species by fiat, in theistic evolution God guides the natural process of helpful genetic mutation that will lead to a split in the genes of a particular creaturely type, eventually resulting in the emergence of a new species.

The differences in these views are typically more pronounced in the literature than in reality. There are areas where they overlap, and sometimes it is difficult to tell where one theory ends and another begins. As such, it can be difficult to categorize one's view because the specifics to which he holds belong to different models. For example, whether a particular model stands as a version of progressive creation or theistic evolution can be a matter of subjective opinion. Suppose one holds that creatures evolve through the accumulation of many genetic mutations that aid adaptability and survivability over many successive generations, but he also holds that God supernaturally and periodically inserts new genetic information that can spur such evolutionary development. The outcome will be virtually indistinguishable from natural evolution, but because of the direct work of God in driving evolutionary change, some may see it as a version of progressive creation. The mere presence of evolutionary processes does not automatically make the model theistic evolution.[12] Similarly, most proponents of immediate creation believe some evolutionary development occurs, though they typically deny that speciation takes place apart from direct creative work of God. But things become murky here, because it is unclear exactly what distinguishes different species one from another, over against creaturely differences within species. Even scientists sometimes have difficulty knowing how to classify newly discovered creatures on the biological taxonomical chart. Thus, not only are the lines between theistic evolution and progressive creation unclear, but even the lines between progressive creation and immediate creation can begin to blur! While these issues are often presented in rather simplistic terms and models, Christians are increasingly becoming aware of their complexities, and attempting to account for the findings of science in their theological models. This, however, does not mean that they do not offer criticism where it is needed.

---

12. See John Jefferson Davis, "Is 'Progressive Creation' Still a Helpful Concept? Reflections on Creation, Evolution, and Bernard Ramm's Christian View of Science and Scripture—A Generation Later," *Perspectives on Science and Christian Faith* 50 (December 1998): 250–59. Some evangelicals who hold to theistic evolution do not like that terminology, believing it to be too deistic-sounding, and thus prefer terms like "evolutionary creationism," "fully-gifted creationism," and the like.

INTELLIGENT DESIGN, MIDDLE KNOWLEDGE, AND THE PROBLEM OF CREATURELY FLAWS

The theory of evolution has almost always engendered controversy. Certainly from the time of Darwin, it has been plagued by constant criticism, though it has had its defenders as well.[13] Daniel Dennett nicely summarizes the mixture of reactions Darwin's idea has engendered: "From the moment of the publication of the *Origin of Species* in 1859, Charles Darwin's fundamental idea has inspired intense reactions ranging from ferocious condemnation to ecstatic allegiance, sometimes tantamount to religious zeal."[14]

The most recent incarnation of criticism of Darwinism (especially as a theory of origins) has come in the form of the modern Intelligent

---

13. Charles Darwin was not the first to propose evolution as a theory. Evolutionary thought can be traced back to the ancient philosophers of many cultures, including the Greek pre-Socratic philosopher, Empedocles. Darwin himself was influenced by the ideas of his grandfather, Erasmus Darwin, who had taught him something of selective breeding, and by the geological work of Charles Lyell, who proposed gradual change over long periods of time as an explanation for strata. These served as the philosophical foundation for Darwin's biological gradualism. However, it is still Charles Darwin who is given credit for suggesting that it is the combination of natural and sexual selection over long periods of time that explains the diversity seen today among creatures. T. H. Huxley became one of its fiercest defenders (even though he was never convinced of the gradualism of Darwin's own idea), being dubbed, "Darwin's bulldog." His debates with Samuel Wilberforce and Richard Owen drew large crowds and created something of a scandal in the British Association for the Advancement of Science.

14. Daniel Dennett, *Darwin's Dangerous Idea: Evolution and the Meanings of Life* (New York: Touchstone, 1995), 17. This comment is telling in its frank admission. Much of the debate surrounding Darwinism and evolution has metaphysical implications and sounds more like religious devotion than scientific detachment. Even Dennett's own work sometimes appears polemical and dismissive of various theological approaches to the natural world. Commenting on the Design argument for God's existence, Dennett boldly proclaims its obsolescence in the face of Neo-Darwinism's proclamation of evolution guided by naturalistic processes based on chance mutation: "[Darwin's theory] has done this by opening up new possibilities of imagination, and thus utterly destroying any illusions anyone might have had about the soundness of an argument such as Locke's *a priori* proof of the *inconceivability* of Design without Mind. Before Darwin, this was inconceivable in the pejorative sense that no one knew how to take the hypothesis seriously. Proving it is another matter, but the evidence does in fact mount, and we certainly can and must take it seriously. So whatever else you may think of Locke's argument, it is now as obsolete as the quill pen with which it was written, a fascinating museum piece, a curiosity that can do no real work in the intellectual world today." Ibid., 83. Not all parties are so antagonistic. It is true that, *in principle*, a wholly naturalistic process of minute, random changes which are naturally selected or rejected based on adaptive advantage could lead to the emergence of life and the vast array of creatures present on Earth, but possibility, actuality, and probability are three very different things. Most Christians who admit that unguided natural selection fueled by means of random genetic mutation is possible, reject that it has been proven to be actual and rate its probability as quite low. Of course, the key word here is "unguided," as there are a number of Christians who believe that natural selection and even random genetic mutation played/plays a substantial role in the emergence and/or development of life on Earth, though they see such activity as still subject to divine providence.

Design (ID) movement. The theory of Intelligent Design was thrust into the limelight in the past few years largely due to the now infamous Dover legal battle, *Kitzmiller v. Board of Education*, in which concerned parents sued the school board after it sought to require science teachers to read a disclaimer regarding the scientific status of Neo-Darwinism and to offer an alternate book which proposed ID as an explanation for the origins and development of life. The school board lost the legal battle and the teaching of ID in public schools was ruled unconstitutional.[15] Even though ID lost this battle, its merits continue to be debated. In this section, a popular criticism of ID will be examined, and an answer drawing upon middle knowledge will be presented.

Problem of Creaturely Flaws

One objection to the theory of Intelligent Design draws upon the existence of undesirable features in creatures that were supposedly designed. The existence of so-called "vestigial organs"—organs that, by definition, are *vestiges* of an earlier form of the creature which made use of the now defunct appendages, organs, or the like—is supposed to point to evolutionary development. As Michael Ruse points out, "Vestigial organs are another piece of evidence for the evolutionary case. . . . Why do these exist? On any theory that makes adaptation totally ubiquitous, they would not have been created. But on a theory of evolution, they follow naturally as relics and evidence of the past—of past ancestors, that is, shared with organisms that still (as did the ancestors) use these features for their own adaptive ends."[16] In many cases, though, these apparently useless (or minimally functional) organs are not only seen as pointing to evolution, but also as evidence against ID.[17] If there were an intelligent designer, so the argument goes, then there would be no unused organs, appendages, or other body parts. This argument has wide appeal. Consider the words of atheist Sam Harris:

> When we look at the natural world, we see extraordinary complexity, but we do not see optimal design. We see redundancy, regressions, and unnecessary complications; we see bewildering inefficiencies that result in suffering and death. We see flightless birds and snakes with pelvises. We see species of fish, salamanders, and crustaceans that have nonfunctional eyes, because they continued to evolve in darkness for millions of years.

---

15. *Tammy Kitzmiller, et al. v. Dover Area School District, et al.,* 400 F. Supp. 2d 707 (M.D. Pa. 2005).

16. Michael Ruse, *Darwinism and Its Discontents* (Cambridge: Cambridge University Press, 2006), 42–43 .

17. There is, in actuality, a rather spirited discussion about exactly what "vestigial" means. The common notion of useless or functionless organs is an oversimplification. One particularly helpful resource is the Talk Origins website: http://www.talkorigins.org/faqs/comdesc/section2.html.

We see whales that produce teeth during fetal development, only to absorb them as adults. Such features of our world are utterly mysterious if God created all species of life on earth "intelligently"; none of them are perplexing in light of evolution.[18]

Similarly, Ken Miller, noted biologist and distinguished professor of biology at Brown University, makes precisely the same argument against ID. In his discussion of the fossil record of proboscidean lineage, Miller claims that ID theorists cannot accept that *Elephas maximus* (Indian elephant) and *Loxodonta Africana* (African elephant) evolved from a common ancestor, the comparatively smaller *Moeritherium*, who does not share their long trunks. He writes:

> Like it or not, intelligent design must face these data by arguing that each and every one of these species was designed from scratch. . . . The hypothesis of design absolutely, positively requires the successive creation of increasingly elephant-like organisms over time. If some of the new "inventions" of structure and skeleton in *Paleomastodon* seem to be carried over in *Gomphotherium*, don't be misled. It's not because of ancestry. One organism has nothing to do with the other.[19]

This leads Miller to object to ID by calling the competence of the Designer into question. He writes, "Almost by definition, an intelligent designer would have to be a pretty sharp fellow . . . biologists can have great fun with that notion. . . . Our bodies do not display intelligent design so much as they reveal the evidence of evolutionary ancestry."[20] He points to the unused yolk sac developed in human embryos, imperfections of the human backbone and feet for upright bipedal locomotion, the appendix, and even the functioning of the human eye— vestigial organs and creaturely flaws—as evidence of evolutionary development and against ID: "Finally, whatever one's views of such a

---

18. Harris, *Letter to a Christian Nation*, 75. Harris goes on to claim that the natural world has so many poor designs that it would take an entire book to catalog them all, suggesting that the evidence speaks against ID [and God as Creator!].

19. Kenneth R. Miller, *Finding Darwin's God* (New York: Perennial, 1999), 95. Just in case the reader thinks this quote an anomaly: "This designer has been busy! And what a stickler for repetitive work! Although no fossil of the Indian elephant has been found that is older than 1 million years, in just the last 4 million years no fewer than nine members of its genus, *Elephas*, have come and gone. We are asked to believe that each one of these species bears no relation to the next, except in the mind of that unnamed designer whose motivation and imagination are beyond our ability to fathom." Ibid., 97. Miller also writes, "This curious pattern of design that resembles succession is repeated countless times in the fossil record; and for each instance, Johnson, Berlinski, and their colleagues must claim that any impression of a sequence is just a figment of our imagination." Ibid., 97, 99.

20. Ibid., 100.

designer's motivation, there is one conclusion that drops cleanly out of the data. He was incompetent."[21]

This form of argument against ID is based on some erroneous assumptions about the claims of ID. First, it makes the misguided assumption that the theory of Intelligent Design is the same as the doctrine of Special Creation. Clearly Miller has equated ID with the belief that each and every variation, even those within species, were specifically intended and created by direct action of God, but ID makes no such claims. For example, Dembski has explicitly stated that ID is compatible with evolutionary processes: "intelligent design is compatible with the creationist idea of organisms being suddenly created from scratch. But it is also perfectly compatible with the evolutionist idea of new organisms arising from old by gradual accrual of change."[22] It is thus a misrepresentation to suggest that ID requires the immediate, sudden emergence of creatures or that it attributes every variation to the direct causative activity of an intelligent designer.

This error could be an unintentional muddle caused by the large amount of support ID has received from creationists of all stripes, including young-earth creationists. This support, largely in the form of political pressure upon school boards to include ID in school science classrooms, has clouded the issues somewhat. Well-meaning creationists have often defended ID by means of creationist arguments, leading many critics (and reporters) to fail to distinguish the two movements. In fact, it has become a common tactic of the opponents of ID to lump it in with scientific creationism in an effort to discredit ID as science. Barbara Forrest and Paul Gross have argued that ID is just a subtle means by which creationists have sought to get their arguments equal hearing alongside Darwinism in the public school classroom; this same point has been made in the now-famous remark that Intelligent Design is "just creationism in a cheap tuxedo."[23] This line of argument is faulty because it is often based

---

21.   Ibid., 102. It is interesting to note, at this point, that Miller refers to himself as a theistic evolutionist; that he claims to hold to a strong belief in God. While his words here may lead some to doubt the sincerity of such claims, it seems to me that such doubt is unwarranted. The better solution is that Miller has simply succumbed to the popular view which sees the spheres of science and religion as completely disparate. One's views on science have no impact on his religion, and vice versa. This is a naïve position at best, but one that has been rather popular among scientists who wish to retain belief in God.

22.   William Dembski, *The Design Revolution* (Downers Grove, IL: InterVarsity, 2004), 178. Dembski seems to have progressive creation in mind here. Elsewhere, he has clearly placed ID in opposition to theistic evolution: "Design theorists are no friends of theistic evolution. As far as design theorists are concerned, theistic evolution is American evangelicalism's ill-conceived accommodation to Darwinism." William Dembski, "What Every Theologian Should Know about Creation, Evolution, and Design," *Center for Interdisciplinary Studies Transactions* 3, no. 2 (1995): 3.

23.   While both Forrest and Gross have contributed numerous articles on the general topic of criticisms of Darwinism, their most substantive work is the book, *Creationism's Trojan Horse: The Wedge of Intelligent Design*, rev. ed. (2004; Oxford: Oxford University Press, 2007). While

on comments about ID by non-specialists or on impugning ID because some of its proponents are religious, but neither of these tactics is fair. It is understandable because ID proponents have sometimes been sloppy in their work, as in the Dover case.

Second, this form of argument is based on the assumption that if ID were true, the designer would have to make a flawless creation. If a creature has flaws, then the designer is not intelligent or the creature was not designed. Either way, ID fails. A moment's reflection will make clear that this objection is not scientific, but theological/philosophical.[24] It may be referred to as the logical problem of creaturely flaws for belief in ID, and can be stated more formally: It is the claim that a logical contradiction exists in simultaneously holding to the following propositions: 1) Creatures are designed; 2) The Designer is intelligent; and 3) Creatures have flaws. If creatures have flaws, then either creatures are not designed, or the Designer cannot be intelligent (or both).[25]

One approach that many advocates of ID have taken to answering this objection is to deny that have flaws by denying vestigial or useless organs/structures. For example, Jerry Bergman and George Howe examine a hundred supposed vestigial organs and offer explanations for their now-discovered use.[26] Similarly, Michael Behe has suggested that pseudogenes will eventually be shown to have a legitimate function, even if we do not now know what that may be.[27] This approach seems best for Calvinists to follow, since the Designer [God] could presumably create whatever he wishes by whatever means he wishes, and therefore, every organ and/or structure was purposely included in the creature's physiology.[28]

---

many people attribute the quote to Richard Dawkins, it was actually made by paleontologist Leonard Krishtalka, professor at the University of Kansas and director of the University's Natural History Museum and Biodiversity Research Center.

24. This is the heart of the complaint against the *way* Darwinism is presented in many science texts. While it is clearly the best naturalistic explanation for the development of life forms, it is lacking in its ability to address the more fundamental question of the origins of life. The proposed naturalistic answers to this question are necessarily speculative, yet they are not presented as tentative or mere possibilities. In this, then, the lines between science and metaphysics are blurred. But this is the very complaint most Darwinists have made against ID-theorists.

25. Some may object to my characterization of the claim because neither Miller nor Harris present a formal logical argument, and may therefore argue that I have set up a straw man. However, given the tenor of their claims and the sarcasm in tone, it seems to be a fair representation. The either/or option posited by Miller: Either creatures are not designed or the Designer is incompetent, suggests a logical argument, even if not laid out as a formal syllogism.

26. Jerry Bergman and George Howe, *"Vestigial Organs" Are Fully Functional: A History and Evaluation of the Concept of Vestigial Organs* (Chino Valley, AZ: Creation Research Society Monograph, 1990).

27. Michael Behe, *Darwin's Black Box: The Biochemical Challenge to Evolution* (New York: The Free Press, 1996), 226.

28. Cornelius Hunter argues not only that many supposed vestigial organs may indeed have a yet-undiscovered function, but correctly points out that the labeling of organs as "vestigial"

The strategy of denying useless organs has its problems; it is unproductive because it is purely reactionary and requires proof of purpose for every example of useless organs or structures. Only one example of creaturely flaws is sufficient to make the argument against ID stand, and new supposed flaws are continuously discovered. Therefore, this approach is ill-equipped to ever dispose of the objection. However, another answer to the objection is available to the proponent of middle knowledge.

The similarities of the argument against ID by appeal to vestigial organs to the atheistic objection to God's existence by appeal to evil is not incidental. Answers given for the logical problem of evil and the emotive problem of evil can help in answering this objection to ID. Just as Christian philosophers have utilized the doctrine of middle knowledge and counterfactuals of creaturely freedom to demonstrate that the logical problem of evil has no force, so also the doctrine of middle knowledge and counterfactuals of genetic mutation may be employed to demonstrate that the logical problem of creaturely flaws has little to commend it; and the emotive problem of creaturely flaws reduces into the logical problem of creaturely flaws.

The logical problem of evil
Recall that the logical problem of evil includes several assumptions regarding God's omnipotence, omniscience, and love, specifically, that an omnipotent, omniscient, and omnibenevolent being will always eliminate every evil it can, that there are no nonlogical limits to what an omnipotent being can do, and that an omniscient and omnipotent being can properly eliminate every evil state of affairs.[29] In a similar way, the logical problem of creaturely flaws makes assumptions about what it means to say that creatures are designed, the designer is intelligent, and that creatures have flaws. For example, it seems beyond dispute that an intelligent designer will design items or creatures with as few flaws as he can, but this modest claim is insufficient to serve as a basis for the objection. Instead, the objection requires the designer to be omniscient and omnipotent.[30]

---

is question-begging: "If a penguin's wing is highly efficient for swimming, then why should we think it is vestigial, aside from presupposing it was formed by evolution? . . . Therefore, when evolutionists identify a structure as vestigial, it seems that it is the theory of evolution that is justifying the claim, rather than the claim justifying the theory of evolution." Still, the complaint of Darwinists is not that the organs are vestigial, but rather that they have no current use, so adjusting terminology from "vestigial" to "useless" does nothing to answer the substance of the objection. Cornelius G. Hunter, *Darwin's Proof: The Triumph of Religion over Science* (Grand Rapids: Brazos, 2003), 46.

29. Alvin Plantinga, *God, Freedom, and Evil* (Grand Rapids: Eerdmans, 1974), 21–22.
30. It relies on the claim that an intelligent designer will design creatures with as few flaws as possible, but even here further assumptions about the level of intelligence of the designer have been made. After all, while human designers meet the qualifications of the first statement (they design items with as few flaws as they can), they surely do not meet the qualifications of the second, though nobody calls their intelligence into question. Consider the design of

Finally, the logical objector to ID also makes assumptions about the kinds of creatures designed and their purposes. He has assumed that an intelligent designer will design creatures for optimal performance (for whatever purpose they are designed), and that creatures are designed with at least a primary purpose in mind, but ID makes no such claim, as Behe has made clear.[31] Pennock has questioned Behe's sincerity here, noting that Paley's Designer was conceived as perfect and thereby obligated to make perfect objects and creatures perfectly suited to their habitats and purposes: "Does Behe really mean to deny that the perfect designer did a perfect job, or is he just making a virtue of vagueness?"[32]

The logical problem of creaturely flaws also assumes that creatures are designed with only one purpose in mind because multiple purposes could conflict and result in some useless organs. This assumption is suspect at best. There seems no good reason to think that there is only one purpose for each creature and thus, there are good reasons for rejecting the logical problem of creaturely flaws from the beginning. Flaws could exist as necessary fallout from more desirable outcomes. Nevertheless, suppose, for sake of argument, that creatures only have one purpose. Even if this is true, and the designer is conceived as omniscient and omnipotent, the belief that the designer can and must eliminate or prevent all creaturely flaws is hardly indisputable; In fact, it is doubtful.

The free will defense

Recall that the free will defense answers the logical problem of evil by claiming that at least some evil exists due to the free decisions of creatures, and that it is possible an all-powerful, all-loving God could not create a world where creatures are free but never commit evil [sin]. Put in biblical terms, the free will defense suggests that it is possible that in every

---

any car. The engineers who work for the auto manufacturer attempt to design their vehicles without any flaws, but if a flaw exists in the design, it does not mean that the engineers are not intelligent. So when the requirement to design items with as few flaws as possible is laid on, something beyond mere intelligence is in use; the designer would have to be maximally intelligent or even omniscient. While ID makes no such claim, it is beyond dispute that most proponents would not take issue with it.

Similar assumptions about the power of the designer have also been made because developing a design and bringing it to fruition are two different things. Intelligence is needed for one, and power/resources are needed for the other. For the argument to work, the designer must have power such that he cannot be thought of as lacking the ability to instantiate flawless creatures. Thus, the argument that the designer can and must properly eliminate/prevent all creaturely flaws requires that the designer is maximally intelligent and maximally powerful (i.e., omniscient and omnipotent).

31. Behe, *Darwin's Black Box*, 223.
32. Pennock, *Tower of Babel*, 248. While Pennock is always quick to point out instances in which *creationists* are unfair to modern Darwinians by mischaracterization, anachronism, or misrepresentation, he himself is guilty of the same here, for modern Intelligent Design theorists, even traditional theists, are under no obligation to hold that God must make a perfect Creation and that insodoing, he only had one option (i.e., "the Best").

case (possible world) where Adam is free with respect to the forbidden fruit, he chooses to eat. It does not require that this *is* the case or that it is even *likely*, but only that it is *logically possible*. Since there is no reason to think it impossible, it might be the case that God could not create a world where Adam is free and he does not sin, and the logical problem of evil fails. The justification for these claims was that a world containing free creatures who love and sometimes commit evil actions is better than a world containing no freedom, no love and no evil. This allows the proponent of the free will defense to claim that an all-knowing, all-loving, and all-powerful being could create a world with evil without violating his essential goodness.

The Intelligent Mutation Defense

Just as the theist only need show that it is *possible* that an all-powerful, all-loving God could not create a world where creatures are free but never commit evil in order to answer the logical problem of evil, so also in order to answer the logical problem of creaturely flaws, the proponent of ID only need show that it is *possible* that the intelligent designer could not have developed creatures with the complexity they have without the flaws they have.[33] Note that this is not the claim that it *has* to be the case or that it *is* the case, but only that it is possible. If the ID theorist can do this, then the logical problem of creaturely flaws fails.[34]

---

33. Or, to be more precise, it is possible that the intelligent designer could not have developed a world with creatures that are as complex as those which exist without some creatures also having flaws.

34. One other point is worth noting, and this is related to the limiting of the discussion to the realm of possibility. The critic of ID may suggest that, while it may be possible that the intelligent designer could not have developed creatures with the complexity they have without the flaws they have, the preponderance of the evidence of vestigial organs still speaks against ID. That is, he may argue that the great number of flaws which exist in the natural world point to a purely naturalistic process devoid of any intelligent guidance or direction. He may argue that the fact that so many species have gone extinct speaks against an intelligent (or benevolent for that matter) designer. Let us call this objection the emotive problem of creaturely flaws, due to the fact that it makes a claim upon our emotional response to the evidence of flaws in the natural world. This would not be an unreasonable objection, especially since ID theorists such as Dembski have suggested that ID is really concerned with inference to the best explanation. However, we will see that this objection does have its problems.

    Most first-year philosophy students will immediately notice the similarity of this sort of argument to the so-called emotive problem of evil (to belief in the existence of God). This form of argument, while seemingly persuasive, is really just a veiled form of the logical arguments, for the attempt to quantify acceptable negative states of affairs always fails. When atheologians are asked to quantify how many instances of evil *would* be acceptable for belief in the existence of God to be rational, they invariably claim none. This same strategy works with the a-ID theorist. If only one flaw speaks against the existence of an intelligent designer, then the Emotive Problem of Creaturely Flaws collapses into the Logical Problem of Creaturely Flaws. Therefore, if the logical problem is answered, then the objection from creaturely flaws is answered.

He can make his case by calling upon the very mechanisms that the proponent of evolution does—random genetic mutation, but he can claim that these mutations still fall within the purview of an intelligent designer (or in the case of Christianity, God), and here is where the doctrine of middle knowledge may prove useful.[35] Of course, the argument presented here to defend ID against its evolutionist critics can also be used to explain how God makes use of middle knowledge in a theistic evolutionary model.[36] In fact, MacGregor has argued that middle knowledge is necessary to theistic evolution because the statistical probability of unguided evolutionary development is so low as to be a virtual mathematical impossibility, and middle knowledge allows God to guide the process without impugning the random nature of the genetic mutations.[37]

Counterfactuals of random genetic mutation
Consider the following two propositions:

If situation S prevails, then random genetic mutation, M, will occur

and

If situation S does not prevail, then random genetic mutation, M, will not occur.

If these propositions are possibly true, then it is possible that the intelligent designer could not have developed creatures with the complexity they have without the flaws they have because S could involve undesirable mutations or the existence of useless organs, and in this way, the

So in some ways, both the Molinist and Determinist could make use of the argument (if the determinist agrees that it is possible). However, if the desire is to move beyond merely responding to the argument and to reflect upon *how* the intelligent designer [for Christians, God] actually did create, then it must be admitted that the argument offered here is not available to the Determinist because he is committed to the claim that the designer must have the ability to have creatures with the complexity they have without the flaws.

35. I understand that many of the opponents of ID have made just this charge, that ID is a veiled attempt to insert Christianity into science, and that my reference to the designer as "God" adds credence to this claim. However, it is somewhat dishonest for me to refuse to refer to the designer as God if I do, indeed, believe him to be such.

36. While I am not a proponent of theistic evolution, I acknowledge that Molinism provides a powerful mechanism for explaining how God could guide evolution in a way that preserves the fundamental scientific claims of neo-Darwinian evolutionary biology without a commitment to naturalistic materialism.

37. Kirk R. MacGregor, "The Impossibility of Evolution Apart from God with Middle Knowledge," paper presented at the national meeting of the Evangelical Theological Society, Milwaukee, WI, 2012. Greg Welty has turned MacGregor's argument on its head, arguing that the statistical impossibility to which MacGregor appeals as proof of God's activity actually speaks against the plausibility of Molinism itself! Greg Welty, "The Evolution of Molinism," paper presented at the national meeting of the Evangelical Theological Society, Milwaukee, WI, 2012.

proponent of ID has answered the objection. Suppose it is true that S is necessary for M to occur. In that case, if God wants mutation M to occur (at least randomly), he would have to actualize situation S (either strongly or weakly). At this point we have the beginnings of an explanation of how an intelligent designer (such as the traditional God of theism) could make use of random genetic mutation to guide evolutionary processes to the end he desires. However, it is not at all clear that these propositions are true or even possibly true. Several items merit further comment.

First, some may complain that they cannot be true because the very wording of the counterfactuals seems contradictory or self-referentially incoherent. This argument claims that there can be no truths regarding when random events would or would not (or will or will not) occur because truly random events must be indeterminate. The indeterminate nature of random events requires that the random mutation could occur (or not occur) whether S prevails or not. This form of argument against the truth of counterfactuals of random genetic mutation is similar in form to the grounding objection to the truth of counterfactuals of creaturely freedom, and I would expect Calvinists and Open Theists to make use of it. There is not time to answer it here, except to say that there is no causal relationship between the antecedent and the consequent in the counterfactuals. Rather, their relationship is merely explanatory.[38]

Second, even if the aforementioned objection can be overcome, the basis for the truth of propositions regarding when a random event will or will not occur cannot be found in God's will, for the random nature of the events preclude a deterministic cause behind their occurrence (even the will of God). This is not to say that God cannot cause genetic mutation, but it is to say that such mutations cannot properly be deemed random. This means that God's knowledge of such propositions must be part of his middle knowledge.

Third, it should be noted that situation S could include a whole host of events, prior mutations, and scenarios. This means that for mutation M to occur, some other undesirable mutations may be required. It is hard to see how, following a random mutation process, one can require that the designer bring about all desired mutations without any undesirable mutations as well. Suppose that mutation, M, is necessary for the complexity of creature, C, and that situation, S, includes flaws in C. Such a supposition seems to not only be obviously possible, but also quite plausible. If creature C evolves by means of evolution, it can rightly be expected to do so by means of certain helpful mutations, and there seems no reason to suppose that situation, S, could not include flaws in C. The possibility of mutation, M, being necessary for the complexity of creature, C, and that situation,

---

38. It is also the case that epistemological uncertainty does not imply metaphysical uncertainty; just because we do not know which of the counterfactuals is true, it does not follow that neither one can be true.

S, includes flaws in C, means that both of the aforementioned propositions [If situation, S, occurs, then random genetic mutation, M, will occur AND If situation, S, does not occur, then random genetic mutation, M, will not occur] are also possible and therefore, it is at least plausible that the designer could not create such complex creatures without flaws if he wished to use a process with randomness.

Two objections need to be considered. First, an explanation for why an intelligent designer might choose to create a world where adaptation is necessary must be given. It is not immediately clear that an intelligent designer would/should choose to include adaptability in his design. Note, again, that what needs to be shown is that an explanation is possible; it need not be the most plausible explanation (though such would be good to offer!). Second, an explanation of why an intelligent designer might choose to utilize a random, rather than determined, process for development must also be proffered. This seems to be the most difficult question to answer.

Problem of intelligent designer's preference for creaturely adaptability
In the same way that the free will defense needed a basis for saying why God would prefer a world with evil and freedom rather than a world with no freedom and no evil, a defense of ID against the logical problem of creaturely flaws needs a premise to explain why an intelligent designer would prefer a world where creatures develop in a way which utilizes random genetic mutation and have flaws, rather than a world where creatures come to be by fiat creation and undergo minor, if any, developmental change and do not have flaws.

Just as there are many possibilities available to the theist for answering the question of why God, who is all-powerful and all-loving, would create a world with evil and suffering, there are also many possibilities available to the ID-theorist for answering the question of why an intelligent designer might use a process such as evolution. For example, he could argue that a world where creatures adapt to a changing environment is better (i.e., more reflective of intelligence) than a world where they do not so adapt. After all, if the environment changes, it just makes sense to give creatures within that environment a chance at survival. So the argument works *given* an environment characterized by change. However, some may wonder why an intelligent designer would not design a stable environment; they may claim that a stable/unchanging environment would be more reflective of the handiwork of an intelligent artificer. Here again, several possibilities exist.

For example, it could be argued that a dynamic environment is more beautiful, and that beauty reflects intelligence. Consider the following proposition:

> A world characterized by change is more beautiful than a world that does not change.

This proposition needs to be augmented in order to get to a justification of an intelligent designer. That is, the further claim that a beautiful world is more reflective of an intelligent designer than a world that is not beautiful, would need to be proven. While this line of argument may be sound (and there is good reason to think it is), it is beyond the scope of this chapter to defend it. Such a defense would need to include an explanation of how change in the world is beautiful while stasis in the divine nature (as classically/traditionally conceived) is preferable. It suggests that an intelligent designer must create the most beautiful world, and so a defense may also require an argument for the supreme beauty of this world.

Fortunately, the aforementioned argument is not the only defense of the intelligibility of an environment characterized by change, and quite frankly, is neither the best nor the most straightforward. Consider the following argument:

> An unchanging environment requires stasis;
>
> Stasis prevents relationality among finite beings;
>
> A world with relationality is more reflective of an intelligent designer than one with no relationality.

The argument here is admittedly basic, but seems sound. Some may wish to contest the last claim, but it is unclear what such an argument would look like. In fact, it is not at all clear how a world populated (in any meaningful sense of the term) with any sort of creatures could possibly not be characterized by relationality. (In this, relationality is being used in a most basic sense—to refer to the fact that there is interaction, in the very least, at the most basic levels.) In fact, a static world may not even be a possibility. No matter how intelligent or powerful the designer may be, it simply may not be within his ability to create a world without change because it simply makes no sense; finitude seems to require movement, interaction, and change. That is, it seems that a world with living organisms requires at least *some* change because of the relationality of finite beings with one another and their environment(s). Change is fundamental to any environment populated by finite beings and is therefore a constituent part of an intelligently designed cosmos. Thus, the claim that a world where creatures adapt is better than a world where they do not, can stand (it is, at least, defensible).

Problem of the intelligence of random mutation
One objection to this argument is to question the intelligence of using random genetic mutation to spur evolutionary development. After all, it is terribly inefficient. It is hard to see why an intelligent designer would choose to create beings with an ability to adapt, but place that ability at the guidance of *random* events. Similarly, it is hard to see why it would not

be more intelligent to use directed genetic mutations. If no good answer can be given, then there may be good reason to doubt the random genetic mutation defense of ID.

However, there are several avenues to follow in answering this objection. One could simply agree that it would be *more intelligent* to use directed mutations, but argue that this does nothing to detract from ID since it only requires that the process followed is intelligent, not that it is *most intelligent*. Although this answers the specific objection, most proponents of ID would find it unsatisfying. However, there are three answers available to the ID theorist who believes the designer is omniscient and omnipotent.

First, some cognitive psychologists have suggested that thoughts and actions are merely the expression of changes and movement at the atomic level in the brain. If all genetic mutations were controlled, then development of brain states would also be determined, and human freedom would be illusory (at least libertarian freedom), but as noted earlier, a good case can be made for preferring libertarian freedom to determinism. Randomness and indeterminacy at the genetic and quantum level may be necessary for (libertarian) human freedom.[39] The problem with this approach is that it smacks of Identity-theory Physicalism, which is clearly antithetical to the idea of an intelligent designer. While some proponents of ID and some theists have made cases similar to this based on Non-reductive Physicalism, it still seems to be at odds with a broad-based dualist view of reality, which ID seems to imply.[40] A better answer can be given.

Second, it could be argued that the use of random processes to produce an orderly system requires more intelligence than it does to use controlled process for the same purpose. Random genetic mutation leading to the evolution of complex life, then, actually points to the glory of God. Van Til hints at this line of reasoning when he calls his own [theistic evolutionary] position the *"fully gifted creation perspective."*[41] According to Van Til, the capabilities for self-organization and transformation necessary for evolutionary development—something he describes as "humanly incomprehensible"—are granted by God's "unbounded generosity and unfathomable creativity."[42] This line of reasoning fits well with the doctrine of

39. For example, Keith Ward suggests that preservation of libertarian freedom may serve as the reason God chose to create by means of random processes. See Keith Ward, "Theistic Evolution," in *Debating Design: From Darwin to DNA*, eds. William A. Dembski and Michael Ruse (Cambridge: Cambridge University Press, 2006), 261–74, esp. 262–63.

40. See, for example, Nancey Murphy and George F. R. Ellis, *On the Moral Nature of the Universe: Theology, Cosmology, and Ethics* (Minneapolis: Fortress, 1996), 32–37; Nancey Murphy, *Beyond Liberalism and Fundamentalism* (Valley Forge, PA: Trinity Press International, 1996), chapter 6, esp. 149–52.

41. Howard J. Van Til, ""The Fully Gifted Creation ('Theistic Evolution')," in *Three Views on Creation and Evolution*, eds. J. P. Moreland and John Mark Reynolds (Grand Rapids: Zondervan, 1999), 173.

42. Ibid.

middle knowledge, for only an infinite mind could comprehend all of the virtually infinite possibilities regarding random genetic mutations and then bring about a world where the desired mutations occur. The fact that God is constrained by the counterfactuals of creaturely freedom and the counterfactuals of genetic mutation detracts nothing from his infinity, conceived either in terms of knowledge (omniscience) or in terms of power (omnipotence).

Third, the random character of mutations could be attributed to the Fall. That is, under a Christian interpretation, one could argue that as a result of the Fall and the emergence of sin into the created order, the cosmos has been characterized by chaos and randomness at the most basic level (e.g., quarks and gluons). Yet, until such time as God recreates or restores the heavens and the earth, he will preserve a measure of peace and order. His use of random mutation and survival of the fittest is due to his grace in extending the current age (2 Peter 3:8–10).

All three options provide a basis for answering the question of why an intelligent designer might use random genetic mutation to allow for creaturely adaptation. The second and the third can be combined to provide a powerful theological statement that is consistent with both theistic evolution and progressive creation.

The logical problem of creaturely flaws does not serve to unseat ID theory, as it is a move into the realm of philosophy and religion. At a minimum, it assumes the designer is both omniscient and omnipotent. A satisfactory explanation of why even a maximally intelligent and powerful being might produce flawed creatures is possible. While other answers can surely be given, the most satisfactory approach is to draw upon the doctrine of middle knowledge and argue that the designer could use his knowledge of how random genetic mutations *would* proceed in order to bring about the adaptations and changes in creatures he desires. However, his ability is constrained by the true counterfactuals of random genetic mutation and therefore, it is possible that undesirable mutations may be required. Satisfactory reasons can be supplied for why an intelligent designer might wish to create creatures with the ability to adapt and to do so by means of random mutation. Ultimately the very process points to the intelligence of the designer and the critique of ID fails.

MIDDLE KNOWLEDGE AND QUANTUM PHYSICS

Another area where Molinism may prove fruitful in the reconciliation of meticulous divine providence with the findings of modern science is quantum mechanics. Most scientists believe there is randomness at the subatomic level, while there is stability, orderliness, and even (dare I say) determinateness at the macro-level. As Heisenberg noted, this recognition of genuine randomness at the quantum level represented a shift in physical thought and in the philosophy of science itself: "quantum theory actually forces us to formulate these laws [of nature] precisely as statistical laws and to depart radically from determinism. . . . With the mathematical formulation of quantum-theoretical laws pure determinism had to be abandoned."[43] If this picture is correct, and there is no good reason to doubt it, apart from *a priori* commitments to some form of determinism, then it seems that Molinism has the necessary tools to handle randomness and orderliness better than its chief competitors, Calvinism/Determinism, Process Theology, and Open Theism.

Determinism, Process, Openness, and Randomness at the Quantum Level

Determinism/Calvinism is ill-equipped to deal with genuine randomness, as should be obvious. Barbour rightly takes issue with William Pollard's suggestion that God's providence is located in his *control* (in a deterministic way) of subatomic and atomic structures/movements; no matter how much the proponent wishes to engage modern physical theory, real indeterminacy is removed under any deterministic scheme of providence.[44] Proponents of Determinism typically claim that there is an indiscernible (through scientific means) determining *cause* of all events (i.e., God's sovereign will) and that the randomness in the universe is only *apparent*, more a reflection of our ignorance or lack of observational ability than of genuine indeterminacy in nature. As theologian Paul Helm puts it, "Heisenberg's Principle does not have to be understood as a statement about the absence of causal preconditions in the case of those events which it says are uncertain, but to be about the limits of our knowledge," and he is correct in this.[45] However, he continues, "And it may be, for all we know to the contrary, that God has freely willed into being a succession of events, some of the latter of which are unspecified and unspecifiable in terms of the earlier."[46]

One would be hard-pressed to take issue with the basic claim in the latter quote; surely God could bring about events that have no discernible relation to previous events. He could conceivably cause all things to go out of existence at each *moment* and bring it all back into existence at each successive moment. The problem is that there is simply no way

43. Werner Heisenberg, *The Physicist's Conception of Nature* (1958), excerpted in Edmund Blair Bolles, ed., *Galileo's Commandment: An Anthology of Great Science Writing* (New York: W. H. Freeman, 1997), 349.

44. He first objects to the *total control* afforded God in this model because it leads to *predestination*, a doctrine Barbour sees as denying human freedom and the reality of evil. While there is good reason to doubt this interpretation of *predestination* itself, Barbour is surely correct that Pollard's view is inconsistent with the reality of chance/indeterminacy. Barbour goes on to criticize the model for its lop-sided view of providence as divine use of unlawful aspects of nature and for its *implicit reductionism*. Barbour, *Religion in an Age of Science*, 117.

45. Helm, *The Providence of God*, 143.

46. Ibid., 144.

to know this. For example, there is no way to know if God brings about the locations of photons in each moment in such a way that their locations have no real relation to anything previous. However, this seems to leave the Determinist with a steadfast faith-claim that is in opposition to observational reality (one that is, ironically enough, perilously close to that of the Process Theologian). Thus, he must presuppose that there is either some kind of indiscernible deterministic relationship causing subatomic particle movement, or God is bringing about the locations of subatomic particles at each moment without reference to earlier states. Neither seems particularly attractive.

It is also hard to see how a Process view of God can inspire the sort of confidence required in any sort of teleological understanding of reality and theology suggested by orderliness at the macro-level. While Process thinkers have consistently maintained the power of persuasion, set against what they see as the only alternative, *coercion*, it seems unable to *ensure* the kind of orderliness observed in the natural world and more importantly, to *secure* a cosmological future that Christian theism proclaims. According to Process Theology, God *preserves* each occasion so that in the midst of the coming-into and going-out-of existence of all *actual entities*, there is something akin to the continuity we observe in the world and infer in theological reflection on the doctrine of divine sustainment (and in scientific work as well), but this only maintains whatever process is already at work. It provides no mechanism for God to govern the process, and may actually result in God's sustainment of processes that work contrary to his ends. The proponent of Process thought must maintain that the eschatological focus of God's self-realization in *becoming* either cannot be guaranteed through persuasion alone, or is met no matter what happens because the process itself *just is* God's self-realization and there is no proper eschatological goal. In the case of the former, God is hopelessly weak. As Basinger writes, "The process theist certainly can hope things will improve. But I see no basis within the system for justifiably coming to believe (having faith) such improvement is probable. . . . Furthermore . . . there is no basis in process thought for assuming that such a 'triumph' would be 'ultimate.'"[47] In the case of the latter, the result is relativistic universalism where *being* and *becoming* are equated, all states of being/becoming are equally ultimate, and randomness/chance and determinacy/orderliness meld into one and are thus, really illusory. But this imposes a metaphysic far more obscure than that of traditional theism, and conflicts with normal notions of observation, assessment, and coherence! Of course, the critique of occasionalism here (and in the previous section critiquing Determinism) could be accused of begging the question, but it still seems more in line with the observational data than the alternatives.

---

47.   David Basinger, *Divine Power in Process Theism: A Philosophical Critique* (Albany: SUNY Press, 1988), 73.

Open Theism is the only model, save Molinism, that seems capable of allowing for genuine randomness at the micro-level and orderliness at the macro-level. So at first glance, one may think it something of a toss-up between the two, with one's proclivities determining (no pun intended) which one adopts. However, it seems that ultimately, Open Theism, like Process Theology, runs into serious trouble in *ensuring* orderliness. That is, the God of Open Theism may get lucky, as it were, so that the random processes at the micro-level just happen to organize themselves in such a way as to produce orderliness, but this outcome has little to do with Open Theism itself. More importantly, the God of Open Theism may not get so lucky, and may find the random subatomic activities leading to chaos. At that point, he has two choices: he can allow chaos to reign and simply work with the new situation as *Plan B* and hope he can non-causally influence things to turn around, or he can intervene and override the natural processes in order to get to outcomes he desires. Both options are available under Open Theist principles, but *that* they are the only seeming options available to God in this situation illustrates the problem: the only way the God of Open Theism can *ensure* orderliness at the macro-level by means of random processes at the micro-level is to violate the most basic principles of the model and, in essence, function like the Determinist/Calvinist God. This is due to the shared assumptions of the Determinist/Calvinist and the Open Theist proponents, namely incompatibilism regarding truths about future contingents and those events truly being contingent, i.e., the grounding objection.

Molinism, Randomness, and Determinism/Orderliness

By contrast, Molinism provides the interpretive means for understanding how God could ensure orderliness while utilizing random processes. In a way similar to how God could use (prevolitionally true) counterfactuals of random genetic mutation to guide an orderly process of evolutionary development, so also God could use (prevolitionally true) counterfactuals of random subatomic particle movement to establish order and determinateness at the macro-level while retaining genuine indeterminateness at the micro-level. That is, propositions such as

> If situation *S* were to obtain, particle *P* would randomly move to location *L*;

could be used by God to guide and/or govern subatomic particles without causally determining their movements by weakly actualizing situations like *S*. Of course, a few caveats must be noted. First, there may be no true counterfactuals of random subatomic particle movement that result in the particle being where God wants it (and so God's options are limited by the true counterfactuals). Second, it may be the case that some minor differences in location of subatomic particles have an effective impact of nil at the macro-level so that the limitations on options have no appreciable effect on God's ability to accomplish his purposes through this random process. Third, there may be no explanation available for what makes counterfactuals of this sort true in that we may not be able to account for the reason why (for example) P moves to L in S rather than (say) $L2$. Note that all of the caveats presented are no different from the caveats that must be made regarding counterfactuals of creaturely freedom (i.e., regular Molinism); no special pleading is required here. As may be expected, some could object that there simply could be no true counterfactuals of random subatomic particle movement because they would not thereby be random or because nothing can be identified which makes them true, but such objections are simply versions of the grounding objection and are subject to the same criticisms/answers already given by Molinists (e.g., they beg the question of the incompatibility of the counterfactual conditionals being true, while the processes they describe are random). However, there are other objections that may demand more comment than reference to the still-unresolved issues of grounding.

First, some may question the feasibility of the process. There may be many ways for situation S to come about so that, on the one hand, there could potentially be many ways for God to weakly actualize S and get particle P to location L by means of random movement, but on the other hand, the virtually infinite layers of complexity involved here may seem to make such weak actualization virtually impossible, for to arrive at S, God would have to weakly actualize another set of random subatomic particle movements, such that an infinite regress results. But this potential complaint seems to just raise the issue of the complexity of the creative work of God in a universe characterized by some processes that are random, and while its comprehension poses problems for finite beings (e.g., humans), its execution poses no problems for an infinite Being. The possibilities regarding particle movement are *virtually* infinite, but they are not *actually* infinite, given the finitude of the creation (though even if they were, it would not, in principle, pose a problem for God anyway). If the concept of a truly infinite Being is coherent, then the many layers of complexity and the many factors involved in the governance of random processes do not make divine providence impossible. If anything, it highlights God's majesty.

Second, some may complain that the randomness of the particle movement is removed due to God's "coercive" activity in actualizing S. That is, they may not have a problem with the notion of true counterfactuals of random subatomic particle movement, but may argue that once any effort at regulating their destination(s) is made (even by *weak actualization*), randomness is, by definition, removed. Notice that this argument is different in structure from the grounding objection in that it allows for truths regarding results from random processes, and it does not require an accounting of how there can be such truths or what makes them true, yet it still has some of the same weaknesses and is based on some of the same assumptions as the grounding objection. At its base is a question-begging assumption that randomness and orderliness cannot be reconciled, and any move toward establishing orderliness is automatically deemed destructive of the random nature of subatomic particle movement. In addition, it fails to appreciate that in the model, God's activity is not directly affecting the particle movement, so there is no coercive, governing, or other such controlling power acting upon the particle in order to determine its ultimate location. An analogous complaint to counterfactuals of creaturely freedom would be to accuse Molinism of destroying freedom because God may set up the conditions where the creature freely acts, but that can hardly be said to destroy freedom in itself unless some variation of the grounding objection has been assumed.

Some perceptive readers may complain that the criticisms of Open Theism and to a lesser extent, Process Theology, are unfair in light of the presentation of the strengths and defenses of Molinism here. For example, it must be admitted that the God of Molinism, like the God of Open Theism, might (as one Calvinist friend put it) "just get lucky" with respect to the true counterfactuals available to him (whether of creaturely freedom, of random genetic mutation, of random subatomic particle movement, etc.), and so, in one sense, Molinism is subject to a similar criticism to that leveled against Open Theism. It should also be admitted that Open Theism (and to a lesser extent, Process Theology) has/have available to it/them similar appeals to the idea that variances at the micro-level may have virtually no impact at the macro-level. However, the latter claim is more a function of true randomness than of the model itself, so it is not so much a strength of one model over another and more a recognition that all three models—Molinism, Open Theism, and Process Theism—can accommodate such randomness. The former charge (of luck) is also not as strong as it first appears, for it fails to account for the fundamental difference between the Molinist and Open Theist models of providence after God's creative act. While there is good reason to question the use of the term "luck" here due to its pejorative (not to mention its *a priori* conflict with sound Christian theories of providence), it will be retained in the answer for consistency. Under Molinist principles, once God decides on a possible world and actualizes it, God is no longer subject to such "luck," whereas neither Open Theism not Process Theology can make that claim at any stage in the history of the cosmos. God's "luck" (or lack thereof) is considered at the front end and worked into the overall scheme such that his decision to actualize a particular world makes provision for all the cases of bad "luck" and he still gets what he desires in the end.

CONCLUSION

In this chapter, I argued that Molinism provides a strong interpretive lens through which theists who are favorably disposed toward Intelligent Design may understand God's providence in creation in such a way that both randomness and orderliness are preserved. It affords the proponent of ID a mechanism by which the designer may intelligently bring about the intricate processes observed in nature, while also explaining the supposed problems in the natural order of development of individual creatures. That is, Molinism allows for creaturely adaptability to a changing environment while also providing an explanatory tool for seemingly useless organs or wasteful/inefficient processes, by appeal to divine middle knowledge of counterfactuals of random genetic mutation. God may use his prevolitional knowledge of these counterfactuals to actualize a world where the creatures he desires will emerge and evolve (through progressive creation wherein he inserts genetic information or through purely naturalistic means). God could know counterfactuals like, *If I were to actualize a world with such and such initial conditions, these particular creatures will evolve, though they will have certain flaws*; but he could also know counterfactuals such as, *If I were to insert this genetic information into this creature's gene pool, some of its descendants will evolve in this way, thus creating this new species, though those who remain the species they are will now have a minor flaw.* In the case of the former, middle knowledge proves helpful to theistic evolution, while in the case of the latter, it serves progressive creation. In both cases, though, there is allowance for some aspects that are undesirable to come along with the desirable.

I have also argued that middle knowledge provides a sound basis for God's providence over a world characterized by true randomness at the quantum level and orderliness at the macro-level, a vision of the natural order shared by most scientists. By appeal to divine knowledge of counterfactuals of random subatomic particle movement, Molinism can provide a powerful interpretive lens for holding to the cherished Christian doctrine of meticulous divine providence while also taking seriously the findings of modern physics and the claims of random movement at the quantum level.

The modern world is dominated by science, and although there is always room for questioning the broad claims of science or the metaphysical implications of a scientific worldview, most Christians still try to reconcile their religious beliefs with the general claims of the scientific community. Only Molinism is able to fully and adequately integrate meticulous divine providence with the claims of evolutionary biology and quantum mechanics. It can, at the very least, serve as an aide to those Christians who take seriously the current claims of science regarding the natural world, and who wish to make sense of the guiding, preserving and directing work of God in light of the extent and reach of those claims.

CHAPTER 9

MOLINISM:
THE BIBLICAL EVIDENCE

INTRODUCTION

The beginning point of theological reflection for many is not natural theology or existential encounter with God, but revealed theology in the Bible. If middle knowledge is true, we should expect the biblical description of how God works to confirm it. Ironically, even though the bulk of the discussion surrounding middle knowledge has taken place among Christian scholars, surprisingly little attention has been devoted to examination of the biblical evidence for its truth. Arguments have tended to remain in the realm of analytical philosophy. Yet, it should go without saying that Christians interested in the doctrine of middle knowledge should search the Scriptures to see if what Molina said was true, much like the Bereans did with Paul's claims about the resurrection (Acts 17:11), and if Molinism is true, it should be adopted.

Objections

As noted earlier, the major objection to Molinism is the so-called *grounding* objection.[1] It has a variety of manifestations, from the simple question of what grounds the truth of counterfactuals of creaturely freedom, to the more complex complaint that middle knowledge is viciously circular.[2] The basis of most of these complaints against Molinism is the claim that counterfactuals of (libertarian) creaturely freedom cannot be true. For ease of study, they will be categorized as Arminian and Calvinist.[3]

---

1. See chapter 2.
2. As noted in chapter 3, it is my contention that the circularity or logical priority objections to middle knowledge are, at their most basic level, derived from the grounding objection because they assume a particular answer to the grounding objection, namely the grounding in the closest possible but not actual world. See also my "Molinism and Supercomprehension."
3. Some may object to my use of "Arminian" here, since most libertarian opponents of middle knowledge are Open Theists. I readily acknowledge this as true, and have already argued that classic Arminian theology assumes the truth of middle knowledge. However, it would also be

Arminian opponents of Molinism—opponents of Molinism who subscribe to libertarian freedom—are typically Open Theists and object to the very concept of true counterfactuals of creaturely freedom. They argue that nothing can serve as the basis for the truth of statements about what persons would have freely done in situations that never arise (i.e., counterfactuals proper). They also often contend that if there are true statements about what persons will definitely do in the future, then libertarian freedom is abrogated. Since Arminian objectors deny the truth of counterfactuals of freedom, what needs to be shown is that the Bible supports the belief that there are such things as true counterfactuals of freedom.

Calvinist (and Thomist) opponents of Molinism—opponents of Molinism who hold to compatibilist freedom—do not normally have difficulty with the concept of counterfactuals of creaturely freedom *per se*, but rather with the Molinist claim that they are counterfactuals of libertarian freedom. One way determinist objectors have attacked this claim is to call into question the prevolitional nature of counterfactuals of freedom.[4] What needs to be shown is that those counterfactuals of creaturely freedom are true independent of God's will, or are true logically prior to God's knowledge of his will, and inform his creative and providential decision(s).

In this chapter, I will argue that the Bible supports the belief that there are true counterfactuals of creaturely freedom, contrary to Open Theist claims and (contrary to compatibilist claims), that God's knowledge of these propositions informs his pre-creative decisions. Molina himself cited three passages as support of his claim that God has knowledge of counterfactuals, but he did not offer proof that counterfactuals of creaturely freedom can be true because it was *assumed* to be the case. However, if there are passages which teach that God knows counterfactuals of creaturely freedom, then it is obvious that the Bible supports the claim that they

---

misleading to categorize *Open Theism* separately, since most Open Theists have come from Arminian roots. My use of the term here is in no way meant to suggest or endorse the idea that consistent Arminian theology leads to Open Theism. Quite the contrary, Molinism is a consistent (and more orthodox) Arminian theology.

4.   Some Calvinists have characterized their own theological positions as *Calvinist-Molinist* and have referred to themselves as *Middle Knowledge Calvinists*. Time and space constraints will not permit a demonstration of why this position is both untenable and impossible, but the very fact that some have attempted to articulate such a position points to the careful distinctions that need to be made in the presentation of the evidence. See my "The Compatibility of Calvinism and Middle Knowledge," *Journal of the Evangelical Theological Society* 47, no. 3 (September 2004): 455–67. These Calvinists have not questioned the prevolitional nature of counterfactuals of freedom, but have placed all of God's knowledge in his natural knowledge. I have argued elsewhere that this leads to Fatalism. See my "Middle Knowledge and the Assumption of Libertarian Freedom: A Response to Ware," paper presented at the National Meeting of the Evangelical Theological Society, Baltimore, MD, 2013. See also John D. Laing, "Calvinism, Natural Knowledge and Fatalism," paper presented at the Southwest Regional Meeting of the Evangelical Theological Society, Fort Worth, TX, 2014; also presented in a revised format at the Houston Baptist University Philosophy Conference, Houston, TX, 2014.

can be true. Each of the passages Molina referenced, in addition to three others that support middle knowledge, will be examined, if only briefly.

CONTRA OPEN THEISM

Matthew 11:22–24

The first passage to which Molina appealed is found in the Gospel of Matthew, in which Jesus's words of rebuke to the inhabitants of the cities of Chorazin and Bethsaida are recorded: "Woe to you, Chorazin! Woe to you, Bethsaida! For if the deeds of power done in you had been done in Tyre and Sidon, they would have repented long ago in sack-cloth and ashes" (Matt. 11:21 NRSV). Molina argued that Jesus was here making a factual claim regarding how the Tyrians and Sidonians would have responded (repentance) if he had performed the same miraculous works in their cities as he had in Chorazin and Bethsaida. Although the wonders were not worked in Tyre and Sidon, God can and does still know it or the truth it represents.[5]

Kenny has criticized Molina, arguing that Jesus was not seriously implying anything factual about what the Tyrians and Sidonians would really do in those circumstances. Rather, Kenny argues, "the passage about Tyre and Sidon is clearly rhetorical," and he is basically correct.[6] Jesus's chastisement of Chorazin and Bethsaida goes on to say, "But I tell you, on the day of judgment it will be more tolerable for Tyre and Sidon than for you. And you, Capernaum, will you be exalted to heaven? No, you will be brought down to Hades. For if the deeds of power done in you had been done in Sodom, it would have remained until this day. But I tell you that on the day of judgment it will be more tolerable for the land of Sodom than for you" (Matt. 11:22–24, NRSV). A consistent hermeneutic demands that Molina read these words of Jesus just as literally as those regarding Chorazin and Bethsaida, but this means Jesus was making several questionable assertions. For example, he appears to claim that on the day of judgment, Tyre and Sidon will receive fewer/less severe punishments than Chorazin and Bethsaida, and Capernaum will receive a greater judgment than Sodom. This suggests various levels of punishment meted out by God at the last day, and while the idea may comport well with modern sensibilities of making the punishment fit the crime, it doesn't fit the biblical description of eschatological judgment, though there is certainly room for disagreement. In addition, Jesus seems to make the rather odd claim

---

5. Molina, *Concordia* 4.49.9 (trans. Freddoso, 116–17). Molina writes, "God knows that there would have been repentance in sackcloth and ashes among the Tyronians and Sidonians on the hypothesis that the wonders that were worked in Chorozain and Bethsaida should have been worked in Tyre and Sidon. . . . But because the hypothesis on which it was going to occur was not in fact actualized, this repentance never did and never will exist in reality—and yet it was a future contingent dependent on the free choice of human beings." Ibid.

6. Kenny, *The God of the Philosophers*, 64.

that Capernaum will be cast down into the realm of Hades; cities may be destroyed by God, but they do not literally go down to the realm of the dead. The language is clearly metaphorical. Jesus also claims that Chorazin, Bethsaida, and Capernaum will receive worse punishments because the inhabitants of Tyre, Sidon, and Sodom *would have* repented if the same deeds of power had been performed in those cities, but a literal reading here would mean the level of punishment one receives is based upon what that individual *would have done* if circumstances had been different, and thus, punishments and rewards have less to do with what one has actually done, and more to do with the true counterfactuals about him. These are questionable theological positions at best and fail to reflect the point Jesus was making. He was not trying to make comparisons about the relative amount of divine wrath to be poured out on particular individuals or cities, and he was not making claims about the relocation of particular cities at the time of God's judgment. It is also doubtful that he was making the theological claim that God punishes (or rewards) individuals or groups based on how they would have acted in any number of possible but nonactual situations. The Bible explicitly states that persons are judged on the works they performed while alive (Rev. 20:12–13), and God's justice and mercy demand that he not punish persons based on what they would have done.[7] It is true that God judges the heart in addition to actions, but this fact in no way allows for punishment for sins not committed or sins that would have been committed in non-realized situations. Jesus meant to condemn the cities of Chorazin, Bethsaida, and Capernaum by offering an unfavorable comparison of their spiritual conditions with the worst cities the Hebrew Bible had to offer. Thus, it seems that Kenny's critique should be sustained.[8] At a minimum, this passage cannot establish the truth of counterfactuals of creaturely freedom.

---

7. Some may wish to point out that my strict reading of the passage can only lead to the claim that God grants grace to some based on what they would have done. In this case, the Tyrians, Sidonians, and Sodomites will receive some measure of grace because they *would have* repented if Jesus had performed his miraculous works in their cities, but the judgment upon the inhabitants of Chorazin, Bethsaida, and Capernaum is for their unbelief in the face of Jesus's actual ministry. While this point is technically correct, for it to overturn the point I am making, it would have to support the idea that God has two standards: one for administering grace, and one for prosecuting judgment, but this does not seem to be the biblical model, where grace and judgment are almost always tied together. Thus, it should still be noted that it is doubtful that God rewards and punishes based on counterfactuals. Interestingly, if it were the case, then *no one* could have assurance of salvation, as personal faith in reality would be only one factor in God's consideration of salvation/judgment. Perhaps counterfactuals regarding our unbelief in various nonfactual situations would override our faith in Christ in actuality.

8. Freddoso concedes that Kenny is correct to claim that Jesus's words are rhetorical. However, Freddoso argues that this is not to say that Molina's interpretation is incorrect: "Often enough, the plain truth has far greater rhetorical force than an obvious exaggeration. So Molinists and Bañezians may justifiably insist that the burden of proof is on those who claim that the words in question are not to be taken in the most natural way." Freddoso, "Introduction," 63.

1 Samuel 23:7–13

The second passage Molina used to defend God's knowledge of counterfactuals of freedom is found in 1 Samuel 23. It tells of a time when David escaped from Saul because he was given special insight into how Saul and the men of the city in which he was hidden would act given certain conditions. The text reads as follows:

> Now it was told Saul that David had come to Keilah. And Saul said, "God has given him into my hand; for he has shut himself in by entering a town that has gates and bars." Saul summoned all the people to war, to go down to Keilah, to besiege David and his men. When David learned that Saul was plotting evil against him, he said to the priest Abiathar, "Bring the ephod here." David said, "O LORD, the God of Israel, your servant has heard that Saul seeks to come to Keilah, to destroy the city on my account. And now, will Saul come down as your servant has heard? O LORD, the God of Israel, I beseech you, tell your servant." The LORD said, "He will come down." Then David said, "Will the men of Keilah surrender me and my men into the hand of Saul?" The LORD said, "They will surrender you." Then David and his men, who were about six hundred, set out and left Keilah; they wandered wherever they could go. When Saul was told that David had escaped from Keilah, he gave up the expedition (1 Sam. 23:7–13, NRSV).

Molina believed the passage to affirm that if David were to remain in Keilah, Saul and his men would (freely) besiege the city, and had they done so, the men of Keilah would (freely) surrender David to Saul, and that although neither of these scenarios would occur, God still knows how they would play out. So God knows two counterfactuals of creaturely freedom:

> If David were to remain in Keilah, Saul would freely besiege the city;

and

> If David were to remain and Saul were to attack, the men of the city would freely hand David over to Saul.

Molina writes, "Notice, God knew these two future contingents [counterfactuals of creaturely freedom], which depended on human choice, and He revealed them to David. Yet they never have existed and never will exist in reality, and thus they do not exist in eternity either."[9]

Although I am sympathetic to Freddoso's desire to defend Molina here, given my analysis of the context, I must side with Kenny here.

9. Molina, *Concordia* 4.49.9 (trans. Freddoso, 117). Molina makes a point of noting this because he is arguing against the position that God knows future free actions because he observes

Kenny thinks these claims are excessive since the instrument of divination (ephod) was so crude. He notes that the ephod probably only had two sides (*yes* and *no*), and therefore, contends that it "would be incapable of marking the difference between knowledge of counterfactuals and knowledge of the truth-value of material implications."[10] Kenny concludes, "Since the antecedent of David's questions was false, the same answers would have been appropriate in each case."[11] Kenny's argument is twofold: on the one hand, he suggests that counterfactuals proper serve as instances of material implication and therefore, offer no value to divine knowledge, and on the other hand, since the ephod could only yield a "yes" or "no" answer, it is unclear if God knew what Saul and the men of Keilah would definitely do (freely), or if he only knew what they would probably do. If God knows that Saul would definitely attack the city and that the men would definitely hand David over, the appropriate answer to David's questions is "yes." However, if God only knows that Saul will probably attack the city or the men will probably hand David over, the appropriate answer to David's question is also "yes." Therefore, Kenny concludes, it is not clear from the text that God really possesses middle knowledge.[12]

This objection may work from a logical standpoint, but it is not the most plausible interpretation of the passage. The most natural reading of the story lends itself to the belief that God indeed had knowledge of how Saul and the men of Keilah would actually act, and not merely of how they would probably act.[13] Two related passages lend insight into the story and support this assertion. One relates to Kenny's understanding of what the ephod was and how it was used, and the other deals with the nature of answers given by consultation of the ephod (i.e., probabilistic or definitive).

Exodus 28 describes many of the robes and other attire utilized by the Levitical priesthood in the Israelite cultus. It is here that the ephod is described as a garment, and not as an object with a "yes" and a "no"

---

them in eternity. Here is an example where God knows how a free agent will act, but there is no event in eternity to observe.

10. Kenny, *The God of the Philosophers*, 64.

11. Ibid.

12. Actually, the argument does not really speak against middle knowledge proper, but rather against divine knowledge of how contingent counterfactual states of affairs would obtain if actual. Although this is the content of middle knowledge, one can believe that God has such knowledge, but it is not middle knowledge. Báñez believed that God has such knowledge, but denied that it is prevolitional or middle knowledge.

13. Freddoso offers an interesting critique of Kenny's interpretation of this passage. On Kenny's interpretation, God does not give good advice and, in fact, may be seen as deceitful. Freddoso writes, "We may safely say that even if *God* knows of the distinction between counterfactual and material implication, *David* did not. But in that case God's affirmative answers were deceptive if His advice presupposed that David's questions involved material implication. At the very least, David would have every right to feel betrayed upon learning that yes was likewise an 'appropriate' answer to the alternative question, 'If I stay In Keilah, will Saul refrain from invading?'" Freddoso, "Introduction," 63.

side. Attached to the ephod was a breastplate which housed, among other things, the Urim and Thummim (Exod. 28:30). Most scholars believe it was these items, and not the ephod itself, which were consulted in ascertaining the will of God. It is unclear whether they were used only to gain either an affirmative or negative answer to simple questions, or were used for more explicit guidance. The Babylonian Talmud suggests that they were part of the high priest's breastplate and gave answers to open-ended questions. Some scholars believe they were used by the priest in conjunction with oral prophecy to deliver the LORD's words.[14] This fits well with normal procedure when one sought guidance from the Lord; he would consult the priests of God after bringing a sacrifice. Since the ephod was reserved for use by the Levitical priesthood, David probably did not consult the LORD directly, but rather consulted him through the mediation of Abiathar the priest. Thus, David would have brought his question to God by way of the priest, and it is unclear if consulting the ephod yielded only a "yes" or "no" answer as Kenny claims, or provided more detailed direction.

A parallel passage exists in which David consulted with Abiathar again, and in this case, he was given more explicit instructions through the ephod (1 Sam. 30:1–19). The Amalekites had attacked the city where David and his men lived, and carried away all their possessions and family members. When David and his men returned, they wanted revenge, but David first sought the guidance of the LORD:

> David said to the priest Abiathar son of Ahimelech, "Bring me the ephod." So Abiathar brought the ephod to David. David inquired of the LORD, "Shall I pursue this band? Shall I overtake them?" He answered him, "Pursue; for you shall surely overtake and shall surely rescue." So David set out, he and the six hundred men who were with him. . . . David attacked them from twilight until the evening of the next day. Not one of them escaped, except four hundred young men, who mounted camels and fled. David recovered all that the Amalekites had taken; and David rescued his two wives. Nothing was missing, whether small or great, sons or daughters, spoil or anything that had been taken; David brought back everything (1 Sam. 30:7–9a, 17–19, NRSV).

The text implies that God knows that if David and his men were to pursue the Amalekites, they will definitely overtake them, and if they pursue the Amalekites and overtake them, they will definitely rescue their families and possessions. David is told what to do and is given definite answers to his questions regarding his success. These are not answers based on probabilities or material implications, but rather based on a knowledge of how things will turn out if David freely pursues the Amalekites. Kenny's analysis of divine knowledge imparted by the ephod suggests God does not know that David and his men would overtake the Amalekites and rescue

---

14.   Babylonian Talmud, *Mishnah Yoomah*; see also Maimonides, *The Guide for the Perplexed* II.45.

their families and possessions, but only that they would probably do so if they took pursuit. But, the answer given by God is a more definite admonishment to go forward to success than one based on probable success. The inclusion of the Hebrew phrase *ki-haseg* in verse 8 does not allow for a probabilistic interpretation of the information known and conveyed by God.[15] Rather, it is certain: David and his men will definitely overtake the Amalekites if they pursue them. Similarly, they will definitely rescue their families and possessions if they pursue. In addition, David received more information than he requested. David asked if he should pursue the Amalekites, but he was told to pursue them *and* that he would rescue that which had been taken. It is likely that David was given this additional information because he was in conversation with a person rather than consulting an impersonal device. The role of the priesthood was to function as mediator between the LORD and humans, and Abiathar fulfilled that role for David. Kenny's claim that David could have only received a "yes" or "no" answer without additional information is most likely false. But even if it is not, the passage from 1 Samuel 30 clearly speaks against Kenny's understanding of divine guidance derived from consultation with the ephod. The Hebrew of the passage connotes definitiveness in tone, even if the English is unclear.

Two possible objections to the use of 1 Samuel 30 for understanding 1 Samuel 23 exist. First, it may be complained that propositions describing the knowledge imparted here are not *counterfactuals proper*. Instead, it refers to events that will (and did) in fact occur, and therefore cannot be compared to the circumstances described in chapter 23, which are *counter*factual. The basic substance of this claim is true—David and his men pursued the Amalekites and rescued their families and possessions—but this is inconsequential to the argument. The purpose of comparing the two passages was to show that Kenny's claims regarding the kind of knowledge available *via* consultation with the ephod were wrong, and 1 Samuel 30 is

---

15. The phrase quoted is a hif'il infinitive absolute followed by the imperfect form of *nsg*. This construction makes the phrase emphatic. The inifnitive absolute is one of the more difficult Hebrew constructions to translate. Burton Goddard has provided a helpful analysis of several of the less common uses, as well as a working hypothesis regarding the development of the function of the infinitive absolute in the Hebrew language of the Bible. See Burton L. Goddard, "The Origin of the Hebrew Infinitive Absolute in the Light of Infinitive Uses in Related Languages and its uses in the Old Testament," ThD thesis, Harvard Divinity School, 1943. Despite the difficulty with some passages, in this passage, the infinitive absolute seems to function in one of the more traditional ways. Haiim Rosén notes that the infinitive absolute "precedes a verbal form (except the inf.) of identical radical probably in such cases where the most emphatically important concept of the sentence is expressed by the verbal stem, i.e. that if the sentence were continued with 'but not', another verb stem had to be used in exactly the same construction." Haiim Rosén, *A Textbook of Israeli Hebrew* (Chicago: University of Chicago Press, 1962), 215. An example of this form in the English is the question, "shall thou *indeed* reign over us?" The implication here is that the individual (Joseph) shall reign over his brothers rather than be their peer.

appropriate for this task. In addition, at the time of the consultation, the propositions were still future conditionals.

Second, it may be complained that propositions regarding David's pursuit and rescue do not refer to free actions and therefore, even if the text requires a rejection of the probabilistic interpretation of David's success, it does not follow that the same should be said for the propositions regarding Saul's and the men of Keilah's actions if David were to remain. Two points can be made in response to this objection, depending on what the objector is really saying. First, as in response to the first objection, the purpose of the comparison is to refute the specific claims of Kenny. Admittedly, the infinitive absolute construction is absent from 1 Samuel 23, but it still seems that counterfactuals about what Saul would definitely do if David were to remain and what the men of Keilah would definitely do if Saul were to attack are implied, and the reading of 1 Samuel 30 seems to confirm that 1 Samuel 23 should be read in definite as opposed to probabilistic terms. Second, if this objection seeks to tie the absence of definiteness in 1 Samuel 23 to the free nature of Saul's and the Keilites actions if David were to remain, then it seems that the objection is really a form of the grounding objection, which has already been addressed. This interpretation of the difference between 1 Samuel 23 and 1 Samuel 30 *as a problem*, seems to presuppose incompatibilism, rather than to present an argument for it.

Wisdom of Solomon 4:10–15

The third passage Molina cited for support of his claim that God possesses knowledge of counterfactuals of creaturely freedom is found in the apocryphal book, Wisdom of Solomon, and will not be discussed here, but other passages also suggest divine knowledge of counterfactuals of creaturely freedom.[16]

---

16. Molina believed that verses 11 and 14 of chapter 4 taught that "God, foreseeing the sins into which the just would fall if they remained in this life for a long time, in His mercy often takes them from this world." Molina, *Concordia* 4.49.9 (trans. Freddoso, 117–18). The entire passage reads as follows:

> There were some who pleased God and were loved by him, and while living among sinners were taken up. They were caught up so that evil might not change their understanding or guile deceive their souls. For the fascination of wickedness obscures what is good, and roving desire perverts the innocent mind. Being perfected in a short time, they fulfilled long years; for their souls were pleasing to the Lord, therefore he took them quickly from the midst of wickedness. Yet the peoples saw and did not understand, or take such a thing to heart, that God's grace and mercy are with his elect, and that he watches over his holy ones (Wis. 4:10–15, NRSV).

Kenny criticizes Molina's interpretation of this passage as well. Kenny believes that the knowledge attributed to God in this passage does not have to come via middle knowledge. Instead, it is knowledge God possesses because he knows the characters and dispositions of the persons spoken of in the passage. Kenny, *The God of the Philosophers*, 64. On such a reading, the

Proverbs 24:11–12

There is a passage in Proverbs which has to do with human awareness of another's tragedy. It refers to some persons being led away to death and includes an indictment of others for their lack of action to save or help:

> Deliver those who are being taken away to death, And those who are staggering to slaughter, O hold [them] back. If you say, "See, we did not know this," Does He not consider [it] who weighs the hearts? And does He not know [it] who keeps your soul? And will He not render to man according to his work? (Prov. 24:11–12, NASB)

While the identity of those being led away is not made clear, the majority of commentators favor a literal rather than figurative or metaphorical interpretation of their fate; the condemned face physical death, and those indicted face God's judgment for failing to rescue or attempting to rescue them.[17] Toy suggests that those being led away were captives of some sort who could be ransomed through various legal means.[18]

The passage also includes a charge against those who did not act, and the charge seems to be based on the fact that God is aware of human motive, thoughts, and feelings. On this basis, Ross believes the principles involved can be universalized, and closer examination of the arguments reveals how this passage supports belief in the truth of counterfactuals of creaturely freedom.[19] The defense of those indicted seems to be based on a claim of ignorance; to wit,

> {D1}: Since we did not know of the plight of the prisoners, we cannot be held guilty for failing to act or supposed callousness.

---

untimely demise (or rapture) of certain saints must be seen as a sort of preventive measure on the part of God. Implicit in Kenny's argument is the assertion that an individual may act out of character or in a way contrary to his/her disposition. This leads Kenny to the conclusion that God cannot know the future if humans are truly free. It must be noted that the basic idea behind Kenny's interpretation does not necessarily conflict with the doctrine of middle knowledge. It may be the case that divine middle knowledge comes from God's knowledge of the character of an individual, but this in no way requires the instantiation of the individual. Rather, it can come from God's knowledge of the individual as he/she existed in his mind prior to the creative act of divine will. See my "Molinism and Supercomprehension."

17. While it is possible to interpret the "death" and "slaughter" referred to as spiritual in nature (e.g., persons who are led to spiritual despondency when they are led away by their own sinful desires), the stark, graphic imagery indicates a more straightforward interpretation.

18. Crawford H. Toy, *A Critical and Exegetical Commentary on the Book of Proverbs*, International Critical Commentary (Edinburgh: T. & T. Clark, 1899), 445.

19. "The general application would include any who are in mortal danger, through disease, hunger, war—we cannot dodge responsibility, even by ignorance." Alan Ross, "Proverbs," in *The Expositor's Bible Commentary*. Vol. 5, *Psalms–Song of Songs*, ed. Frank E. Gaebelein (Grand Rapids: Zondervan, 1991), 1075.

Implicit in this defense is the claim that, had they known of the plight of the prisoners, those indicted would have done something about it.

The indictment is less clear, for it could be based on their lack of action or on their poor attitude (that would have resulted in their doing nothing even if they knew). That is, God's indictment could be of one of the following forms:

> {I1}: You knew of the plight of the prisoners (and weighed the pros and cons) and did nothing to help them. Therefore, you are to be held guilty for your inaction and callousness.

or

> {I2}: You did not know of the plight of the prisoners, but even if you had known, you would not have done anything about it. You did nothing to help the prisoners, and therefore, you are to be held guilty for your inaction and callousness.

Two related questions are worth considering. First, which of {I1} or {I2} presents a stronger case against the person(s) indicted? Second (and more importantly), which of {I1} or {I2} serves as the basis of the indictment in the passage? Of course, if {I1} is correct, the passage fails to support the doctrine of middle knowledge because no true counterfactual of creaturely freedom is included in the argument. Although the defense makes use of a counterfactual, it does not support middle knowledge because the accused could be lying or just mistaken. In the structure of the passage, comments made in the indictment (most likely because they come from God) are presented as true, while comments made in the defense are not necessarily so. Thus, the passage only supports counterfactual truth if {I2} is true.

Several considerations favor {I1} over {I2}. First, {I1} appears to present a stronger case against the violator because of the volition required by its construction. That is, a conscious choice had to be made to ignore the plight of the prisoners. By contrast, {I2} includes an element of ignorance, and this may remove guilt under biblical law. The Levitical sacrificial system included sacrifices for sins committed in ignorance, but they were separated from the other sacrifices, suggesting a different standard. Second, it is unclear whether God holds persons responsible for actions they *would have* committed if things had been different than they were. As noted earlier in the discussion of Matthew 11, condemnation based on sins one *would* have, *but did not* commit, seems unjust and out of step with God's holy character. Third, it may be the case that the defense presented above is not an accurate interpretation of the passage. Scott has suggested an alternate translation of the key defense section (verse 12): "If you say, 'See, this is none of our business,' will not he who weighs men's hearts take note of it? He who keeps watch on your life will know, and will require a man according to his acts."[20] If Scott is right in seeing the construction as a colloquialism similar to the expression, "I was just minding my own business," then the defense may look something like the following:

> {D2}: We were aware of the plight of the prisoners, but it was none of our business to interfere with the actions being taken against them. Therefore, we cannot be held guilty for our inaction or callousness.

In this case, the indictment presented in {I1} would probably need to include the additional point that it was/is the business of persons to interfere with the actions being taken against others.

This approach to the passage presents at least two problems for opponents of Molinism in using {I1} and rejecting true counterfactuals of creaturely freedom. First, there seems to be no good reason for translating the passage this way. There is virtual unanimity regarding the translation of *yada* in verse 12; it refers to knowledge or awareness, and since Scott offers no reasons for his alternate translation [not our concern], it must be concluded that the passage speaks of *claimed* ignorance.[21] Second, if the passage were translated this way, it would reintroduce counterfactuals of creaturely freedom into the argument because the defense is based on the additional claim:

> If it were our business to interfere with the actions being taken against the prisoners, we would have freely intervened.

While the indictment would certainly dispute this claim, the converse counterfactual would not be necessary for the argument to stand. Ultimately, the alternate translation adds nothing to the argument presented by {I1}, and its defense {D2} has a weaker claim to legitimacy than the original {D1} and therefore, it should be rejected. However, there are good arguments in favor of {I2}, some of which seem to stem from the passage itself.

First, it may be argued that {I2} is stronger than {I1} because it is more inclusive. While {I1} is based only upon inaction of the individual, {I2} includes both inaction and callousness (a problem of the heart). The strength of the indictment is tied to the strength of the defense and thus, we must ask if the additional claim of what the indicted party would have done had they known makes the defense stronger than it would be with only a claim of ignorance. Adding comments about how the indicted would have acted differently only presents a stronger case if the indictment is for

---

20. R. B. Y. Scott, *Proverbs, Ecclesiastes,* The Anchor Bible 18 (New York: Doubleday, 1965), 145. Unfortunately, Scott offers no textual justification for his alternate translation of *yada*.

21. It may be that Scott is attempting to take into account the fact that the indictment suggests that the guilty parties did, in fact, have knowledge of the plight of the prisoners. An appeal to ignorance makes little sense in that case. But given the fact that there is no warrant for the unusual rendering of *yada*, this line of reasoning must be rejected.

both inaction and an unrighteous attitude. The more inclusive indictment {I2} leads to a stronger defense, namely the one which claims they would have intervened had they known.

Second, the requirement of a sacrifice for sins committed in ignorance under the Levitical system speaks for the argument presented by {I2} rather than detracts from it. The fact that a sacrifice is required speaks to the culpability of the perpetrator, regardless of his intentions or awareness. The seriousness of the situation is highlighted by the fact that the offering for unintentional sins is the same as that for intentional sins, an unblemished bull, goat, lamb, or ram (Lev. 4:3, 14, 23, 28, 32; 5:15, 18), and the blood of the sacrifice is applied to the horns of the altar by the priest. The differentiation in the situation was on the part of the human who erred, not on the part of God—sins committed in ignorance are still condemnable and the offending party is still culpable (Lev. 5:19).

Third, the passage itself indicates that the indictment includes subjective as well as objective elements. As already noted, the claim that they would have acted as a defense suggests that the indictment was understood by the accused as being closer to {I2} than {I1}. In addition, God's weighing of the heart indicates that the judgment is primarily for a lack of love or concern for his fellow man. Thus, it seems that {I2} serves as indictment, and therefore, the counterfactual,

> If you had known the plight of the prisoners, you would not have done anything about it;

is true. The passage supports the claim that counterfactuals of creaturely freedom can be true.

1 Corinthians 2:6–16

In another supporting passage, the Apostle Paul refers to a message of wisdom the mature possess, as distinguished from the wisdom of this age or the wisdom of the rulers of this age.

> Yet we do speak wisdom among those who are mature; a wisdom, however, not of this age, nor of the rulers of this age, who are passing away; but we speak God's wisdom in a mystery, the hidden [wisdom,] which God predestined before the ages to our glory; [the wisdom] which none of the rulers of this age has understood; for if they had understood it, they would not have crucified the Lord of glory; but just as it is written, "Things which eye has not seen and ear has not heard, And [which] have not entered the heart of man, All that God has prepared for those who love Him." For to us God revealed [them] through the Spirit; for the Spirit searches all things, even the depths of God. For who among men knows the [thoughts] of a man except the spirit of the man, which is in him? Even so the [thoughts] of God no one knows except the Spirit of

God. Now we have received, not the spirit of the world, but the Spirit who is from God, that we might know the things freely given to us by God, which things we also speak, not in words taught by human wisdom, but in those taught by the Spirit, combining spiritual [thoughts] with spiritual [words]. But a natural man does not accept the things of the Spirit of God; for they are foolishness to him, and he cannot understand them, because they are spiritually appraised. But he who is spiritual appraises all things, yet he himself is appraised by no man. For who has known the mind of the LORD, that he should instruct Him? But we have the mind of Christ (1 Cor. 2:6–16, NASB).

The identity of the mature is somewhat ambiguous. Some have thought it refers to those who are mature in their faith, over against new Christians, but it seems to be a more general reference to believers.[22] The contrast with the wisdom and rulers of "this age" in verse 6, along with the continuing contrast between the natural (*psychikos*) or carnal (*sarkinos*) on the one hand, and the spiritual (*pneumatikos*) on the other hand, supports this assessment.[23] Thus, those who understand God's secret wisdom are the regenerate who have the Holy Spirit. The identity of the rulers of this age should also be clarified. While it is possible that Paul is here referring to spirits, demons, or demonically controlled humans, the most likely meaning is human rulers, specifically those responsible

22. The Greek term used by Paul is *teleioi*, which can refer to persons who are *older* or *more developed*, but it can also simply mean *complete*. Robertson and Plummer note that although Paul does distinguish between the *teleioi* and *nepioi en Christō*, there is no restriction placed upon the possibility of progress for the *nepioi*. So *teleioi* does not refer to a "select body" of the initiated. Archibald Robertson and Alfred Plummer, *A Critical and Exegetical Commentary on the First Epistle of St Paul to the Corinthians*, International Critical Commentary (New York: Charles Scribner's Sons, 1911), 39. W. Harold Mare, "1 Corinthians," in *Expositor's Bible Commentary*, ed. Frank E. Gaebelein (Grand Rapids: Zondervan, 1976), 10:200. Fee agrees, noting, "On the one hand, those who are still of *this* age, who have not received the Spirit, do not understand the wisdom of God in Christ crucified. But their wisdom is under divine judgment and already on its way out. Those who have the Spirit, on the other hand, have 'the mind of Christ' and thus understand God's activity, revealed to them by the Spirit. This is why Paul comes down so hard on his Corinthian friends. They do have the Spirit; they are part of the new age that God is ushering in. But their present conduct and stance toward wisdom betray them. Paul includes them among the 'spiritual' (vv. 7–13), yet later addresses them as 'fleshly' and 'merely human' because their quarrels indicate that they are acting just like those who do not have the Spirit (3:1–4). The real contrast is therefore between Christian and non-Christian, between those who have and those who do not have the Spirit." Gordon D. Fee, *The First Epistle to the Corinthians*, The New International Commentary on the New Testament (Grand Rapids: Eerdmans, 1987), 100–101.
23. It is further buttressed by Paul's assumption that those to whom he writes have this wisdom (note the first person plural pronouns in vv. 10, 12, 13, and 16). It strains credulity to think that Paul considered all of the Corinthians as mature Christians. On the contrary, Paul makes it clear that they are nowhere close to being mature in the faith. See, for example, Paul's words in the very next chapter: "I gave you milk to drink, not solid food; for you were not yet able [to receive it.] Indeed, even now you are not yet able" (1 Cor. 3:2, NASB).

for Jesus's crucifixion.[24] Paul's reference to their lack of understanding accords well with Jesus's prayer for forgiveness of those who crucified him (Luke 23:34).

In verse 7, Paul speaks of God's secret wisdom that was "hidden" (*en musteriō*) for a long time but has now been made known to all who receive it. While Paul could be referring to a special knowledge (*gnōsis*) reserved for a select group, this is doubtful, in spite of the fact that he calls it a mysterious wisdom (*musterion sōphia*; literally, he calls it the "wisdom of God, a mystery"). Rather, the wisdom seems to be the gospel of Jesus Christ in its totality.[25]

In the next verse, Paul states that the rulers of this age did not understand the secret wisdom, as evinced by their crucifying Christ. This suggests a truth about what would have been the case if things had been different. That is, it appears that Paul is here affirming the truth of the counterfactual of freedom,

> If the rulers of this age understood God's secret wisdom, they would (freely) refrain from crucifying the Lord of glory;

and denying:

> If the rulers of this age understood God's secret wisdom, they would (freely) crucify the Lord of glory.

The Open Theist may argue that Paul's words are not meant to be taken as a statement of what *actually* would be the case if the rulers had understood God's secret wisdom, but rather only of what *probably* would be the case. Under this view, Paul is seen as making the weaker claim that

---

24. While the majority of recent commentators reject this view, Conzelmann prefers the spiritual powers interpretation. He writes, "The mythical context suggests the interpretation demons, and so also does the solemn prediction *tōn katargoumenon*, 'which are being brought about to nothing.' They are the minions of the 'god of this aeon' (2 Cor. 4:4)." Hans Conzelmann, *1 Corinthians*, trans. James W. Leitch, ed. George W. MacRae, Hermeneia (Philadelphia: Fortress, 1975), 61. I have transliterated the Greek text. Of course, Conzelmann's point could be buttressed with references to Romans 8:38; 1 Corinthians 15:24; Colossians 2:15; and John 16:11.

25. As Robertson and Plummer write, the wisdom of God spoken of here "comprises primarily Christ and Him crucified; the preparation for Christ as regards Jew and Gentile; the great mystery of the call of the Gentiles and the apparent rejection of the Jews; the justification of man and the principles of the Christian life; and (the thought dominant in the immediate context) the consummation of Christ's work in the *doxa emōn*." Robertson and Plummer, *Critical and Exegetical Commentary on First Epistle to the Corinthians*, 39. I have transliterated the Greek in the quote. Conzelmann's interpretation of the rulers of the age as spiritual powers leads him to argue that Paul allows for a higher insight into the meaning of the cross; "an insight into the cosmic background of the crucifixion." Conzelmann, *1 Corinthians*, 63.

> If the rulers of this age understood God's secret wisdom, they would prob-
> ably (freely) refrain from crucifying the Lord of glory;

is true.[26] On this interpretation, the rulers still might have crucified the
Lord, even if they understood God's secret wisdom. How is the Molinist
to respond to this interpretation of the passage? While this interpretation
is *possible*, it is not the most likely for two reasons, one grammatical and
the other theological.

The grammatical problem has to do with the conditional statement
presented in verse 8. Paul's use of the aorist indicative here leads Robertson to conclude that it is a *determined as unfulfilled* conditional, or second
class conditional, with the conclusion following logically from the premise.[27] Thiselton agrees, noting that Paul's words indicate that the rulers
of this age "would not have lent their aid unwittingly to furthering these
purposes."[28] At first glance, this point may seem to undermine libertarian
freedom, but it does not. While Robertson uses the language of *logical
inference,* his point is merely that the conditional is definite; there is a fact
of the matter about what will be the case if the conditions (i.e., the rulers
understanding God's secret wisdom) are met.[29] There is no formal logical
connection between antecedent and consequent.

The theological problem is that it suggests Christians could participate in the crucifixion, which contradicts Scripture. In order to see why,
consider the following principle: to curse someone is to wish ill fortune,
even death, for him. If this principle is true, then it seems that if one is
willing to kill another, he is willing to curse him. Robertson and Plummer
suggest that cursing functions this way in the Bible, noting that Jesus was
cursed by the very persons who crucified him.[30] Jesus also seems to have

---

26.   It is worth noting that even on the probabilistic interpretation, the counterfactual, *If the rulers
      of this age understood God's secret wisdom, they would (freely) crucify the Lord of glory,* would
      still be false, as would a corresponding probabilistic counterfactual (i.e., *If the rulers of this age
      understood God's secret wisdom, they would probably (freely) crucify the Lord of glory*).

27.   A. T. Robertson, *A Grammar of the Greek New Testament in the Light of Historical Research,* ed.
      (Nashville: Broadman, 1934), 1015. Regarding determined conditionals, Robertson writes, "A
      positive statement is made in either case and the conclusion follows logically from this prem-
      ise." Ibid., 1004. He goes on to explain the second class conditional: "In this somewhat difficult
      condition only past tenses of the ind. occur. The premise is assumed to be contrary to fact. The
      thing in itself may be true, but it is *treated* as untrue. Here again the condition has only to do
      with the *statement,* not with the actual fact." Ibid., 1012.

28.   Anthony C. Thiselton, *The First Epistle to the Corinthians: A Commentary on the Greek Text,*
      The New International Greek Testament Commentary (Grand Rapids: Eerdmans, 2000), 248.

29.   Even though Robertson speaks of the conclusion following logically from the premise, it is
      clear, even to the determinist, that properly speaking, this is not the case.

30.   They write, "The blasphemous *Anathema Iesous* would be more likely to be uttered by a Jew
      than a Gentile; *faciebant gentes, sed magis Judaei* (Beng). It is possible that it was uttered
      against Jesus by his bitter enemies even during his life on earth. It is not improbable that Saul
      himself used it in his persecuting days, and strove to make others do so (Acts xxvi. 11). When
      the Gospel was preached in the synagogues the fanatical Jews would be likely to use these very

viewed cursing in this way when he condemned those who curse as being in danger of hellfire (Matt. 5:22; cf. James 3:9–11, 15–16, where blessing is a work of God and cursing is a work of earthly and demonic forces). Of course, all that needs to be shown is the weaker claim that if one is willing to kill another, he would be willing to curse him, and this seems obviously true, at least if murder is a sin of equal or greater consequence than cursing. Later in the letter, Paul sets up a parallel contrast, noting that "no one speaking by the Spirit of God says, 'Jesus is accursed'; and no one can say, 'Jesus is Lord,' except by the Holy Spirit" (1 Cor. 12:3, NASB).[31]

A straightforward reading of Paul's words regarding the ability of those who have the Spirit to curse Jesus suggests the following argument: Those who have the secret wisdom of God have the Holy Spirit; Those who have the Holy Spirit cannot say, "Jesus is accursed"; Those who cannot say, "Jesus is accursed" cannot crucify Jesus; Therefore, those who have the secret wisdom of God cannot crucify Jesus [the Lord of glory].[32] It follows from this that the probabilistic reading of the passage fails and instead, that which affirms the truth of the counterfactual,

> If the rulers of this age understood God's secret wisdom, they would (freely) refrain from crucifying the Lord of glory;

stands, and the passage supports belief in true counterfactuals of creaturely freedom.

---

words when Jesus was proclaimed as Messiah (Acts xiii. 45, xviii. 6)." Robertson and Plummer, *Critical and Exegetical Commentary on First Epistle to the Corinthians*, 261. I have transliterated the Greek in the quotation.

31. The situation which gave rise to this particular teaching of Paul has been widely discussed and disputed. Hypotheses regarding the origin of the "Jesus is accursed" saying range from the suggestion that there were Christians who said it while in a sort of spiritual ecstasy and were supposedly speaking by the power of the Holy Spirit, to a rebuttal of Gnostic attempts at separating Christ from Jesus, to the belief that it arose out of Christian controversies with Jewish antagonists. The third hypothesis seems most accurate. As Orr and Walther point out, the idea of cursing Jesus was "not hypothetical, even for this comparatively early date. In Paul's defense before Agrippa he says that he 'tried to make [the Christians] blaspheme' (according to Acts 26:11); and this would presumably be an abjuration of Jesus. Later in the century there are hints of the same sort of challenge, coming both from within and from outside the church; cf. I John 4:1–6 and Rev 2:13, 3:8, 12:17, 17:14." William F. Orr and James Arthur Walther, *1 Corinthians*, Anchor Bible 32 (New York: Doubleday, 1976), 278. Robertson and Plummer agree. These considerations leave little doubt regarding the validity of relating cursing to murder.

32. Some may object to the claim that those who have the Holy Spirit cannot say, "Jesus is accursed" because Paul's words only refer to one speaking *by* the Holy Spirit, or *in the power of* the Holy Spirit, as opposed to *having* the Holy Spirit (e.g., Paul's words may have allowance for so-called *carnal Christians* to curse Christ). This is faulty reasoning, for as Orr and Walther point out, these affirmations ["Jesus is Lord" and "Jesus is accursed"] are not meant to be taken as purely verbal in nature. They write, "They are rather commitments of the whole life. The one statement is a rejection of the one who determines what Christian life is; the other means that one accepts the lordship of Jesus Christ and is willing to live by his commandment. The enablement for this latter commitment comes by God's Holy Spirit." Ibid.

John 15[33]

Jesus's farewell speech to his disciples may indicate that there are true counterfactuals of creaturely freedom. Consider Jesus's words to the disciples: "If the world hates you, you know that it has hated Me before [it hated] you. If you were of the world, the world would love its own; but because you are not of the world, but I chose you out of the world, therefore the world hates you" (John 15:18–19, NASB). Jesus seems to argue that the world hates the disciples *because* they are not of the world and that the reaction of those in the world to the disciples would be different if they were of the world, to wit, the counterfactuals of creaturely freedom,

> If the disciples were of the world, those in the world would freely love them;

is true, and

> If the disciples were of the world, those in the world would freely hate them;

is false. Likewise, the conditionals of creaturely freedom,

> If the disciples were not of the world, those in the world would freely hate them;

is true, while

> If the disciples were not of the world, those in the world would freely love them;

is false. Robertson denies the possibility of a probabilistic interpretation of the conditional statement in verse 19 because it is a second class conditional statement, and therefore, the argument that verses 18 and 19 support belief in counterfactuals of freedom seems unassailable.[34]

Included in the discourse is an interesting discussion of the impact of the incarnation and Jesus's ministry upon the guilt of those who hate God. Consider his words:

> But all these things they will do to you for My name's sake, because they do not know the One who sent Me. If I had not come and spoken to them, they would not have sin, but now they have no excuse for their sin. He who hates

---

33. I wish to give credit to my former research assistant, Steven Hays, for suggesting this passage for investigation.
34. He writes, "In verse 19 of John 15 we have *ei ek tou kosmou ete, ho kosmos an to idion efilei.* 'The addition of *an* to an indicative hypothesis produced much the same effect as we can express in writing by italicizing '*if*'' or by adding to the apodosis 'in that case.' This is the definite use of *an*." Robertson, *Grammar of the Greek New Testament*, 1014. I have transliterated the Greek.

Me hates My Father also. If I had not done among them the works which no one else did, they would not have sin; but now they have both seen and hated Me and My Father as well. But [they have done this] in order that the word may be fulfilled that is written in their Law, 'THEY HATED ME WITHOUT A CAUSE'" (John 15:21–25, NASB).

He seems to imply that if he had not come and worked miracles, those of the world would have been ignorant of God and thereby, innocent of sin, and so the incarnation gave godless men an opportunity for sin they would otherwise not have been given.[35] While this may seem to allow ignorance to stand as an excuse for sin, it doesn't necessarily.[36] It may be that Jesus was referring to the specific sin of rejecting him (and by extension, the Father) rather than to sin in general.[37] If both love and hate are free responses with

---

35.   Most commentators neglect to discuss the implications of the conditionals included in this passage. Morris is an exception. Commenting on verse 22, he writes, "The seriousness of rejecting Christ is brought out. Jesus does not mean, of course, that the Jews would have been sinless had he not appeared. But he does mean that the sin of rejecting God as he really is would not have been imputed to them had they not had the revelation of God that was made through him." Leon Morris, *The Gospel according to John*, rev. ed., The New International Commentary on the New Testament (Grand Rapids: Eerdmans, 1995), 604. Robertson notes that the conditional statements found in verses 22 and 24 are both second class conditionals, and therefore refer to definite events that would occur if the requisite conditions were met: "But in Jo. 15:22 (and 24) *ei me ēithon kai elalēsa autois, hamartian ouk eichosan*, how is it? Is it a simple historical narrative about a past situation? Is it a hypothesis about the present time in terms of past time to suggest its unreality? Fortunately here the context shows. The very next words are *nun de prophasin ouk echousin peri tēs hamartias autōn* (Cf. also *nun de* in verse 24). The contrast with the present and actual is made in plain terms." Robertson, *Grammar of the Greek New Testament*, 1013–14. As before, I have transliterated the Greek.

36.   Several commentators see the charge (against the world) of ignorance of God referenced here as the same charge Jesus made earlier in John's gospel against "the Jews" who did not know the Father (John 5:37; 7:28; see also 8:54–58). This issue is not, then, one of *awareness* of Jesus or the Father, but rather of *intimate knowledge*. So, Raymond Brown: "There are several instances in the NT where those responsible for the suffering of Jesus are said to have been ignorant (Luke xxiii 34; Acts iii 17); yet when in John xv 21 and again in xvi 3 Jesus says that those who persecute his disciples have not known the Father (nor himself), there is no suggestion that such ignorance lessens culpability. Rather the ignorance itself is culpable. Jesus has come to these men both with words (22) and with works (24); yet they have refused to know him, and this refusal to believe is the root of sin. Because the words and works of Jesus are the words and works of the Father (v 36, xiv 10), rejection and hatred of Jesus are rejection and hatred of the Father, as 23 makes clear." Raymond E. Brown, *The Gospel according to John XIII–XXI*, Anchor Bible 29A (Garden City, NY: Doubleday, 1970), 697.

37.   Interestingly, this reading may ultimately reduce Jesus's claims to a tautology, which would leave them meaningless. Consider the following argument:
       [1] If I had not come into the world to be known, those of the world would not have known me;
       [2] If I could not be known, then those of the world could not have known me;
       [3] If I could not be known, then I could not be known.
       Of course, this is not a tightly constructed argument. Perhaps more thought on this issue is needed.

love the desired and hate the undesirable sinful response, then Jesus's argument looks something like the following: If Jesus had not come and worked
miracles, those of the world would have been ignorant of God (Jesus and
the Father), and they would not have had an opportunity to respond to Jesus
and the Father with love or hate. If that were the case, then they would not
be credited with freely loving God or guilty of freely hating God, and therefore, if Jesus had not come and worked miracles, those of the world would
not be credited with freely loving God or be guilty of freely hating God. This
argument appears to be based on a couple of principles:

> One can only be held guilty for inaction or credited with action if he can act;

and

> An individual cannot act if he does not have an opportunity to act.

On the second reading of Jesus's statements (in verses 21–25), no counterfactuals of freedom have been presented, and the opponents of Molinism
may argue they do not prove that there can be true counterfactuals of creaturely freedom. Still, no alternate reading has been proposed for verses
18–19, which are also dependent upon counterfactuals, and none seems
possible, and therefore, the overall thrust of Jesus's teaching here supports
the claim that counterfactuals of creaturely freedom can be true.

We have considered five passages that appear to support the Molinist
contention that there are true counterfactuals of freedom, and shown that a
responsible interpretation confirms this claim. I first argued that the passage
regarding the faith of the inhabitants of Chorazin and Bethsaida is incon-
clusive, and its support of the existence of true counterfactuals of creaturely
freedom is doubtful at best. However, I also demonstrated that the reading
of the text from 1 Samuel which supports the doctrine of divine knowledge
of counterfactuals of creaturely freedom is more probable than the reading
proposed by Kenny. Likewise, it has also been shown that middle knowledge can be maintained on either Molina's or Kenny's understanding of the
passage in Wisdom of Solomon, and that the most likely reading of Proverbs
24 relies upon counterfactuals of freedom. Similarly, the passage in 1 Corinthians 2 requires a true counterfactual of freedom to have any force at all.
Last, the passage in John 15 was shown to be based upon a counterfactual
of freedom, though an alternate interpretation which does not appeal to any
counterfactuals of freedom could be used, but is less likely. The burden of
proof now belongs to the Arminian detractors of Molinism.

CONTRA CALVINISM

Thus far, I have argued that the biblical text supports the Molinist claim
that there are true counterfactuals of freedom and therefore, the Open

Theist critique cannot stand. I will now show that the Bible also supports the Molinist position against its Calvinist detractors by questioning some of the common tenets of Calvinist soteriology. Specifically, I wish to explore two: Calvinist conceptions of the order of salvation and unconditional election.

Ordo Salutis

The concept of *ordo salutis* (literally, "order of salvation") is similar to the idea of the pre-creative divine decrees. It has to do with the *logical* order of the various facets of God's saving work. While it is acknowledged that many of the aspects of salvation occur simultaneously, there still may be dependency relationships among them, and a number of biblical passages seem to allude to such an order (Rom. 8:29–30; 1 Cor. 1:26–30; Eph. 1:11–14; 2 Thess. 2:13–15; 2 Tim. 1:8–10; 1 Peter 1:1–2; 2 Peter 1:9–11).[38] For example, John Murray, following the wording of Rom. 8:30, suggests the following order: calling, regeneration, faith/repentance, justification, adoption, sanctification, perseverance, and glorification.[39] Louis Berkhof offers a similar construction: calling, regeneration, conversion, justification, sanctification, perseverance, and glorification.[40] Suppose, then, that talk of an *ordo salutis* is legitimate.[41] What if Romans 8:30 does give insight

---

38. A word of caution is in order. As G. C. Berkouwer has noted, focusing on theoretical questions like *ordo salutis* could have the negative effect of detracting from a proper perspective on salvation; there should be greater concern for the riches of salvation than for the order. G. C. Berkouwer, *Faith and Sanctification*, trans. Lewis B. Smedes (Grand Rapids: Eerdmans, 1954), 25–26.

39. John Murray, *Redemption—Accomplished and Applied* (Grand Rapids: Eerdmans, 1955), 104–5.

40. Berkhof, *Systematic Theology*, 416.

41. In a helpful discussion, Hoekema rejects talk of an order of salvation conceived of as a succession of separate steps (even if only *logical* succession) and instead suggests thinking of salvation as a unit with different aspects. Hoekema's concern seems to be twofold: First, the traditional way of expressing an *ordo salutis* almost always devolves into a chronological conception (despite attempts to avoid this; see, for example, Berkhof's qualifications regarding the reformed approach), as if a Christian can be justified without also being sanctified (or regenerate without being justified, or effectually called without being regenerate, etc.); and second, the step-by-step process conception leads to problematic views of the Christian life which we characterize by hierarchies of believers. By way of example, he points to both the way belief in Holy Spirit baptism functions in much Pentecostal theology and the way talk of carnal Christianity is employed among some evangelicals. In both cases, a sort of hierarchy of Christians emerges. Hoekema, *Saved by Grace*, 17–26. Still, Hoekema is unable to completely free himself from all speculation regarding a proper ordering of the different aspects of salvation, and following traditional reformed dogma, he argues that regeneration must precede repentance and justification. He writes, "Before we take up this question, we should consider the relationship between regeneration and the other aspects of soteriology. By regeneration we mean the work of the Holy Spirit whereby he initially brings us into a living union with Christ and changes our hearts so that we who were spiritually dead become spiritually alive. It will be obvious that regeneration as thus defined must precede conversion (including faith and repentance), justification, sanctification, and perseverance, since the last-named experiences

into the order of salvation, as Murray thought? It would, of course, only mean that the following order can be confirmed: predestination, calling, justification, glorification. This order, though, is not problematic for anyone, Calvinist or Arminian. Yet many contemporary Calvinists have rejected the use of Paul's words here as indicative of the *ordo salutis*. Most have attempted, along the lines of Hoekema, to claim that this was not Paul's primary purpose here.

While it is true that this was not Paul's *primary* purpose, there still seems to be an order communicated. The important point to note (and the motivation behind Calvinist rejection of using this passage for *ordo salutis* considerations), is that when verse 29 is also considered, the order of salvation includes a reference to divine foreknowledge: foreknowledge, predestination, calling, justification, glorification.[42] This order is problematic because in the Calvinist system, God's foreknowledge must be logically posterior to predestination; he foreknows who will be saved because he predestined them to salvation by an act of his will. Molinists typically claim that middle knowledge functions as a sort of proto-foreknowledge such that God's predestining work is logically dependent upon his (logically prior) knowledge of how all possible persons would act in all possible situations. So the Molinist can argue that Paul provides an order of salvation in which predestination (and election) logically follows from a type of God's foreknowledge (Rom. 8:29–30). This discussion should lead to the greater question of the nature of God's election.

Unconditional Election

As noted in chapter 5, most Calvinists—even those who are not "five-pointers"—hold to the doctrine of unconditional election. Indeed, many Molinists hold to a form of it, understood as the truth that God's election is not based on good works the individual will perform or upon foreseen merit. Nevertheless, Calvinists and Molinists often disagree over this doctrine concerning foreseen faith. Calvinists typically argue that there is nothing to explain God's choice of particular individuals to salvation except his own gracious choice (his "good pleasure"), while Molinists often argue that election is based on God's knowledge of how persons would respond in faith.

Use of "To Know"

The use of *yada* in several Old Testament passages suggests a sort of deliberation in God's will that is commensurate with the doctrine of middle knowledge and the idea of election based on foreseen faith. Four such

---

presuppose the existence of spiritual life. In this sense we could speak of a kind of order in the process of salvation: regeneration must be first." Ibid., 14.

42. It is worth noting that none of the passages place foreknowledge after election. The passage in First Peter (1 Peter 1:1–2) also suggests that election and calling follow divine foreknowledge.

passages will be examined: Genesis 18:19, 2 Samuel 7:19–20, Jeremiah
1:5;, and Exodus 33:14–23; further allusions to this process can also be
found in Isaiah 40:14, 1 Chronicles 28:9, and elsewhere.

Genesis 18:19
The Abrahamic covenant is first recorded in Genesis 12, but is referenced
again several times throughout the book. It is normally considered a grant
covenant in which God makes a covenant with Abraham independent of
Abraham's actions and faith. As sovereign king, God blesses his subject
with no requirement as a condition for its reception. Yet, later in the story
as Yahweh reflects on whether to tell Abraham of his decision to destroy
Sodom and Gomorrah, he references the covenant and seems to indicate
that his reasons for entering into that relationship with Abraham had to do
with his intimate knowledge of Abraham. Consider the following passage:

> The LORD said, "Shall I hide from Abraham what I am about to do, since
> Abraham will surely become a great and mighty nation, and in him all the
> nations of the earth will be blessed? "For I have chosen him, so that he may
> command his children and his household after him to keep the way of the
> LORD by doing righteousness and justice, so that the LORD may bring upon
> Abraham what He has spoken about him" (Gen. 18:17–19, NASB).

The word translated as "chosen" in this verse is from the Hebrew root *yd*.
The translation of *yada* as "chosen" makes Abraham's covenant faithfulness appear to be dependent upon God's choice, or predestination. That
is, it gives a sense of divine causation behind Abraham's covenant faithfulness. Abraham is going to command his children and household to keep
the way of the LORD *because* God *chose* him (and, implicitly, because God
caused him to respond positively). Yet there are good lexical reasons for
rejecting this translation of *yada* in favor of the more common, "known."
    First, the translation of *yada* as "choose" or "chosen" is uncommon
by all counts. The word occurs almost 950 times in the Old Testament
and it is given this reading only one or two times by most translators.
For example, the New American Standard translates *yada* in this way only
twice (including this passage), and in both cases, "know; known" fits the
context. The other passage is Amos 3:2: "Hear this word which the LORD
has spoken against you, sons of Israel, against the entire family which He
brought up from the land of Egypt, 'You only have I *chosen* among all
the families of the earth; Therefore, I will punish you for all your iniqui-
ties.' Do two men walk together unless they have made an appointment?"
(Amos 3:1–3, NASB). The immediate context suggests that *yada* should
be understood in a relational sense (i.e., "know; known"). The reference to
two walking together in verse 3 points to the familial relationship apparent in verse 2. "Known," or an intimate knowledge, seems to fit the passage
better than the less intimate "chosen," and under this interpretation, the

punishment comes as a result of a broken relationship, not a broken promise or rejection of God's choice.

Many commentators have acknowledged that *yada* is best translated as "known," even though they still opt for the less common, "chosen" in Genesis 18 anyway, with little or no explanation. For example, Gordon Wenham notes that *yada* is literally, "known," but then points the reader to a variety of other passages which also presumably have a sense of choosing or electing (Exod. 33:12, 17; Deut. 34:10; 2 Sam. 7:20; Amos 3:2). No further explanation is given and the reader is expected to simply agree that the verses listed do, indeed, have such a sense.[43] Speiser has attempted to walk a line between knowledge and choice by translating it as "singled out" (i.e., "I have singled him out"). Speiser writes, "Another aspect of the flexible stem *yd'* ; cv. Comment on iv.1. Here the stress is on 'to acknowledge.' The verse as a whole gives an excellent summary of the way of life ('way of Yahweh') that is expected of Abraham and his descendants."[44] Speiser's interpretation seems closer to that being proposed here; namely, that God's knowledge of Abraham has led to a covenant relationship. Skinner argues that *yada* here is a reference to intimate knowledge and translates it as "entered into personal relations with."[45]

Ironically, many OT scholars defend the use of "chosen" here because "known" may not include the requisite intimacy. They criticize translating *yada* as "known" here and in Amos 3:2 because it could be misinterpreted as mere intellectual awareness instead of personal knowledge of Abraham (by God). Commenting on the Amos passage, McComiskey writes, "The word *yada* bears a special sense of intimacy. . . . Thus the word connotes more than simple awareness or acknowledgment. It includes the idea of God's sovereign activity whereby the object of that knowledge is set apart or chosen for a divine purpose."[46] However, it is unclear exactly how "chosen" remedies this possible deficiency of the English term. It seems that, while "known" *could* possibly be misinterpreted in this way because of its semantic range, "chosen" is even more misleading because it connotes a dispassionate action on God's part and introduces decision into the passage; God is *picking*. In fact, some Calvinist explanations of unconditional election require a lack of *directed* passion in the choice (i.e., that God loves this particular individual over against an individual not chosen), lest one infer that the choice is based on something in the

---

43. Wenham goes on to discuss the implications of God's covenant love/choice of Abraham. He writes, "If the ground of election was God's promise (v. 18), its fuller purpose is now stated for the first time: to create a God-fearing community (v. 19)." Gordon J. Wenham, *Genesis 16–50,* Word Biblical Commentary 2 (Dallas: Word, 1994), 50.

44. E. A. Speiser, *Genesis,* Anchor Bible 1 (New York: Doubleday, 1962), 133.

45. John Skinner, *A Critical and Exegetical Commentary on Genesis,* vol. 1, 2nd ed., International Critical Commentary (Edinburgh: T. & T. Clark, 1930), 304.

46. Thomas E. McComiskey, *The Expositor's Bible Commentary.* Vol. 7, *Daniel–Minor Prophets,* ed. Frank E. Gaebelein (Grand Rapids: Zondervan, 1985), 298.

individual elected. Thus, if the concern is for the reader to catch the personal aspect of God's relationship to Abraham, "known" is better than "chosen." In addition, it is clear enough that "known" has a range of meaning to include intimate relations (as epitomized in sexual union). Thus, it is hard to see how "chosen" serves as a less misleading term for translating *yada*.

The second reason for favoring "known" over "chosen" is the fact that both the Septuagint and the Vulgate translate *yada* as "known" here. The Septuagint translates *yada* with *ēdein* (first person singular pluperfect active indicative of *oida*), while the Vulgate uses the common *scio*, from *scientia*. Of course, this does not prove error by modern translators, but it gives some indication of the beliefs prevalent at the time these two translations were prepared. Neither opts for a sense of choosing, and it may call into question the preference for the more unusual translation over the more common ("chosen" over "known").

Third, a word exists in Hebrew that would have been better to use if the writer of Genesis wished to convey the sense of *choice* presented by that translation of *yada* and the Calvinist interpretation of God's election of Abraham for covenant relationship. The Hebrew word most commonly translated as "choice, choose, chosen, etc." is *bachar*, from the *bchr* root. Of the eighty-five occurrences of "chosen" in the New American Standard version, eighty are from this root; and of the twenty-one occurrences of "chose" and the twenty-two occurrences of "chooses" in the New American Standard, one hundred percent are from this root; and of the forty-two occurrences of "choose" in the NASB, forty are from this root. Clearly, *bachar* is the dominant Hebrew word for "choice." So the question that must be answered by translators who wish to render *yada* as "chosen" in Genesis 18:19 is, "Why did the writer of Genesis not use *bachar* if he wanted to say, 'chosen'?"

It may be thought that *bachar* was not available to the writer of Genesis, that the word had not yet developed to have the connotations of *choice* needed for use in the Genesis 18 passage and that therefore, *yada* was used, but this is not the case because *bachar* is used seven times to connote *choice* in Job, widely thought to be the oldest book in the canon, and it is found in Genesis on two occasions with both references prior to the narrative between Abraham and the *men*.[47]

It may be argued that the writer of Genesis uses *yada* for "chosen" here for some of the very reasons already cited regarding the nature of *yada* and the relationship of God—because the choosing of Abraham was personal in nature; because God chose Abraham for an intimate, personal relationship. Under this interpretation, *yada* is seen as the preferred Hebrew word

---

47. Job 7:15; 9:14; 15:5; 29:25; 34:4, 33; 36:21. The two occurrences both refer to choice: "the sons of God saw that the daughters of men were beautiful and they married anyone of them they *chose*" (Gen. 6:2); "So Lot *chose* for himself the whole plain of the Jordan and set out toward the east" (Gen. 13:11).

for covenant choosing, while *bachar* is seen as a somewhat disinterested or impersonal choice. This seems to be the line of thought Ken Matthews follows. He writes, "Exceptional to the Deuteronomic language of covenant is the term for 'chosen,' which translates *yada* ('to know'), rather than the common Deuteronomic word *bachar* ('to choose'). *Yada* conveys the idea of election with the nuance of familiarity, intimacy (e.g., Jer 1:5; Hos. 13:5; Amos 3:2)."[48] Related to this argument is the claim that *bachar* indicates unacceptable choosing; a choice with negative consequences, or that *bachar* refers to human choice, while *yada* refers to divine choice. Proponents of this line of reasoning can point to the Israelites' choice [*bachar*] of Saul as king, which was a disaster. For example, in warning the people against getting a human king, Samuel told them everything the king would do and that, when those events occur, they would cry out for relief from the king they had *chosen* (1 Sam. 8:18). Similarly, in a speech before Israel, Samuel recounted the history of God's deliverance, from the time of the exodus through the judges, and he confronted them because of their desire to have a king. In that condemnation, he charged them with *choosing* the king (1 Sam. 12:13). In both cases, the *choice* [*bachar*] was a human endeavor and had negative outcomes.

While this argument has an initial plausibility, it cannot be sustained, for *bachar* is used in many places to refer to God's choice of both individuals and groups for covenant relationship. It refers to God's choice of Palestine for his people twenty-one times in the Pentateuch alone.[49] It is used in reference to God's choice of Israel as his covenant people and of his choice of the Levites.[50] It is used to refer to God's choice of Moses (Ps. 105:26) and Jacob (Ps. 135:4; Isa. 41:8; 44:1–2) as well, and it is used to refer to God's choice of Saul (1 Sam. 10:24) and of Solomon (1 Chron. 28:4–5, 10; 29:1), and even of God's choice of David (1 Kings 8:16; 2 Chron. 6:6; Ps. 78:70), thus eliminating the suggestion that it cannot refer to covenant choice of nations or persons. However, some may wish to argue that Abraham's covenant relationship with God was unique because it was the first covenant or was more intimate and needed *yada* rather than *bachar*. After all, Abraham is described as the "friend of God," and so it may be that God's covenant choice of Abraham was of a different nature from his covenant choice of David or Moses.[51] Even this argument fails because

---

48. Kenneth A. Matthews, *Genesis 11:27–50:26*, The New American Commentary 1B (Nashville: Broadman & Holman, 2005), 223.

49. Deut. 12:5, 11, 14, 18, 21, 26; 14:23, 24, 25; 15:20; 16:2, 6, 7, 11, 15, 16; 17:8, 10; 18:6; 26:2; 31:11.

50. Israel (note: I have only included reference found in the Pentateuch): Deut. 4:37; 7:6, 7; 10:15; 14:2; 17:15. Levites: Deut. 18:5; 21:5; 1 Sam. 2:28.

51. There is, however, one other argument advanced in favor of reading *yada* as "choice" here. In an oft-cited article, Herbert Huffmon argued that *yada* can serve as a technical term for treaty relationships between a suzerain and vassal; for recognition of the status of the vassal in covenant with the king (in this case, Yahweh). If this argument is correct, then it may help explain

Nehemiah uses *bachar* to refer to God's choice of Abraham (Neh. 9:7), and the very next verse seems to indicate that the covenant choice of Abraham was based on his faith: "You are the LORD God, who chose Abram and brought him up from Ur of the Chaldees. *You found his heart faithful before You*, and made a covenant with him to give him the land of the Canaanite, of the Hittite and the Amorite, of the Perizzite, the Jebusite and the Girgashite—to give it to his descendants" (Neh. 9:7–8, NASB; emphasis mine). Note that the covenant is entered subsequent to God's finding Abraham faithful. Thus, there seems to be no good explanation for why the writer of Genesis used *yada* instead of *bachar* for "choice" in 18:19, apart from plain literary license.[52]

Now consider the implications of reading the passage with *yada* translated as *known*: "The LORD said, 'Shall I hide from Abraham what I am about to do, since Abraham will surely become a great and mighty nation, and in him all the nations of the earth will be blessed? For I have *known* him, so that he may command his children and his household after him to keep the way of the LORD by doing righteousness and justice, so that the LORD may bring upon Abraham what he has spoken about him'" (Gen. 18:17–19, NASB, with change of *yada*). The change seems to add a different nuance, one that is not insignificant. The blessings of God's covenant promise to Abraham appear directly related to Abraham's faithfulness in teaching his family the way of the LORD. The second half of the passage makes it clear that the granting of the covenant blessings is tied to Abraham's future faithfulness. That is, God will bring upon Abraham what he has spoken about him (i.e., that he will become a great and mighty nation and that he will be the means of blessing for all the nations of the earth) when (because) Abraham is obedient to the covenant requirements by faith. This understanding is consistent

---

the translation of *yada* as "chose"; God *knew* Abraham in covenant relationship. However, to move from covenant recognition to *choice* goes beyond the point Huffmon makes. In fact, Huffmon concludes that *yada* in the passages cited (Genesis 18:19 among them) should be rendered as "acknowledge" or "recognize." Herbert B. Huffmon, "The Treaty Background of Hebrew *YADA*," *Bulletin of the American Schools of Oriental Research* 181 (February 1966): 31–37. But this does not alter the point I am making here. It does not carry the connotation of choice without regard to intimate knowledge of the individual. Rather, it still suggests intimate or personal knowledge and does not denote choice.

52. Perhaps this is why Hamilton suggests that the writer of Genesis used *yada* in order to make a play on words, but this is hardly compelling (if the writer *really* wanted to communicate a sense of choice), especially given the overwhelming use of *bachar* and the lack of use of *yada* for "choice." He writes, "The choice of the verb 'know' may be deliberate in the light of the context. Yahweh knows Abraham; yet he goes to Sodom in order to know (v. 21b) what is going on there. Certainty and uncertainty are placed alongside each other. Or again, perhaps the narrator wants to draw a contrast between Yahweh who knew Abraham and the Sodomites who wanted to 'know' Lot's guests (19:5). Here benign knowledge and diabolical knowledge are juxtaposed." Victor P. Hamilton, *The Book of Genesis, Chapters 18–50*, The New International Commentary on the Old Testament (Grand Rapids: Eerdmans, 1995), 18.

with the passage in Nehemiah noted earlier. Wenham agrees, noting that the pattern of promise-obedience-fulfillment of promise is found throughout Old Testament covenant theology and indicates that the covenant is conditional (at least in some sense).[53] Yet, this is not to say that the covenant is based on works; the Bible is abundantly clear that Abraham was justified by believing God.[54] It is to say that the covenant was effected because God had a kind of knowledge of Abraham whereby he knew Abraham would respond in faith if he were to call for such a response. That is, God knew several counterfactuals. For example, he knew that if he were to tell Abraham to sacrifice Isaac, he would respond in faith. Similarly, he knew that if he were to call upon Abraham to enter into a covenantal relationship, Abraham would respond positively, and that if they were to enter into such a relationship, Abraham would teach his descendants to honor and worship the LORD. So God's knowledge of these truths, among others, informed his decision to enter into a covenant with Abraham. (Molinists would typically make the further claim that it impacted God's decision about what sort of world to actualize.) This is not a particularly controversial claim insofar as some moderate Calvinists could agree that something like this does indeed take place, though they view the nature of faith and the freedom involved in the responses differently. It does, however, call into question the view of those [Calvinists] who see God's decision to enter into covenant with Abraham as an expression of God's good pleasure with no reference to Abraham's future response. Instead, then, God's decision to enter into covenant with Abraham is based on his knowledge of how Abraham would respond to his call.

2 Samuel 7:19–20

There is also a hint (and perhaps only a hint) that the Davidic covenant is also based on God's knowledge of the recipient [David]. The covenant was made after David expressed his wishes to build a Temple for the LORD. After initially telling David to proceed with his plans, Nathan received a word from God to the contrary. Instead of David building a house of cedar for the LORD, God would build a house for David (2 Sam. 7:5–7, 11). This promise includes a descendant who "will build a house" and it includes an everlasting relationship between David's house and the LORD, manifested in an everlasting kingship.

---

53. Wenham, *Genesis*, 50.
54. As the text says, "Abraham believed God and it was credited to him as righteousness" (Gen. 15:6, 22; Rom. 4:3; Gal. 3:6; James 2:23). The very idea of belief being credited as righteousness suggests an *ordo salutis* in which faith/belief precede regeneration/justification. In biblical usage, the language of crediting is most often associated with justification, and it appears to be God's gracious response to human faith.

In response to this covenant, David offers a humble prayer of thanksgiving. There is a sense of awe in David's words. He wonders at God's grace to him and his household as set over against God's reaction to Saul and his household: David's posterity will enjoy the blessings of God's love, even when he sins: "I will be to him a father, and he shall be to me a son. When he commits iniquity, I will discipline him with the rod of men, with the stripes of the sons of men, but my steadfast love will not depart from him, as I took it from Saul, whom I put away from before you" (2 Sam. 7:14–15, ESV). David asks *why* this is the case. From his own perspective, he is not worthy of such favor. In fact, David's words belie a curiosity about the *reason* for the bestowal of covenant love upon him and his household such that it will endure: "Who am I, O LORD God, and what is my house, that you brought me thus far?" (2 Sam. 7:18b, ESV). So David cannot make sense of the *reason*. He can, however, make sense of God's *ability* (for lack of a better term) to make such a promise. He offers up two explanations.

First, David attributes it to God's immeasurable power and providence: "And yet this was a small thing in your eyes, O Lord GOD" (2 Sam. 7:19a, ESV). Second, he points to God's immeasurable love and grace: "Because of your promise, and according to your own heart, you have brought about all this greatness" (2 Sam. 7:21, ESV). Interestingly, though, sandwiched between these two explanations, David refers to God's knowledge of him. David has asked for a *reason* why God would make the covenant with him and admits that he, himself, is perplexed; so much so that he is rendered speechless (2 Sam. 7:20a)! He sees himself (and his household) as unworthy, but resigns himself to God's providence. It is at this point that he apparently suggests that the answer to his question may be found in God's knowledge of him: "And what more can David say to you? For you *know* your servant, O Lord GOD!" (2 Sam. 7:20, ESV). This phrase could mean several things. On the one hand, it could be a reference to David's inability to articulate his feelings in response to God's gracious offer and God's ability to know without such articulation; that is, it could simply be David's way of reveling in God's grace to him. On the other hand, it could also be an expression of David's resignation to God's wisdom and providence. In essence, David may be saying, "I do not understand why you did what you did, but you know me better than I know myself, so I trust your decision to grant me this grace." God's knowledge in verse 20 appears to be directly related to his love [the reference to God's "heart"] in verse 21. Read in this way, we may surmise that David is suggesting that God considered the outcomes of his making everlasting covenants with both Saul and David and elected David based on that knowledge. God knew that if he were to offer Saul an everlasting kingdom, Saul would freely reject it by acting in ways contrary to faith, and if he were to make the same offer to David, he would freely respond in faith. We already know that God would have granted Saul an everlasting kingdom if Saul had been faithful (1 Sam. 13:13). That is, the following counterfactual of divine freedom is true:

> If Saul were faithful to the LORD, God would grant him an everlasting kingdom.

Yet this fact poses a problem for the Calvinist: It makes no sense for this counterfactual to be true if God is the cause of Saul's unfaithfulness, even if only as a secondary cause by creating Saul so that he will freely (in the compatiblistic way) choose to reject God. Under a Molinist conception regarding Saul's freedom to respond in faith, we can deal better with how such a counterfactual of divine freedom can be true while the corresponding counterfactual of creaturely freedom (i.e., *If God were to offer an everlasting kingdom to Saul, he would respond with unfaithfulness*) is as it is.

If God did consider how Saul and David would respond to the offer of an everlasting kingdom in deciding whether to offer it or not, then it seems that the following counterfactuals were also true and considered by God in his electing decision(s):

> If I were to offer an everlasting kingdom to Saul, he would fail to raise his son to be faithful;

> If I were to offer an everlasting kingdom to David, he would raise his son to be faithful.

On this reading, then, the Davidic covenant should be seen as, like the Abrahamic, conditioned on a faith response (by David, as well as on Saul's lack of faith response) to God. It is not conditioned on David's works, but on his being a person of faith. God's knowledge of how Saul and David would respond to God's calling on their lives informed his pre-creative decision regarding his election of David for covenant relationship. God's election or predestination of David to covenantal love is directly tied to God's intimate knowledge of him. Notice that it will not do to note the obvious nature of God's love for David after David existed, for the covenant was part of the original decree of God. A similar argument may be developed regarding the predestination of Jeremiah and his call to prophetic ministry.

Jeremiah 1:5

This, of course, is one of the most oft-quoted passages in support of the pro-life movement. It is a reference to Jeremiah's call to the prophetic ministry. In verse 5, the consecration of Jeremiah and the appointment of Jeremiah as a prophet to the nations is linked to God's knowledge (*yada*) of him. Prior to Jeremiah's physical existence, God had knowledge of him which is tied to God's decision to set Jeremiah apart as a prophet. The text does not elaborate on the details of the relationship between that prior knowledge and God's decision, but that there is a relationship is abundantly clear. It seems that God's call on Jeremiah's life was based on his knowledge of how Jeremiah would act or respond in various circumstances. Molinism claims that something like the following propositions were true (and we know they were, given the events that happened) and served as a basis for God's decision to actualize a world where Jeremiah exists and God calls and equips him for the prophetic ministry:

> If God were to call Jeremiah to be a prophet, he would (freely) respond positively.

> If God were to give Jeremiah his words (v. 9), Jeremiah would (freely) speak them to the nations, to pluck up and break down, destroy, overthrow, and to build up and plant (v. 10).

God's knowledge of these propositions forms the basis of his predestining work with regard to Jeremiah's prophetic ministry. While some Calvinists would not take issue with this claim (as long as the freedom noted were understood as compatibilism), most would because it undercuts unconditional election as it is traditionally conceived in reformed circles. It makes predestination to ministry dependent upon the individual's ability, foreknown actions, or foreknown faith. I would argue the latter—that election is based on foreseen faith (if God were to actualize a world where the individual is born and the appropriate circumstances prevail)—and that godly actions follow from that faith.

In each of the cases considered thus far, we have seen that God's election of individuals seems to be tied to his knowledge of them. I have argued that the presence of *yada* in the discussion of the Abrahamic and Davidic covenants, as well as Jeremiah's call to prophetic ministry, indicates that this relationship exists. Interestingly, a similar point can be made with regard to Moses in the passage quoted by the apostle Paul in Romans 9.

Romans 9 (Moses and Pharaoh; Jacob and Esau)

In his most developed discussion of predestination (and a favorite passage of Calvinists for their view of unconditional election), Paul notes that God says to Moses, "I will have mercy on whom I have mercy and I will have compassion on whom I have compassion" (Rom. 9:15, ESV). This is often cited as evidence that Paul believes God's predestining persons for salvation is based on nothing but his own good pleasure; that nothing regarding how the individual acts or responds (or more properly, *will act* or *will respond* if created) is considered in that decision. While most Calvinists claim ignorance regarding what God considers in his electing decisions, they tend to argue that it is at least *not* based on foreseen merit or foreseen faith. A quote from John Calvin himself may be representative: "And what pray, does this mean? It is just a clear declaration

by the Lord that he finds nothing in men themselves to induce him to
show kindness, that it is owing entirely to his own mercy, and, accordingly, that their salvation is his own work."[55] However, an examination of
the context of the Old Testament passage Paul quotes seems to indicate
otherwise. In fact, I want to suggest that God's decision to show mercy is
directly related to the faith of the individual and that Paul does not quote
it in an effort to teach that God will show mercy to anyone he chooses
without regard to the individual's faith position. The quotation comes
from Exodus 33:19, where God reveals himself to Moses as he hides in
the cleft of the mountain. The passage reads as follows:

> And He said, "My presence shall go [with you,] and I will give you rest."
> Then he said to Him, "If Thy presence does not go [with us,] do not lead us
> up from here. "For how then can it be known that I have found favor in Thy
> sight, I and Thy people? Is it not by Thy going with us, so that we, I and Thy
> people, may be distinguished from all the [other] people who are upon the
> face of the earth?" And the LORD said to Moses, "I will also do this thing of
> which you have spoken; for you have found favor in My sight, and I have
> known you by name." Then Moses said, "I pray Thee, show me Thy glory!"
> And He said, "I Myself will make all My goodness pass before you, and will
> proclaim the name of the LORD before you; and I will be gracious to whom
> I will be gracious, and will show compassion on whom I will show compas-
> sion." But He said, "You cannot see My face, for no man can see Me and live!"
> Then the LORD said, "Behold, there is a place by Me, and you shall stand
> [there] on the rock; and it will come about, while My glory is passing by, that
> I will put you in the cleft of the rock and cover you with My hand until I have
> passed by. Then I will take My hand away and you shall see My back, but My
> face shall not be seen" (Exod. 33:14–23, NASB).

There are at least two points worth noting here: First, it should be noted
that the phrase, "I will have mercy on whom I will have mercy," refers to
a *special blessing* God wished to give to someone, not to an *initial entry*
into covenant relationship. Specifically, he will allow Moses to see him and
live.[56] Second, and more importantly, the text notes that he did so because
Moses had found favor in his sight (v. 17); that is, the showing of mercy
to Moses was a response to Moses's request and to Moses's faithfulness
to God. Ultimately, it was based on God's personal and intimate knowledge of Moses. God *knew* (*yada*) Moses to be a person of faith. Of course,
in this case, God's knowledge of Moses is not *middle knowledge*; it does
not refer to knowledge of how Moses *would* react or *would* be if he were

55. John Calvin, *Institutes of the Christian Religion* 3.22.6, trans. Henry Bevridge (Peabody, MA:
     Hendrickson, 2008), 619.
56. This may not be terribly important, as Paul appears to apply it to the salvation of Gentiles:
     their initial entry into the blessings of the Abrahamic covenant.

created. Rather, it refers to God's present knowledge of Moses's character as he truly is. Nevertheless, the point still stands that the granting of mercy here is responsive to Moses's character and faith.

Now we must ask how Paul is using the passage in Romans 9. If it is determined that Paul is using the passage to argue that God shows mercy for his own internal reasons, with no reference to the actions/faith of the people, then it is hard to see how Paul has not misapplied the passage or at least quoted it out of context.[57] Fortunately, this is not the only option; it may be that what Paul has in mind is this—although salvation is by grace, not of works (Eph. 2), it is nevertheless God's gift to persons as they respond to his call in faith.

This interpretation accords well with the other reference from Romans 9 used by Calvinists to argue their point: the comment regarding God's love for Jacob and hatred for Esau. There are actually two quotes/allusions to Jacob and Esau in the chapter. First, Paul notes that, prior to either child doing anything good or bad, and prior to their birth, their mother, Rebekah, was told that the older would serve the younger. This is a reference to Genesis 25:23 and is essentially just as Paul notes. Yet to make his point about election, Paul goes on to quote Malachi 1:2–3: "I loved Jacob, but I hated Esau." In context, this is a prophecy to Israel, to call the nation to properly worship the LORD. It includes the possibility of cursing if the people do not offer proper sacrifices, and ultimately includes a warning about the coming Day of the LORD. The people are exhorted to "Remember the law of my servant Moses, the decrees and laws I gave him at Horeb for all Israel" (Mal. 4:4, NIV), and recalls Moses's warnings given in his farewell discourse (Deut. 28:15ff.; 30:15ff.). It is also a prophecy against the people of Edom, as a nation, similar to that offered in Obadiah. The love and hatred, then, seem to apply to the nations represented by Jacob and Esau.

Throughout the latter part of his letter to the Romans, Paul is addressing the Jew/Gentile question; how is it that those for whom Jesus came (i.e., Israel; Matt. 15:24; John 1:11) are not saved, while those to whom he did not come are saved? Paul is arguing that Israel is not lost, but that there is a hardening for a time, and that the hardening figures into God's plan for the ages so that the Gentiles may enter into the fellowship of faith (Rom. 10–11). That is, it is not clear that Paul is using the passage to argue for election of particular persons, but rather for people groups— here he is speaking of the Gentiles entering into the kingdom of God and how that fits into the overall plan of God for the ages. God shows mercy to the Gentiles because he knew they would respond in faith to his call when the time was right. God has allowed the Jews to be hardened so that the Gentiles *could* enter into covenant relationship with him

---

57. Of course, some may agree that Paul has done just this, and argue that this is fine since he does so under the inspiration of the Holy Spirit.

through Christ (Rom. 11:25). So the Molinist believes that God considered the following counterfactuals:

> If I were to offer covenant relationship to the Gentiles in the first century,
> they would freely respond in faith;

> If the Jews were to respond in faith to the Gospel in large numbers, the
> Gentiles would not freely respond in faith;

> If the Jews were hardened to the Gospel, the Gentiles would freely respond
> in faith;

> If the Jews were hardened so that Gentiles could respond, the Jews will still
> one day freely respond in faith;

and others like them in his plan for Jews and Gentiles, and that they served
as a basis for his decisions regarding election of Jews and Gentiles.[58] Only
God could know truths of this sort and set forth a perfect plan for all
peoples, and it is this truth that leads Paul to worship God for the depth
of his knowledge and wisdom (Rom. 11:32–36). If a reading following this
model is seen as correct, then Paul is not misapplying the Old Testament
texts, or interpreting them in some colorful ways. Rather, he is being true
to the sense of the passage quoted.

Does what I have presented here prove the superiority of Molinism
to Calvinism? I think not. There are several places at which the Calvinist
could object to the argument. For instance, he could dispute my initial
claim that *yada* should be translated as "know" in these passages. After all,
most translators have rendered it "chosen," and it is unlikely that there is a
vast Calvinist conspiracy among translators to subvert the *true* meaning of
the text. Still, a more satisfying answer to the question of why it should be
translated as "chosen" is required. Even if my initial argument on translation is accepted, *unconditional election* as traditionally conceived among
Calvinists is not conclusively overturned. Rather, all that was shown is
that the passages suggest that God considers future faith (for example,
of Abraham) in his decisions to enter into covenant relationship, call to
ministry, or grant mercy. The moderate Calvinist could grant *this* point
and still discount Molinist claims regarding libertarian freedom and the
independence (from God's determining will) of the truth of counterfactuals of creaturely freedom. That is, the moderate Calvinist could agree that
God's decisions to enter into covenant relationships are based on foreseen faith, but still claim that God determines the truth of counterfactuals

---

58. Of course, many other counterfactuals could be presented in order to perverse God's justice
    by his weakly actualizing the hardening of the Jews or by nothing that there may be no other
    way for the Gentiles to believe.

of freedom because he causes or grants faith. This, though, would be a major concession to Arminian theology. To grant that predestination is based on foreseen faith or that election is unconditional with respect to good works, but conditional with respect to future faith just is to agree with traditional Arminian soteriology. It would seem to be a strange position for a Reformed theologian to take. Nevertheless, I have argued that the presence of *yada* in passages referencing the Abrahamic and Davidic covenants, Jeremiah's call to prophetic ministry, and even Paul's use of God's decision to grant special mercy to Moses, at least suggests that election (to salvation and service) is tied to God's intimate knowledge of the individuals in question. Specifically, I argued that predestination is based on God's middle knowledge regarding individual faith.

CONCLUSION

In this chapter, I have argued that there is good reason to believe that the Bible teaches that God knows counterfactuals of creaturely freedom (and therefore, they can be true). Those who object (primarily Open Theists) have either presupposed the grounding objection, or have unwittingly superimposed their philosophical commitments onto the biblical text. I have also demonstrated that biblical references to election of persons to covenant relationship and ministry suggest conditions of faithful response of those called. This best accords with the Molinist picture and avoids the difficulties of Calvinist soteriology.

CHAPTER 10

EXISTENTIALLY SATISFYING

INTRODUCTION

An important facet of any model of providence is how it impacts the believer's understanding of the life of faith. At different stages throughout this book, I have attempted to highlight the value of the Molinist view of providence for the Christian life. For example, it helps explain how God's foreknowledge is related to his providence in a way that retains human moral responsibility.[1] It also offers an explanation of providence and evil that speaks to the concerns of both those who find solace in the idea that God exercises meticulous providence over all events (even those that result in great suffering for them), and those who find comfort in the claim that evil may sometimes be gratuitous (in the sense that it may not have a direct link to some future good). Molinism is also best able to make sense of issues related to verbal/plenary inspiration and inerrancy, wherein the choices of words are the human authors' own, but also reflect the very words of God, and it provides a mechanism whereby conservative Christianity may be reconciled to current scientific thought with orderliness at the macro-level, and randomness at the micro-level. In addition, Molinism is able to clarify the nature of salvation through faith and how election/divine predestination may be a sovereign choice of God that is neither capricious nor dependent upon human goodness, and is able to explain the strange phenomenon of redeemed, regenerate persons that are new creatures with new natures and yet who continue to struggle with sin. Similarly, it can offer eschatological hope that God's plan will come to fruition, even while affirming that some creatures will rebel against a glorified, presently reigning Christ.

---

1. The idea is that libertarian freedom best accords with the concepts of human morality/moral responsibility, even though proponents of compatibilism have successfully argued that agents may be morally praiseworthy and blameworthy under more restrictive views of freedom. See for example, John Martin Fischer and Mark Ravizza, *Responsibility and Control: A Theory of Moral Responsibility* (Cambridge: Cambridge University Press, 1998).

In this chapter, I hope to discuss a few other practical issues that Molinism may address. The primary concern will be with questions related to unfulfilled prophecy and petitionary prayer, though some discussion of spiritual gifts and eschatology remain.

Unfulfilled Prophecy

As noted in the introduction to the book, Open Theists have often pointed to places in the Bible where God seems to have changed his mind or been wrong about the future. They find instances of unfulfilled prophecy most promising. Most often, these are prophecies of judgment against a nation or people, but the judgment announced never comes to fruition. Open Theists reason that, in these situations, God may have simply been wrong. This explanation, of course, accounts for prophecies whose outcomes do not come to pass, but it fails to address the requirement of accuracy for legitimate prophecy (Deut. 18). The biblical test for determining whether an individual is a true prophet of God or a false prophet is the level of accuracy he/she has with regard to predictions, and the only acceptable level of accuracy for a true prophet is one hundred percent. The test is so determinative and important (because the spiritual life of Israel is so important) that failure is a capital offense. The Open Theist claim that God was wrong and thus led the prophet astray, not only fails to account for this requirement, but suggests that a prophet could utter a false word and deserve death through no fault of his or her own! In cases like this, the prophet could justifiably complain that he really did speak the word Yahweh gave to him and that it is God's fault that the prophecy was wrong. Since it was God's word that was in error and it is God's word that demands the prophet who utters an erroneous prophecy be executed, there is good reason to question God's justice (not to mention his coherence) under this model!

But the Bible does not treat unfulfilled pronouncements of judgment as false prophecies or mistakes by God, but rather recognizes them as conditional in nature. That is, judgment prophecies almost always include an implied conditional: if the person or nation were to repent, God may show mercy after all.[2] The book of Jonah offers a clear example. God sent

---

2. Sanders questions this move under a model that assumes comprehensive divine foreknowledge because there aren't any conditionals; the outcome is certain: "How can a conditional promise be genuine if God already foreknows the human response and so foreknows that he will, in fact, never fulfill the promise?" Sanders, *The God Who Risks*, 131. Sanders sees the typical application of the principle as suspect, wherein "failed" prophecies are claimed to be conditional, while "fulfilled" prophecies are not. He rightly notes that some fulfilled prophecies were also conditional. Still, Sanders fails to account for the human element in the recipient. It is likely that, if the prophecy were given in a conditional format, it would not be taken as seriously as when given in a definite format. Procrastination, even in repentance, is an all-too-common problem. These are theological arguments. Kaiser argues that biblically, the majority of Old Testament prophecies are conditional, and follow the pattern of blessing/curse found in Leviticus 26 and Deuteronomy 28–32. Kaiser and Silva, *Introduction to Biblical Hermeneutics*.

Jonah to Nineveh to preach God's judgment upon the city. Jonah instead tried to flee and was swallowed by a fish until he repented of his disobedience, eventually arriving in Nineveh to deliver the message. Upon hearing, the people conducted a city-wide fast and repented (Jonah 3:6–9), averting God's wrath and saving Nineveh. Irritated at God's manifest grace, Jonah explained that his anticipation of divine mercy was why he had fled and its realization was now the source of his anger with God (Jonah 4:1–2). Two important points surface: 1) Although the prophecy was given in definite terms ("God will destroy the city," Jonah 3:4), it included an unspoken element of mercy; and 2) Jonah's anticipation of God's mercy indicates that this element was a common feature of Old Testament prophecy. Jonah feared that the people would repent in response to his message of impending doom and that God would relent in his anger; he assumed mercy was available in spite of the more definite-sounding nature of the message God gave him for the Ninevites.

Calvinists and Molinists both appeal to this facet in explaining how it is the case that many Old Testament prophets are not false prophets worthy of death due to their supposed errors. Both also argue that although God knew ahead of time how the recipients of the pronouncement of judgment would respond, their actions in either repenting and turning from sin or continuing in sin stand to justify or condemn them. However, the proclamation of conditional judgment raises issues more problematic for Calvinism than Molinism. Recall that in the Calvinist model, God has the ability to control the free decisions of persons in such a way that he can guarantee they will respond in precisely the way he desires, while Molinism proclaims that God can arrange circumstances so that people will act the way he desires so long as there are true counterfactuals of freedom that allow for such action. The Molinist model allows more room for exploring God's just condemnation of those who fail to turn/repent.

Consider the situation of Judah during the time of the second Babylonian Empire. Jeremiah continually warned of the coming judgment of God and called the people to repent. They did not, and as a result of political concerns and intrigue, the Babylonian army laid siege to Jerusalem, conquered it, carried away its most prominent citizens and artifacts, and destroyed the Temple. Both Calvinists and Molinists claim that God knew the following counterfactual to be true:

> If I were to send Jeremiah to Jerusalem to preach a message of repentance, the people would fail to freely turn from their wicked ways;

and the counterfactual,

> If I were to send Jeremiah to Jerusalem to preach a message of repentance, the people would freely turn from their wicked ways;

to be false. However, the Molinist can make the further claim that God could not make it such that the people would repent because of the true counterfactuals. Under a Calvinist analysis, God could have made the Judeans so that they would freely choose to repent upon hearing Jeremiah's message of impending judgment, but he chose not to. Instead, he chose to make them so that they would develop into people who stubbornly refuse to repent, even in the face of divine judgment and an overwhelmingly superior enemy. Just as the problem of evil is more acute for the Calvinist than the Molinist, so also the problem of God's judgment and unfulfilled prophecy is more acute for the Calvinist.[3]

Efficacy of Petitionary Prayer

A second area of interest to Molinism is that of petitionary prayer. As Basinger rightly notes, most Christians believe that at least some of the time, God's intervention in the world depends on whether they ask or not, and he highlights James's own words: "we have not because we ask not."[4] Basinger notes that Calvinists can, in a sense, maintain that prayer changes things because God ordained that his actions be in response to prayer (and that he would not have acted without the prayer), but he also argues that there is a bit of sophistry in this claim [my words, not his] because under Calvinist principles, God can always ensure that the prayer is offered. He writes, "Thus, for proponents of specific sovereignty, it can never be the case that God is prohibited from bringing about that which he can and would like to bring about—a healing, guidance and the like—because we have not requested that he do so."[5]

By contrast, other views of providence do not believe that God can ensure that the petitionary prayer is offered because the petitioner may choose to refrain from praying. If no prayer is offered and God has decreed that he will only act if someone prays, then God will not act, even though he would have, if asked. At a certain level, then, there seems to be an advantage of the Open view over the Calvinist view, but at another level, petitionary prayer poses problems for all models of providence. Consider prayers for others that involve some kind of change in them (e.g., prayers that he change his behavior or come to faith, etc.). On an Open model, it is doubtful that God would override the individual's freedom simply because someone else asked him to.[6] On a Calvinist model, it makes no sense for God to make his action depen-

---

3. And in a similar way to how he handles the problem of evil, the Calvinist can appeal to the maximizing of God's glory as the explanation.
4. David Basinger, "Practical Implications," in Pinnock et al., *The Openness of God*, 158.
5. Ibid.
6. A fundamental feature of Open Theism is God's respect for human freedom. If he won't abrogate someone's freedom to bring about his own will, he surely won't do so to bring about a creature's (limited and perhaps sinful) will.

dent on creaturely responses, in part because God can make the creature freely perform the desired action and in part because God's will is determinative. Molinism has similar problems. After all, the question, "Why wouldn't God go ahead and intervene without our prayers?," seems problematic for all positions.[7] Nevertheless, Molinism seems to have the benefits of each. It can explain why God created a world where some are never saved or why some prayers do not elicit the desired effect without impugning God's goodness and love, but it also claims that God's plan will come to fruition and that his will cannot be thwarted.

Boyd tells the story of a young woman who accosted him one evening after he preached a sermon on how God directs our paths. She told him of her Christian upbringing, early salvation experience and call to missions, and of how she earnestly prayed for a godly husband to serve with on the field. She met a young man at college and after many years of courting/dating, praying, seeking godly counsel, and all the other "right" steps to discerning God's will, they were married, convinced it was God's plan for their lives. Unfortunately, her husband had an affair and fell further and further away from God. He eventually became abusive and divorced her. As Boyd tells it, her deep disappointment was tied to God's foreknowledge: "Understandably, Suzanne could not fathom how the Lord could respond to her lifelong prayers by setting her up with a man he *knew* would do this to her and her child."[8]

She had some friends who suggested she had been wrong about God's will, but she reasoned that this leads to complete ignorance and uncertainty about God's will: No one can ever be sure! Other friends suggested that the ordeal was God's will and he was using it to teach her something. She responded that God is a very poor teacher, and noted that it had only left her bitter and that abuse, adultery, and divorce were clearly against God's will.

Boyd tried to help Suzanne see that the situation was her ex-husband's fault and not God's, but as he puts it, "her reply was more than adequate to invalidate my encouragement: If God knew exactly what her husband would do, then he bears all the responsibility for setting her up the way he did."[9] He could not argue with her point, but did offer an alternative: God was as disappointed with how things turned out in her marriage as she was. In fact, it was God's will when she married because at the time, her husband was a godly man and their marriage had really good prospects for success. Boyd goes so far as to suggest that God prodded the two to go to the same college with their marriage in mind![10]

7. See David Basinger, "Why Petition an Omnipotent, Omniscient, Wholly Good God?," *Religious Studies* 19 (1983): 24–41.
8. Boyd, *God of the Possible*, 105.
9. Ibid.
10. Ibid., 106.

So the answer to Suzanne's dilemma is that she was correct in ascertaining God's will, but God was wrong in his predictions about how things would turn out because her husband refused to respond appropriately to his promptings and repent of his sin. Boyd sees this perspective as a positive development: "[Suzanne] didn't have to abandon all confidence in her ability to hear God and didn't have to accept that somehow God intended this ordeal 'for her own good.' Her faith in God's character and her love toward God were eventually restored and she was finally able to move on with her life."[11]

There is surely something attractive about Boyd's answer to the problem of getting God's will wrong. After all, we want to have confidence that when we do all the right things, we can properly discern God's will in the various decisions that come our way, especially the "big ones." Still, there is something off-putting about Boyd's approach, perhaps its apparent smugness—we need not worry about our own error, because it was God's error that got us into this mess! To be fair, Boyd does not mean the account to be read this way, but the contrast between God's error and our [Suzanne's] wisdom is striking and disconcerting. Why can it not be the case that she *was* wrong? Why can it not be the case that, while she took precautions prior to marrying the man, she was blind to his history, or patterns, or the like, that might have given some indication that he would act the way he did?

This gets to the heart of the problem of providence and petitionary prayer. In the case of marriage, we may affirm that the persons we married were those identified in God's plan and that they married us of their own free will. Both Molinism and Calvinism can maintain this, but Molinism also allows for the possibility of mistakes. Molinism allows us to speak of some marriages as not ideal—the abusive relationship, the marriage of Christians and non-Christians, etc.—by appeal to the same categories used to address the issue of gratuitous evil. Some bad marriages may not be God's will (taken as desire), but may, nevertheless, be part of God's plan, given the particular possible world actualized. Calvinism can make no such distinction, and instead must appeal to differing wills in God (permissive/declarative, secret/revealed, etc.) and mystery to explain why God would decree something evil when he could have met his end goals without it. Thus, petitionary prayer is sometimes seen as a stumbling block for Calvinism.

Calvinist Paul Helm seeks to meet the challenge head-on. He notes that the Bible depicts petitions as having efficacy, as promoting action in the one petitioned (at least sometimes); Jesus suggested that fervent, persistent, heart-felt prayers can move God to action in a way that weak, intermittent, half-hearted prayers do not (cf. Luke 18:7). Helm correctly notes that if the impression of petitionary prayer in the Bible—that it

---

11. Ibid.

influences God to act—is true, then it forms part of the order of divine providence, "that great matrix of causes and effects through which God governs the world."[12]

Some libertarians have argued that petitionary prayer makes little sense in a Calvinist framework, not so much because the response of God or the outcome is determined, but because compatibilist freedom some-how detracts from personal relationship, and petitionary prayer is predi-cated upon it. According to this view, only in the context of free relations does the concept of a request make sense. Helm responds by questioning the underlying assumption that personal relations require that both parties possess libertarian freedom and neither party has power over the other. He points to familial relations as examples of deeply personal relations where one party often wields significant power over the other.[13] Helm goes on to rightly point out that the assumption that personal relationships can only exist between equals is at the heart of the objection, and it is clearly unbiblical; God and humans are certainly not equal, but personal rela-tionship exists between them, and petitionary prayer is at least one of the interactions characteristic of that relationship.

Helm asks if his Calvinist view of providence conflicts with the bibli-cal picture of prayer moving God to action (so that he seems *respon-sive*) or even making up and changing his mind because of prayer. This concern forms one of the chief criticisms by Open and Process Theists against Calvinism and Molinism. Helm begins his answer by suggesting that prayer ought to be considered no different from any other action one might take, and to note that in concrete terms, if anyone *has prayed*, then that prayer was (or those prayers were) ordained by God. Helm takes this to mean that, in one respect, it is unprofitable to ask questions about what might have happened if the prayer had not been voiced: "It is easy to ask, 'if A had not prayed, would God have done what he did?' But to do so is in effect to prise apart the action of praying from the total matrix of events and actions of which it forms a part."[14] The point he hopes to make is that, in the complex but delicate relations between God's providence and human actions, the prayer itself is an integral component; to remove the prayer is to change the whole formula, so to speak, but then the question becomes so difficult to answer that it verges on meaninglessness. Human ignorance about the interrelation-ships between events in this world, not to mention those between the spiritual and physical, make assessment of counterfactuals of prayer

---

12. Helm, *Providence of God*, 146.
13. He writes, "It is clear, however, that personal relations are jeopardized by *some* kinds of manipulation or coercion by one of the parties; for example, by brain washing or intimidation. But it is surely not a necessary condition of any personal relation that no coercion between the parties can take place." Ibid., 149.
14. Ibid., 154.

efficacy virtually impossible.[15] We simply cannot know what would have been the case if one had not prayed when he in fact did, and vice versa.

Of course conceptually, Helm is absolutely correct. Apart from special revelation, we simply cannot know what appreciable difference our prayers for help, healing, others, etc., actually make. Helm also correctly notes that although prayer's primary efficacy is sometimes psychological for the petitioner (e.g., prayer for help on a test inspires the student to study more and thus, be better prepared), this cannot be our only answer to the question if prayer changes things.[16]

Helm goes on to consider what we know about God, petitions, and his promises. In some cases, God has made it clear that if he is asked, he will grant the request (e.g., request for salvation). It can thus be known that if an individual were to ask God for forgiveness (and truly mean it and ask in faith in Christ), God will grant the request and forgive. In other cases, God has not so obligated himself and he may answer any given request, at any given time, by any given person, in either the affirmative or negative, as he chooses. Similarly, in these cases, sometimes God's actions (or the eventual results) will depend on petitions being offered, and sometimes they will not; that is, sometimes the prayer makes a difference to the ends, and sometimes, at least conceivably, it does not.[17]

Two issues must be considered here: first, the ends that God has ordained, and second, the means to those ends. When the ends are considered in the abstract, then the answers to questions about efficacy of prayer are negative: God's preordained ends will be met no matter what prayers are, or are not, uttered. However, as noted earlier, such abstract conceptions fail to appreciate that the prayers offered or failed to have been offered *just are* an integral part of the means God has preordained to meet those desired ends.

---

15. Helm writes, "Whether the question 'If A had not prayed, what would have happened?' is worth discussing very largely depends upon how much general information there is about such cases, and therefore in how warranted we are in making generalizations about them. For instance, we have sufficient general information about the germination of seeds to accept the truth of the statement, 'If the seeds had not been watered they would not have germinated.' But we do not have sufficient information to determine the truth or otherwise of the statement, 'If A had not prayed for examination success, he or she would have failed?'"[sic]. Ibid.

16. He writes, "It is clearly unsatisfactory as an account of petitionary prayer to limit the efficacy of the praying to the petitioner, as if the sole effect of the prayer to God were to make the petitioner redouble his or her efforts and so succeed. Perhaps the examinee's prayer did have this effect; but if this is all that such prayer even accomplished then prayer would be nothing more than talking to oneself." Ibid., 154–55.

17. Here things get a bit confusing because on the one hand, things are the way they are, at least in Helm's deterministic framework, because of the events that have preceded, and so they could not be the same if the prayer situation were different; but on the other hand, if God determined that the end result will be a certain way, it will be that way no matter what someone prays or doesn't pray.

Ironically, though, Helm considers prayers that seem to request something that God has already clearly promised he would do (e.g., bring about his kingdom), and asks what sense it makes to pray for something that will be the case, whether we pray or not. His answer is that the prayer is not really a request *per se*, but is instead an expression of desire or "an affirmation of solidarity with the unfolding will of God."[18] Helm's answer illustrates the real concern many have with Calvinism and its conception of petitionary prayer. If it is asserted that everything happens by necessity, then there should never be a prayer offered as a request. Rather, prayer should always represent resignation or affirmation of solidarity with God's pre-ordained plan, *even if the petitioner does not know what that plan is*, because if he is a Calvinist, he knows that the ends and means just are already determined by God's sovereign will in a way that is not dependent upon counterfactuals of prayer efficacy. Such an approach to life and prayers were characteristic of Stoicism.

Two responses to this complaint are available to the Calvinist. First, he can argue that the objection really only stands against forms of Fatalism because in Calvinism, everything depends on the will of God, not *necessity*. This seems to skirt the issue without seriously addressing the underlying concern. Second, he may appeal to the ignorance of the petitioner regarding God's plan and desires for the particular situation in order to argue that the appropriate action is to humbly request while maintaining an attitude of faithful acceptance of whatever answer he may get from God. That is, the Calvinist can note that the one praying only knows *that* God has determined the end, but not *what* the end is, and so truly requesting something specific is still appropriate. Calvin seems to adopt this approach in his discussion of petitionary prayer, where he labels the critique "profane" and "foolish."[19] So, on the one hand, Calvinists have given answers to the specific objection. On the other hand, though, the criticism still seems to have some force, for if an appropriate prayer to a situation with a known outcome is faithful resignation and acceptance and not request, it seems that the same type of prayer is appropriate for a situation with a determined, though unknown outcome. Why should ignorance of the pre-ordained outcome change the nature of the petitioner's posture? It is hard to see why it should. However, it seems to me that the Calvinist has a third option: accept the substance of the claim in the criticism while denying that it is a negative thing; he can agree that there is a sense in which all Christians should approach petitionary prayer with an attitude of resignation and submission to God's sovereign will and

---

18. Ibid., 158

19. Calvin writes, "The profane make such a bluster with their foolish puerilities. . . . Nay, these trifles even infer, that the prayers of the faithful must be perverse, not to say superfluous, since they intreat the Lord to make a provision for things which he has decreed from eternity." Calvin, *Institutes of the Christian Religion* 1.17.3 (trans. Bevridge, 103).

plan, and that such an attitude is nothing to be maligned. In fact, Calvinist Richard Phillips notes that it leads to a proper posture of thanksgiving, worship, and surrender.[20]

Most Molinists would agree with everything Helm has said up to this point, except they may point out that there can be value in considering how counterfactuals of prayer efficacy may be used *by God*, even if *we* do not know their truth values. Recall that counterfactuals of divine freedom are known by God's free knowledge. So, for example, God's knowledge of the counterfactuals,

> If Hezekiah were to pray for healing, I will give him fifteen more years;

and

> If Hezekiah were to fail to pray for healing, I will not give him fifteen more years;

are thus dependent upon his will (Isa. 38:3–5). Suppose that God wants Hezekiah to rule another fifteen years, but only if he has been through the terrifying and life-changing ordeal of having been confronted with his impending death. In that case, God would need knowledge of some counterfactuals of freedom in order to ensure Hezekiah would pray for healing and Isaiah would submit to God's instruction to confront the king. In other words, in order to meet his desires for Hezekiah, God may have needed middle knowledge of the following two counterfactuals of creaturely freedom (among perhaps others):

> If Isaiah were called to confront Hezekiah with his sin, he would freely submit to God's calling and faithfully execute his charge;

and

> If Hezekiah were confronted by Isaiah for his sin, he would freely repent.[21]

---

20. Richard D. Phillips, "Prayer and the Sovereignty of God," in *Let Us Pray: A Symposium on Prayer by Leading Preachers and Theologians* (Orlando, FL: Northampton, 2011), electronic resource. Phillips writes, "But far from being outraged at the idea that prayer does not change God's will, Christians should be profoundly grateful." He goes on to point out God's omniscience and our inability to add to his good thoughts, intentions, and wisdom.

21. For example, some of the others could include: *If Hezekiah were confronted by Isaiah, he would not only freely repent, but his response to the events would shape his personality in such a way that he would become the king God wants; There is no other means by which Hezekiah will freely become the king God desires;* or *There is no other means by which Hezekiah will freely become the king God desires that better serves God's other purposes (e.g., least amount of evil, most revelatory, etc.).*

In addition to defending the Calvinist model's view of petitionary prayer, Helm offers a critique of Open Theism. He suggests that on a risky view of providence (like that of Open Theism), the upshot of maintaining absolute efficacy of prayer is that petitioners are to be blamed for failing to pray sufficiently fervently, faithfully, or persistently, and are thus responsible for evil not averted: "Who is to blame for Auschwitz?.... [O]n this view of petitionary prayer, the blame at least for the continuation of the atrocity (once it has come to the notice of a potential intercessor) falls not on Nazi Germany, or on God, but on the numerous potential intercessors who did not pray as hard or as sincerely as they might have done."[22]

It is hard to take Helm seriously here for a number of reasons. First, it is doubtful anyone would make such a positive argument for assignment of blame and the fact that Helm produces no documentation of any such argument evinces this. Second, Open Theists rightly blame Auschwitz on those who perpetrated the evil there (Nazis), and consider the free nature of their actions to be a central component of their ideology. They would no more blame potential intercessors who failed to pray than they would God, who had perfect knowledge of the atrocities and power to stop them, but failed to do so. The point made by Open Theists is that their system removes more of the force of the problem of evil than does either Calvinism or Molinism, and as already noted, they are in at least some respects correct. Helm would have Open Theists adopt a deterministic view of providence with regard to God's prevention of sin, so long as someone else prayed for his intervention, but this seems more consistent with a Calvinist view than an Openness view. If Helm is going to make such a preposterous claim with no allowance for nuance in the Open Theist's view of providence, then his own determinist framework fails miserably on the problem because he can only soften its force by nuanced appeals to God's two wills, to God's transcendence and infinite holiness and wisdom, and to mystery. Third, Helm cannot honestly suggest that the culpability of one who failed to intercede is the same or greater than that of the perpetrator, no matter how one conceives of the efficacy of potential intercessory prayers. Fourth, Helm's argument may be turned in on his own position, for he argued that prayer can move God if God has built it into his order of means and causes. If God chose to not do so (i.e., decree that he will intervene to save the Jews if enough people pray and then decree that enough people pray), then does God not, yet again, bear blame? Not only has God decreed the actions of the Nazis, but he has failed to decree that people pray or he has failed to decree that he would intervene if they pray, etc.). Under Helm's standards of blame here, it would seem God is culpable, but Helm rejects this. Ultimately, his argument smacks of a desperate attempt to criticize the Open Theist position, but it need not here.

22.   Helm, *Providence of God*, 159.

Molinism, Evangelism, Discipleship, and Prayer

One specific type of intercessory prayer that we often utter has to do with spiritual growth, either of ourselves or others. With regard to evangelism, we ask God to move in the hearts of others so that they will accept the truth of the gospel and be born again. Similarly, with regard to discipleship, we ask God to mold us into the image of Christ, conforming our wills to his and changing us from the inside out. Some have complained that such prayers cannot honestly be uttered by Molinists because they conflict with basic Molinist principles. For example, Garrigou-Lagrange writes, "The Molinist in his hours of intense prayer, forgets this doctrine and says with the Scripture: 'Have mercy on me, O God. . . . Convert me, O Lord, to thee and I shall be converted.'"[23] Similarly, Toner notes, "It seems obviously less than optimal to be a Molinist in the classroom, when teaching philosophy of religion, but a Thomist when at prayer. Truth does not contradict truth—why should prayer contradict truth?"[24] Both Garrigou-Lagrange and Toner mean to say that the way we pray ought to speak to our theological commitments, but more than this, the way we pray points to theological truth. That is, their objection is this: if you have to resort to a differing model's terminology because it works better for spiritual growth than your own model's terminology, then the other model is probably more correct. Since Molinists pray like Thomists when it comes to evangelism and discipleship, then it is likely that Thomism (akin to Calvinism) is true.

There are at least two points that the Molinist can make in response to these charges. First, the argument fails to account for the fact that most people exhort others to holiness as if Molinism were correct, even if their prayers do not. In Protestant circles, it may be put this way: We evangelize as if Arminianism is correct, and we pray for the lost as if Calvinism is correct. But this is far too colloquial to be taken seriously as a strong theological argument for/against either position, for both Arminian and Calvinist theologians are prepared to discuss in greater detail all the nuances of their positions vis-à-vis evangelism praxis and intercessory prayer for the lost. When a Calvinist gives an altar call like an Arminian or when an Arminian prays for his lost friend like a Calvinist, each does so keeping in mind his own background beliefs about how salvation works—the work of the Holy Spirit enabling or causing faith and the human response in faith—and he works it into his own understanding of what he is specifically requesting of God, despite his use of somewhat loose language. Second, this overly pragmatic approach to truth seems naïve. After all, the great spiritual directors to whom Garrigou-Lagrange and Toner refer as teaching Thomistic providence in their spiritual exercises do not offer up prolonged explanations of primary and secondary

23. Reginald Garrigou-Lagrange, *God: His Existence and His Nature*, vol. 2, trans. Dom Bede Rose (St. Louis: Herder, 1934; repr. Albany, NY: Preserving Christian Publications, 1993), 378.
24. Patrick Toner, "The Prayer of the Molinist," *Heythrop Journal* 49 (2008): 944.

causation in their writings on spiritual growth precisely because their works are not strict theological treatises. In other words, while theological precision is desirable in the way we practice and teach others to practice the faith, there is more room for colloquial language and imprecision in our praxis than in our dogmatics. To expect one's spiritual expression to be as technical as his theological articulation is probably unrealistic, unnecessary, and even unfair. At any rate, it seems that persons of all theological persuasions fail here, so it does not stand as a critique of any one position.

Worthy of Worship

The question of worship-worthiness often arises in discussions of providence, with all sides jostling for position and suggesting that others present a portrayal of God that is less than impressive. For example, in his discussion of the difficulty the Calvinist position has with the problem of evil, Roger Olson has claimed that he could never worship a deity like that presented by Calvinism because he appears as a "moral monster."[25] In this, Olson is joined by many Open Theists and atheists. This is not to indict Olson through guilt by association, but rather to note that these concerns are wide-ranging and that the question of worship-worthiness gets to the heart of the faith.

Calvinists have often pointed to God's absolute control of all things as the key to his worthiness for being worshipped, and have criticized Molinism for its seemingly weak portrayal of God.[26] Under Molinist principles, they complain, God is somehow weak, or subject to the whims of his creatures. Some have even charged that Molinism turns the proper relations between creator/creature upside down with the creator serving the creature. I trust that it has been made abundantly clear that such a portrayal is grossly misleading. While Molinism does suggest that there are restrictions upon what sort of world God can actualize (as does Calvinism), and that some of those restrictions are tied to creaturely freedom (unlike Calvinism), it also maintains that God is in no way obliged to create, to create creatures with libertarian freedom if he chooses to create, or to refrain from overriding creaturely freedom if he chooses to create and to endow some creatures with libertarian freedom. In other words, Molinism allows God to function very much like the God portrayed by Calvinism, if he were to so choose, though it seems he rarely does so. To be fair, Open Theism makes similar claims about God: he reserves the right and has the ability to override creaturely freedom at any time he sees fit, though almost never chooses to exercise that right. So both Molinism and Open Theism can overcome the "weak God" complaint of their Calvinist critics.

---

25. Olson, *Against Calvinism*, 85. Surprisingly, Olson also admits that he can and does worship with Calvinists "without cringing." Ibid., 13.

26. For example, Turretin complains that middle knowledge makes God dependent upon the creature. Turretin, *Institutes of Elenctic Theology* 3.13.13 (trans. Giger, 1:215).

In addition, there is good reason to question the general assertion that God's worship-worthiness is tied to his control of all things, at least as it is typically expressed. It suggests that worship-worthiness is directly proportional to the deity's direct control; the more direct control of earthly affairs the deity exercises, the more worthy he is of worship. There are two flaws with this reasoning (apart from the fact that it is simply taken for granted). First, and I suspect my Calvinist friends will agree, God's worship-worthiness *just is*, because he is, at the most basic and fundamental level, worthy of worship. That is, worship-worthiness is not somehow dependent upon what he does or does not do, as if it is contingent on his doing the right thing, or on our approval of his sovereign choices. He is worthy of worship because of who he is. To be fair, of course, the point of raising the question of worship-worthiness is really to raise the question of the types of actions and/or the model of providence that best accords with our understanding and knowledge of the God who is worthy of worship, so this first objection can rightly be dismissed as correct, but missing the mark of the original concern.

Second, it is just as likely that a deity who is able to make use of the free actions of creatures—actions he cannot, by their very nature, control—to achieve his purposes is most worthy of worship. It has been argued by many Open Theists that it takes a greater Being to use undetermined events to achieve his desired ends than to simply cause all events to do so. It is hard to decide between these two competing claims. At face value, both have merit. However, other considerations that impact the discussion lead me to conclude that the portrayal of God by Molinism is most worthy of worship, over against the portrayals of Calvinism and Open Theism.

As already noted in Olson's quote above and in the chapter on the problem of evil, the stronger causal view of providence held by Calvinists comes at a great cost. While it was admitted that all positions on providence (save perhaps Process Theology) have some difficulty with the problem of evil, the difficulty is particularly acute for Calvinism. Any worship-worthiness gained by the exceptionally strong emphasis on divine control is subsequently lost by the added divine culpability for evil that comes along with that emphasis.

By contrast, the portrayal of God by Open Theism fails precisely because God seems unable to ensure his desired ends really are met. Open Theists do not think this should be cause for concern because, as Sanders argues, God has the power, love, and wisdom "to continue working with his project until he brings it to the fulfillment he intends."[27] Bruce Ware rightly questions Sanders here, and argues that the examples of divine mistakes and regret offered by Open Theists undermine confidence in both the future and God's wisdom. He is worth quoting at length:

---

27. Sanders, *The God Who Risks*, 133.

> If God is not sure that what he does is best, can we be sure that he really knows what he is doing? The simple fact is that a God who can only speculate regarding what much of the future holds, at times second-guesses his own plans, can get things wrong, can falsely anticipate what may happen next, and may even repent of his own past conduct is a God unworthy of devotion, trust, and praise. What open theists have "gained" by their insistence on God as a risk-taker has been won at the expense of God's full wisdom, knowledge, trustworthiness, majesty, sovereignty, and glory; and it leads inevitably to doubt, worry, and fear regarding the fulfillment of God's plans.[28]

The depiction of God in Molinism fares better on both of these counts. It handles the problem of evil better than Calvinism because it has the means to account for why evils may be necessary for greater goods and why some evils may not themselves directly lead to greater goods. It handles the future better than Open Theism because it has the means to account for God's certainty of the future, God's confidence in his own choices and how they will contribute to his plan, and God's sovereignty over all things such that his ultimate purposes will come to fruition. The constraints the counterfactuals of freedom place upon God allow the Molinist to speak of gratuitous evil in a way the Calvinist cannot, and the use God makes of the counterfactuals of freedom allows the Molinist to speak of God's meticulous providence and sovereignty over all things in a way the Open Theist cannot.

However, these issues give rise to two final concerns that some may have with the Molinist picture. Ironically, these two concerns appear to be at odds with one another, for one complains that under Molinist principles, God's providence is too deterministic, while the other complains that it is not sufficiently direct. Both appeal to the way Molinism places so much emphasis upon God's pre-creative reflection and his use of the counterfactuals of creaturely freedom.

First, some proponents of Open Theism and simple foreknowledge have complained that Molinism is particularly problematic because of how God's use of the counterfactuals of creaturely freedom seem to determine the future. Very similar complaints were discussed in the chapter on the grounding objection, but here I want to consider the complaint as it is expressed by those Arminians who maintain that God possesses foreknowledge. According to the simple foreknowledge view, God's predestination of some for salvation is based on his knowledge of how they will respond in faith to his call. They see this as preserving the freedom of the individual because there are no external influences placed upon the individual regarding his choice to follow Christ. Molinism, they charge, does bring external influences to bear when God

---

28. Bruce A. Ware, *God's Lesser Glory: The Diminished God of Open Theism* (Wheaton, IL: Crossway, 2000), 159.

chooses to actualize one possible world instead of another. Once God does so, then the counterfactuals of freedom that are true in the world now actual are set, and those individuals whose counterfactuals say they will accept *must accept*, and those whose counterfactuals say they will refuse *cannot accept*. Thus, the individual responses to the gospel call (among other things) are not free. Even worse, any evils that occur in this world are tied to God's choice to actualize this world rather than another world, and so he is responsible for evil.

In response to this objection, I must first note that there is really nothing new here; it is a conflation of the issues addressed in chapters 2 and 4. A number of strategies are available to the Molinist, from distinguishing between *bringing about* and *causing* or strong and weak actualization (on the part of God), to the difference between counterfactuals being descriptive and being causal, to differences between *will* and *must*. The true counterfactuals do not make it so that the individual *must* accept or *must* refuse the offer of salvation. Rather, they merely say what the individual *will* do; he *may* (taken as *could*, not *might*) refuse the offer of salvation, even if the true counterfactual says that he *will* accept the offer. Of course, simple foreknowledge has something of a problem of its own with regard to creaturely freedom, as noted in chapter 4. What is important to note here is that, although proponents of simple foreknowledge have concerns about the greater level of divine action in the Molinist picture, their fears can be allayed. In fact, the very strategies they utilize in order to overcome the problem of foreknowledge and freedom in their own model are the same strategies the Molinist uses to answer this objection.

Second, some may fear that Molinism presents a picture of divine providence that seems eerily close to Deism. Molinism puts a lot of the onus for its claims of meticulous providence upon the pre-creative deliberation of God regarding possible and feasible worlds, and thus, some may leave with the impression that Molinism says that once God chooses to actualize one of those worlds, he just lets it play out according to what he has foreseen. That is, one could get the idea that Molinism has God, prior to creating, conceiving of how all the histories of all possible worlds would play out, and once he finds one that suits his desires (or finds several that equally meet his desires/goals), he actualizes it and then takes a laissez-faire approach from then on because he has no need to intervene. Such a portrayal seems very close to deistic conceptions of God, and such a God is hardly worthy of worship.

Fortunately (Providentially!), this is not the picture Molinism paints, properly conceived. First, Deism was predicated on the assumption that an omnipotent, omnibenevolent Being must create the best possible world and therefore, the actual world must be the best possible, a perfect world in need of no intervention. Intervention, under these presuppositions, was seen as evidence of a deficiency in the creation and thus, the Creator. Molinism makes no such claims about the implications of God's perfection. Second, Molinism allows for divine intervention. In some ways, it is very much like Calvinism; divine intervention is built into the divine plan/decree. In other ways, it is different because it involves more variables. God considers how his intervening will affect the course of events in world history, the truth of counterfactuals of creaturely freedom (and random events), and his own dispositions when he reflects upon which world to actualize. Once he chooses to actualize a world, then the events occur as he knew they would, but the playing out of that knowledge in reality includes his own involvement with the created order (as well as the free actions of creatures). Just as creaturely actions are meaningful even though pre-planned and foreknown, so also are divine actions. Third, as already suggested, Molinism claims that some of the true counterfactuals include divine action in them. Even some counterfactuals of creaturely freedom include divine action in them such that God's plan could not be met without his active involvement with, and intervention in, the created order. Numerous examples have already been given, but the most obvious are those referencing God's active movement upon the hearts of sinners, enabling them to repent and believe the gospel. Molinists affirm that persons could not be saved without this work of God because the counterfactuals do not support it. There is no world where

> If John were presented the gospel and there were no work of the Holy Spirit upon his heart, he will freely repent of his sin and believe the gospel;

is true. By contrast, the counterfactual,

> If John were presented the gospel and God were to move in his heart in a particular way, he will repent and believe the gospel;

is true in the actual world. Thus, God can only ensure that John freely repents and believes the gospel by his active movement in John's heart. So the complaint that Molinism appears deistic falls flat.

Ethics, Providence, and End-of-Life Decisions

One important pastoral concern has to do with end of life decisions. When, if ever, is it right to remove life support from a terminally ill and suffering family member? Many persons are plagued by questions of this sort because they do not want to "kill" their loved ones, and they see the decision in these terms.[29]

---

29. Underlying these concerns and feelings is an assumption that there is a correct answer to the moral conundrum. To be more a little more precise, in asking the moral question, one assumes that there is a correct time at which it becomes morally good to remove life support, but before which, removing life support would have been immoral and after which, failure to remove life support would also be immoral. Of course, it could be the case that there is a period of time, as

Sometimes, especially when the person on life support is young, family members cling to the hope of recovery. In these cases, the decision to suspend artificial life support is especially agonizing and has the potential to be terribly contentious. Families can be torn apart by disagreement, and individuals can be overcome with guilt if they doubt their decisions. Thus, it is worth asking if one's theory of providence can help provide guidance for decision-making or help provide comfort and peace to the family. Family members will surely wonder about counterfactuals such as

> If we leave our family member on life support for five more days, he will begin to respond and eventually recover;

and

> If we leave our family member on life support for five more days, he will suffer needlessly and die on the fifth day;

among others. If they can know that the former is true and the latter false, they can make an informed decision, and the decision to keep the family member on life support would presumably be God's will. If the former is false and the latter true, then the decision to keep the family member on life support would be contrary to God's will (or evil), and so they should go ahead and cease artificial life support.[30]

So how do the three primary models of providence fare here? If the patient's recovery (or death) is fully and comprehensively determined by all the factors already extant in his body and environment, then all three models will offer God the same amount of knowledge and therefore, they are on a par with one another. God would provide the same wise counsel under each model. If, however, the patient's recovery is in some way tied to random events (such as the movements of bacteria, etc.), then Open Theism does not fare well because God cannot know which counterfactual is true, short of his intent to miraculously and supernaturally intervene. Of course, he could choose to do just that, and cause the family member to recover or die, but this violates basic openness principles. Molinism and Calvinism seem to be at relative parity in most ways, for under both, God could know which is true, in Molinism due to his middle knowledge, and in Calvinism due to his knowledge of all relevant causal factors.

---

opposed to a mere moment, in which removal is good, but the principle remains (the period would be demarcated by a prior time during which removal would have been evil and a later time during which failure to remove would also have been evil). These natural assumptions give rise to pastoral questions and concerns to which one's model of divine providence and knowledge may speak.

30. It should be clear that the counterfactuals do not exhaust all options here, but represent typical thinking on the subject.

However, there is one way in which each of Calvinism and Molinism may be seen as superior to the other. Calvinism seems better equipped to deal with the nagging doubts that follow such agonizing decisions, for grieving family members can ostensibly comfort themselves with the belief that the decision they ultimately made *just was* in accord with God's will, while Molinists can only claim that the decision was part of God's plan, but not necessarily his will. Molinism is superior in its handling of the problem of prolonged suffering resulting in death (i.e., the second counterfactual was true). In these cases, Molinism can affirm that the family members may have made the wrong decision or that the suffering itself may have had no direct greater good, and that God knew the correct counterfactual. This can bolster the believer's confidence in God, even while he struggles with his own error. That is, some may find comfort in the belief that they made an error in discerning God's will, even when such error results in pain for their loved one because they can still rely on God. Still others may find comfort in the belief that no matter what—even prolonged suffering of a loved one prior to his death—God willed what happened and therefore, their decisions were in accord with that will. Others may find comfort in the belief that God did not know how things would turn out and that, while they properly discerned his will, his prognosis for the family member's recovery was overly optimistic. Each has strengths, but each also has vulnerabilities.

Eschatology

Eschatology, or the study of last things (colloquially, end times), deserves brief mention here, for it seems that Molinism is best able to account for some key features in certain understandings of its outworking. Christians are sometimes sharply divided over issues related to eschatology, especially when it comes to the meaning of the millennium (thousand-year reign of Christ; Rev. 20) and the events surrounding the coming of Christ. Premillennialism typically teaches that evil will grow in the world, culminating in a large-scale rebellion of humans against God and persecution of his people, followed by a miraculous intervention of judgment by God upon the world prior to a recreation of the heavens and earth. Postmillennialism and amillennialism both typically teach that the church will progressively succeed in its mission of transforming the world so that God's righteousness reigns, at which time God will miraculously re-create the heavens and the earth.

Although these two visions for the future are very different—some would say opposites—they both require that God know how humans will respond to the Gospel and how they will act far into the future. Of course, Open Theism struggles here, as there can be no assurance that people will respond negatively *en masse* (and God knows that they will) as premillennialism predicts, and there can be no confidence that people will respond positively *en masse* (and God will know that they will) as post-

and amillennialism predict. Thus, Open Theism has to cast its eschatological vision in terms of God's observance of patterns in order to offer up as good a prediction as can be given (because he has comprehensive present knowledge), but it cannot speak of how the future definitely will turn out. It faces particular difficulty the further into the future one looks due to the compounded unpredictability of generations of free beings. By contrast, both Molinism and Calvinism have the tools needed for certainty regarding the future and God's knowledge of it. Molinism is at a slight advantage because Calvinism has to explain why we should expect a marked increase in evil in the premillennial model without impugning God's character. If the future is determined by the will of God alone, then it seems reasonable to expect that righteousness will increase, and this natural expectation may be the reason many Calvinists favor post- and amillennialism. Molinism is able to account for the expectations of either vision of the future by appeal to categories already discussed on the problem of evil for premillennialism, and by appeal to the sanctifying work of the Holy Spirit in the church for post- and amillennialism.

CONCLUSION

In this chapter, many pragmatic issues were considered. The problem of unfulfilled prophecies was addressed first. Molinism can explain how judgment prophecies may be conditional in nature while retaining God's just condemnation when the people fail to repent of their sins. In addition, Molinism is best able to deal with petitionary prayer for guidance because it can have the certainty that Open Theism lacks, but it can also have the contingency that makes *request* rather than *resignation* appropriate, something Calvinism struggles to explain. It was also shown that Molinism's commitment to free will does not conflict with intercessory prayers for spiritual growth or salvation because of the colloquial way in which our prayers are uttered. Just as our exhortations to holiness are given as though persons can, of their own free will, choose to be holy (even though they cannot), so also prayers for salvation of others suggest that they have no part in coming to faith (even though they do). These two types of intercessory prayer typically seem at odds in most people's piety; one seems based on compatibiism while the other seems based on libertarianism, but in reality, the prayers are more expressions of our desires and less expressions of our strictly articulated theological commitments. The question of worship-worthiness (i.e., what type of God is worthy of worship?) was also briefly addressed. It is especially difficult to answer, but a relatively strong view of divine control, along with divine innocence of evil, seem compelling factors to consider, and it was argued that they are best balanced by appeal to middle knowledge. The last concern addressed was eschatology. In particular, it was argued that Open Theism cannot account for the confidence the Bible has in God's victory over the powers of darkness. It was also shown that the premillennial conception of a future where evil seems to run rampant is best handled under a Molinist view of providence, while the amillennial conception of a future where the church progressively grows, eventually overthrowing the forces of darkness in this age and ushering in God's kingdom, is best handled under a Calvinist view of providence.

Much of the work in this book has left it to the reader to decide the superior view of providence. All approaches have strengths and weaknesses, and there is something attractive in each. Open Theism offers the most robust view of human freedom, and is able to account for the existence of evil in the world.[31] Calvinism offers the most robust view of divine control, and is able to account for the attaining of God's plan. Both, however, have their problems. While it is not quite accurate to portray Molinism as some kind of *via media* between the two, it does have features that allow it to borrow from the strengths of each. Ultimately, each model's coherence with the Scriptures and its portrayal of God's governance should determine which is deemed most accurate. I have tried to argue that Molinism best deals with the theological concerns at stake, and best accords with that Scriptural portrayal.

---

31. Technically, Open Theism and Molinism subscribe to the same view of creaturely freedom, but what I mean here is that Molinism is sometimes charged with violating libertarianism, while Open Theism is not.

BIBLIOGRAPHY

BOOKS

Abailard, Peter. "Exposition of the Epistle to the Romans." In *A Scholastic Miscellany: Anselm to Ockham*, edited by Eugene R. Fairweather. Translated by Gerald E. Moffait. Philadelphia: Westminster, 1956.

Abbott, Edwin A. *Flatland*. 1884. New York: New American Library, 1984.

Abraham, William. *The Divine Inspiration of Holy Scripture*. New York: Oxford, 1981.

Alston, William. *Perceiving God: The Epistemology of Religious Experience*. Ithaca, NY: Cornell, 1993.

Anselm. *Cur Deus Homo*. In *St. Anselm: Basic Writings*. 2nd ed. Translated by S. N. Deane, 191–302. La Salle, IL: Open Court, 1962.

Anselm. *Monologion*. In *St. Anselm: Basic Writings*. 2nd ed. Translated by S. N. Deane, 81–190. La Salle, IL: Open Court, 1962.

Aquinas, Thomas. *Summa Theologica*. In *Great Books of the Western World*. Edited by Robert Hutchins. Translated by Laurence Shapcote. Vol. 17. Chicago: Encyclopedia Britannica, Inc., 1952, 1990.

Aristotle. *De Interpretatione,, in Aristotle: The Organon I [The Loeb Classical Library]*. Translated by Harold P. Cooke. Cambridge, MA: Harvard University Press, 1938.

————. *De Interpretatione*. In Aristotle: Categories and *De Interpretatione*. Translated by J. L. Ackrill. Oxford: Oxford University, 1975.

Arminius, James. *Arminius Speaks: Essential Writings On Predestination, Free Will and the Nature of God*. Edited by John D. Wagner. Eugene, OR: Wipf & Stock, 2011.

Augustine. *Confessions*. Translated by Henry Chadwick. New York: Oxford, 1991.

————. *On Christian Teaching*. Translated R. P. H. Greene. New York: Oxford University, 1997.

————. *On Free Choice of the Will*. Translated by Thomas Williams. Indianapolis: Hackett, 1993.

Barbour, Ian. *Religion in an Age of Science*. San Francisco: Harper Collins, 1990.

Barth, Karl. *Church Dogmatics I.2 Doctrine of the Word of God*. Edited by Geoffrey W. Bromiley and Thomas F. Torrance. Edinburgh: T & T Clark, 1956.

Basinger, David. *The Case for Freewill Theism: A Philosophical Assessment*. Downers Grove, IL: InterVarsity, 1996.

————. *Divine Power in Process Theism: A Philosophical Critique*. Albany: SUNY Press, 1988.

Beothius, Anicius Manlius Severinus. *The Consolation of Philosophy*. Translated by William Anderson. Carbondale, IL: Southern Illinois University Press, 1963.

Bergman, Jerry, and George Howe. *Vestigial Organs Are Fully Functional: A History and Evaluation of the Concept of Vestigial Organs*. Chino Valley, AZ: Creation Research Society Monograph, 1990.

Behe, Michael. *Darwin's Black Box: The Biochemical Challenge to Evolution*. New York: The Free Press, 1996.

Berkhof, Louis. *Systematic Theology*. 1939. Reprint, Grand Rapids: Eerdmans, 1993.

Berkouwer, G. C. *Faith and Sanctification*. Translated by Lewis B. Smedes. Grand Rapids: Eerdmans, 1954.

Bloesch, Donald G. *Holy Scripture: Revelation, Inspiration & Interpretation*. Downers Grove, IL: IVP, 1994.

Boettner, Loraine. *The Reformed Doctrine of Predestination*. Phillipsburg, NJ: Presbyterian & Reformed, 1932.

Boyd, Gregory A. *God of the Possible: A Biblical Introduction to the Open View of God*. Grand Rapids: Baker, 2000.

Brodrick, James. *Robert Bellarmine: Saint and Scholar*. London: Burns and Oates, 1961.

Brown, Raymond E. "The Gospel According to John XIII–XXI." *The Anchor Bible*. Vol. 29A, Garden City, NY: Doubleday, 1970.

Calvin, John. *Institutes of the Christian Religion*. Edited by John T. McNeill. Translated by Ford Lewis Battles. 2 vols. Louisville: Westminster, 1960.

_____. *Institutes of the Christian Religion*. Translated by Henry Bevridge. Peabody, MA: Hendrickson, 2008.

Chisholm, Roderick. *Person and Object: A Metaphysical Study*. LaSalle, IL: Open Court, 1976.

Cobb, Jr., John B., and David Ray Griffin. *Process Theology: An Introductory Exposition*. Philadelphia: Westminster, 1976.

Conzelmann, Hans. *1 Corinthians. Hermenia*. Edited by George W. MacRae. Translated by James W. Leitch. Philadelphia: Fortress, 1975.

Cooper, John W. *Panentheism: The Other God of the Philosophers: From Plato to the Present*. Grand Rapids: Baker, 2006.

Cornwell, John. *Hitler's Pope: The Secret History of Pius XII*. New York: Viking, 1999.

Craig, William Lane. *Divine Foreknowledge and Human Freedom*. Leiden: E.J. Brill, 1991.

_____. *The Only Wise God: The Compatibility of Divine Foreknowledge and Human Freedom*. Grand Rapids: Baker, 1987.

_____. *The Problem of Divine Foreknowledge and Future Contingents from Aristotle to Suarez*. Leiden: E.J. Brill, 1988.

Creegan, Nicola Hoggard. *Animal Suffering and the Problem of Evil*. New York: Oxford, 2013.

Davis, Stephen T., Editor. *Encountering Evil: Live Options in Theodicy*. Atlanta: John Knox, 1981.

_____. *Logic and the Nature Of God*. Grand Rapids: Eerdmans, 1983.

Demarest, Bruce. *The Cross and Salvation*. Wheaton, IL: Crossway, 2006.

Dembski, William. *The Design Inference: Eliminating Chance through Small Probabilities*. Cambridge: Cambridge University Press, 1982.

_____. *The Design Revolution*. Downers Grove, IL: InterVarsity, 2004.

_____. *No Free Lunch*. Lanham, MD: Rowman & Littlefield, 2002.

Dennett, Daniel C. *Darwin's Dangerous Idea: Evolution and the Meanings of Life*. New York: Touchstone, 1995.

Dougherty, Trent. *The Problem of Animal Pain: A Theodicy for All Creatures Great and Small*. New York: Palgrave Macmillan, 2014.

Dulles, Avery. *Models of Revelation*. Rev. ed. Maryknoll, NY: Orbis, 1992.

Edwards, Jonathan. *The Justice of God in the Damnation of Sinners*. Newark, NJ: John Tuttle & Co., 1814.

Ehrman, Bart D. *Misquoting Jesus: The Story Behind Who Changed the Bible and Why*. San Francisco: HarperOne, 2007.

Eliade, Mircea. *Shamanism: Archaic Techniques of Ecstasy*. Translated by Willard R. Trask. Trenton, NJ: Princeton University Press, 1964.

Erickson, Millard. *Christian Theology*. 3rd ed. Grand Rapids: Baker, 2013.

Fee, Gordon D. "The First Epistle to the Corinthians." In *The New International Commentary on the New Testament*. Grand Rapids: Eerdmans, 1987.

Feinberg, John S. *No One Like Him*. Wheaton, IL: Crossway, 2001.

Finney, Charles G. *Lectures on Revivals of Religion*. Rev. ed. New York: Fleming H. Revell, 1868.

Fischer, John Martin, and Mark Ravizza. *Responsibility and Control: A Theory of Moral Responsibility*. Cambridge: Cambridge University Press, 1998.

Flint, Thomas. *Divine Providence: The Molinist Account*. Ithaca, NY: Cornell University Press, 1998.

Forrest, Barbara, and Paul Gross. *Creationism's Trojan Horse; The Wedge of Intelligent Design*. Oxford: Oxford University Press, 2007.

Foster, Richard. *Celebration of Discipline: The Path to Spiritual Growth*. 1978. Reprint, San Francisco: Harper, 1998.

Frame, John. *The Doctrine of God: A Theology of Lordship*. Phillipsburg, NJ: Presbyterian & Reformed, 2002.

Fretheim, Terence. *The Suffering of God: An Old Testament Perspective*. Philadelphia: Fortress, 1984.

Fülüp-Meiller, René. *The Jesuits: A History of the Society of Jesus*. Translated by F. S. Flint and D. F. Tait. New York: Capricorn, 1963.

Garrigou-Lagrange, Reginald. *God: His Existence and His Nature*. 1934. Translated by Dom Bede Rose. 2 Vols. Reprint, Albany, NY: Preserving Christian Publications, 1993.

Geisler, Norman. *Systematic Theology, Volume 1: Introduction, Bible*. Minneapolis: Bethany House, 2002.

Gregory of Nyssa. *The Great Catechism*. In *Nicene and Post-Nicene Fathers*. Vol. 5. Edited by Phillip Schaff and Henry Wace. Translated by William Moore and Henry Austin Wilson, 471–509. Peabody, MA: Hendrickson, 1994.

Grotius, Hugo. *A Defence of the Catholic Faith Concerning the Satisfaction of Christ, against Faustus Socinus*. Translated by Frank Hugh Foster. Andover, MA: Warren F. Draper, 1889.

Grudem, Wayne. *Systematic Theology: An Introduction to Biblical Doctrine*. Grand Rapids: Zondervan, 1994.

Gunton, Colin. *The One, the Three and the Many*. Cambridge: Cambridge University Press, 1993.

Hamilton, Victor P. "The Book of Genesis, Chapters 18–50." *The New International Commentary on the Old Testament*. Grand Rapids: Eerdmans, 1995.

Harney, Martin P. *The Jesuits in History: The Society of Jesus Through Four Centuries*. New York: The America Press, 1941.

Harris, Sam. *Letter to a Christian Nation*. New York: Alfred K. Knopf, 2006; Vintage, 2008.

Hartshorne, Charles. *Omnipotence and Other Theological Mistakes*. Albany: SUNY, Press 1984.

Hasker, William. *God, Time and Knowledge*. Ithaca, NY: Cornell University Press, 1989.

Helm, Paul. *The Providence of God*. Downers Grove, IL: IVP, 1994.

Henry, Carl F. H. *God, Revelation and Authority*. 1976. 6 vols. Reprint, Wheaton, IL: Crossway, 1999.

Hoekema, Anthony A. *Saved by Grace*. Grand Rapids: Eerdmans, 1989.

Horton, Michael. *For Calvinism*. Grand Rapids: Zondervan, 2011.

Howard-Snyder, Daniel, Editor. *The Evidential Argument from Evil*. Bloomington: Indiana University Press, 1996.

Hume, David. *Dialogues Concerning Natural Religion*. Edited by Martin Bell. New York: Penguin, 1990.

Hunter, Cornelius G. *Darwin's Proof: The Triumph of Religion over Science*. Grand Rapids: Brazos, 2003.

Irenaeus. *Against Heresies*. In *Ante-Nicene Fathers*. Vol. 1. Translated and Edited by Alexander Roberts and James Donaldson, 309–567. Peabody, MA: Hendrickson, 1994.

Justin. *Apologie pour les chrétiens*. Edited by C. Munier. *Sources Chrétiennes* 507. Paris: Cerf, 2006.

Kaiser, Walter Jr., and Moisés Silva. *Introduction to Biblical Hermeneutics: The Search for Meaning*. 2nd Ed. Grand Rapids: Zondervan, 2007.

Keathley, Kenneth. *Salvation and Sovereignty: A Molinist Approach*. Nashville: Broadman & Holman, 2010.

Kenny, Anthony. *The God of the Philosophers*. Oxford: Clarendon, 1979.

Kren, George M., and Leon Rappoport. *The Holocaust and the Crisis of Human Behavior*. New York: Holms & Meier, 1980.

Kittelson, James M. *Luther the Reformer: The Story of the Man and His Career*. Minneapolis: Augsburg, 1986.

Kvanvig, Jonathan. *The Possibility of an All-Knowing God*. New York: St. Martin's Press, 1986.

Lewis, David K. *Counterfactuals*. Cambridge: Harvard University Press, 1973.

Lindsell, Harold. *Battle for the Bible*. Grand Rapids: Zondervan, 1978.

Little, Bruce A. *A Creation-Order Theodicy: God and Gratuitous Evil*. Lanham, MD: University Press of America, 2005.

Luther, Martin. *The Bondage of the Will*. Edited by Philip S. Watson. Translated by P. S. Watson. *Luther's Works*. Vol. 33, *Career of the Reformer III*. Philadelphia: Fortress, 1972.

————. *De Servo Arbitrio*. In *D. Martin Luthers Werke: Kritische Gesamtausgabe*, 18:600–787. Weimar: Hermann Böhlaus Nachfolger, 1908.

Mackie, J. L. *The Miracle of Theism*. Oxford: Clarendon, 1982.

Madden, Edward H., and Peter H. Hare. *Evil and the Concept of God*. Springfield, IL: Charles H. Thomas, 1968.

Mare, W. Harold. "1 Corinthians" in *Expositor's Bible Commentary*, Vol. 10: *Romans-Galatians*. Edited by Frank E. Gaebelein, 173–298. Grand Rapids: Zondervan, 1976.

Matthews, Kenneth A. "Genesis 11:27–50: 26." *The New American Commentary*. Vol. 1B. Nashville: Broadman & Holman, 2005.

McBrien, Richard P. *Lives of the Popes: The Pontiffs from St. Peter to John Paul II*. San Francisco: Harper, 1997.

McComiskey, Thomas E. *Daniel-Minor Prophets*. *The Expositor's Bible Commentary*. Vol. 7. Grand Rapids: Zondervan, 1985.

McGrath, Alister E. *Christian Theology: An Introduction*. Cambridge: Blackwell, 1994.

McTaggart, J. M. E. *The Nature of Existence*. 1927. 2 Vols. Reprint, Cambridge: Cambridge University Press, 1968.

Mesle, C. Robert. *Process Theology: A Basic Introduction*. St. Louis, Chalice, 1993.

Miley, John. *Systematic Theology*. 3 Vols. New York: Hunt & Eaton, 1893.

Miller, Kenneth R. *Finding Darwin's God*. New York: Perennial, 1999.

Molina, Ludovicus. *Liberi Arbitrii Cum Gratiae Donis, Divina Praescientia, Providentia, Praedestinatione et Reprobatione Concordia*. Edited by Johannes Rabenek. Oña and Madrid: Soc. Edit. "Sapientia", 1853.

————. *On Divine Foreknowledge (Part IV of the Concordia)*. Translated by Alfred J. Freddoso. Ithaca, NY: Cornell University Press, 1988.

Morris, Henry. *Scientific Creationism*. 2nd ed. Green Forest, AR: Master Books, 1985.

Morris, Leon. "The Gospel According to John." *The New International Commentary on the New Testament*. Rev. ed. Grand Rapids: Eerdmans, 1995.

Morris, Thomas V., Editor. *The Concept of God*. Oxford: Oxford University Press, 1987.

Murphy, Nancey. *Beyond Liberalism and Fundamentalism*. Valley Forge, PA: Trinity Press International, 1996.

Murphy, Nancey, and George F. R. Ellis. *On the Moral Nature of the Universe: Theology, Cosmology, and Ethics*. Minneapolis: Fortress, 1996.

Murray, John. *Redemption-Accomplished and Applied*. Grand Rapids: Eerdmans, 1955.

Murray, Michael. *Nature Red in Tooth and Claw: Theism and the Problem of Animal Suffering*. New York: Oxford, 2011.

Oden, Thomas C. *The Word of Life*. San Francisco: Harper Collins, 1989.

Olson, Roger E. *Against Calvinism*. Grand Rapids: Zondervan, 2011.

Origen. *Contra Celsus*. Edited by P. Koetschau. Vol. 1 of *Origenes Werke. Die Griechischen Christlichen Schriftsteller der ersten drei Jahrhunderte*, vol. 2. Leipzig: J. D. Hinrichßche Buchhandlung, 1899.

_____. *Contra Celsum*. 1953. Translated by Henry Chadwick. Cambridge: Cambridge University Press, 1980.

Orr, William F., and James Arthur Walther. "1 Corinthians." In *The Anchor Bible*. Vol. 32, New York: Doubleday, 1976.

Osborne, Grant R. *The Hermeneutical Spiral*. Downers Grove, IL: IVP, 1991.

Pastor, Ludwig von. *The History of the Popes from the Close of the Middle Ages*. 40 Vols. Translated by E. F. Peeler. London: Routledge and Kegan Paul, 1899–1953.

Pennock, Robert. *Tower of Babel: The Evidence against the New Creationism*. Cambridge, MA: MIT Press, 1999.

Peterson, Michael L., Editor. *The Problem of Evil: Selected Readings, Library of Religious Philosophy 8*. Notre Dame, IN: University of Notre Dame Press, 1992.

Pike, Nelson. *God and Timelessness*. New York: Schocken, 1970.

Pinnock, Clark, et al. *The Openness of God: A Biblical Challenge to the Traditional Understanding of God*. Downers Grove, IL: IVP, 1994.

Plantinga, Alvin. *God and Other Minds*. Ithaca: Cornell, 1967.

_____. *God, Freedom and Evil*. Grand Rapids: Eerdmans, 1974.

_____. *The Nature of Necessity*. Oxford: Clarendon, 1974, repr. 1982.

_____. *Warranted Christian Belief*. Oxford: Oxford, 2000.

Plantinga, Alvin, and Nicholas Wolterstorff, Editors. *Faith and Rationality: Reason and Belief in God*. Notre Dame, IN: University of Notre Dame Press, 1983.

Plato. *Timaeus*. Edited by Oskar Piest. Translated by Francis M. Cornford. Indianapolis: Bobbs-Merrill Co., 1959.

Plotinus. *The Enneads*. Translated by Stephen MacKenna. London: Penguin, 1991.

Polkinghorne, John. *Science and Theology: An Introduction*. Minneapolis: Fortress, 1998.

_____. *Serious Talk: Science and Religion in Dialogue*. Valley Forge, PA: Trinity Press International, 1995.

Ratzsch, Del. *The Battle of Beginnings: Why Neither Side Is Winning the Creation-Evolution Debate*. Downers Grove, IL: IVP, 1996.

Rice, Richard. *God's Foreknowledge and Man's Free Will*. Minneapolis: Bethany House, 1985.

_____. *The Openness of God*. Minneapolis: Bethany House, 1980.

Robertson, Archibald T. *A Grammar of the Greek New Testament in the Light of Historical Research*. 4th ed. Nashville: Broadman, 1934.

Robertson, Archibald, and Alfred Plummer. "A Critical and Exegetical Commentary on the First Epistle of St. Paul to the Corinthians." *International Critical Commentary*. New York: Charles Scribner's Sons, 1911.

Robinson, Michael. *Eternity and Freedom: A Critical Analysis of Divine Timelessness as a Solution to the Foreknowledge/free Will Debate*. New York: University Press of America, 1993.

Rooker, Mark F., and Kenneth D. Keathley. *40 Questions about Creation*. Grand Rapids: Kregel, 2014.

Rosén, Haiim. *A Textbook of Israeli Hebrew*. Chicago: University of Chicago Press, 1962.

Ross, Alan. "Proverbs." *The Expositor's Bible Commentary, Psalms-Song of Songs*. Vol. 5. Grand Rapids: Zondervan, 1991.

Rubenstein, Richard L. *After Auschwitz: Radical Theology and Contemporary*. Indianapolis: Bobbs-Merrill, 1966.

Rubenstein, Richard L., and John K. Roth. *Approaches to Auschwitz: The Holocaust and Its Legacy*. Atlanta: John Knox, 1987.

Ruse, Michael. *Darwinism and Its Discontents*. Cambridge: Cambridge University Press, 2006.

Sanders, John. *The God Who Risks: A Theology of Providence*. Downers Grove, IL: InterVarsity, 1998.

Scott, R. B. Y. *Proverbs, Ecclesiastes. The Anchor Bible*. New York: Doubleday, 1965.

Skinner, John. *A Critical and Exegetical Commentary On Geneses, ICC*. 2nd ed. Vol. 1. Edinburgh: T & T Clark, 1930.

Speiser, E. A. *Genesis. The Anchor Bible*. New York: Doubleday, 1962.

Sproul, R. C. *Chosen by God*. Wheaton, IL: Tyndale, 1988.

Steinmetz, Andrew. *History of the Jesuits*. 39 Vols. London: Richard Bentley, 1848.

Steward, Kenneth. *Ten Myths About Calvinism: Recovering the Breadth of the Reformed Tradition*. Downers Grove, IL: IVP, 2011.

Stott, John R.W. *The Cross of Christ*. Downers Grove, IL: IVP, 1986.

Suchocki, Marjorie Hewitt. *The End of Evil*. Albany: SUNY Press, 1988.

Swinburne, Richard. *The Coherence of Theism*. Rev. ed. Oxford: Clarendon, 1993.

_____. *The Existence of God*. Rev. ed. Oxford: Oxford Universty Press, 1990.

The Racovian Catechism. Translated by Thomas Rees. London: Longman, Horst, Rees, Orme and Brown, 1818.

Tertullianus. *Apologeticum. Corpus Christianium, Series Latina*. Edited by Dom Eligius Dekkers, 1:77–172. Turnhout, Belgium: Brepols, 1954.

Thiselton, Anthony C. "The First Epistle to the Corinthians: A Commentary on the Greek Text." *The New International Greek Testament Commentary*. Grand Rapids: Eerdmans, 2000.

Toy, Crawford H. *A Critical and Exegetical Commentary on the Book of Proverbs, International Critical Commentary*. Edinburgh: T & T Clark, 1899.

Turretin, Francis. *Institutes of Elenctic Theology*. Edited by James T. Dennison Jr. Translated by George Musgrave Giger. 3 Vols. Phillipsburg, NJ: Presbyterian & Reformed, 1994.

van Inwagen, Peter. *An Essay on Free Will*. Oxford: Clarendon, 1983.

von Ranké, Leopold. *History of the Popes: Their Church and State*. 3 Volumes. Translated by E. Fowler. New York: Colonial, 1901.

Ware, Bruce A. *God's Greater Glory: The Exalted God of Scripture and the Christian Faith*. Wheaton, IL: Crossway, 2004

_____. *God's Lesser Glory: The Diminished God of Open Theism*. Wheaton, IL: Crossway, 2000.

Warfield, Benjamin B. "Biblical Idea of Inspiration." In *Inspiration and Authority of the Bible*, Edited by Samuel G. Craig. Philadelphia: Presbyterian & Reformed, 1970.

Wenham, Gordon J. "Genesis 16–50." In *Word Biblical Commentary*. Vol. 2. Dallas: Word, 1994.

Wierenga, Edward. *The Nature of God: An Inquiry into Divine Attributes*. Ithaca, NY: Cornell Universty Press, 1989.

Wiesel, Elie. *Night*. Translated by Stella Rodway. New York: Bantam, 1960.

————. *The Trial of God*. Translated by Marion Wiesel. New York: Schocken, 1979.

William of Ockham. *Ordinatio*. In *Philosophical Writings: A Selection*. Translated by Philotheus Boehner. Indianapolis: Bobbs-Merrill, 1964.

————. *Predestination, God's Foreknowledge, and Future Contingents*. 2nd ed. Translated by Marilyn McCord Adams and Norman Kretzmann. Indianapolis: Hackett, 1983.

Williams, J. Rodman. *Renewal Theology*. Grand Rapids: Zondervan, 1996.

Wright, R. K. McGregor. *No Place for Sovereignty: What's Wrong with Freewill Theism*. Downers Grove, IL: InterVarsity, 1996.

Zagzebski, Linda. *The Dilemma of Freedom and Foreknowledge*. New York: Oxford University Press, 1991.

ESSAYS AND ARTICLES

Adams, Marilyn McCord. "Is the Existence of God a 'Hard' Fact?" *Philosophical Review* 76:4 (1967): 492–503.

Adams, Robert Merrihew. "Middle Knowledge and the Problem of Evil." *American Philosophical Quarterly* 14:2 (April 1977): 109–17.

————. "Must God Create the Best?" *Philosophical Review* 81:3 (1972): 317–32.

————. "An Anti-Molinist Argument." In *Philosphical Perspectives 5: Philosophy of Religion*. Edited by James E. Tomberlin, 343–54. Atascadero, CA: Ridgeview, 1991.

Aikin, Scott, and Brian Ribeiro. "Skeptical Theism, Moral Skepticism, and Divine Commands." *International Journal for the Study of Skepticism* 3 (2003): 77–96.

Almeida, Michael, and Graham Oppy. "Evidential Arguments from Evil and Skeptical Theism." *Philo* 8:2 (Winter 2005): 84–94.

Alston, William P. "Does God Have Beliefs?" *Religious Studies* 22:3/4 (1986): 287–306.

————. "The Inductive Argument from Evil and the Human Cognitive Condition." In *Philosophical Perspectives 5: Philosophy of Religion*. Edited by James E. Tomberlin, 29–68. Atascadero, CA: Ridgeview, 1991.

Anderson, C. Anthony. "Divine Omnipotence and Impossible Tasks: An Intensional Analysis." *International Journal for Philosophy of Religion* 15 (1984): 109–24.

Bar-Hillel, Maya, and Avishai Margalit. "Newcomb's Paradox Revisited." *British Journal for the Philosophy of Science* 23 (1972): 295–304.

Basinger, David. "Divine Control and Human Freedom: Is Middle Knowledge the Answer?" *Journal of the Evangelical Theological Society* 36:1 (March 1993): 55–64.

————. "Divine Omniscience and Human Freedom: A 'Middle Knowledge' Perspective." *Faith and Philosophy* 1:3 (July 1984): 291–302.

————. "In What Sense Must God Be Omnibenevolent?" *International Journal for Philosophy of Religion* 14:1 (1983): 3–15.

————. "In What Sense Must God Do His Best: A Response to Hasker." *International Journal for Philosophy of Religion* 18 (1985): 161–64.

————. "Middle Knowledge and Divine Control." *International Journal for Philosophy of Religion* 30:3 (1991): 129–39.

————. "Practical Implications." In *The Openness of God: A Biblical Challenge to the Traditional Understanding of God*. Clark Pinnock, et al., 155–76. Downers Grove, IL: IVP, 1994.

————. "Why Petition an Omnipotent, Omniscient, Wholly Good God?" *Religious Studies* 19 (1983): 24–41.

Beaudoin, John. "Skepticism and the Skeptical Theist." *Faith and Philosophy* 22:1 (January 2005): 42–56.

Bergmann, Michael. "Skeptical Theism and Rowe's New Evidential Argument from Evil." *Nous* 35:2 (2001): 278–96.

Bergmann, Michael, and Michael Rea. "In Defense of Skeptical Theism: A Reply to Almeida and Oppy." *Australasian Journal of Philosophy* 83:2 (June 2005): 241–51.

Boyd, Gregory A. "Neo-Molinism and the Infinite Intelligence of God." *Philosophia Christi* 5:1 (2003): 187–204.

————. "The Open Theism View." In *Divine Foreknowledge: Four Views*. Edited by James K. Beilby and Paul Eddy, 13–47. Downers Grove, IL: IVP, 2001.

Bromiley, Geoffrey W. "The Church Doctrine of Inspiration." In *Revelation and the Bible: Contemporary Evangelical Thought*. Edited by Carl F. H. Henry, 203–18. Grand Rapids: Baker, 1958.

Chrzan, Keith. "God and Gratuitous Evil: A Reply to Yandell." *Religious Studies* 27 (1991): 99–103.

————. "Necessary Gratuitous Evil: An Oxymoron Revisited." *Faith and Philosophy* 11:1 (January 1994): 134–37.

————. "When is a Gratuitous Evil Really Gratuitous?" *Philosophy of Religion* 24 (1988): 87–91; reprinted *Sophia* 30:2–3 (1992): 23–9.

Craig, William Lane. "Hasker on Divine Knowledge." *Philosophical Studies* 67 (1992): 88–110.

————. "Men Moved by the Holy Spirit Spoke from God: A Middle Knowledge Perspective on Biblical Inspiration." *Philosophia Christi* 1:1 (1999): 45–82.

————. "Middle Knowledge: A Calvinist-Arminian Rapprochement?" In *The Grace of God and the Will of Man*. Edited by Clark H. Pinnock, 141–64. Minneapolis: Bethany House, 1989.

————. "Nice Soft Facts: Fischer on Foreknowledge." *Religious Studies* 25:2 (1989): 235–46.

————. "On Hasker's Defense of Anti-Molinism." *Faith and Philosophy* 15:2 (April 1998): 236–40.

————. "Robert Adams's New Anti-Molinist Argument." *Philosophy and Phenomenological Research* 54:4 (December 1994): 857–61.

Davis, John Jefferson. "'Is 'Progressive Creation' Still a Helpful Concept? Reflections on Creation, Evolution, and Bernard Ramm's Christian View of Science and Scripture-A Generation Later." *Perspectives on Science and Christian Faith* 50 (December 1998): 250–59.

Davis, Stephen T. "Free Will and Evil." In *Encountering Evil: Live Options in Theodicy.* Edited by Stephen T. Davis, 69–100. Atlanta: John Knox, 1981.

Dembski, William. "What Every Theologian Should Know about Creation, Evolution and Design." *Center for Interdisciplinary Studies Transaction* 3:2 (1995): 1–3.

Draper, Paul. "Pain and Pleasure: An Evidential Problem for Theists." *Nous* 23 (1989): 331–50.

Durston, Kirk. "The Complexity of History and Evil: A Reply to Trakakis." *Religious Studies* 42 (2006): 87–99.

_____. "The Consequential Complexity of History and Gratuitous Evil." *Religious Studies* 36 (2000): 65–80.

_____. "The Failure of Type-4 Arguments from Evil, in the Face of the Consequential Complexity of History." *Philo* 8:2 (2006): 109–22.

Dyson, R.W. "St. Augustine's Remarks on Time." *The Downside Review* 100 (July 1982): 221–30.

Feinberg, John. "God Ordains All Things." In *Predestination and Free Will: Four Views of Divine Sovereignty and Human Freedom.* Edited by David Basinger and Randall Basinger, 17–60. Downers Grove, IL: IVP, 1986.

Fischer, John Martin. "Freedom and Foreknowledge." *The Philosophical Review* 92:1 (January 1983): 67–79.

_____. "Putting Molinism in its Place." In *Molinism: The Contemporary Debate.* Edited by Kenneth Perszyk, 208–26. Oxford: Oxford University Press, 2012.

_____. "Snapshot Ockhamism." In *Philosophical Perspectives, Volume 5: Philosophy of Religion.* Edited by James E. Tomberlin, 355–72. Atascadero, CA: Ridgeview, 1991.

Fischer, John Martin and Mark Ravizza. "Responsibility and Inevitability." *Ethics* 101 (January 1991): 258–78.

Fitzgerald, Paul. "Stump and Kretzmann on Time and Eternity." *The Journal of Philosophy* 82 (1985): 260–69.

Flint, Thomas P. "Divine Sovereignty and the Free Will Defense." *Sophia* 23 (July 1984): 41–52.

_____. "Hasker's *God, Time, and Knowledge.*" *Philosophical Studies* 60 (1990): 103–15.

_____. "In Defense of Theological Compatibilism." *Faith and Philosophy* 8:2 (April 1991): 237–43.

_____. "Middle Knowledge and the Doctrine of Infallibility." In *Philosophical Perspectives, Volume 5: Philosophy of Religion.* Edited by James E. Tomberlin, 373–94. Atascadero, CA: Ridgeview, 1991.

_____. "A new anti-anti-Molinist argument." *Religious Studies* 35:3 (September 1999): 299–305.

_____. "Two Accounts of Providence." In *Divine and Human Action.* Edited by Thomas V. Morris, 147–81. Ithaca, NY: Cornell University Press, 1988.

Flint, Thomas P. and Alfred J. Freddoso. "Maximal Power." In *The Existence and Nauture of God.* Edited by Alfred J. Freddoso, 81–113. Notre Dame, IN: Notre Dame University Press, 1983, also in *The Concept of God.* Edited by Thomas V. Morris, 134–167. New York: Oxford University Press, 1987.

Foster, J., and Daryn Lehoux. "The Delphic Oracle and the Ethylene-Intoxication Hypothesis." *Clinical Toxicology* 45:1 (2007): 85–89.

Frankfurt, Harry G. "Alternate Possibilities and Moral Responsibility." *Journal of Philosophy* 66 (1969): 828–39.

————. "Freedom of the Will and the Concept of a Person." *Journal of Philosophy* 68 (1971): 5–20.

Freddoso, Alfred J. "Accidental Necessity and Logical Determinism." *Journal of Philosophy* 80:5 (May 1983): 257–78.

————. "Accidental Necessity and Power Over the Past." *Pacific Philosophical Quarterly* 63 (1982): 54–68.

————. "Human Nature, Potency and the Incarnation." *Faith and Philosophy* 3:1 (1986): 27–53.

————. "Introduction." In *On Divine Foreknowledge: Part IV of the Concordia*, Translated and Edited by Alfred J. Freddoso, 1–81. Ithaca, NY: Cornell University Press, 1988.

Friedman, R. Z. "Evil and Moral Agency." *Philosophy of Religion* 24 (1988): 6–17.

Gaskin, Richard. "Conditionals of Freedom and Middle Knowledge." *The Philosophical Quarterly* 43:173 (October 1993): 412–30.

————. "Middle knowledge, fatalism and comparative similarity of worlds." *Religious Studies* 34:2 (May 1998): 189–203.

Gowen, Jule. "God and Timelessness: Everlasting or Eternal?" *Sophia* 26 (March 1987): 15–29.

Gunton, Colin. "Time, Eternity and the Doctrine of the Incarnation." *Dialog* 21 (Fall 1982): 263–68.

Hasker, William. "Anti-Molinism Undefeated!" *Faith and Philosophy* 17:1 (January2000): 126–31.

————. "The Antinomies of Divine Providence." Paper presented at the Eastern Division meeting of the American Philosophical Association, Washington, DC, December 1998. *Philosophia Christi* 4:2 (2002): 361–75.

————. "Are alternative pasts plausible? A reply to Thomas Flint." *Religious Studies* 36:1 (March 2000): 103–05.

————. "Chrzan on Necessary Gratuitous Evil." *Faith and Philosophy* 12:3 (July 1995): 423–25.

————. "Defining 'Gratuitous Evil': A Response to Alan R. Rhoda." *Religious Studies* 46:3 (2010): 303–09.

————. "Explanatory Priority: Transitive and Unequivocal, A Reply to William Craig." *Philosophy and Phenomenological Research* 57:2 (June 1997): 389–93.

————. "Foreknowledge and Necessity." *Faith and Philosophy* 2:2 (April 1985): 121–57.

————. "The Hardness of the Past: A Reply to Reichenbach." *Faith and Philosophy* 4:3 (1987): 337–42.

————. "How Good/Bad is Middle Knowledge? A Reply to Basinger." *International Journal for Philosophy of Religion* 33:2 (1993): 111–18.

————. "Middle Knowledge and the Damnation of the Heathen: A Response to William Craig." *Faith and Philosophy* 8:3 (July 1991): 380–89.

————. "Middle Knowledge: A Refutation Revisited." *Faith and Philosophy* 12:2 (April 1995): 223–36.

————. "Must God Do His Best?" *International Journal for Philosophy of Religion* 16:3 (1984): 213–23.

————. "The Necessity of Gratuitous Evil." *Faith and Philosophy* 9:1 (January 1992): 23–44.

————. "A New Anti-Molinist Argument." *Religious Studies* 35:3 (September 1999): 291–97.

————. "O'Connor on Gratuitous Natural Evil." *Faith and Philosophy* 14:3 (July 1997): 388–94.

————. "A Philosophical Perspective." In *The Openness of God: A Biblical Challenge to the Traditional Understanding of God.* Clark Pinnock, et al., 126–54. Downers Grove: IVP, 1994.

————. "Providence and Evil: Three Theories." *Religious Studies* 28:1 (March 1992): 91–105.

————. "A Refutation of Middle Knowledge." *Nous* 20 (1986): 545–57.

————. "Reply to Basinger on Power Entailment." *Faith and Philosophy* 5:1 (January 1988): 87–90.

————. "Response to Thomas Flint." *Philosophical Studies* 60 (1990): 117–26.

————. "Simplicity and Freedom: A Response to Stump and Kretzmann." *Faith and Philosophy* 3:2 (April 1986): 192–201.

————. "Yes, God Has Beliefs." *Religious Studies* 24 (September 1988): 385–94.

————. "Zagzebski on Power Entailment." *Faith and Philosophy* 10:2 (April 1993): 250–55.

Hoffman, Joshua, and Gary Rosenkrantz. "Hard and Soft Facts." *The Philosophical Review* 93:3 (July 1984): 419–34.

Horgan, Terence. "Counterfactuals and Newcomb's Problem." *Journal of Philosophy* 78 (1981): 331–56.

Huffmon, Herbert B. "The Treaty Background of Hebrew Yada." *Bulletin of the American Schools of Oriental Research* 181 (February 1996): 31–37.

Hunt, David Paul. "Divine Providence and Simple Foreknowledge." *Faith and Philosophy* 10:3 (July 1993): 394–414.

————. "Middle Knowledge: The 'Foreknowledge Defense." *International Journal for Philosophy of Religion* 28 (1990): 1–24.

————. "Prescience and Providence: A Reply to My Critics." *Faith and Philosophy* 10:3 (July 1993): 428–38.

Inman, Ross. "Gratuitous Evil Unmotivated: A Reply to Kirk R. MacGregor." *Philosophia Christi* 15:2 (2013): 435–45.

Keene, G.B. "A Simpler Solution to the Paradox of Omnipotence." *Mind* 69 (January 1960): 74–75.

Keene, G.B. "Capacity-Limiting Statements." *Mind* 70 (1961): 251–52.

Kripke, Saul. "Semantical Considerations on Modal Logic." *Acta Philosophica Fennica* 16 (1963): 83–94.

Laing, John D. "The Compatibility of Calvinism and Middle Knowledge." *Journal of the Evangelical Theological Society* 47, no. 3 (September 2004): 455–67.

————. "The New Atheism: Lessons for Evangelicals." *Southwestern Journal of Theology* 54:1 (Fall 2011): 13–28.

Leftow, Brian. "Eternity and Simultaneity." *Faith and Philosophy* 8:2 (April 1991): 148–79.

Lehoux, Daryn. "Drugs and the Delphic Oracle." *Classical World* 10:1 (2007): 41–56.

Lewis, Delmas. "Eternity, Time and Tenselessness." *Faith and Philosophy* 5:1 (January 1988): 72–86.

Lewis, Gordon. "The Human Authorship of Inspired Scripture." In *Inerrancy*. Edited by Norman Geisler, 229–66. Grand Rapids: Baker, 1980.

Linville, Mark. "Ockhamists and Molinists in Search of a Way Out." *Religious Studies* 31:4 (December 1995): 501–15.

Locke, Don. "How to Make a Newcomb Choice." *Analysis* 38 (1978): 17–23.

Looper, Bernard M. "Process Theology: Origins, Strengths, Weaknesses." *Process Studies* 16:4 (Winter 1987): 245–54.

Luther, Martin. "The Bondage of the Will." In *Martin Luther's Basic Theological Writings*. Edited by Timothy F. Lull, 173–226. Minneapolis: Fortress, 1989.

Mackie, J.L. "Evil and Omnipotence." *Mind* 64:254 (April 1965): 200–12.

MacGregor, Kirk. "The Existence and Irrelevance of Gratuitous Evil." *Philosophia Christi* 14, no. 1 (2012): 165–80.

Madden, Edward H. "The Many Faces of Evil." *Philosophy and Phenomenological Research* 24:4 (1964): 481–92.

Madden, Edward H., and Peter H. Hare. "Evil and Inconclusiveness." *Sophia* 11:1 (April 1972): 8–12.

————. "Evil and Unlimited Power." *Review of Metaphysics* 20:2 (1966): 278–89.

Mavrodes, George. "Necessity, Possibility, and the Stone Which Cannot Be Moved." *Faith and Philosophy* 2:3 (July 1985): 265–71.

————. "Some Puzzles Concerning Omnipotence." *Philosophical Review* 72:2 (1963): 221–23.

Mayo, Bernard. "Mr. Keene on Omnipotence." *Mind* 70:278 (1961): 249–50.

McBrayer, Justin. "Evidential Arguments from Evil and the 'Seeability' of Compensating Goods." *Auslegung* 27:1 (Winter/Spring 2004): 17–22.

————. "CORNEA and Inductive Evidence." *Faith and Philosophy* 26:1 (2009): 77–86.

Mele, Alfred R., and M. P. Smith. "The New Paradox of the Stone." *Faith and Philosophy* 5:3 (July 1988): 283–90.

Nelson, Herbert J. "Time(s), Eternity, and Duration." *International Journal for the Philosophy of Religion* 22:1–2 (1987): 3–19.

Novak, David. "Arguing Israel and the Holocaust" *First Things* 109 (January 2001): 11–14.

Nozick, Robert. "Newcomb's Problem and Two Principles of Choice." In *Essays in Honor of Carl G. Hampel*. Edited by Nicholas Rescher, 114–46. Dordrecht: D. Reidel, 1969.

Oaklander, L. Nathan. "A Defense of the New Tenseless Theory of Time." *The Philosophical Quarterly* 41:162 (January 1991): 26–38.

_____. "The New Tenseless Theory of Time: A Reply to Smith." *Philosophical Studies* 58:3 (March 1990): 287–92.

O'Connor, David. "Hasker on Gratuitous Natural Evil." *Faith and Philosophy* 12:3 (July 1995): 380–92.

_____. "The Impossibility of Middle Knowledge." *Philosophical Studies* 66 (1992): 139–66.

O'Leary-Hawthorne, John, and Daniel Howard-Snyder. "God Schmod and Gratuitous Evil." *Philosophy and Phenomenological Research* 53:4 (December 1993): 861–74.

Otte, Richard. "A Defense of Middle Knowledge." *International Journal for Philosophy of Religion* 21 (1987): 161–69.

Parsons, Keith. "Evil and the Unknown Purpose Defense: Remarks Addressed to Theodore Drange's Nonbelief and Evil." *Philo* 8:2 (Fall/Winter 2005): 160–68.

Perszyk, Kenneth. "Free Will Defense with and without Molinism." *International Journal for Philosophy of Religion* 43 (1998): 29–64.

_____. "Molinism and Theodicy." *International Journal for Philosophy of Religion* 44 (1998): 163–84.

_____. "Stump's Theodicy of Redemptive Suffering and Molinism." *Religious Studies* 25:2 (June 1999): 191–211.

Phillips, Richard D. "Prayer and the Sovereignty of God." In *Let Us Pray: A Symposium On Prayer by Leading Preachers and Theologians*. Orlando, FL: Northampton, 2011.

Pike, Nelson. "Divine Omniscience and Voluntary Action." *Philosophical Review* 74:1 (January 1965): 27–46.

_____. "Of God and Freedom: A Rejoinder." *Philosophical Review* 75:3 (July 1966): 369–79.

_____. "Plantinga on the Free Will Defense: A Reply." *Journal of Philosophy* 63:4 (1966): 93–104.

Pinnock, Clark. "God Limits His Knowledge." In *Predestination and Free Will: Four Views of Divine Sovereignty and Human Freedom*. Edited by David Basinger and Randall Basinger, 141–77. Downers Grove, IL: InterVarsity, 1986.

_____. "Systematic Theology." In *The Openness of God: A Biblical Challenge to the Traditional Understanding of God*. Clark Pinnock, et al., 101–25. Downers Grove, IL: IVP, 1994.

Piper, Mark. "Why Theists Cannot Accept Skeptical Theism." *Sophia* 47:2 (July 2008): 129–48.

Plantinga, Alvin. "On Ockham's Way Out." *Faith and Philosophy* 3:3 (July 1986): 235–69.

_____. "Replies." In *Alvin Plantinga: Profiles*. Edited by James E. Tomberlin and Peter van Inwagen, 313–98. Dordrecht: D. Reidel, 1985.

Quinn, Philip L. "Divine Foreknowledge and Divine Freedom." *International Journal for Philosophy of Religion* 9:4 (1978): 219–40.

Reichenbach, Bruce. "God Limits His Power." In *Predestination & Free Will*. Edited by David Basinger and Randall Basinger, 99–140. Downers Grove, IL: InterVarsity, 1986.

_____. "Hasker on Omniscience." *Faith and Philosophy* 4:1 (1987): 86–92.

Rhoda, Alan R. "Gratuitous Evil and Divine Providence." *Religious Studies* 46 (2010): 281–302.

Rice, Richard. "Biblical Support for a New Perspective." In *The Openness of God: A Biblical Challenge to the Traditional Understanding of God*. Clark Pinnock, et al., 11–58. Downers Grove. IL: IVP, 1994.

Rogers, Katherin A. "Eternity Has No Duration." *Religious Studies* 30 (March 1994): 1–16.

Rowe, William. "The Problem of Evil and Some Varieties of Atheism." *American Philosophical Quarterly* 16:4 (1979): 335–41.

_____. "Ruminations About Evil." In *Philosophical Perspectives, 5: Philosophy of Religion*. Edited by James E. Tomberlin, 69–88. Atascadero, CA: Ridgeview, 1991.

_____. "Skeptical Theism: A Response to Bergmann." *Nous* 35:2 (2001): 297–303.

Rubenstein, Richard L., and Elie Wiesel. "An Exchange." In *Holocaust: Religious and Philosophical Implications*. Edited by John K. Roth and Michael Berenbaum, 349–70. New York: Paragon House, 1989.

Rubenstein, Richard L. "Some Perspectives on Religious Faith after Auschwitz." In *The German Church Struggle and the Holocaust*. Edited by Franklin H. Littell and Hubert G. Locke, 256–61. Detroit: Wayne State University Press, 1974.

Russell, Bruce. "Defenseless." In *The Evidential Argument from Evil*. Edited by Daniel Howard-Snyder, 193–205. Bloomington: Indiana University Press, 1996.

_____. "The Persistent Problem of Evil." *Faith and Philosophy* 6:2 (1989): 121–39.

Sanders, John. "God as Personal." In *The Grace of God and the Will of Man*. Edited by Clark H. Pinnock, 165–80. Minneapolis: Bethany House, 1989.

_____. "Historical Considerations." In *The Openness of God: A Biblical Challenge to the Traditional Understanding of God*. Clark Pinnock, et al., 59–100. Downers Grove, IL: IVP, 1994.

Saunders, John Turk. "Of God and Freedom." *Philosophical Review* 75:2 (April 1966): 219–25.

Savage, C. Wade. "The Paradox of the Stone." *Philosophical Review* 76 (1967): 74–79.

Schlesinger, George. "Omnipotence and Evil: An Incoherent Problem." *Sophia* 4:3 (1965): 21–24.

_____. "The Problem of Evil and the Problem of Suffering." *American Philosophical Quarterly* 1:3 (July 1964): 244–47.

Senor, Thomas D. "Incarnation and Timelessness." *Faith and Philosophy* 7:2 (April 1990): 149–64.

Sheppard, Gerald T., and William E. Herbrechtsmeier. "Prophecy: An Overview." In *The Encyclopedia of Religion*. Edited by Mircea Eliade, 12:8–14. New York: Simon & Schuster Macmillan, 1995.

Smith, Quentin. "Problems with the New Tenseless Theory of Time." *Philosophical Studies* 52 (November 1987): 371–92.

Spiller, Henry A., John R. Hale, and Jelle Zeilinga de Boer. "The Delphic Oracle: A Multidisciplinary Defense of the Gaseous Vent Theory." *Clinical Toxicology* 40:2 (2002): 189–96.

Stalnaker, Robert C. "A Theory of Conditionals." In *Studies in Logical Theory, American Philosophical Quarterly Monograph No. 2*, 98–112. Pittsburgh/Oxford: University of Pittsburgh Press/Basil Blackwell, 1968.

Stegmüler, Friedrich. "Molinas Leben und Werk." In *Geschichte des Molinismus*. Edited by Friedrich Stegmüler, 1*–80*. Münster: Verlag der Aschendorffschen Verlagsbuchhandlung, 1935.

Stump, Eleonore and Norman Kretzmann. "Eternity." *Journal of Philosophy* 78 (1981), 429–458; Reprinted in *The Concept of God.* Edited by Thomas V. Morris, 219–252. Oxford: Oxford University Press, 1987.

————. "Eternity, Awareness, and Action." *Faith and Philosophy* 9:4 (October 1992): 463–482.

————. "Prophecy, Past Truth, and Eternity." In *Philosophical Perspectives, Volume 5: Philosophy of Religion.* Edited by James E. Tomberlin, 395–424. Atascadero, CA: Ridgeview, 1991.

Sturch, R. L. "Problem of the Divine Eternity." *Religious Studies* 10 (December 1974): 487–493.

Talbott, Thomas B. "On Divine Foreknowledge and Bringing about the Past." *Philosophy and Phenomenological Research* 46:3 (March 1986): 455–469.

Toner, Patrick. "The Prayer of the Molinist." *Heythrop Journal* 49:6 (2008): 940–47.

Trakakis, Nick. "Evil and the Complexity of History: A Response to Durston." *Religious Studies* 39:4 (2003): 451–58.

————. "God, Gratuitous Evil, and van Inwagen's Attempt to Reconcile the Two." *Ars Disputandi* 3:3 (2003): 1–10.

van Inwagen, Peter. "Against Middle Knowledge." *Midwest Studies in Philosophy* 21:1 (1977): 225–36.

————. "The Argument from Particular Horrendous Evils." *Proceedings of the American Catholic Philosophical Association* 74 (2000): 65–80.

————. "The Magnitude, Duration, and Distribution of Evil: A Theodicy." *Philosophical Topics* 16:2 (1988): 161–87.

————. "The Problem of Evil, the Problem of Air, and the Problem of Silence." In *Philosophical Perspectives 5, Philosophy of Religion.* Edited by James E. Tomberlin, 135–65. Atascadero, CA: Ridgeview, 1991.

Van Til, Howard J. "The Fully Gifted Creation ('Theistic Evolution')." In *Three Views on Creation and Evolution.* Edited by J. P. Moreland and John Mark Reynolds, 159–218. Grand Rapids: Zondervan, 1999.

Wachterhauser, Brice. "The Problem of Evil and Moral Skepticism." *International Journal for Philosophy of Religion* 17:3 (1985): 167–74.

Ward, Keith. "Theistic Evolution." In *Debating Design: From Darwin to DNA.* Edited by William A. Dembski and Michael Ruse, 261–74. Cambridge: Cambridge University Press, 2006.

Warfield, B. B. "Revelation." In *International Standard Bible Encyclopedia.* Edited by James Orr. 4 Volumes, 4:2573–82. Grand Rapids: Eerdmans, 1939, repr. 2002 (Peabody, MA: Hendrickson).

Werther, David. "Open Theism and Middle Knowledge: An Appraisal of Gregory Boyd's Neo-Molinism." *Philosophia Christi* 5:1 (2003): 205–15.

Widerker, David. "Two Fallacious Objections to Adams' Soft/Hard Fact Distinction." *Philosophical Studies* 57:1 (September 1989): 103-07.

Wierenga, Edward. "Prophecy, Freedom, and the Necessity of the Past." In *Philosophical Perspectives, Volume 5: Philosophy of Religion*. Edited by James E. Tomberlin, 425–445. Atascadero, CA: Ridgeview, 1991.

Wykstra, Stephen. "The Humean Obstacle to Evidential Arguments from Suffering: On Avoiding the Evils of 'Appearance.'" *International Journal for Philosophy of Religion* 16:2 (1984): 73–93.

Yandell, Keith. "Gratuitous Evil and Divine Existence." *Religious Studies* 25:1 (1989): 15–30.

Zagzebski, Linda. "Rejoinder to Hasker." *Faith and Philosophy* 10:2 (April 1993): 256-60.

Zemach, Eddy, and David Widerker. "Facts, Freedom, and Foreknowledge." *Religious Studies* 23:1 (1987): 19–28.

THESES AND DISSERTATIONS

Goddard, Burton L. "The Origin of the Hebrew Infinitive Absolute in the Light of Infinitive Uses in Related Languages and its Uses in the Old Testament." Th.D. thesis, Harvard Divinity School, 1943.

Laing, John D. "Molinism and Supercomprehension: Grounding Counterfactual Truth." Ph. D. diss., Southern Baptist Theological Seminary, 2000.

Layne, Ronald Ross. "Exodus 32:7–14 in Richard Rice's Argument for the Openness of God." Th.M. thesis, The Southern Baptist Theological Seminary, 1998.

BOOK REVIEWS

Freddoso, Alfred J. Review of *God, Time and Knowledge*, by William Hasker. *Faith and Philosophy* 10:1 (January 1993): 99-107.

Hasker, William. Review of *Divine Providence: The Molinist Account*, by Thomas P. Flint. *Faith and Philosophy* 16:2 (April 1999): 248–53.

UNPUBLISHED MATERIALS

The Chicago Statement on Biblical Inerrancy. International Council on Biblical Inerrancy. Chicago, IL, 1978.

"Declaration of the Establishment of the State of Israel." May 14, 1948. Accessed July 9, 2014. http://mfa.gov.il/mfa/foreignpolicy/peace/guide/pages.

Hasker, William. "The God Who Risks." Unpublished paper, 1999.

Laing, John D. "On Molinism, Question Begging and Foreknowledge of Indeterminates." paper presented at the Randomness and Foreknowledge Conference, Dallas, TX, October 25, 2014.

_____. "Intelligent Design, Middle Knowledge, and the Problem of Creaturely Flaws." Paper presented at the annual meeting of the Evangelical Theological Society, Milwaukee, WI, November 14, 2012.

MacGregor, Kirk R. "The Impossibility of Evolution Apart from God with Middle Knowledge." Paper presented at the annual meeting of the Evangelical Theological Society, Milwaukee, WI, November 14, 2012.

Perman, Matt. "What Does Piper Mean When He Says He's a Seven-Point Calvinist?" *http://www.desiringgod.org* (blog), January 23, 2006. Accessed July 28, 2015.

Piper, John. "The Freedom and Justice of God in Unconditional Election." *http://www. desiringgod.org* (blog), January 12, 2003. Accessed July 28, 2015.

Truman, Harry S. "Speech before the National Jewish Welfare Board." Lecture, Washington, DC, October 17, 1952.

Welty, Greg. "The Evolution of Molinism." Paper presented at the annual meeting of the Evangelical Theological Society, Milwaukee, WI, November 14, 2012.

_____. "Molinist Gunslingers: God and the Authorship of Sin." Paper presented at the annual meeting of the Evangelical Theological Society, Atlanta, GA, November 18, 2010.

Wolterstorff, Nicholas. "Address to the Evangelical Philosophical Society." Address presented at the annual meeting of the Evangelical Philosophical Society, Boston, MA, November 18, 1999.

SCRIPTURE INDEX

AUTHOR INDEX

SUBJECT INDEX